Practical Sales Managei

Practical Sales Management

Gordon J. Bolt
BSc(Econ), MA, FInstM, FInstBIM
Chairman of Faculty of Accounting, Business & Management
Head of Department of Business Studies
Bristol Polytechnic

Pitman

Pitman Publishing
128 Long Acre London WC2E 9AN

© Gordon J. Bolt 1987

First published in Great Britain 1987

British Library Cataloguing Publication Data
Bolt, Gordon J.
  Practical sales management.
1. Sales management
  I. Title
  658.8'1   HF5438.4

ISBN 0–273–02736–0

Phototypeset by Wyvern Typesetting Limited, Bristol
Printed and bound in Great Britain

Contents

Preface

'A born salesman' is a phrase often used to describe someone whose persuasive or 'wheeler-dealer' characteristics are admired. But men and women are no more born sales people than they are born doctors or lawyers. There must always be the aptitude for, the right attitude and inclination towards, and the ability to perform, any work the basis of which is skill. Some persons' skills can be developed by encouragement and early experience in life; some can be developed further by work experience over a period of time when the flair for selling emerges. It is part of the sales manager's role to develop the sales flair in the individual.

It is also necessary for the sales person to be organised, otherwise the flair for selling does not get the optimum opportunity to be employed. Training can help and, coupled with good direction, good product and market knowledge and fair conditions of service, can form the basis of the organisation component of the successful sales person.

The proportions of flair and organisation needed to produce the optimum sales person will vary from one sales job to another and from one time period to another. What is common to the effectiveness of all jobs in selling is that they all need to be underpinned and supported by effective sales management.

Sales management was once described as 10 per cent inspiration (or flair?), 40 per cent organisation and 50 per cent perspiration. This book aims to inspire by suggesting new ideas as well as describing existing methods and approaches, improving the reader's ability to organise and, although energy and drive are needed to apply the contents of the book, I am seeking to reduce the perspiration content to make more time available for the first two.

This book is intended for three groups of readers:

(a) for students of sales/marketing/management, including those on BTEC courses, undergraduates at polytechnics and universities, post-graduate diploma students and others;
(b) for sales personnel and aspiring sales managers;
(c) for practising sales managers.

The importance of this book and its subject content depends on the perception one has of the role of sales management and selling. This role can be seen as the vital link between an organisation and its customers. It is indisputable that it is the sales team, field and internal sales personnel, and sales management, in the final analysis, who convert everyone else's time, money and effort in a company into orders. While this does not necessarily make the sales function the most important in an organisation, the fact remains that should it not be effective, the very existence of an organisation may be endangered.

This book follows a traditional, sequential structure; it is organised on the assumption that the chapters will be treated in the order in which they are presented. However, it is possible to selectively read particular chapters bearing in mind that within sections one chapter follows logically from the previous one.

Section One examines the basics of management in the broadest sense and how it applies to the specialist sales management area. Section Two examines the actual planning and organisation of sales management in action while Section Three covers operations and control activities necessary for effective sales management. Section Four covers the administrative role of the sales manager, the necessary support activities of a sales office and analyses six key sales support activities. Section Five examines the relationship interface between sales management and the various environments within which it operates, both internally and externally. It also acknowledges the environment of 'time' by identifying current trends and predicting future developments that can be expected in sales management.

The content of the book has been influenced from a number of directions. My early work experience in selling has obviously influenced me. I learned a lot by observing, working with and talking to sales managers (and other functional managers) and individual members of sales teams in the many sales management/sales training/marketing consultancy assignments I have carried out in many widely differing industries/markets. I have been influenced by talking to, and/or reading articles/publications of, recognised experts in selling and associated fields. Many of these are quoted and acknowledged in the text but there are others whose personal influence it is difficult to connect with specific writings and conversations over a long period of time. The influence of fellow members of professional bodies and of friends and relations 'in selling' has been valuable. The contribution to my thinking by my colleagues at Bristol Polytechnic and the students (and often the companies with whom they were placed for industrial experience) has been considerable.

To all the people involved in the above experiences, I say 'thank you' as they have helped me to develop and clarify my own views as to what sales management is about.

I would also extend my thanks to Diane Cromwell for her perseverance in deciphering my hieroglyphics and producing a high-quality (as always) manuscript. Finally, my thanks to my wife Peggy for her support, understanding and patience.

The management role

Section Two

The management role

CHAPTER 1

Sales management in context

Objectives

This first chapter examines the scope and nature of management related to the sales function and therefore the work/role of the sales manager. It fits the major functions of a business, including sales management, into the overall management process and identifies aspects/activities that are common in all forms of corporate management. This chapter also examines the relationships of sales management with other functional areas of management within a company, identifying the different sectional aims, objectives and potential areas of conflict, all of which need to be reconciled. Finally it defines selling, the various activities of sales management and describes the job of the sales manager.

Management and the sales function

The term 'sales management' is ambiguous. In the widest sense it could mean the management or manipulation of the sales of an organisation. For example, a board of directors 'manages sales' in various ways, e.g. by allocating a level of resources to the sales function, by making customer-type policy decisions (i.e. dealing through wholesalers rather than retailers), by determining the level of advertising/sales promotional support or by pricing policy, or by making a policy decision not to have a field sales force at all, perhaps using instead an inside telephone selling operation or by direct marketing through mail and/or press. All these policy decisions can affect the management (quantity, quality and profitability) of the sales of an organisation.

Alternatively 'sales management' could mean the planning and effective day-to-day running of the sales department of an organisation. It is in this context that 'sales management' is defined for the purposes of this book although it will be affected by the factors mentioned in the first definition. Sales management, as one of a number of functional activities within a company, will need to operate within the approved company plan while the sales plan itself will essentially form part of the company's marketing plan, which in turn is part of the company overall plan. Sales management will operate within a number of other internal and external 'environments' and the impact of these will affect its nature, scope and operation.

Sales management is essentially a management function/process and as such has basic characteristics that are common to the other company functional activities that make up the total corporate administration. Figure 1.1 illustrates a three-dimensional approach to management and shows marketing and sales on one dimension as one of a number of functional management types and implies that the factors on the other two dimensions of the model apply, at the same time, to a greater or lesser degree to all the functions shown.

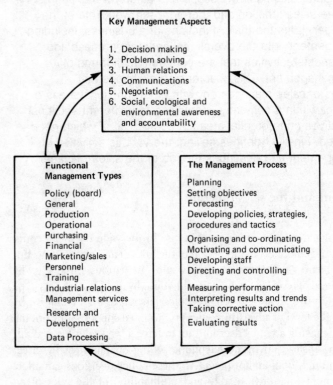

Fig. 1.1 A three-dimensional approach to management

The management process

Management, being the activity of getting things done through others, requires a manager to perform certain tasks. These are identified in the management process dimension of Fig. 1.1 and all have implications for the sales management function.

Planning

This has been described as the thoughtful determination and systematic arrangement of the factors that will be required in the successful operation of an enterprise. As such, planning is concerned with identifying and determining organisational goals and developing the policies, procedures, strategies and tactics necessary to achieve them. The sales manager needs to actively plan and develop a sales function plan; this will be covered in depth in Chapter 2.

When setting objectives/goals it is important for the sales manager to consider and set long- and medium- as well as short-term goals. Further, the manager is responsible for organisational results and personal responsibilities and therefore directional and performance objectives need to be identified for himself, the sales function as a whole, for specific geographic and/or product areas and for sales personnel, individuals as well as those who manage/supervise.

Normally, objectives will fall into five categories:

(a) Goals for routine duties – measured by exceptions.

(b) Emergency or problem-solving goals – measured by solutions and time.

(c) Creative goals – measured by results against stated objectives.

(d) Personal goals – measured by assessment.

(e) Organisational goals – measured by performance of each sub-function.

During the year the sales manager should check each subordinate's goals at suitable periods and should not hesitate to eliminate inappropriate ones or add new targets if special opportunities arise or situations change. All sales management goal-setting must take into account what is feasible and practical as well as what is desirable, and be compatible with the corporate and/or marketing plan.

Planning also entails forecasting events, performance, potential, sales and identifying changes that may be expected in demand, competition, technology, the international and national economy, finance, social and cultural pressures. The sales manager has a special responsibility in forecasting because every budget in a company ultimately depends on how many units of a company's product/service are sold.

Developing policies, procedures, strategies and tactics are also part of planning. Many company policies that affect sales management will originate from the board of directors and/or a company's marketing 'committee', and it is the role of sales management to execute them.

However, some policies will need to be formulated at sales management level to provide guidelines to specific decisions so that they are consistent, without the need for constant clearance with superiors. Acceptable procedures need to be developed as these are chosen ways (identified by the sales manager) to implement policies and to do specific tasks and are therefore a means of 'managing at a distance'.

The sales manager needs also to develop strategies and tactics, i.e. the 'mix' and/or disposition of his/her resources so as to impose upon the market (including competition) the time, place and conditions preferred to carry out sales activities so as to give the sales function the greatest possible advantage and/or the least possible disadvantage.

Organising and co-ordinating

Just as policy and the setting of objectives are the basis of management, so organisation is its framework. Organisation is concerned with:

(a) the optimum arrangement of resources (manpower, machines, methods, money) to achieve company objectives;

(b) the setting up of efficient information systems to ensure effective internal and external communications;

(c) the definition of the role, status, authority and responsibilities of all named individuals, jobs, sections and departments in the company;

(d) the definition of interrelationships established by virtue of such authority, responsibility and accountability. Authority is the right to require compliance by subordinates on the basis of formal position and control over rewards and sanctions; it should be given in line with responsibility given while accountability relates to the obligation of the subordinate to carry out his responsibility and exercise authority in terms of the established policies.

An organisation chart is not in itself an organisation structure but merely reflects the descriptive definition of the arrangement/grouping of responsibilities, authority and accountability, and expresses the relationships that arise at the interface between the various functional groups within a company.

Several types of organisation structure are available from which to choose/modify to suit an organisation's needs.

Line organisation
Each manager is connected to his immediate subordinate by a straight vertical line on the organisation chart, e.g. the sales manager's vertical line relationship upwards with the marketing manager or managing director and his/her vertical line relationship downwards to area managers. Examples of line organisation are shown in Figs 1.2(a) and (b). The more 'horizontal' the organisation, the greater the control of grassroots activity.

Line and staff (functional) organisation

As organisations grow and become more complex, it becomes necessary to integrate personnel with specific knowledge and functions into the system to provide specialist services and/or advise the line manager, i.e. to provide a 'staff' function.

An example would be the sales manager operating in a line relationship vertically with his area managers and the marketing manager, paralleled by a specialised, functional personnel manager/department providing aid in recruiting sales personnel, i.e. the dotted line in Fig. 1.2(b).

Further specialised functional relationships would be the legal department advising the sales manager on sales contracts etc. and the medical director in a pharmaceutical company advising the sales function on medical implications etc.

Departmental/divisional organisation

Vertical divisions of authority, responsibility and accountability is implied above, but organisations typically have some basis for horizontal differentiation of activities. Primarily there are five bases of departmentalisation:

(a) by function, i.e. production, marketing, purchasing, finance etc.;

(b) by product group and/or brand or service, e.g. semi-conductors, government and industry apparatus, materials, and geosciences, consultancy services etc.;

(c) by location, i.e. where all organisational activities performed in a particular geographic area are brought together into a single unit;

(d) by immediate or ultimate customer type, i.e. industry or consumer type wholesale or retail, large/medium/small scale;

(e) by unrelated business organisation, e.g. computer division, food products division, insurance division, publishing division etc.

Whether the overall company structure is one or a combination of these, departmentalised/divisionalised structures will affect the sales manager's decision-making on what structures are feasible in the sales function. However, at the sales manager's level in the organisation, versions of all except (e) could be applied to the sales function.

Strategic business units

A distinguishing characteristic of organisation in some diversified companies is the formal grouping of related 'business' into strategic business units (SBU), large and homogeneous enough to exercise effective control over most factors affecting their businesses. The SBU concept recognises two distinct strategic levels: corporate decisions that affect the shape and direction of the enterprise as a whole and business unit decisions that affect only the individual SBU operating in its own environment. It is in the latter activity that the sales manager is involved (unless acting in a director role).

The SBU is a specific part of the business for which one executive is responsible and who is following a distinct 'mission', competing with an identifiable set of competitors and able to formulate and implement a strategic plan with little input from others.

Matrix management

This form of organisation combines the vertical flow of authority into the various functional activities/departments of production, research and development, marketing/sales, finance etc. which are treated as cost centres, with the horizontal flow of authority into 'business'/projects/programmes set up on the basis of product type, e.g. food products, tobacco, semi-conductors, medical etc., which are treated as profit centres. In this form of structural arrangement, 'business boards' are established for each business which has a distinct 'mission' competing with an identifiable set of competitors and able to formulate and implement a strategic plan with little help from 'outside'. The managers of the 'business' have direct responsibility for profits but they rely on the resources allocated from the functional managers. Thus there could be a separate sales organisation for each of the businesses, but the implication for the sales manager of each business is that he/she is responsible to both the 'business' manager and the company functional head of marketing and/or sales, but within the 'business' unit the sales manager may adopt the form of structure mentioned above.

The effectiveness of all these organisation structures depend on certain basic acknowledged principles.

Authority and responsibility

The authority and responsibility of an organisation flows vertically from the highest level to the lowest. Depending on the needs of the company, some organisations are horizontal or 'flat' with few levels of management, some are vertical or 'tall' with many levels, while others are combinations of both, e.g. it is possible to have one particular part of a vertical or 'tall' structure organised in a horizontal or 'flat' arrangement. Figures 1.2(a) and (b) are examples of the first two.

As the size of a company increases and new levels are created and new managerial appointments made, it is important that the revised chain of command is clearly understood by everyone in the organisation and that responsibility, authority and accountability balance each other in all posts.

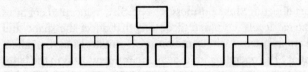

Fig. 1.2(a) Horizontal or 'flat' organisation structure

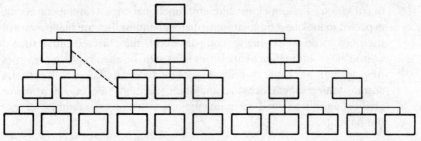

Fig. 1.2(b) Vertical or 'tall' organisation structure

The more levels of management in an organisation, the greater the difficulty of effective communication and complexity of information systems and the greater the cost (overheads).

Span of control
A number of levels is often necessary in organisation to relieve those managers who have too much responsibility or too many people under their control. The span of control (or responsibility) relates to the number of subordinates that a superior can supervise. It is of particular relevance to sales managers because of the geographical spread of the field sales force and the flexible nature of the sales person's work. Traditional management theory advocates a narrow span of control (five or six subordinates) to enable the manager to provide adequate integration of all the activities. Five or six subordinates is often the size suggested, but it will ultimately depend on the job, the circumstances and the personality of the particular manager. Implicit in the span of control (or responsibility) is the need for the co-ordination of the activities of subordinates by the manager.

Job descriptions/person profiles
Each post/job at each level should be defined in terms of responsibility, authority and accountability by means of job descriptions and by person profiles, i.e. descriptions of the personal characteristics, experience, qualifications etc. of the person most appropriate to perform a particular job.

Co-ordination
The division of a company into separate functions under managers and further sub-dividing into sub-functions under more junior managers creates the need for some means (and even the right attitudes) to integrate, relate and blend together the work of various people/departments so that they work effectively in harmony. There is also the need to ensure that the activities of one component part of the organisation do not negate/obstruct/diminish the efforts of another part. These harmonising activities are co-ordination and are usually involved in actions horizontally across the

organisation. Personnel in different functional areas cannot always be expected to look beyond their immediate job unless they are made aware of the need to do so. At higher company level, the chief executive should ensure the co-ordination of marketing sales with the other functions. At sales management level, the co-ordination of the field sales force, with the sales administration support activities and/or the telephone sales operation and/or credit controllers, will exercise the sales manager's abilities of co-ordination.

Informal relationships
Co-ordination implies that, in addition to the formal relationships depicted in the organisation chart, lateral and/or informal relationships will need to develop across formal boundaries and their effectiveness will depend on the attitudes of the personnel concerned.

Delegation
Delegation needs to take place, i.e. the passing 'down' of work to subordinates. It operates on the basis that the work delegated will be better performed by persons concentrating on a specific area and, secondly, the functions retained by the manager will be better performed and he/she will also have more time to 'think' and develop policy/strategy. In the case of the sales manager, the delegation of training, supervision and control to regional/area managers, the delegation of training to a sales trainer and of administration to a sales office manager are examples, but the ultimate responsibility for their actions is still that of the sales manager.

Duplication
In some cases, duplication instead of delegation will need to take place, i.e. where delegated work is of such a nature (quality) and quantity it cannot be further delegated, the established post must be duplicated. For example, in a multi-product company, a number of brand/product group managers' posts are 'duplicated' to 'manage' groups of brands/products. In the case of sales management organised geographically, delegated work is organised in areas each under the duplicated control of an area manager.

Resources
Clearly, for organisation structures to operate they must be adequately resourced in terms of personnel, machinery and organised in terms of methods and systems. As all other factors operate through people, staffing the organisation is a key organisational factor. It covers manpower planning, job analysis, development of job descriptions and personal profiles, recruitment and selection, training and development, transfers, promotions, demotions and dismissals. All these activities are necessary to keep the organisation adequately staffed with suitably qualified personnel so

that organisational objectives can be achieved and so that it operates at optimum.

Overall system

The various component parts of the managerial task examined so far will be effective collectively if operated within an appropriate system. The manager needs to develop, operate and maintain a total system comprised of a number of integrated sub-systems that take into account external situations/factors (e.g. economic, political, legal, cultural etc.) as well as internal situation factors (e.g. technical, political, behavioural, structural etc.). The overall objectives of these information/administrative sub-systems must be the optimum effectiveness of the overall business or the specific function (e.g. sales management). There will need to be technical and organisation/structure sub-systems (covering role/task specialisation, co-ordination and integration), also information sub-systems concerned with identifying data type, collection, storage, retrieval, analysis and presentation of policy, strategic operating and control-type information. There will also need to be sub-systems that encourage/influence the development, improvement and momentum of the managerial process, involving role identification and analysis, motivation/leadership/communications effectiveness, analysis of performance, feedback from sub-systems, development of personnel (including levels of management) and the development of the organisation generally.

All these need to be serviced by effective/efficient administrative procedures that are supportive of the organisation as a whole or of the specific function (e.g. sales management).

Directing operations, motivating and communicating

Directing operations is concerned with responsibility, authority and accountability relationships. The manager's aims, apart from his personal motives and obligations which ideally should coincide with those of the company, is to see that his staff implement company plans and achieve the company's objectives. To do this and to get the organisation structure operating, orders, instructions and directives must be given and the particular management style in specific circumstances will determine how effectively they are carried out.

But instructions alone are not enough: effective communication and the ability to motivate are crucial to the direction of operations. For the manager, it is basically a matter of leadership which has been defined as '. . . that combination of persuasion, compulsion and example that makes men and women do what you want them to do . . .' and a leader has been defined as '. . . someone who guides and directs other people to work together towards certain known objectives . . .'.

Closely linked with the concepts of the leadership is that of motivation. This is based on motive defined as '. . . the inner driving force that dictates how great an effort will be made . . .'. Therefore motivation is identifying how to get the best out of subordinates by understanding why they behave the way they do, what their motives are, and what makes them work well or badly, and then using this information and a variety of techniques to motivate subordinates to a higher level of performance.

All managers need a motivation plan which should:

(a) Develop and stimulate, through dynamic leadership, a keen sense of loyalty to the organisation as a whole and to the manager's department in particular.

(b) Induce into personnel the sense of prestige and pride of belonging to the organisation and, in fact, being partly responsible for the progress it is making.

(c) Foster the unqualified acceptance of the management of the company.

(d) Inject into the working groups a friendly competitive spirit.

The ideal motivator has a genuine and sincere interest in his/her staff and possesses a breadth of mind that enables him/her to treat all members of the work team with a friendly, fair, helpful, but always positive, attitude.

But leadership and motivation will get nowhere unless the manager is able to communicate effectively not only with the next level of management and 'lateral' executives, but also with subordinates in his/her department. Communication includes all human behaviour that results in the exchange of meaning; as such it consists of transmitting, receiving, sharing and exchanging ideas, knowledge, data, opinions, information and attitudes through interpersonal and social skills using, where possible, the five senses of hearing, sight, touch, smell and taste.

Organisations cannot operate internally or externally without the two-way exchange of information which can only take place with the four communication components of an originator or sender, a message, a channel and a receiver. But of prime importance will be the explicit and/or implicit attitudes of the sender and receiver, both to each other and to the actual communication.

A formal system of information flow is crucial to the communication/decision-making process but needs to be backed by an informal system reflected in interpersonal relations between managers and personnel at varying organisation levels. Such systems must be designed for feedback as well as transmission of data.

The differential nature of the information needs of various levels of managers requires information sub-systems to be developed, supported by human and/or computer databases. The level and scope of data provided by the information system is necessarily geared to the needs of the end user, thus the nature of information needed for strategic planning will be different than that required for operational control. The technological advances of electronic mainframe and microcomputers, which have greatly reduced the costs of computer processing power, and data storage permits increasingly sophisticated information/decision systems to be evolved.

Computer-operated information systems fall into three main categories graded according to their 'question answering' power. At the relatively simple level there are data storage and retrieval systems which make it easy to bring accumulated data/information to bear on questions and problems. At the next level are monitoring systems which provide measurements/readings enabling managers to find out how things are going. Many companies' efforts to change to computer-operated information systems are concentrated at this level to report on such activities as daily production levels, stockholding/inventory situation, profits, marketing and sales. At a higher level are the analytical information systems designed to answer the managers' more probing questions such as 'Why did that happen?' or 'What does it mean to the business that it happened that way?' or 'What will happen if . . ?' etc. The analytical tools built into systems of this type, range from simple cross-tabulation to complex mathematical models. Among the many exploratory diagnostic, evaluative or predictive analyses that are useful for the sales manager are those that are based on:

(a) evaluating alternative pricing strategy;
(b) manipulating current and/or historical sales data to provide projections of future sales trends;
(c) sales territory assignments etc.

The use of mathematical models to evaluate alternative outcomes of business decisions is increasingly a common feature of such information systems. The key management areas of directing operations, motivating and communicating are fundamental to effective sales management. Not only has the sales manager management problems normally found in these areas of activity but also the additional problems of individual members of the sales force operating, often at considerable distances away from the manager's immediate supervision, 'closed', one-to-one conversations with customers, the contents of which are difficult to verify. The sales manager's problem is how to ensure that field sales force personnel are operating/selling the same way when he/she is not working with them as when he/she is. The answer can be only through dynamic leadership and effective motivation and communication. This is an area of such importance to sales management that customer motivation and communication and sales management organisational motivation and communication are dealt with separately and in depth later in this book.

Developing staff

This part of the management process covers not only the fundamental activity of training personnel but also the wider one of encouraging and allowing them to develop mentally within the organisation.

Development of staff is about using the basic approach of jointly agreed goals for coaching, training, developing and improving each person's performance on a continuous basis. It is also concerned with reinforcing good results by the feedback of success when it is seen by the sales manager. Acknowledgement (either 'publicly' or privately as appropriate) of what is being done and positive recognition of the individual and his/her contribution are important parts of human relations in management. It is a process of building on strengths, of trying to remedy weaknesses and even using failures as a platform for coaching/training.

Staff development in its various forms is aimed at the employee to make him/her more effective, but where the main element of motivation is in the character of the work itself (as opposed to promotion or material incentive) then a number of approaches such as job enrichment, job satisfaction, job sharing, job restructuring, job rotation, team work and flexitime can be used.

In sales management, staff development and training will need to be personally intensive and orientated to the needs of the individual and the company in the market-place. On one dimension it is about giving the individual knowledge, skills and understanding in the five main areas of product/service, sales techniques, the market (customers and competitors), product/service application and administration. The other dimension is concerned with initial training, supervised experience, continuous training and training for promotion.

Directing and controlling

Good supervision and control is that which interferes least with the individual's freedom of initiative; it leads and directs along a route of greater achievement with the maximum amount of leadership and instruction and the minimum amount of domination, constraint and 'bossing'. It suggests rather than commands, and harnesses the pride and ambition of individuals to stimulate all-out effort. This particularly applies to sales personnel especially with regard to the field sales force where the supervision of new sales personnel means the continuation of initial training, the building of confidence and showing that the company sales policy and methods really do work. With established sales personnel, supervision should take the form of working with them, ensuring that company sales policy and methods are observed, eradicating bad work habits, ensuring that the relationship between company/sales person and the customer is constantly improving, assisting in the establishment of new methods and advising in every way. The direction of effort and the quality of effort and commitment are inseparable.

Supervision can only get results through people and most effectively takes place by letting each employee know what progress he/she is making. The 'supervisor' must decide what he/she expects of the individual and point out ways of improving performance, and should always give credit where it is due by looking for extra or unusual performance. Personnel should be told in advance about changes that will affect them, telling them why it is happening and 'selling the benefits' of the change to them. Good supervision builds on the individual strengths and abilities, and encourages initiative.

Control as a management activity is concerned with checking performance against pre-determined objectives set in plans to ensure progress and performance. It means:

(a) Having the optimum information/feedback system so as to be informed of any relevant situations (e.g. through sales persons' reports, field sales management reports, company sales/profit data of various market segments etc.).

(b) Having an effective system of measuring performance from the data obtained in (a) therefore implies the prior setting of agreed standards/ objectives/expectations against which performance can be measured (sales targets, individuals' sales or call quotas, personal goals, organisational goals etc.). It also implies having a system of highlighting deviations from sales plans.

(c) Comparing and verifying results with objectives and past performance and meaningfully interpreting trends and results. For example, the reason for a sales person not reaching a targeted 10 per cent increase in sales in a sales period may not be due to his/her lack of commitment or effort but because of a good customer leaving the area, the company's inability to supply certain products, a considerably improved product/service 'deal' by competitors, i.e. events beyond the control of the sales person. However, care must be taken not to simply rationalise the 'non-performance' but to objectively identify what factors held performance below, or pushed performance above, the original expectations.

(d) Knowing where, how and when to take remedial action. This means exercising authority, regulating, giving directions/orders, curbing or restricting the activities of the sales function. If necessary, it will require re-forecasting, re-setting objectives and re-developing the sales management plan.

A further aspect of control is recording performance data for use as a guide to future planning and operations.

If sales personnel are committed, well-trained and motivated, individuals will identify problems, interpret deviations from objectives/plans and take corrective action without waiting for the sales manager to act. Observation of self-correcting activity of this kind is an indicator to the sales manager of potential supervisors/area managers.

Evaluating results

The success of a company generally and/or one of its functions in particular (e.g. sales management) can be measured against the specific objectives it sets itself, or was set for it as in the case of a subsidiary company. Measurement includes, for example, return on capital invested, profit level, sales levels in particular market segments, market share, production levels etc. A comparison of results against objectives will normally produce differences/variations and it is the analysis of these and what is learned that should make future performance more effective. Evaluation of results should be carried out with adequate information on a psychological/ qualitative plane as well as on an actual 'black and white'/quantitative level and considered along the three time horizons of short-, medium- and long-term time periods.

Key management aspects

These are certain aspects/activities of the manager's job that can be necessary at particular points or throughout the overall management process just described. Those being considered are shown in Fig. 1.1.

Decision-making and problem-solving

No matter how a company's success is measured, it will depend for its effectiveness on how well decisions are made and problems identified and solved. The overall management process from planning and setting objectives to controlling and evaluating results is inevitably a series of analysing situations, identifying problems and solving them, and making decisions at all levels in the organisation.

Because management is getting work done through others (sales management is not so much the management of sales as the management of people), managers are involved with making decisions that influence/affect other people.

Basically, decision-making implies that there are two or more alternative courses from which the manager has to make up his/her mind and choose; it can also mean to pass judgement on situations. The import of any decision is that it will affect subsequent decision-making; the individual decision should be seen as merely one of a series with the consequences for future decisions fully appreciated.

Another dimension of decision-making is that of the use of experience. Rarely is complete information available; there is either no time or money available to collect it and, in fact, some data will be qualitative and cannot be measured. Decisions are based sometimes on conscious thought, common-sense and intuition which are influenced/fashioned by past experience or even following a hunch. The most common way of solving problems and making decisions is to do what was done last time when this problem arose or situation happened, i.e. it is based on past experience.

It is not difficult to show that experience, commonsense or hunches are not always good enough for the problems/decisions that managers face. A wide range of systematic approaches to problem-solving/decision-making has been developed to enable the manager to make a more logical, objective and rational approach: a suggested approach follows.

Identification/recognition that a problem exists

Some problems are brought to the manager, others have to be searched for or anticipated. There is also the aspect of dealing with small problems before they become large and a need to identify whose responsibility the problem situation is in the organisation.

The real problem

There is a need to define the real problem rather than the apparent, avoiding generalisation and oversimplification, identifying by whose and what standards it is a problem and to get as much reliable information about the situation.

Objectives

It is necessary to identify what is to be achieved or the objectives to be met; these can be recognised as being at three levels: *must* achieve objectives are conditions which must be met and any solution without them would not be acceptable; *should* achieve objectives are conditions that would add to the quality of a just adequate solution; and *could* achieve objectives are those that add to the previous two elements that either ensure the conditions that caused the problem do not occur again or even continue to exist. Some problems cannot be completely solved immediately and therefore should be considered in a short-, medium- or long-term context with the objectives reflecting an appropriate time horizon.

Alternative solutions

The next stage is to generate alternative solutions. There are many ways of doing this, e.g. by using past experience, intuition, commonsense, experts, pure logic, group discussion techniques, brain-storming, key personnel, rationality, model building, computational approach, pay-off matrices, decision trees etc. Which of these the manager uses will depend on the appropriateness of a particular method and how much time or even money is available.

Consequences

In the decision-making stage, the alternative solutions obtained are tested against the 'must', 'should' and 'could' achieve objectives and rated or scored. It is then necessary to consider the consequences of such decisions and, if possible, draw up comparative lists of favourable and adverse consequences before a final decision is made. This can be made by the manager alone but as the final decision will have to be implemented by others it is best to involve them at an early stage, as more brain power/experience can be brought to bear on the problem. Also, they may be able to contribute more knowledge of the problem and its causes, more facts and possibly may be able to think of other alternative solutions. Involving those who will have to implement the decision gains commitment to the chosen solution or in turn may bring to the surface other latent problems that in themselves may have prevented the proposed solution from operating effectively.

This latter approval is imperative in sales management where commitment by personnel and motivation by the manager is crucial to ensure sales personnel work to the same high level of performance when the manager is not there as when he is.

Implementation

The first part of this stage is to determine the degree to which the decision should be implemented (whole or in parts) and its timing. The second part is to determine how the decision will be communicated (media), explaining why the change is necessary, what the change will be, who will be affected and why it was the best decision. As with all communication processes, some feedback is necessary to check that it is fully understood. The third part is actually implementing the decision by listing the tasks to be carried out with regard to a time scale and the resources needed, developing some logical sequence of change, briefing everyone concerned, checking that each stage of implementation is happening on time and having contingency plans for each stage.

Monitor progress and review results

As the decision is implemented, it should be monitored to see that it is happening as intended; it should also be confirmed that the 'must', 'should' and 'could' achieve objectives have or are being met and determine whether the main problem has been solved. There is also a need to observe whether any unexpected adverse effects have emerged, e.g. are the effects of implementing the decision adversely affecting other parts of the company's function/structures as a whole or the sales function in particular?

Human relations

As management is about getting things done through people, relationships between the sales manager and the sales personnel are very important. However, there is no one thing that could be described as the key human relations factor. Between different people in different situations there is a combination of factors of varying intensities (some favourable and some unfavourable) that will make up the overall interpersonal relationships of a manager with his sales personnel. It is rather like a profit and loss account in human terms where the adverse human relations factors of a manager are set against the favourable ones that are credited to a manager. An example of the concept of a number of management credits and debits in the form of a sales manager's profit and loss account in human terms is shown in Fig. 1.3.

Debit	Credit
Satisfied with things as they are	Strong but fair leadership
Unique problems	Flexibility
Interested only in existing methods	'Approachability' (simple but effective chain of command)
Rule by committee	Energy – enthusiasm
Divided management	Self-analysis
No specialist help	Balanced sales team
Conservative policies	Contact and care
Always done it before	Reward for job well done etc.
Poor liaison	

Fig. 1.3 Sales manager's profit's and loss account in human terms

It is recommended that sales managers draw up such a profit and loss account, noting the unfavourable 'debits' and aiming to improve their human relations profile; such a checklist should be examined and amended to reflect the current situation every 4–6 months.

Management by objectives

This is the process whereby each manager in an organisation jointly identifies common aims and objectives with each person reporting to him/her and defines each person's responsibility in terms of performance expectations. The manager uses the jointly agreed objectives to guide the activities of individuals and to monitor and assess performance.

Although many complex programmes of management by objectives have been developed and used by companies, the concept means simply that every manager should jointly agree with the individual staff member his/her short- and long-term objectives so that each knows what job is expected of them, what is to be achieved within a certain time scale and the standard required. It implies that the manager will ensure that resources are available to carry out the job to be done. The manager regularly monitors and reviews progress towards the jointly agreed goals, discusses progress with individuals and guides/advises them through training. Ideally, at the point of achievement of the objectives there should be some reward/recognition.

By concentrating on jointly agreed objectives, the sales manager should provide the optimum motive and sense of achievement by allowing individuals to evolve their own way of working, to develop initiative and to encourage the application of new or adapted methods to meet changing situations.

Leadership

This is a particular quality necessary throughout the management process but essential to the sales manager who has to ensure that geographically spread sales persons are motivated to work effectively without immediate/ instant supervision. Leadership was defined earlier as '. . . that combination of persuasion, compulsion and example that makes men and women do what you want them to do . . .'. It has also been defined as '. . . Leadership is the ability to persuade others to seek defined objectives enthusiastically, it is the human factor that binds a group together and motivates it towards goals . . .'*

The underlying nature of leadership has been described as:

1. Support. Behaviour that enhances someone else's feeling of personal worth.
2. Interaction facilitation. Behaviour that encourages members of the group to develop close, mutually satisfying relationships.
3. Goal emphasis. Behaviour that stimulates an enthusiasm for meeting the group's goal or achieving excellent performance.
4. Work facilitation. Behaviour that helps goal attainment by such activities as scheduling, co-ordinating, planning, and by providing resources such as tools, materials and technical knowledge.†

But the way and extent in which these four factors are applied will depend on which of three basic types of leadership is adopted by a particular sales manager. The three leadership/management styles are

---

* K. Davis, *Human Behavior at Work*, 5th edn. McGraw-Hill Book Co., New York, 1977, p. 107.
† Reprinted from 'Predicting organisational effectiveness with four factor theory of leadership' by David G. Bowers and Stanley Seashore, published in *Administrative Science Quarterly*, Volume 11–2 (Sept 1966) p. 247, by permission of *Administrative Science Quarterly*. All rights reserved.

(a) The task-centred or autocratic or, at the extreme, the dictatorial type of leadership. This type of leader will think, plan and decide by himself what is to be done and then tell his/her subordinates or simply issue instructions as to what he/she has decided and what has to be done. Subordinates have little or no influence on the decision reached, little opportunity to discuss ways of implementing them and usually there is no avenue of appeal against them.

(b) The group-centred or democratic or consensus approach to leadership. This type of leader delegates decision-making to the group of subordinates and decisions reached reflect the opinion of the majority (or the worst, vocal minority!) or, ideally, will reflect something of the thinking of all members of the subordinate group.

(c) The individual-centred or free rein or non-manager approach to leadership. This type of leader may be a genuine delegator who places trust and confidence in his subordinates, encourages them to make their own decisions and then supports/defends them whether they are right or wrong. Alternatively, this type of leader may simply not be 'managing', and problems tend to arise later as the sum of the individuals 'doing their own thing' tends not to go in the same direction as overall sales management or company objectives.

The leadership-effective manager is one that has the ability to identify and adapt the type of leadership that is appropriate to the needs of the company in the market-place, its overall objectives, its traditional style and values, its size, its structure and attitudes.

Social and environmental awareness, responsibility and accountability

Expectations/pressures by government, the public generally, specific groups, employees, consumers, the media etc. are such that increasingly they are requiring 'business' to have social and environmental awareness, responsibility and accountability. The best reason why business in general and company executives in particular should have a high degree of social responsibility is simply that a policy/course of action to cover this is the morally right thing to do. It may be that it is a question of conformity not only to the law but to the spirit of the law. It may also come from pressures of the need for a good corporate image through 'public relations'.

The pressures are to consider ways of planning and/or measuring the impact/effect that companies' activities have on society and the environment generally but also on specific areas. For example, in providing products, services and jobs, the current pressures are that 'business' act with sensitivity to changing social values, priorities and the 'quality of life'. This would be reflected in such issues as environmental conservation, health and safety at work, consumerism and the more rigorous expectations of consumers for information, influence, fair trading practices etc. The area of environmental conservation is particularly sensitive in the various 'public' expectations of 'business' of social awareness, responsibility and accountability. This includes air and water pollution, the effect of the discharge of effluents on wildlife, the creation and disposal of radioactive waste, experimentation on animals, changes in the balance of ecological systems by commercial exploitation etc.

It is not suggested that all these factors are in the control of individual managers but they are often within the control of large companies or groups of companies. Even so, some are outside the control of the individual corporation, e.g. the social consequences on corresponding British industries and their supporting communities of the economic shift to prime steel producers and/or shipbuilders in the Far East or the impact of increased imports of television receivers and motor cycles from Japan on UK industries.

Nevertheless, social and physical environmental issues will require companies and managers to re-assess and/or take account of priorities, concepts and operating methods, and consider their effect on environmental and ecological situations, the better use and conservation of resources, on social progress and the 'quality of life'.

The relationship of sales management to other functional management types

The main role of the sales function is to sell profitably the output of the company, but it cannot operate in isolation and therefore organisational relationships will exist between it and the other functional/activity areas of the company which were listed in Fig. 1.1. In the context of the organisational terms used earlier, these relationships with the sales function can be either line (e.g. with the board of directors and/or general management), lateral (e.g. as with production) or 'staff'/functional (e.g. as with personnel which provides a service or gives advice). Some of the aspects of these relationships are:

The production function

The relationship between sales and production is based on the fact that in a manufacturing organisation they are interdependent. Without production's output of goods, sales have nothing to sell; and without the sales function, production has no way of selling its output. Production, operating either job, batch or mass/continuous production systems, will have to convert the sales/market demand pattern into viable/profitable production schedules for its machines. Usually it would like long order lead times through the medium of sales forecasts. On the other hand, the sales function would ideally like to operate on short order lead times so that it will be able to react quickly to the demands of the market. Also, the sales manager will need to reconcile production's desire for long production runs with few models and no model changes with his/her own desire to help the sales force (internal or field) by having short production runs with many models and frequent model changes to give a wider customer choice thereby making selling easier. Further, the sales function's desire for product/service combinations specifically made to customers' individual requirements, aesthetic appearance and tight quality control to eliminate customer complaints may not be matched with the ideals of production. These tend to concentrate on standard orders, ease of manufacture and average quality control, all in the interest of manufacturing economics and/or production convenience. Obviously the cost and quality of the work done by production will affect the quality of the end product/service combination and the prices at which the sales function can sell.

The research and development (R & D) function

Every company which manufactures a product or provides a service has the choice of one or a combination of the following alternatives:

(a) buying in its product/service/process knowledge from outside by contract or licence;

(b) inventing its own entirely new products/services/processes;

(c) developing improved products/services/processes from existing designs/specifications;

(d) employing other companies/consultancy agencies to develop improved new products/services/processes.

The necessity for taking one or a combination of these courses of action arises from the inescapable facts that business is dynamic, that technology is constantly evolving, that customers' requirements change and that production/services/processes need updating.

It is the R & D department's role to provide products/services/processes that will appeal to customers and which can be sold by the sales department. The latter will ideally be pressing for high quality and low cost/prices and preferably with unique selling features that differentiate the 'deal' being offered from those of competitors. R & D will have to balance the quality and cost/price factors, will tend to develop functional rather than sales features and want to develop few models/types with standard components compared with the sales function's desire for many models with custom components.

Ideally, sales would like R & D to develop product/service/process combinations that can be covered by patents and/or trademarks which can be registered and give the company a 'monopoly' of certain special features in the market-place, thus enabling the sales function to offer a unique selling proposition.

The purchasing function

In a 'trading' as opposed to a manufacturing company, purchasing will take over the prime role of providing the items to sell. But even in the latter type of company where much of purchasing's role is the buying of raw materials, components and sub-assemblies for processing, it is the activity that sets the cost threshold (by the quality and terms it negotiates) of the prices at which the sales function can sell the various product/service combinations the company markets. The purchasing activity tends to concentrate on the price of materials, components and equipment, economic lot sizes and standard parts whereas the sales function emphasis tends to be on the quality of the materials, components and equipment, large lot sizes to avoid being out of stock and non-standard parts to differentiate the product/service. Further, the purchasing approach of buying at infrequent intervals has to be reconciled with the sales function's preference of frequent and immediate purchasing to meet customers' specific needs.

The financial/accounting function

The provision and control of financial resources affects all aspects of a company, e.g. it can affect the type and size of production facilities. This in turn can affect the availability of products for the sales function to sell and the ability of the company to spread its overhead/prime costs over a greater output thereby reducing the overhead cost on each product/service item produced. It can therefore affect the basic threshold costs on which prices are set and at which the sales function must sell.

On the other hand, in most companies the sales marketing function will be expected to produce a market and sales forecast, on which all budgets in the company should be based. All budgets in a company depend fundamentally on how many units are sold and/or how much revenue is produced.

The financial function tends to emphasise pricing to cover costs whereas the sales/marketing approach is for pricing to further market development and/or pricing based on what the market will bear. The finance function can also be expected to want strict, rational reasons for spending and rigid budgets whereas the sales/marketing function can be expected to prefer intuitive reasons/arguments for spending (sometimes earlier or later than scheduled) and for flexible budgeting to meet changing market situations and the sudden need to respond to competition in the market place.

In addition to the pricing area, other financial activities that directly affect the actions of the sales function are those of financing customer credit. Every industry has accepted customer credit time periods, i.e. from when the goods are sold to when they are paid for. A financially imposed 1 month credit period will not help the sales function to sell if competitors are giving 3 months' credit. On the other hand, no sale is completed until the goods have been paid for and so the sales function does have some responsibility in ascertaining creditworthiness of customers and for ensuring that accounts are paid in line with company credit policy and, where possible, for avoiding bad debts.

Financial credit management will tend to emphasise the need for full financial disclosures by customers and low credit risk-taking whereas the sales function tends to prefer minimum financial disclosures and credit examination with medium risk-taking. The sales function tends to be sensitive to probing too deeply the financial affairs of potential new customers for fear of upsetting them, but the sudden change of a company from one supplier to another could mean that its credit has run out with one and it is seeking to extend credit facilities as opposed to being convinced it will get a better 'deal' from the new supplier.

Financial credit management will also tend to concentrate on tough credit terms and collection procedures whereas the sales function prefers easy credit terms and collection procedures; this, it claims, helps to foster good customer relations and the image of an understanding friendly supplier.

In some companies, customer credit control is the responsibility of the finance/accounting function; in others, sales managers prefer to maintain control over this activity and are responsible for it. They wish to maintain good sales person/customer relationships and avoid conflict between the sales person's role in selling from that of credit maintenance and debt collection. In this case the sales manager operates a credit control office so that the potentially unpalatable role (from the sales person's viewpoint) can be off-loaded from the sales person and good friendly relations always maintained.

Another financial activity which directly affects the scope and operation of the sales department is the financing of adequate and possibly geographically dispersed stocks of products. It is really a balance between economic central stocking and protracted customer delivery service or, alternatively, dispersed (and therefore more costly because of duplication) stocking and speedier customer delivery service. Further, financial stock management tends to favour a narrow, fast-moving product range with 'economic' levels of stock whereas the sales department would prefer a broad, multi-model product range with large/peak size level of stocks. Many companies calculate the level of business likely to be lost at varying 'stock-out' levels, e.g. it may be more profitable for a company to be out of stock of a particular line (and perhaps lose business) on 5 per cent of the occasions when orders are received than to maintain 100 per cent of stock of all lines on all occasions. It will depend on the levels of service customers are willing to accept and on the difficulties and problems such a policy will cause to effective selling by the sales department.

Selling prices will be affected by the methods of accounting used (marginal, absorption, average costing/pricing) and the balance between considering the profit per each item sold or the overall profit based on stock turn. For example, a stock turn of 12 times per year on £100 stock at 15 per cent profit (i.e. £180) will produce less profit than a stock turn of 20 times per year at 10 per cent profit (i.e. £200). The accounting function tends to prefer standard transactions whereas sales tend to prefer the flexibility of being able to carry out special deals and use special terms and discounts.

The personnel, training and industrial relations functions

These activities have the overall responsibility of commencing, maintaining and improving relationships between the company and personnel. They cover:

(a) employment: recruitment and selection, keeping personnel records, grading, transfers, dismissals;

(b) education and training;

(c) joint consultation, negotiation, maintaining labour relations;

(d) remuneration: advising parties in wage negotiations, developing incentive schemes in conjunction with work measurement and other specialists;

(e) welfare: administering welfare schemes, providing social and re-creational clubs/facilities, advising on personal problems, providing or being responsible for catering and other facilities;

(f) health and safety: ensuring that the provisions of the Health and Safety Acts and employment legislation are complied with, maintaining medical services, acting as a link between the company and group health insurance schemes;

(g) manpower planning, operating review and appraisal schemes, identification and forecasting future manpower needs.

However, the sales function often makes a special case for carrying out a number of these itself, e.g. recruiting and training its own personnel with or without the help of the personnel and training functions. The special case is based on the fact that sales personnel often work unsupervised for long periods in geographically dispersed locations and that the sales manager's and the sales person's personalities must be compatible; they must be able to 'get on' together. The sales manager's leadership/management style, ability to motivate and train, and methods of supervision and control must be such that the sales person works the same way whether the sales manager is present or not. A special case is also often made for the training of telephone sales personnel.

Even so, the sales manager may seek advice about personnel matters and may even be involved in joint operations with personnel, i.e. jointly defining a job, or a job advertisement, or carrying out joint recruitment or development interviews. In some situations it will be difficult for the central service of personnel to be operationally involved, e.g. recruitment and training for branch sales offices. In others, recruitment and training of staff whose basic role is the same across the company (i.e. office staff, computer operators etc.) will tend to stay with personnel.

However, it is impossible to lay down definite organisational demarcation lines and the relationship of sales management and personnel will be dependent on past company policies and the current needs of the company in terms of its organisation and the needs of the market-place.

The relationship of the sales function/management with other aspects of marketing are considered in depth in Chapters 11 and 12, i.e. the sales/marketing interface.

There will be points of contact and therefore relationships with other parts of the organisation not mentioned, i.e. the areas of central administration/ company secretary's office/legal, computer services, data processing, work measurement and value engineering, operations research, organisation and method study etc. All have a job to do, all will have a preferred course of action or objectives which may not correspond with those of the sales function. In each case, negotiations should take place to find common ground, reconcile points of view and to effect a compromise course of action. If this cannot be achieved, the problem will need to be pushed upwards by the sales manager through 'line' management to (depending on the structure of the organisation) the marketing manager/director or the managing director.

What is sales management?

Following an examination of the nature and scope of the management process and its relevance to sales management, and the relationships with other functional parts of a company, it is now appropriate to more clearly define selling and the role of the sales manager and sales management.

Selling can be defined as: 'Personal, individual, two-way, persuasive communication aimed at achieving specific objectives, notably profitable sales, within specific market segments. It implies the need for particular knowledge, skills and understanding of the needs and problems of the market.'

Although sales management must be concerned with managing a

company's selling activities, it needs to be put into a management context. It can therefore be described as:

> . . . a management function which, through dynamic leadership and in the context of the overall company Marketing Plan,
> (a) plans, sets objectives, forecasts, develops strategies and tactics for optimum effect in the market-place;
> (b) defines sales roles, recruits, selects appropriate personnel for present and future company needs;
> (c) organises, co-ordinates, directs operations, motivates, communicates and develops individuals and collectively an effective sales team, that can achieve the stated objectives;
> (d) supervises, controls and evaluates results;
> (e) sets up effective administrative information and other sales support systems;
> (f) achieves profitable sales.

Because of the different objectives of companies, resource situations, the needs of customers in specific market segments, competition etc., job descriptions for sales managers vary from company to company. However, an illustrative, overall job description for a sales manager* is shown in Fig. 1.4.

Some sales managers' job descriptions are far more detailed and some contain specific objectives, but all need to be integrated with corresponding job descriptions for regional and/or area managers and sales office managers, examples of which are shown in Chapter 9 (pp. 257–8).

A company lives by its sales; but the best sales personnel and the best product/service combinations are of little effect unless supported by first-class sales management.

Summary

This chapter first identified the subtle difference between the management of sales and sales management. The latter was then considered against an examination of recognised management process activities, i.e. the need to plan, set objectives, forecast, develop policies, procedures, strategies and tactics, to organise and co-ordinate, direct operations, motivate, communicate, develop staff, supervise and control and evaluate results. There are certain activities necessary to ensure the effectiveness of all forms of management which therefore need to take place in the management of the sales function, i.e. decision-making, problem-solving, human relations, management by objectives, leadership, social and environmental awareness, responsibility and accountability. The main role of the sales function is to sell profitably the output of the company, but it cannot operate in

---

* *Training for Marketing*, Department of Employment Report. HM Stationery Office, p. 88, reproduced with permission of the Controller of Her Majesty's Stationery Office.

Job description

Date:	
Job title:	Sales Manager
Reports to:	Marketing Manager
Job location:	Head Office
Controls:	Salesmen Area Managers 3 Sales Office Staff
Objectives:	To achieve the agreed sales and profit targets through the sales of the company's products.
Authorities and responsibilities:	1 To establish the product's sales potential and its characteristics and draw up sales forecasts based on these. 2 To prepare annual budget and control company's selling activities within the agreed sales budget. 3 To recruit, select, train, appraise and develop field sales and sales office staff. 4 To set targets, both financial and by products, for field staff to meet sales budget. 5 To determine salesmen's geographical territories and the number of calls per journey cycle, eliminating unprofitable calls. 6 To arrange and conduct field staff meetings, ensuring that staff are aware of company's sales policy, advertising and promotion activities. Encouraging suggestions from salesmen and informing them of current sales situations. 7 To promote sales in conjunction with marketing and advertising managers, through exhibitions, advertising, display and general promotional activities. 8 To co-operate with marketing manager deciding pricing strategy and to be responsible for issuing price lists and conditions of sale. 9 To be responsible for the administration of the sales office, ensuring acceptable cash flow from debtors. 10 To give immediate attention to any complaint and decide on action to be taken according to company policy.
Appraisal:	Performance against these objectives, and specified targets, will be appraised annually and promotion and salary increases given against these appraisals.
Standards to be derived from	1 Territory performance in terms of sales target. 2 Key account performance as percentage of territory target. 3 Development of sales staff.

Figure 1.4 Job description for a sales manager

isolation. Therefore the relationships of the sales function with general management, production, research and development, purchasing, finance and accounting, personnel training, industrial relations and other parts of marketing need to be developed, fostered and discussions carried out to reconcile/reduce conflict and to make decisions jointly as to what is good for the company in the market-place. Selling, sales management and the role of the sales manager need to be researched and defined to meet specific, individual company needs in terms of objectives, the various environments in which the company operates, company resources available, the needs of customers in the market-place and the pressures of competition if the sales function is to make its optimum contribution to the success of a company.

Questions

1. Why is the difference between managing sales and sales management significant to the effective running of a company?
2. 'It is not only the individual parts of the management process that are significant but the sequence/order of how and when they are carried out.' Explain this statement and describe how the content and sequence of the management process apply to sales management.
3. Identify those activities or parts of activities of sales management that the sales manager could delegate to regional and/or sales office managers and those that should be retained.
4. In all functional parts of management, the underlying activities common to all include decision-making, problem-solving, human relations, management by objectives, leadership and social and environmental awareness, responsibility and accountability. Indicate how these would apply to the sales management function of a company of your choice.
5. Consider the definitions given of selling and sales management, and the job description for a sales manager. Construct a person profile, i.e. a description of the ideal person to fill the sales management post described. Write this in the context of an industry/product/market area with which you are conversant.

Sales management in action (1): developing the profile

CHAPTER 2

Sales management planning and organisation

Objectives

This chapter considers initially an action plan sequence of the sales management process starting with an examination of key external and internal influencing 'environments', followed by identifying sources of necessary input. A progressive list of various forms of analysis is then suggested to provide the sales manager with a good information base. These include an assessment of the current situation of the company's strengths, weaknesses, opportunities and threats, the identification of assumptions and objectives, past performance analysis and potential strategies, analysis into the financial implications of the sales plan and an examination of the risks involved. The various stages and content of the sales plan are examined in detail. To be effective, a sales plan must have the appropriate organisation/structure for it to be implemented. Various organisational alternatives available to the sales manager are examined together with methods of determining how many field sales personnel are needed.

The sales management planning process

All sales management decisions (policy, strategy, structure, operations) take place in the context of an increasingly complex total business environment. Externally, this will include a number of environmental 'component parts', e.g. economic, political, social, cultural, technological, institutional, legal, the market, competition and demand, and others, all interacting upon each other, all changing inevitably at different speeds and thereby creating a changing set of opportunities, problems and constraints to the company/ organisation. The process of environmental change is sometimes rapid, dramatic and easily perceived; on other occasions, important environmental changes are slow, subtle and easily overlooked by the sales manager.

Internally, the environmental 'component parts' include operating within the overall corporate/marketing plan and the objectives set for the sales management function, operating within the informal political and social networks of the organisation, relationships with other functional areas of the company (production, purchasing, finance and accounting, personnel etc.), relationships with other parts of the marketing 'mix' (marketing research, product strategy, pricing, branding, forecasting, advertising, distribution etc.) and others.

The success of sales management decisions depends initially on there existing an understanding of the component parts of the total business environment mentioned above, that there is a willingness to accommodate the changes taking place with regard to them and that there exists a generally favourable (to the company/organisation) set of environmental circumstances and an acceptable probability of success.

In fact, it must be recognised that sales of any product/service originate from, and are merely the result of, the above external and internal factors, all changing inevitably at different speeds and with different emphasis and all interacting upon each other.

Planning was described earlier as setting objectives/goals, forecasting, developing policies, procedures, strategies and tactics. Sales management planning is no exception and the sales manager needs to develop and apply an action planning sequence of the kind shown in Fig. 2.1 which indicates the stages through which ideally sales management planning should progress.

However, the sales manager may not always have the time (or money) to cover each stage in the depth suggested, in which case the overview planning process should be used as far as possible as guidelines rather than a managerial strait-jacket.

The key environmental factors (stage 1) have already been considered in the opening paragraphs of this chapter.

Information inputs (stage 2)

The sales manager needs to compile an appropriate list of sources of information, external and internal. The external sources can be divided into secondary or published sources, e.g. government statistics such as Business Monitor Series or specialised private sources such as A. C. Neilsen and many other marketing research agencies, and information obtained by original field research carried out either by a specialist marketing research agency or by the company's own marketing research department or sales force. However, it is important when using the sales function for research that it is realised that their main role is to sell; gathering marketing information, although important, must be given appropriate priority.

The internal sources of information can be divided into desk research covering internal records and research information that can be provided by

Stage 1 Identify key influencing environments	Stage 2 Obtain information inputs	Stage 3 Analysis	Stage 4 The sales plan
External: economic international political social technological legal industry markets competition demand etc. Internal: organisation structure informal political and social networks relationships with (a) other functional parts of the company (b) other parts of the marketing mix etc.	External information, e.g. economic social business market etc. Internal information, e.g. past record corporate plan, objectives and direction financial and other resources marketing plan, objectives and direction R & D ability and capacity production and/ or purchasing capacity level of technology etc.	Current situation SWOT analysis Plan analysis Performance analysis Cost analysis Risk analysis	Specific sales function objectives Identify main and alternative contingency plan concepts Strategies to be used to achieve objectives Organisation to enable strategies Time scales and cost schedules Tactics in detail Schedule of who does what, where and when Methods of testing sales plan

Fig. 2.1 An action planning sequence for the sales management planning process

other functional parts of the company (e.g. accounting and finance who carry out financial analysis and/or data gathered by the marketing research function).

For details of many hundreds of sources of information, the reader is recommended to read 'The collection of data' (Bolt, 1981). *

Analysis (stage 3)

This stage of the sales management planning process is that of carrying out a series of progressive analyses which are now described.

* Gordon J. Bolt, 'The collection of data' in *Market and Sales Forecasting*. Kogan Page, 1981, pp. 90–115.

Current situation analysis

This is an analysis of the company's present situation and is based on the answers to a wide range of searching questions.

General

What are the company's objectives, e.g. profit optimisation, sales maximisation, increased market share, expansion, product innovation, leadership etc.?

What is the nature and scope of the company's current business?

What are its product and/or service combinations and what are their immediate and end uses?

What are the market segments in which the company operates and, within them, what are its market share and market position?

Industry

How could the industry, in which the company competes with others providing the same or similar product and/or service combinations or substitute product and/or service combinations, be defined?

How big is the industry and what were its historical growth rates, what are they at present and what are they likely to be in the future?

What are the key influences to growth in the industry, and are there barriers to entry and deterrents to leaving the industry?

What is the status of production facilities in the industry generally and the company in particular; is it seen as old-fashioned/modern, over- or under-capitalised, over- or undermanned, well or badly managed?

What is the current stage of the industry's life-cycle?

Competition

How many competitors does the company have, are they large, medium or small scale, what resources have they available (internally or externally from a larger group)?

What are the competitors' production/sales volumes and market shares generally and particularly in those areas relevant to the company?

How important to competitors are the various market segments in which the company operates; what is competitor reaction likely to be to company changes of strategy in existing markets and in others if it decides to enter?

What are the general competitive directions/thrusts of competitors with regard to product and/or service combinations and the overall product/service range or mix?

What are competitors' corporate strategy in terms of integration, i.e. are they reaching forward to control next stage sales outlets, are they reaching backwards to control supplies thereby achieving cost economies, are they integrating horizontally thereby controlling larger sections of the industry, or are they operating a nil integration policy?

What is the nature of current competition: price, performance, technology, quality, design, service, delivery, lower costs, quantity or performance discounts, before- and/or after-sales service, spares availability, company image, product and/or service image, product/service mix or range, or various combinations of these?

Considering the nature of competition in each market segment, is the company secure, dominant brand or technology leader, strong, favourable, acceptable, weak, at a disadvantage or non-viable?

What criteria can be used to assess the company's competitive position, e.g. price leader, technology advantage, market share, profitability, fundamental strength, risk-taking, customer spread etc.?

A useful comparative analysis of competition is illustrated in Fig. 2.2.

Comparative market: assessment of competitors						
Names	Estimated share (%)	Increasing share	Holding share	Declining share	Corporate image	Rank in order of threat posed
					Gaining Losing	
Own standing						

Fig. 2.2 Competition comparison

Market

What markets are being serviced and what are their size and segmentation by competitors and/or customer type?

What are the potential key changes and trends?

Are there any significant seasonal, cyclical or business cycle patterns?

What are the traditional methods and channels of distribution open to the company?

What is the geographic distribution, age, sex, socio-economic group, industry type, of customers?

At what stage of the life-cycle are the various product and/or service combinations being offered?

SWOT analysis

Very simply this is an analysis of the company's Strengths, Weaknesses, Opportunities and Threats from the point of view of the sales function. The sales manager can carry out the analysis, but it is a good idea to involve sales personnel in identifying the factors in each of the four areas in SWOT analysis. This may be carried out simply as a discussion in a training session or monthly sales meeting or even more effectively in a brainstorming session.

The effective sales person sells not only the product and/or service combinations produced by the company but also himself/herself as a 'consultant' and the company. It is in this latter area that the strengths are important sales tools to be converted into buying reasons and benefits that come from dealing with the company. What is interesting is that in a brainstorming/discussion session, some sales people will see one aspect of the company as a strength whilst others will see it as a weakness. It is the discussion between the 'two factions' that provides the sales manager with information how different colleagues have differing views/perceptions of the company's activities upon which strong selling themes can be developed.

The identification by members of the sales department in general and the sales manager in particular of sales opportunities and threats will enable many minds to be brought to bear on the possibilities/potentials for future sales management planning.

The sales manager should also identify and consider other opportunities such as ways of optimising/maximising present sales operations, and major market alternatives for present and potential product/service combinations. What are the opportunities and threats to the need for new/increased earnings and to the adoption of new strategies and tactics? What are the opportunities and threats to entering new market segments each with a unique set of customers and competitors?

Plan analysis

This should be carried out in the context of the results from the current situation and SWOT analyses above, and with realistic and feasible objectives being set.

But initially, key assumptions/forecasts have to be made for such areas as the following:

(a) The *economy*, e.g. national and regional growth, inflation rates (affecting prices and purchasing power), interest rates (affecting purchases of capital items, financing of new projects, stocks, credit etc.), foreign exchange rates (if company markets or purchases abroad), recession or boom and their effect on the competitive climate.

(b) The *market*, e.g. market potential growth or decline, becoming more fragmented or being rationalised into larger individual units, demand for ever-changing product and/or service combinations, price trends linked with volume and deviations from pricing policy such as functional and performance discounts, promotional pricing etc.

(c) The *industry*, e.g. growth, economies of large-scale production, fragmentation, technological change, capacity changes, new entrants and their associated resources and markets, exits from the industry, specialisation or diversification, maturity, foreign competition etc.

(d) *External influences*, e.g. government actions, political stance towards business generally and the company's industry/markets in particular, legislation, labour relations climate, social and cultural trends and influences.

(e) The *company*, e.g. production output (if manufacturing), purchases (if trading), scale of activities (if service), sales in units and/or value by products, market segment, region, industry, wholesale and/or retail outlet, market share, market position, optimum profit product mix.

After making assumptions and/or forecasts covering the above five areas, the sales manager should identify the alternative objectives that could be set for the sales department generally. Whenever possible, these objectives should be quantified, given a time horizon and, where appropriate, costed. For example, the objectives could be to:

(a) sell successfully to a certain target group of customers, i.e. increase customer conversion from enquiries to sales by 10 per cent in 6 months;

(b) increase market share by 4 per cent in the industrial chemicals market in the next 12 months:

(c) sell 5 per cent more to existing customers over the next two sales periods;

(d) sustain customer loyalty and reduce customer mortality rate by 20 per cent in next sales period;

(e) register over the next three sales periods a particular sales message, i.e. a 10 per cent increase in product performance at the same price;

(f) get potential customers to take a particular course of action, i.e. a 20 per cent increase in requests for demonstrations and/or opportunities to quote in the next two sales periods;

(g) open 15 per cent more new accounts in the next 12 months;

(h) increase the sales of a particular product/service combination by 20 per cent within 12 months;

(i) increase sales by 10 per cent in relation to sales costs.

There are many other objectives and each sales manager will need to identify specific ones in relation to particular market segment potential and/or company situation.

Performance analysis

What strategies has the company used in the past and what were the results; which were the successful ones and why?

What are the strategies and tactics appropriate to the future (based on three previous analyses); should they be an up-dated continuation of those used in the past or should new ones be implemented?

It is also at this stage that alternatives/contingency plans must be considered as possible courses of action, should basic situations change radically, necessitating a modified/new plan.

Initially, future business strategies need to be discussed by the sales manager with the company chief executive and/or the board of directors because future overall business strategies will obviously affect decisions on appropriate sales function strategies.

The decision as to which overall business strategy to adopt will depend on the strategic posture of the company. Research by Miles and Snow* suggests that companies tend to adopt four main strategic postures:

Prospectors – firms which seek new product/market segments
Defenders – firms which penetrate a narrow product/market domain and guard it
Analysers – firms adopting both prospector and defender postures
Reactors – firms that realise the environment is changing but cannot effect the necessary realignment of strategy within the environment

These strategic postures will influence which of the following overall business strategies a company can adopt and will in turn restrict and/or have implications for the sales manager's alternative choice of sales function strategies and tactics.

Primary demand development

This strategy is used when marketing new generic types of products as opposed to new brands of an existing product type. It needs a good basis of marketing research to ensure that the right product has been identified to satisfy a latent need in a particular market segment. Because it tends to be a new product type, it may take longer to develop volume markets. The sales function will need to provide 'missionary' sales persons who are used to convert customers from an old product type or system often in an unfamiliar market segment.

Market acquisition

Instead of developing primary demand, an alternative strategy is to acquire an existing company operating in that new market segment. The sales department problem here is that it will either have to absorb a new sales force into its present structure or allow it to continue as a separate entity.

---

* R. E. Miles and C. C. Snow, *Organizational Strategy: Structure and Process*. McGraw-Hill, New York, 1978.

Whichever course is adopted, a major training programme is likely to be needed. The same problems arise when competitor companies are acquired in the company's existing markets, but the added problems of selling former competitors' products occur.

Market rationalisation

This strategy is appropriate where there are a number of market segments being covered both by product and by particular sections of the sales force specialising by individual market segments, this causing, in some cases, considerable overlapping/duplication of sales effort. The strategy causes like-market segments or unique sets of customers to be grouped together to make for greater sales force effectiveness. The crucial factor will be what reduction in service is likely to be acceptable to customers.

Product line and/or range adjustment

This strategy can be used to extend, maintain, rationalise or withdraw individual products and/or product ranges. The problems of sales management in the case of extending the product line/range will be the extra training needed for the sales force and whether individual sales people will be able to cope with the extra lines to be sold. If the increased work is considerable, the sales manager may even have to consider re-organising the sales force into smaller geographic areas. Rationalisation and withdrawal of products may mean that some specialised salesmen will have to be retrained and/or transferred to other work or made redundant. The sales force may also have to cope with antagonism of customers faced with the need to find other sources of supply for part of their needs.

Production/purchasing capacity change

The strategy of increasing or decreasing a manufacturing company's production capacity or a trading company's purchasing capacity will tend to increase/decrease costs which, in turn, could affect the prices at which the sales function will be required to sell. Economies of scale could reduce the cost per each item produced (unless the increased production requires extra manufacturing plant); conversely, a decrease in manufacturing capacity may not only reduce economies of scale but may mean existing plant will run at less than full capacity, thereby reducing profits. Further, old equipment will last longer, putting the company in a disadvantageous competitive position in the market-place. With a trading company, an increase in purchasing capacity may mean that it can purchase at increasingly favourable prices which in turn could mean either increased profits or these could be converted into lower resale prices, which could be an extra selling benefit for the sales force. Conversely, lower purchasing capacity could mean lower profits or increased resale prices at which the sales force will be required to sell. Further, increases/decreases in production and/or purchasing capacity could mean that either more or fewer sales people will be needed to sell the increased/decreased capacity unless these changes can be accommodated by the existing sales force. If they are accommodated, increased capacity will increase sales force cost-effectiveness whilst decreased capacity will reduce it.

Market share/market position defence

In the middle stages of the product life-cycle when the demand for a product/service combination has levelled out, any new entrants to an industry can only take sales volume/market share from those companies already in the market. The strategy therefore is to defend a company's sales volume and/or market share. The three main methods are particular ways of advertising, pricing and service. Advertising appeals to brand/company loyalty of customers. Prices must not be reduced directly as the price image of the product/service combination being sold must not be undermined or its market position will be adversely affected. The provision of an additional service or services is a way of enhancing the attractiveness of purchasing a particular product/service combination in real terms without affecting its price image or market position. The role of the sales department with this strategy is to reflect/emphasise the advertising appeal to brand loyalty of customers and/or wholesale or retail stockists. It will also need to concentrate on selling quality and/or performance rather than lower prices and may find itself supplying some aspects of the extra service benefit, e.g. the giving of technical advice and/or installation or maintenance with industrial products/services and performing merchandising activities etc. in retail outlets with consumer products and/or service combinations.

Forward, backward or horizontal integration

In times of recession when there is a battle for sales volume to maintain economies of scale, one strategy with consumer goods can be to reach forward and acquire wholesale and/or retail outlets or start a retail chain to ensure the availability of outlets in the market-place or to acquire distributors etc. This can only be done if retail customers are widespread as, in effect, the company is competing with its customers. With industrial products, forward integration means to be involved in the next stage of utilisation of a company's products/components, e.g. a components manufacturer acquiring a machinery company that uses large quantities of its components. In times of boom and shortages of raw materials/components, one strategy can be to reach backwards and acquire suppliers to guarantee supplies or to influence quality and/or design. In all these cases, the aim is to 'add value' and thereby make profits at each level. Further, by selective pricing at the lower stages, competing companies can be made to subsidise (by economies of scale if nothing else) the product/service combinations being sold by the sales forces. By horizontal integration, the strategy is to take over companies at the same level of the manufacturing process and/or place in the market, to obtain a larger market share or greater influence in the market. The danger here is that the interest of the Monopolies Commission can be attracted if the company is close to a 'monopoly' situation. Whether forward, backward or horizontal integration, the sales function's responsibilities are those of effective retraining to get the companies taken over to conform to the parent company's strategies and methods of operation and selling.

Technological efficiency change

This strategy can take several forms. The technological efficiency of production can be improved, thereby reducing costs. The administrative/accounting functions can be more highly computerised so that invoicing can be done centrally, thereby reducing costs, improving cash flow and providing more control information for management. The technological efficiency of marketing/sales can be improved by computerised ordering systems, selling by telephone and by the marketing and sales managers using computers for data collection, storage, retrieval and, in an interactive mode, to simulate the anticipated situation in the market-place if certain key factors change (e.g. the effect of a 5 per cent increase on sales volume). Generally these strategies call for more investment and are more effective the larger the operation. If technological efficiency change is applied to the product/service combination being sold, then it may mean that the sales force will need more technologically trained sales persons to cope with the increased complexity of product. An intangible 'spin-off' of adopting these strategies is that the corporate image could be enhanced, with the sales force being able to 'sell' an up-to-date, super-efficient company and/or technological leadership.

Quality change

In many markets there are often demands for a number of levels of quality of product/service combinations. As a minimum, there are usually three: high quality (usually accompanied by high prices because quality costs more), medium quality and standard or basic quality. The term low quality should not be used as this implies unfit materials and bad workmanship, whereas the scale of high, medium and basic means an adequate level of quality and therefore performance to meet the specific needs of particular market segments. For example, government and local authority agencies may wish to purchase high-quality concrete mixers that will last 20 years for maintenance and emergency work. A medium-sized builder may wish to purchase a low-cost (basic quality) concrete mixer that will be 'written-off' in the process of building a project development of forty houses. The quality charge may be upwards or downwards to meet the needs of specific market segments. Some companies will make different quality products for each of the high, medium and basic levels.

The implications for the sales function are complex: a sales person used to selling a high-quality product at a high price may have difficulty in selling a basic-quality product. Also, this sales person will have to find a new set of customers to whom to sell as his former ones are unlikely to be interested in the basic product. Conversely, the sales person used to selling basic-quality, low-priced products/services may have difficulty in selling high-quality, high-priced ones and will again have to find a new set of customers. Companies selling at a variety of levels need to train sales people strongly in identifying the specific quality needs of customers and where possible to upgrade the order being placed.

Hesitation strategies
These include postponing investment in new projects, scaling back of existing projects or at least increasing the time scale for completion, investment restriction (generally or to specific projects) and a general cost-cutting programme. All these will have implications for sales management and the sales department. The appearance of updated or new product/service combinations may be delayed, putting the company at a competitive disadvantage. New or updated equipment may be delayed (e.g. replacement of sales personnel cars or computerised telephone ordering system). A general cost-cutting programme could also affect the operational expenses of a sales force and greater emphasis may need to be given on sales training courses as to journey/territory planning and the more effective use of travelling/entertaining expenses.

Future strategies/objectives
From the strategies being proposed and/or accepted by corporate management, the sales manager will be able to identify the future strategic thrusts/broad objectives of the company. For example, it has been suggested* that there are four product/service strategy approaches open to most companies in an industry based on changing technology:

(a) *First to market*, based on strong research and development, technical leadership and risk taking.
(b) *Follow the leader*, based on strong development resources and the ability to react quickly when the market starts its growth phase.
(c) *Applications engineering*, based on product modifications to fit the needs of particular market segments in mature markets.
(d) *'Me-too'*, based on superior manufacturing efficiency and/or cost control.

It is important to identify the strategy being adopted by the company because the particular choice can affect sales management strategy and sales team performance.

* Reprinted by permission of the *Harvard Business Review*. Excerpt from 'Strategies for technology-based business' by H. Igor Ansoff and John M. Stewart, November/December 1967, Copyright © 1967 by the President and Fellows of Harvard College; all rights reserved.

Other strategic thrusts/objectives could be the starting up of new projects, introducing new product lines, to grow at the same rate, faster or more slowly than the industry, to attain/maintain cost and/or brand leadership, to diversify, to project a competitive difference, to concentrate on certain parts of present operations/activities, to find a special market segment or niche in the market-place, to recover ground previously lost to competitors etc. All should affect/influence the sales manager in considering, from the sales management point of view, possible corporate strategies and their direct and indirect effect on the sales functions, contributing towards implementing them operationally.

The sales manager will now need to identify and choose from a number of marketing/sales strategies.

Will specific target groups of customers be best reached by selling direct or going through middlemen, i.e. franchised dealers, retailers, wholesalers, agents, distributors?

Do the product/service combinations being sold by the sales department in consumer markets need to be displayed and sold extensively (e.g. basic food products, confectionery, cigarettes) or intensively in specialised outlets (e.g. high-quality porcelain china, specialised video and/or home computer equipment)? In industrial markets, will the company's product/service combinations need to be sold widely over many industries (e.g. silver solder, paint, timber, typewriters, etc.) or will the appropriate strategy need to be to concentrate on a relatively few user companies (e.g. outlets for diesel electric locomotives, specialised computer or communications equipment)?

Will the appropriate strategy be to concentrate sales activities by industry user type, by geographic area, by product usage area, by type of sales outlet or by market segment?

What is the appropriate communication combination strategy, i.e. the proportion of the sales department activity to advertising, public relations, sales promotion, merchandising, before- and after-sales service? For example, in consumer goods, marketing/selling product/service combinations may be heavily 'pre-sold' by advertising, supported by sales promotion and by the sales force 'selling in'. In some industrial markets it may be an appropriate strategy for the field sales force to personally sell to large potential customers supported by some selling by telephone; medium potential customers mainly contacted by telephone supported by infrequent calling by the field sales force and direct mail; with small potential customers mainly contacted/sold to by direct mail with some selling by telephone activities. The question arises, even in consumer goods service industries, how much of the sales effort should be by telephone as opposed to personal field selling?

Strategies within the sales department activities will also need to be decided upon. For example, in industrial/technical selling, should sales teams be only of highly qualified (and consequently highly paid) technical specialists or would it be appropriate to have teams of four or five sales persons with basic technical knowledge supported by one highly qualified specialist? In marketing/selling consumer goods, should the sales person, in addition to selling, carry out merchandising/display activities or should these be the job of a team of special merchandisers?

Will the degree of customer service necessary require a decentralised operation strategy, i.e. with the sales force (and perhaps distribution/ availability centres) based on branch offices, or will a centralised form of operation strategy be appropriate with the individual sales person working from his or her home?

By identifying appropriate alternative strategies, the sales manager can develop his/her main and contingency strategies.

Financial/cost analysis

An evaluation in terms of the financial implications of organising and implementing the chosen strategies needs to take place, e.g. the size of the investment implied, in terms of money and time, the return on this investment etc. Further, what are the opportunity costs, i.e. are there more profitable alternatives that the company will have to forego if the proposed objectives/goals/strategies are implemented?

The form of the financial/cost analysis will necessarily vary from company to company because of differences in scope and nature of organisations, markets, resources, structures, complexity of product range, accounting and information systems, appropriate time horizons etc.

A hypothetical and simplified example of financial analysis and evaluation of a particular market segment or product group could be based on the following information:

		1	2	3
(a)	From Marketing Department			
	Sales ('000 units)	1000	1250	1500
	Selling price (£/unit)	1.5	1.5	1.5
	Expenditure –			
	sales force costs (£000)	150	100	110
	Advertising and promotion	250	200	50
	Other costs	15	2	2
(b)	From Production (and Research)			
	Variable cost (£/unit)	0.9	0.9	0.9
	Additional fixed overheads (£000)	50	50	50
	Capital expenditure	200	—	—
(c)	From Finance Department			
	Stocks (5 weeks' sales)	96	120	144
	Debtors (3 weeks' sales)	58	72	86

This could then be summarised to produce a financial analysis statement as illustrated in Fig. 2.3.

	1	2	3
SALES (000 units)	1000	1250	1500
£000			
Net sales value (NSV) @ £1.5/unit	1500	1875	2250
CONTRIBUTION @ £0.6/unit	600	750	900
(i.e. £1.5 NSV unit−variable cost of £0.9)			
less Sales force costs	150	100	110
Advertising and promotion	250	200	50
MARKETING/SALES CONTRIBUTION	200	450	740
less Fixed costs − production	50	50	50
marketing	15	2	2
NET PROFIT	135	398	688
CAPITAL EMPLOYED			
Plant and machinery	200	200	200
Stocks	96	120	144
Debtors	58	72	86
TOTAL	354	392	430
1. Profit % of capital employed	38%	102%	160%
2. Profit % of sales	9%	21%	30%
3. Contribution % of sales	40%	40%	40%
4. Sales force costs % of sales	10%	5%	5%
5. Advertising % of sales	17%	11%	2%
6. Fixed costs % of sales	4%	3%	2%
7. Sales: capital employed	4.2	4.8	5.2

Fig. 2.3 Financial statement

The sales forecast in the above example is in units to avoid the problems of inflation and is multiplied by the net sales value per unit of £1.5 to produce the sales revenue or net sales value. The contribution of £0.6 per unit is obtained by subtracting the variable cost per unit (£0.9) from the net sales value per unit (£1.5).

An examination of the financial statement (Fig. 2.3) reveals that the return on the investment rises from 38 per cent in period 1 to 160 per cent in period 3. This appears to be extremely good; in reality, this should cause a searching examination of the assumptions/predictions used to ensure that this is not too optimistic. The other ratios/analyses would need to be compared with earlier periods and confirmed as being acceptable.

It is often very useful for the sales manager to apply probability and percentage analysis to the financial/cost analysis and to put it in the context of the market place by identifying a market share value. This adds another dimension to this analysis as it enables comparisons to be made within the

	Period 1		Period 2		Period 3	
Sales forecast (units)	180,000		450,000		720,000	
Market share (value) Market share (units)	4% 2%		9% 5%		13% 8%	
Sales forecast probability ± %	90%		75%		60%	
Average realisation price per unit	£4.50		£4.50		£4.50	
	£000	%	£000	%	£000	%
Sales forecast (value)	809		2,025		3,240	
Cost of goods Distribution	108 28	13 4	270 71	13 4	432 113	13 4
Gross margin	673	83	1,684	83	2,695	83

Expenditure:
  Sales function direct
    costs
  Sales function
    support material
  Samples
  Direct mail
  Advertising
  Other media
  Marketing research
	340
	55
	45
	54
	90
	20
	30
		4	340
			22
			—
			30
			100
			—
			30
				2	340
					22
					—
					30
					70
					—
					30
						1

Total expenditure	634	78	522	26	492	15
Net profit/contribution per period Cumulative net profit	39 39	5	1,162 1,201	57	2,203 3,404	68

Fig. 2.4

total and between periods as well as causing the sales manager to think more deeply about assumptions, decisions and alternative courses of action. An example is shown in Fig. 2.4.

Risk analysis

How favourable are the current and likely sets of internal and external circumstances and what is the probability of success of proposals of plans?

An analysis format with risk factors appropriate to the company can be used by the sales manager to assess the element of risk of particular plans. For example, assumptions/predictions made with regard to certain factors could be analysed in the form of Fig. 2.5.

Factor	Rank order of importance of weighting factor	Risk				
		Considerable Value 5	Some Value 4	Average Value 3	Little Value 2	None Value 1
Economy						
Industry						
Company						
Resources						
Markets						
Social						
Customer						
Competitive position						
Sales forecast						
Fashion						
Strategy						
Past performance						
Product/service combinations						
Over risk						

Fig. 2.5 Risk analysis format

The risks of all assumptions/predictions can be ascribed a rating or value and also, if appropriate, they can be weighted either by the rank order of importance or by a subjective weighting factor.

The sales plan (stage 4)

A sales plan provides a disciplined approach to solving selling and sales department problems by ensuring that all aspects of the problems are considered in a systematic way and where possible converts them into selling opportunities. The written plan provides a mechanism for achieving basic agreement, prior to any commitments, as to what constitutes the problem or opportunity. It then forces an evaluation of the various methods/means to overcome it and sets priorities or lays down alternative courses of action if certain contingencies arise. It guides the sales manager in making long-range plans and identifies strategies by which to implement them; further, it obviates the need/likelihood of costly improvisation and changing direction. A sales management plan provides a time-proven method for achieving continuity of effort and direction, and the morale-boosting factor of working in a well-organised team, that is vital for the successful achievement of a company's and/or the sales department's objectives and goals.

A sales plan can be defined as a written detailed document which assembles in one place all the up-to-date facts and thinking regarding the market/marketing/selling and company situations under consideration. It establishes specific long-, medium- and short-term sales objectives, and proposes long- and medium-range strategies to build on company strengths, avoid or change weaknesses, solve problems and capitalise on opportunities. It also recommends specific selling and promotional tactics to carry out the short-term strategy and to accomplish the objectives set for the next sales period.

The cost of planning (in time and money) is insignificant compared with the rewards that come from a well-orchestrated sales effort that is integrated into a company's overall customer communications mix as part of the total corporate plan.

Initially, specific sales plans that have been quantified have objectives, time horizons and, where possible, costs (as identified in the Plan Analysis, pp. 38 and 39); these should be set to be compatible with objectives set in other areas such as market share, position, penetration; customer awareness, acceptance and action; manufacturing, production, product design, quality, size and range; pricing and discount structure; advertising, public relations, sales promotion, merchandising, packaging, branding; before- and after-sales service; methods and channels of distribution; competition; stock turn, return on investment and profits.

The next stage is to identify the main thrust or concept of the sales plan (e.g. to increase sales and market share) and identify alternative courses of action that will only be substituted for the main plan if certain contingencies arise (e.g. the rumoured arrival of a major new competitor in a key market segment occurs, whereupon the thrust of the contingency sales plan will be to help defend market share).

A useful part of the sales plan could be to identify the activities to be undertaken by the sales function to improve the company's standing in the market, as illustrated in Fig. 2.6.

The third stage is to identify from the performance analysis exercise (pages 39–40) appropriate strategies for the sales plan. Strategy is essentially the proposed specific method or plan to use to accomplish the sales plan objectives over the next three or four sales periods or years. The development

Activities to improve standing in the market				
Description	Expected effect	Immediate	Short term	Long term

Fig. 2.6 Improvement activities format

of medium- and long-term methods or strategies needs an awareness of trends and/or new developments, imagination, ideas, creativity and the appreciation of the combined effect of various change agents. The purpose of initially defining objectives is to guide the sales manager's mental and creative process of selecting a strategy or method which will achieve the set goal.

Strategy covers the medium and long term; tactics covers the short term and determines in detail who does what, to whom, when, where, why and how and what costs are involved for the next sales period or year. In this section of the sales plan, the sales manager should define the target group of customers or potential customers, whom the field sales force and/or the telephone sales operation should contact. He should also identify the sales message to be conveyed, the promotional material, literature and samples. They need to sell the company's product and/or service combinations, categorise customer types, determine length and scope of the field sales force journey cycle, and decide how to co-ordinate and integrate the message carried by advertising and sales promotion with the sales department's activities.

In fact, in relation to the potential of, and the market conditions in, particular sales territories, the sales manager should set the individual sales person's objectives within the context of the overall sales objectives and/or strategies above. For example, typical quantified objectives set for sales persons could be to:

(a) obtain an increase of 10 per cent in sales volume during the year;

(b) obtain an increase of 15 per cent in call quota over the next two sales periods;

(c) open three new accounts per month for the company's two major products;

(d) maintain the same share of the business for the five best customers in No. 4 area during the next two sales periods;

(e) carry out a full-scale presentation to fifteen purchasing executives of companies not at present buying from the company;

(f) obtain an additional 10 per cent, or a total of 90 per cent, of sales volume on a contract basis by the end of the year;

(g) increase orders-to-calls ratio by 10 per cent in next sales period etc.

One method is to itemise the sales mix by broad product/service group, or by industry, by market segment, by type of wholesale and/or retail outlets etc., and to state the sales target to be achieved in each and the proportion this is of the total (see Fig. 2.7).

Product/service or market segment or industry or type of outlets		Sales area 1	Sales area 2	Sales area 3	Sales area 4
1	£000s or units % of total				
2	£000s or units % of total				
3	£000s or units % of total				
4	£000s or units % of total				
5	£000s or units % of total				

Fig. 2.7 Sales targets format

In some market/competitive situations, fairly tight schedules of activities need to be laid down for the sales function as a whole or for individual sales persons or sales territories; for example, the format in Fig. 2.8 could be used.

Week No.	Objective to be achieved	Success achieved (%)	Action to be taken
1			
2			
3			
etc.			

Fig. 2.8 Action to be taken format

In the marketing of pharmaceutical products, priorities of selling particular products are established by assigning them numbers and using a 'detail' sheet, setting the priorities in which they will be 'detailed' or sold to the doctor or pharmacist (see Fig. 2.9).

Priority	Period 1	Period 2	Period 3	Period 4	Period 5
A	4	4	1	1	4
B	1	1	4	4	1
C	3	3	2	2	2
D	2	2	3	3	3

Fig. 2.9 Priority/Detail schedule

This method ensures that the appropriate priority is given to products whether because they are new and need special emphasis or because they are lagging and need a boost. It also ensures that the individual sales person does not simply sell what he/she finds easiest to sell, which may not coincide with the optimum profit product mix.

The costs of all sales department activity need to be assembled in the sales plan whether these are capital items (the cost of which can be spread over a number of years/sales periods, i.e. the replacement of cars for sales personnel) or operational costs such as:

(a) the direct costs of the field sales force (i.e. salaries, commission, bonus, car expenses, entertainment expenses plus the spread of a portion of the sales management cost over the whole of the sales force);

(b) the direct cost of the company's selling by telephone operation such as salaries, commissions, cost of telephone calls etc., plus the opportunity cost of office space;

(c) sales office and administration costs;

(d) the cost of supporting activities by sales area, i.e. advertising, sales promotion, support literature, samples, sales aids, exhibitions etc.;

(e) sales training (internal and external) costs;

(f) costs of operating branch offices and warehouses if appropriate;

(g) costs of physical distribution, if part of the branch or warehouse operation;

(h) costs of agents' commission, consignment stocks etc. if appropriate;

(i) cost of any marketing research activities directly affecting or applicable to the sales operation, e.g. journey planning, frequency of call, territory potential etc.

Finally, it is important that the sales manager, key people in the company and all members of the sales department regard the sales plan as an action document, i.e. things are expected to, and will, happen because of it. It is essential to communicate to all concerned about the parts of the sales plan they need to know and, when delegating the responsibility for the carrying out parts of it, it is important to delegate the authority also.

Organisation

In Chapter 1 it was proposed (page 6) that just as policy and the setting of objectives are the basis of (sales) management, so organisation is its framework, i.e. the vehicle by which the chosen strategies and tactics are implemented.

It also stated that the setting up or taking over of an organisation implied the use of job descriptions to describe each job and of person profiles to describe the ideal persons to perform them. Further, it implied an effective span of control (i.e. a viable number of persons reporting to each level of management/supervision) and the use of methods of co-ordination and delegation of responsibility by the sales manager.

There are a number of ways in which the sales function may be organised:

(a) by function (Fig. 2.10)
(b) by product/service combination type (Fig. 2.11)
(c) by customer type (Fig. 2.12)
(d) by geographic region (Fig. 2.13)
(e) by industry type (Fig. 2.14)

The way that the sales department is organised, the methods used to communicate with customers and the scale of the operation, will have a direct effect on the number and type of sales persons employed. For example, direct marketing operations or the use of manufacturers' agents

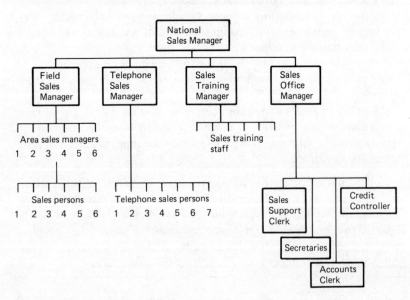

Fig. 2.10 Organisation by function

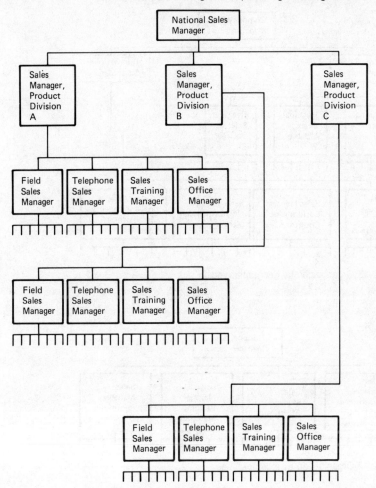

Fig. 2.11 Organisation by product/service combination

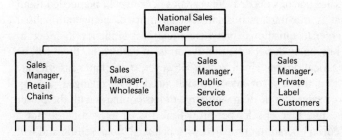

Fig. 2.12 Organisation by customer type

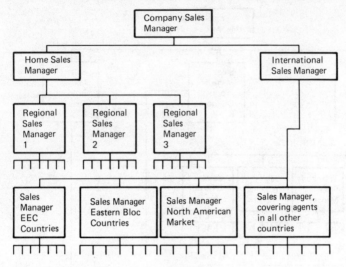

Fig. 2.13 Organisation by geographic region

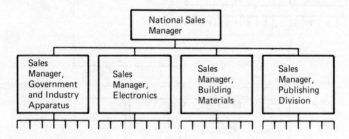

Fig. 2.14 Organisation by industry type

will mean that the company needs no field sales force. The use of such methods as franchising networks, retail agents, consignment stocks, forward contract ordering, commando or specific task sales forces reduces the number of sales persons needed. Fewer sales persons will be needed in an industry that is moving towards larger-scale units or being rationalised through mergers/acquisitions, or where there is a tendency to move to centralised buying by dispersed customer units; in both cases, there will be fewer buying locations on which to call. However, in the latter cases it may mean also that the type of salesman will need to be changed, i.e. an executive type salesman dealing with large orders/contracts with the power to negotiate. The type of sales person will also need to be different for a telephone selling operation compared with personal 'field' selling and will tend to reduce the number of salesmen needed because it substitutes telephone calls for personal calls and because many more can be made in the same time period and/or made more frequently.

If the product/service combination being marketed is offered nationwide and applies to large numbers of homes or industries, and personal selling is necessary, not only will a large number of field sales personnel be needed but, as they will need to be organised in teams, there will also be a need to appoint combinations of district, area, regional managers. The teams may also need different sales person types within them, e.g. in industrial selling, to a team of four technical sales persons may be added a more highly qualified sales engineer.

It will be necessary for the sales manager to estimate the number of sales persons needed to staff the type of organisation chosen.

Accurate measurement is essential and this depends on two basic requirements. First, the planning of workloads and territories and, secondly, the provision of information in the form of quantifiable facts and details, allowing standards of performance to be set and contrasted. This method is generally referred to as the workload approach.

From the many different methods of allocating areas and workloads, a simple but sound approach is outlined below. It is by no means all-embracing and is hypothetical in its examples, but it does incorporate the major principles used by many sales managers.

(a) Establish and list both existing and potential customers.
(b) Give each customer a category based on potential.
(c) Endeavour to equalise workloads, balancing with the respective sales potentials. The way to do this is to:

(1) Decide call frequency based on categorisation, for example:
High potential   – A Once a week
Good potential   – B Once a fortnight
Moderate potential – C Once a month

(2) Decide the number of calls feasible per month. To do this, consider the 'average length' of a call and the 'average time' taken on travelling, waiting, paperwork, etc. If the figures are:
160 per month in urban areas
120 per month in country areas

(3) If the categories for the whole market are:

A_1 75 urban   ⎫ High potential
A_2 25 country   ⎬ Call rate once per week

B_1 200 urban   ⎫ Good potential
B_2 300 country ⎬ Call rate once per fortnight

C_1 500 urban   ⎫ Moderate potential
C_2 500 country ⎬ Call rate once per month

the total calls required per month are:

Urban   *Country*

$(75 \times 4) + (200 \times 2) + (500 \times 1)$ $(25 \times 4) + (300 \times 2) + (500 \times 1)$
= 1200 urban calls + 1200 country calls

$\therefore$ Number of salesmen required $\dfrac{1200}{160} + \dfrac{1200}{120} = 18$ salesmen

(4) Obtain an appropriate map and divide it into 20 miles square. Each square should be analysed to show, for example:

Number of customers	*Number of calls per month*
A_1 ...	No. of $A_1 \times 4$
A_2 ...	No. of $A_2 \times 4$
B_1 ...	No. of $B_1 \times 2$
B_2 ...	No. of $B_2 \times 2$
C_1 ...	No. of $C_1 \times 1$
C_2 ...	No. of $C_2 \times 1$

The amount of a salesman's time required to cover the square will therefore be:

No. of $A_1 \times 4 \times \frac{1}{160}$ of a month =
+ No. of $A_2 \times 4 \times \frac{1}{120}$ of a month =
+ No. of $B_1 \times 2 \times \frac{1}{160}$ of a month =
+ No. of $B_2 \times 2 \times \frac{1}{120}$ of a month =
+ No. of $C_1 \times 1 \times \frac{1}{160}$ of a month =
+ No. of $C_2 \times 1 \times \frac{1}{160}$ of a month =

When sufficient squares have been drawn to add up to a complete month's work, then the area covered will constitute one salesman's territory. The process can be applied in reverse to check existing territories and workloads with a view to re-allocation.

The second basic requirement of quantifiable information could include:

(a) *General essential information*
Total market potential for area
Estimated total sales per area of the national volume
Number of customers and/or potential customers per area
Time taken to cover area
Total turnover from area
Total selling expenses
Total marketing expenses

(b) *Information specific to the controlling function*
Number of working days
Number of calls
Average calls per day
Cost per call

Number of orders
Average size of order (value)
Percentage of orders to calls
Average value of order per call
Cost per sale per £
Cost of opening new accounts
Delivery cost
Miles travelled

These are not all meant to be applied literally by every sales manager. Nor in turn, is it suggested that they constitute a totally comprehensive list. Instead, they should be used selectively and there should be added those items which particularly relate to a specific business or industry.

A number of other ways of determining the size of the sales force have been put forward by different researchers. For example, one method suggested by Bullock* is where the size of the sales force is determined by the amount that the company can 'afford' to budget for field selling. However, it does not consider market potential or customer needs. Another method is suggested by Semlow† who proposed a system of measuring the sales productivity of a sales force in different sized territories. He observed that '. . . sales representatives recorded higher sales in territories which were graded as having a high potential but that their sales were less than proportional to the increase in sales potential on which the whole approach depends'.

Heyman's relationship between additional 'sales persons and new business' approach‡ operates on the principle that a company systematically records the amount of new business obtained when sales people are added or removed from sales territories. A further method is that of Lambert's marginal responses to sales effort approach which uses the differences in the number of sales persons in X number of territories to explain variations in sales. This method does not take into consideration variations in the size and number of customers per area and assumes that selling ability is the same for all members of the sales force.

While the workload approach is very popular with sales managers, it can be modified by adding certain aspects of the other methods mentioned to suit the needs of different markets and companies.

Finally, successful organisation does not simply depend on the type and pattern of the organisation structure but also on co-ordination (see page 9).

---

* 'How many sales people?' by D. Dalrymple and L. Parsons in *Marketing Management – Text and Cases*, copyright © 1980. Reprinted by permission of John Wiley & Sons, New York, USA.
† W. Semlow, 'How many salesmen do you need?', *Harvard Business Review* paper, 1959.
‡ D. Dalrymple and Leonard Parsons, 'How many sales people', *Marketing Management*, 1980.

The sales manager's style and systems should encourage the formal and informal integration and blending together of the activities of the field sales force, the telephone sales operation, sales support and administrative personnel, training staff etc. to produce a unified organisation and a team determination to achieve the set of objectives.

Summary

This chapter concentrated on basic management principles and concepts applied to sales planning and to the organisation needed to implement the sales plan. It proposed a set of guidelines to help the sales manager to develop a comprehensive sales plan, and an action planning sequence that progresses logically through the various necessary stages was suggested. This recognised the various key, external and internal influencing environments and identified sources of appropriate information inputs and was therefore a logical starting place. This was followed by in-depth analysis of the current situation, of the strengths, weaknesses, opportunities and threats facing the company, of the appropriate objectives and goals, and of the possible strategies and tactics likely to achieve them. An important type of analysis is that of costing the proposed plan activities and an examination of risk factors. From this comprehensive analysis, it should be possible for the sales manager to put together a viable sales plan together with several contingency alternatives. The plan sequence suggested was to identify specific sales objectives, main and contingency concepts, strategies to achieve the stated objectives, time scales and cost schedules, tactics, the kind of organisation to carry out the strategies, short-term tactics in detail, schedules of who does what, where and when and, finally, methods of testing the sales plan.

The need to monitor, control and evaluate the sales plan is examined in Chapter 8.

Crucial to the success of a sales plan is having the appropriate organisation structure to carry it out so that the activities of the various parts of the sales organisation are integrated and co-ordinated towards common objectives. The basic organisation principles covered in Chapter 1 were extended to cover the specific needs of the sales function. The next chapter will deal with sales management operations.

Questions

1. What are the key external and internal business environment factors to be recognised and how do they affect the sales management process?

2. What are the various stages of analysis appropriate for planning and why are they so crucial to the effectiveness of the sales plan?

3. Identify the ideal stages in an actual sales plan?

4. In addition to planning and organising the activities of the field sales force, what other activities should be included in the sales plan?

5. The sales function can be organised in a number of ways; identify three and indicate what you perceive to be their advantages and disadvantages.

Sales management in action (2): operations

CHAPTER 3

Defining the job and the sales person

Objectives

This chapter examines the initial steps in building a dynamic sales team by identifying objectives, considering the alternative selling roles/tasks available to the sales managers, applying techniques of job analysis and evaluation, evolving an effective job description and developing a 'person profile' that identifies the ideal person to carry out a particular sales task.

Setting sales force role objectives

Whether the sales manager is required to set up a new sales force for a new company, a new sales force for a new activity in an existing company or whether he 'inherits' an existing sales force, he will need to clarify the objectives of its role by asking the questions: What, Why, How, Where, Who, When.

What is the role of the sales force? While the prime task is obviously to sell, it may have secondary tasks. For example, in the industrial situation it may be to ensure the customer has enough technical performance/information on which to make a decision, or in a consumer goods situation to obtain the best possible display positions in a retail outlet.

What are the immediate sales force objectives? To increase sales, to increase profitability, to open more accounts, to increase market share, to develop brand/company loyalty, to improve the corporate image etc

The sales manager may, because of the size of the sales force task, need to delegate some management/supervisory functions to senior salesmen, area managers or regional managers, and their management, selling, training roles will need to be clearly defined.

Why does the company need a particular type of sales force and will it need to plan for expected future changes in market situations? The different field and internal sales force tasks (examined later) in a variety of combinations together with selling by telephone activities and other internal sales support will need to be considered in answering this question.

How should the ideal sales force be developed? Are existing staff capable of being retrained and who should do the training? If new staff are to be recruited, from where are they to be obtained? How should the sales force be structured and organised (by industry, geographic area, by product type, customer outlet type etc.) and, if necessary, management/functions delegated?

Where should the sales force be based: on Head Office (with sales personnel working from their home), on branch offices, on production facilities?

Who is the ideal person to perform the sales task and what experience, qualifications, education, personality and background should he/she possess?

When should the new sales force combination be ready to operate or the existing sales force combination (field, internal, support functions) retrained or confirmed? What is the optimum time scale for any type of expansion or contribution whether by product type, geographic area, distributive outlet?

When the sales manager has been able to answer these and other relevant questions, he/she will be able to determine the sales operations objectives as they relate to the sales force; all set within the context of the company's overall marketing plan.

Alternative selling roles/tasks

The prime role/task of the individual sales person is to sell the product/service 'deal' that the company is marketing, to sell himself/herself as an adviser/consultant/friend, and to sell confidence in the company and its image.

This broad definition can be applied to every selling job, but effective sales management means going further and identifying the type of sales task required to be done before it is possible to identify the ideal type of person to do it.

There are many types of selling jobs and although titles may mean slightly different sales roles in different companies/industries, it is useful to identify the different ones even though some may overlap or combinations of them may be necessary in practice.

Industrial sales person

One whose sales calls range across more than one industry with a common range of products/services, i.e. a silver solder salesman, a centre lathe salesman, industrial security salesman. Needs high-level knowledge of the requirements of a warranty of industries, i.e. selling in breadth.

Technical sales person

One whose sales calls are to a narrow range of industries but gives advice and answers questions about technical performance and/or shows that the product/service 'deal' being sold solves certain technical problems. Needs highly specific technical knowledge of narrow range of industrial situations, i.e. selling in depth.

Sales engineer

One whose main role is to secure sales but who is involved also in identifying and solving customer problems relating to the application of his company's plant/equipment/process to a particular customer situation. Needs high-level technical applications knowledge and problem-solving ability.

Designer salesman

One whose role contains a considerable element of creativity/application by designing a product to meet specific customer's needs/problems. For example, the sales person designing an in-plant conveyor system; the microcomputer software salesman who needs to 'design' a special software package; and packaging salesman who designs a new pack for an existing customer or with the purpose of attracting the business of a potential customer. Needs high creativity and conceptualisation ability in addition to the ability to perceive unique solutions to ongoing problems.

Sales adviser/consultant

While there needs to be an element of advising based on an understanding of the customer needs in all types of selling, it may form the whole basis of some selling tasks. For example, in the selling of life insurance, consultancy services, central heating, planned kitchens etc. Needs considerable empathy and understanding of the customer's needs/situations.

Retail sales person

As the name suggests, this sales person sells to the public in a retail outlet. Usually employed by the retailer but could be employed by another (i.e. in the case of 'shops within shops') or by a manufacturer (e.g. cosmetics sales personnel, hosiery consultants or 'demonstrators' of household equipment).

Delivery sales person

One who delivers the product as well as sells. At the consumer end, the sales element may be small as in the case of milkmen or baker's roundsmen, or considerable as in the case of brush or household item sales people. At the 'trade' end of the spectrum, a van sales person delivering/selling perishable foods, tea/coffee, electric batteries and torches etc. to retailers must not only be able to sell but also merchandise/display products and/or collect payment for current or previous delivery. Needs in some cases to be able to cope with 'anti-social' hours and endurance because of the sheer number of calls this type of person is expected to make.

Consumer goods sales person

One who sells a product/service 'deal' to retail outlets and who may be employed by manufacturers, manufacturers' agents or wholesalers needs to have knowledge of a broad range of prices (own and competitors), trade deals and promotions, and achieve a high but effective call rate.

'Missionary' sales person

One who works for a manufacturer, manufacturer's agent, franchisee or wholesaler whose main role is to 'convert' outlets not stocking or using a line at present (e.g. wholesalers, builders' merchants, retail outlets etc.). Usually works with his customers' sales team with any orders obtained going to the latter. For example, a 'missionary' sales person for a company manufacturing a new range of pvc rainwater building products working with a builders' merchant's sales person selling to builders and whose customer company wants proof that the 'new type' of product will 'sell' before investing money in stocks. Needs to be able to sell himself/herself to the potential stockists and sell product/service concepts to the end user or stockist.

Creative tangibles sales person

One who has to 'create' a need or persuade a potential customer there is a latent need, perhaps not previously appreciated, before it is possible to sell the actual tangible product/service 'deal'. An example would be selling a computer or office system to a company which may consider that its scale of operation may not warrant it. Double glazing and cavity wall insulation are further examples of where need has to be sold first. Sales persons need to be very perceptive to identify specific needs and make instant appreciation of a variety of situations, i.e. possess a high degree of empathy, ability to bring latent needs to the surface.

Creative intangibles sales person

Like the creative tangibles sales person, one who has to 'create' a need before it is possible, in this case, to sell an 'intangible' deal, i.e. one that cannot be seen at the time of selling. Examples are types of service selling such as insurance, computer services, ship-broking, advertising services, consultancy/training etc. The needs of this type are the same as for the creative tangibles sales person but with a greater emphasis on selling service.

'Political' sales person

One who by knowing the 'right' people or moving in the 'right' social or business circles is able to 'set up' the broad framework of a contract, negotiation, 'deal' and who, after the initial stages have been completed, tends to withdraw or play a continuing but more 'public relations' role while technical, commercial, financial considerations are negotiated/'sold' by executive specialists. Examples in these areas would be the 'setting up' of large government contracts, the initial stages of the sale of a complete oil refinery or large steel strip mill, or a 'deal' relating to aircraft new to a particular airline. The 'political' sales person needs to be well 'connected', socially acceptable at the appropriate levels, persuasive, with an appreciation of the wider business/economic issues relating to the needs of an organisation or business.

Negotiator

In sales situations that are not standard or customer needs can be met in a variety of combinations (qualities or quantities) of products and/or services and where there is room to manoeuvre, supplier and customer will seek to obtain the most advantageous 'deal'. Each tend to start negotiations at different levels and gradually meet at a compromise 'deal' somewhere in the middle. Such a sales person needs a strong character, resilience, ability to 'read' the real situation behind the apparent one, and a high level of sensitivity and understanding of human and corporate behaviour.

'Multiples' sales person

One who sells a wide range of products, often working for a middleman or wholesaler usually with sales activity based on a catalogue sometimes of massive proportions, to a variety of outlets/users. Examples are sales persons working for builders' merchants, or those working for large household/food wholesalers where the number of product lines 'carried' is considerable. These are often highly competitive, low profit margin situations with competitors selling exactly the same supplier products with apparently the same base price. The need is for a sales person who can build personal relationships, sell himself, sell his company, sell an extra service because the basic product is the same as that offered by competitors.

Sales executive

In situations where the apparent status of the sales person is important or where the 'buyers' are senior managers or directors of customer companies or where large-value orders or contracts are involved, often a different type of salesman is needed. A sales person who can handle 'higher level' sales situations that are more difficult or need a more sensitive approach or with more protracted negotiation than the 'ordinary' sales person in the company. For example, the sales executive negotiating large contracts with 'house accounts' or government departments rather than with single retailers. In some cases, the term sales executive is used by some companies to add status, or give psychological advantage to members of a sales force who could be more properly described by one of the other categories.

Merchandisers

Merchandising has already been defined as 'psychological persuasion at the point of purchase without the aid of a sales person'. But the merchandiser is not a passive display person, but often has to 'sell' the retailer (manager or owner) on giving him a better 'display hot spot' in the store and to allow the right number (usually based on market share) of 'facings' on a display unit. Qualities are understanding the character of the store, spatial concepts of the overall merchandising of the store, display techniques, ability to establish a rapport with retail store managers and/or owners. Examples are merchandisers employed by manufacturers of fast-moving consumer goods servicing supermarkets and hypermarkets.

Telephone sales person

Selling by telephone is a unique selling job whether it is when the supplier takes the initiative and telephones a customer or potential customer to either sell a product and/or service, to obtain an appointment, to obtain information, to give information or to handle and sell on a complaint; in this case it could be considered as a dynamic internal sales force. Or whether the customer takes the initiative and telephones the supplier to obtain information, to place an order or to make a complaint; in which case, the activity may be one that supports the field sales force. Such a person needs (because the lack of visual contact) an acceptable telephone sales personality, a pleasant voice, the ability to 'paint word pictures', a good sales vocabulary and considerable empathy with customer situations. Telephone sales persons are used by a wide range of companies in a variety of industries from industrial companies contacting relatively small users to manufacturers of fast-moving consumer goods 'topping up' stocks in retail outlets. In addition to the sales support activity given by an internal telephone sales person, there are others that need to be identified and analysed. These could be sales correspondents who look after the internal administrative activities of one or more field sales personnel, or technical data support personnel, accounts and credit controllers, order progressers and/or despatchers etc.; but all need job analysis to be carried out as to content.

Similarly, if the general/national sales manager delegates any management functions to regional or area sales managers, to senior sales representatives or sales administration/office managers, these roles all need analysis in terms of the context and balance of their sales role, their administrative role, their management of resources role and their training role. These management roles could be analysed within the management functions mentioned in Chapter 1: planning (setting of objectives, policies and procedures), organising and co-ordinating, motivating and communicating, controlling by taking action and developing staff.

There are other selling roles/tasks and also combinations of those shown, but the range and scope of those mentioned indicate the magnitude of the sales manager's job in determining the type of selling job to be done at present and how this will evolve in the future. It also indicates the need for the sales manager to objectively analyse the individual sales job.

Job analysis and evaluation

Sales force roles/tasks can be analysed to determine the level of the qualities that are needed for them to be performed effectively. Most jobs can be analysed under the following headings; selling roles/tasks are no exceptions.

Physical requirements

Included under this heading are strength, endurance and resistance to fatigue, speed of movement, overall physical co-ordination, the fine co-ordination of specific muscle groups, physical adaptability, ability to learn new motor (physical) skills, general physical fitness and well-being.

The carrying of heavy sample cases, long hours and/or distance driving in congested traffic conditions and intense activity in short periods are all general factors in the selling role/task, but any combination of levels of these can be appropriate for specific selling jobs and must be identified.

Sensory qualities

An extension of physical requirements are the sensory qualities needed to perform a specified sales task. An acuteness of each of the five senses (sight, hearing, touch, taste and smell) may indicate a general fitness. However, the acuteness of certain of these might be fundamental to the job. For example, highly intricate drawings/specifications may put special demands on sight; for those requiring the recognition or changes of levels of pitch, tone and volume, well-tuned hearing is vital; where recognition of coarseness, smoothness, texture is important, well-developed touch sensitivity is crucial; taste is often a key factor in the food and drink areas (especially in wines, spirits, beer etc.); and well-developed sense of smell is vital in a number of selling situations with regard to cosmetics, perfumes, wine, even air-conditioning.

Specific job requirements

Under the broad heading of perceptual qualities, these can range from the speed of perception for each of the senses and the accuracy of discrimination for each sensory attribute to the perception (and assessment) of physical situations (e.g. the layout of machinery in a factory) through to the perception of psychological/'political' situations (e.g. the relationships between persons in the customer organisation and between persons who can influence the decision to make a purchase).

Level of intelligence

The level of intelligence needed to effectively sell in specific areas can be analysed by considering a number of qualities needed under the heading of intellectual attributes. Verbal comprehension, literacy, numeracy, deductive and inductive reasoning, mechanical comprehension, systems awareness and spatial visualisation (ranging from the total layout of an oil refinery in relation to the sale and installation of one machine, to the application of a merchandising concept within the overall spatial impact of a supermarket).

Qualities and levels of knowledge

These are reflected in academic skill requirements of a particular selling task/role and should be analysed generally and then specifically in terms of scientific knowledge, mathematical knowledge, fluency and accuracy in the mechanics of verbal and written expression, together with the intellectual ability to appreciate and assimilate new knowledge. Maximum, as well as minimum, levels of intelligence need to be established because although sales personnel with higher levels of intelligence than the basic selling job requires may later be promoted to manager, in some cases it also makes for high levels of labour turnover often with the loss of 'sunk investment' in training. One dairy products distribution company involved in door-to-door delivery realised that it (and its fairly elementary but effective sales training scheme) was being used as a means of gaining entry to selling. By placing a maximum (but appropriate) intelligence level on entrants, it reduced its sales personnel labour turnover by 58 per cent.

Professional application of social skills

This is a large part of the selling role/task in the pursuit and achievement of specific goals. The social qualities and requirements of specific selling roles/tasks are crucial to the acceptance, and in some cases the credibility of, the sales persons. This aspect can be considered under the headings of interpersonal skills, communication skills, pleasing and acceptable manner and appearance, and the understanding of the behaviour of others (empathy), tact/discretion in dealing with others and being a 'good mixer'.

Interest/attitude requirements

These requirements of a sales role/task can be analysed under a variety of headings. As selling is an interpersonal skills area, the general interest in, and attitude towards, people is important. But a variety of other interests in, and attitudes towards, such factors as the industry, the product, particular materials, mechanical/electrical/electronic 'things', abstract ideas, adventure, excitement, change and personal challenges may be highly desirable in specific selling situations.

Emotional requirements

All sales force roles/tasks have emotional situations and therefore there is a need to analyse the necessary emotional requirements. These cover the ability to function under various pressures of speed, complexity, time limitations, as well as personal stability and personal adjustment needed. There is also the need to identify the necessary level of the frustration threshold, whether an easy-going or more dynamic personality is necessary. Will the role/task involve the sales person in accepting the *status quo* or does it need a degree of dissatisfaction with, or to effect changes in, the existing circumstances? What will the demands be on the role/task holder regarding pressures on one side from the employing company and from the other pressures from the customer, i.e. company loyalty versus customer loyalty? Also, what degree of flexibility, adaptability and ability to cope with change is necessary?

Organising/management requirements

All sales force roles/tasks have organising/management requirements either explicitly stated as in the case of area or regional managers, or implicitly stated as in the case of a field sales person who is expected to manage the particular geographical territory allocated and to organise his or her time, i.e. the proportion of time spent on existing customers, potential customers or looking for new prospects.

The information suggested in these nine areas should be available through:

(a) *Written material,* i.e. updated existing job descriptions, field sales persons' reports, organisation charts and scenarios, feedback from training courses, training manuals, reports of sales conferences and meetings and, if available, consultants' reports. In some cases it is possible to ask a sales person to keep a diary of activities during one complete journey cycle.

(b) *Current job holders' reports* either from a request for a report on the job or from job appraisal interviews.

(c) *Colleagues' reports.* Assembling information from a number of salesmen doing similar work will ensure all aspects of a sales task/role are identified. Reports from area/regional managers, production executives, accounts and credit managers, marketing department personnel, and brand and product group managers on their expectations of the job of the sales force will highlight a variety of the aspects of the sales role/task.

(d) *Direct observation.* Working with the sales force in the 'field' should be a normal activity for effective management and continuous training but also provides the data for job analysis. However, it should be realised that the sales activity during a programme of 'double calls' with a sales person could be an enhanced version of what normally happens when the sales manager is not present.

(e) *Previous experience.* The sales manager's previous sales experience should not only provide a yardstick to measure the particular job being analysed but may also provide some new basic parameters for developing sales situations or updating existing job descriptions.

(f) *New sales role/task consultation.* Discussion with production, marketing, accounts, credit control, brand or product group managers as to their expectations of a new sales role/task, as well as with the existing sales force and area/regional managers, will not only enable job analysis of the actual potential job but also the role as it is perceived, which may not be the same thing.

Job analysis data can be used as the basis for a number of sales management activities. It can be used for recruitment, advertising, for the basis of selection, to determine the content of sales training programmes, for giving applicants some understanding of a particular sales job and, most important of all, as the basis for developing a credible job description.

Job descriptions

After analysing the existing or potential job to be done, the next stage is to develop a job description which should be explicitly a specification of the job/task and not the person in the job; it should then focus upon the major end results that must be accomplished in order to fulfil the purpose of the sales role/task; it should identify the essential characteristics of the environment in which the job holder operates; and it should list the key financial and other resource dimensions. In the case of senior representatives such as area managers and regional managers (i.e. those with delegated supervisory management and training responsibilities), these aspects should be clearly defined.

The job description should be seen as the basis on which the job holder is to be employed by the company, focusing critically upon the essential features of the sales role/task and the results the job holder is paid to achieve. A good job description is sufficiently flexible to accommodate a reasonable amount of change in the job content, but if there is any fundamental change in the role/task then a new one is necessary. It should also be updated by agreement during employment as new instructions and/or duties arise; consequently, the basic job description can be filed and re-activated when a new recruitment situation arises.

It is important that the sales person and the sales manager agree that the job description is a fair account of the particular sales role/task. From such an authentic description it will be possible to make evaluating judgements that will be both technically and emotionally acceptable.

It is recognised that different companies will have different needs and practices, but it is recommended that the format of job descriptions of all sales roles/tasks in a company be standardised to enable comparisons to be made in content and in different time periods. Ideally, they should include the following information section headings:

(a) Job title and location.

(b) Name and title of person to whom the job holder reports and who has agreed the job description.

(c) Purpose of job; what are its objectives and role in the organisation.

(d) Description of job; its scope in terms of knowledge or experience it requires in the areas of product/process/technical/service, sales techniques, the market-place (customers, potential customers, competitors), applications (e.g. the applications of computers to banking) and administration (e.g. prices, terms of sale, delivery dates, reports etc.).

(e) Responsibilities; principal, regular and occasional duties.

(f) Working relationships within the organisation; with the immediate line manager (e.g. area, regional, national sales manager), in terms of functional relationships (e.g. with brand or product managers whose product/services the job holder is expected to sell; and the priority relationships if there are several of these) and lateral relationships (e.g. with the credit control function or delivery service function etc.).

(g) Job appraisal and evaluation – the basis of how the job will be measured and evaluated.

(h) Scope of authority over operations, personnel, prices, terms of sale, expenditure, expenses etc., and freedom to act.

(i) Remuneration and conditions of service. Remuneration to cover basic salary, bonuses, commission, composite schemes (e.g. one rewarding effort integrated with sales volume reward), the terms of remuneration in times of illness, the operation of sales quota and/or target schemes. Conditions of service to cover basic hours of work, holiday use of company car, pension arrangements etc.

Because the needs of companies are different and situations in industry/markets vary, job descriptions need to be designed specifically for sales personnel recruitment in the context of the particular company situations using as many as possible of the factors listed above.

An example of the adaptation of the job description concept to specific company needs is shown in Fig. 3.1 which is a job description outline used by Business Press International. Note the introduction of percentage weighting in the sections on 'Function' and 'Principal Accountabilities' and the use of diagrams in the section on 'Reporting Relationships'.

An example of a shorter, but still effective, job description that would be generally applicable for a salesman selling consumer products to retailers is shown in Fig. 3.2. This was recommended by the Department of Employment* and could be used as a basis to develop a specific sales job description in a specific company.

Person profiles

When the job description has been written, it should then be possible to identify the ideal type of person needed to do a particular sales job. This should take the form of developing a person profile under four broad headings: quantitative elements, experience, qualitative elements and job motivation. Each of these should be further sub-divided according to the complexity of the sales job to be done and the accuracy of 'fit' required. For example, the description of the ideal person for selling computer systems to banks at director level may need to be more detailed than a person selling heavily advertised groceries to retailers.

It is useful to rate/grade the various elements of the person profile in terms of importance or priority (high, medium or low) either by marking

---

* *Training for Marketing*, Department of Employment report. HMSO.

appropriate columns with an 'X' or by assigning a value 1 to 5; with 5 being high rating and 1 low rating in each category (see Fig. 3.3). This will add a degree of objectivity to a relatively subjective judgement, and although it can appear to be rather mechanical, if rating values are applied the ensuing total marks can form the basis of comparison between applicants.

Quantitative elements

(a) Age – although there is no correlation between age and sales ability, certain ranges of age may be more appropriate than others, e.g. a younger person may be more appropriate where a sales job is very physically demanding or is selling a 'young person' product than in a situation where apparent credibility and confidence comes from a more mature person.

(b) Education – it is important not to set the level too high, but this factor may be crucial for some sales tasks (e.g. educational qualification in mathematics in a scientific sales job) while in others the educational experience alone (public school or university) may be the real educational asset.

(c) Qualifications – these can be divided into two categories, those that are directly relevant to a specific sales job and those, although not directly relevant, indicate that the applicant has mental capacity and can assimilate new changes or complex knowledge.

(d) Personal background – some combinations of personal background factors can be more appropriate/relevant than others. This section should include marital status (i.e. whether married or single etc.), has a clean driving licence, is a householder, has any disabilities, state of health, and whether candidates speak foreign language(s), availability to start employment, any legal or personal special commitments, hobbies, leisure pursuits and other interests.

(e) Personal appearance – mode of appearance, dress, personal impact will need to be appropriate for the type of outlet/buyer/customer conditions likely to be faced in a particular selling role, but there will be a basic level of standards of personal hygiene and appearance that need to be present in a representative of a company.

Experience

This can be divided into recent and past, business and other, relevant and not directly relevant (all experience is relevant to a degree as it has helped to shape the applicant mentally and perhaps physically).

(a) Work experience generally.
(b) Experience related to sales activity.
(c) Experience involving a particular product and/or service.

JOB DESCRIPTION

JOB TITLE	Advertisement Sales Executive
JOURNAL/DEPARTMENT	Middle East Health/Far East Health(Advertising)
SUB-DIVISION	Reed Business Publishing Developments
REPORTS TO (Name/Job Title)	Advertisement Manager

JOB PURPOSE — concise statement of the overall purpose of the job (limited, if possible, to one sentence):

To sell advertisement space in the areas defined

JOB DIMENSIONS — statement of relevant annual money sums on which the job has an impact, and of the total number of staff (if any) under its control:

Definition(s)   **Amount(s) * £**

Advertisement Sales on Middle East Health and
Far East Health

Total number of staff (if any) under its control: Nil

* Based on actual results in the fiscal year:

REPORTING RELATIONSHIPS — a diagram of the organisation structure incorporating the job, those of its peers (if any), that of the person to whom it/they report(s) and those of any people reporting to it, directly and indirectly.

Fig. 3.1 Job description for a sales executive

STAFF REPORTING DIRECTLY (if any) — a list of the job titles of staff reporting directly to the job holder *together with* a brief summary of the main responsibilities of each of them:

Nil

ENVIRONMENT — a brief statement of the product, market, commercial, technological, and PHYSICAL environment (both internal and external) within which the job functions:

Sales on monthly, controlled circulation titles, Middle East Health and Far East Health. Journals are circulated within respective regions with advertising sold to U.K. and International medical equipment and pharmaceutical companies. Job located at Times House with extensive U.K. travel and occasional European travel required.

FUNCTION — a description of the main functions and activities involved in the job (indicate roughly the proportion of time spent on each):

	% weighting
Servicing of clients to sell advertising to agreed targets by personal calls and by telephone/telex	80%
Keeping good records	10%
Monitoring competitive titles	5%
Obtain and updating first calls market knowledge	5%

... continued

FUNCTION (continued) . . .

DECISION-MAKING — examples of decisions made by the job holder WITHOUT REFERENCE to others:

Planning and implementing sales calls

— examples of matters WHICH ARE APPROVED OR REVIEWED by others:

Approval of expenditure for European sales visit

— examples of matters WHICH ARE SUBJECT TO INTERNAL OR EXTERNAL
CHECK (e.g. audit):

Claims for bonus payments

CONTROL INFORMATION — a list of the main records, and written or verbal reports prepared by the job holder for whom and how frequently:

Complete details on all clients in representatives area.
Weekly sales report and plan of next weeks sales calls
to Advertisement Manager.
Verbal and/or written reports on follow up on special
features/issues to Advertisement Manager as required.

PRINCIPAL ACCOUNTABILITIES — a description, by use of broad statements, of the main objectives of the job. Each accountability should define an end result which the job is aiming to achieve. Please number each accountability (usually there are not more than eight although there may be fewer). Please also rank the importance (or significance) of each accountability by assigning a percentage weighting in relation to the job as a whole (the sum of the weight given must add up to 100%):

% weighting

Achievement of agreed advertisement target. 30%

Servicing of clients
Performance standard - to call regularly and build-up a good
relationship with both actual and potential clients/agents. 30%

Market knowledge and the application of it
Performance standard - first calls knowledge of your journal
and its competitors.
Monitoring of competitive titles for leads on new business
and background on existing clients. 20%

Ability to work within a team
Performance standard - to establish and maintain a good
relationship with all other members of the journal staff. 10%

Effort, Loyalty and Industry
Performance standard - willingness to work without constant
supervision, to persevere, to be self-starting. 10%

Please use continuation sheets for any additional information.

AGREEMENT OF JOB DESCRIPTION (to be completed upon appointment)

	JOB HOLDER	PERSON TO WHOM JOB HOLDER REPORTS
NAME		
SIGNATURE		
DATE		

Job description

Date:	
Job title:	Salesman (Consumer)
Reports to:	Sales Manager
Job location:	Territory No. 1 – London
Objectives:	To sell profitably, retaining existing customers and securing new customers, reaching his sales objectives and targets.
Authorities and responsibilities:	1 To sell profitably the company's products to the retailer in accordance with sales objectives and targets.
	2 To call on customers according to the call plan agreed by his manager and plan and control his journey cycle.
	3 To plan sales presentation in order to show the benefits of the product, always carrying a full range of samples.
	4 To maintain and upgrade customer relationships.
	5 To negotiate display space, distribute point of sale material and sales literature.
	6 To collect overdue accounts as advised by credit department.
	7 To keep customer record cards up to date and process orders promptly.
	8 To submit weekly reports, including comments on competitor activity.
	9 To abide by the company policy on cars, expenses, appearance, etc.
Appraisal:	Performance against these objectives, and specified targets, will be appraised annually and promotion and salary increases given against these appraisals.
Standards to be derived from:	1 Profitable sales.
	2 Achievement of sales targets, particularly promotional lines.
	3 Economic journey planning.
	4 Skill in presentation of sales story.
	5 Ability to merchandise at retail stores economically and effectively.
	6 'Days of credit'.

Figure 3.2 Job description for a consumer goods salesman

PERSON PROFILE	Importance factor		
Quality	High	Medium	Low

Fig. 3.3 Person Profile rating format

(d) Experience related to a particular market or industry.
(e) Experience involving a particular type of sales outlet or customer.
(f) Number of jobs held in last 5 years.

Qualitative elements

The particular personal qualities or character traits the ideal applicant should bring to a particular sales job are difficult to identify and even more difficult to measure. They should be identified by defining those that are essential, those that are desirable and those that are acceptable.

Ideally, consideration should be given to such qualities/traits as:

(a) First and/or overall impression.
(b) Intelligence – if it is intended to measure this characteristic, it could be considered under Quantitative elements above; it will be covered later under psychological testing. Care should be taken in not setting the intelligence level too high because if the job does not require such a level, job holders may feel there is no mental challenge, become bored and a high labour turnover can result. In some cases, it may be even appropriate to set a ceiling on intelligence levels, otherwise a very routine selling job may become the 'training ground' for persons wishing to 'get into selling' but who lack initial basic 'qualifications'.
(c) Acceptable personality.
(d) Stability.
(e) Good verbal expression – a good communicator.
(f) Good attitude to work.
(g) Self-starter.
(h) Perseverance.
(i) Appropriate degree of sophistication.
(j) Likes people and is able to 'get on with others'.
(k) Empathy – the ability to understand others.

    (l)   Loyalty.

    (m) Honesty and integrity.

    (n)   Sincerity.

    (o)   Sense of humour.

    (p)   Willingness to accept responsibility.

    (q)   Adequate level of numerate dexterity.

    (r)   Adequate level of literacy.

Job motivation

The intensity of different combinations of desires/needs will motivate different people to different levels of work performance; these should be identified as part of the ideal person profile.

    (a)   Money – either because of the need for a regular income on basic salary or the opportunity to make money through high commission, bonuses, incentive schemes.

    (b)   Challenge and competitiveness.

    (c)   Likes working with people.

    (d)   Security and/or safe job.

    (e)   The degree of independence the selling role gives.

    (f)   Status – this may also be linked with the type/size of car or other peripheral benefits.

    (g)   Sense of power (real or apparent).

    (h)   Being of service.

    (i)   Opportunity to apply academic knowledge.

    (j)   Opportunity to pursue a personal interest commercially.

    (k)   A step towards future career progress.

    (l)   To experience the role of management as a territory manager.

    (m) To travel.

Some companies operate a weighting and rating system with the person profile, i.e. not only rating the particular element but also giving a higher weighting to some than to others. For example, while the need for experience in an industry might be rated at 3 (on a 1 to 5 scale), the level of computer knowledge needed may be relatively higher and therefore although willing to accept a rating of 3 (and train to a higher level later) the element may be weighted 4 (important), thus the score needed would be 3 × 4, i.e. 12 points.

Summary

Carrying out job analysis, preparing the job description and the person profile causes the sales manager to think objectively about the job he wants done and the ideal person for doing it. The work involved in doing this initially (it can be updated as a job evolves over the long term) is seldom wasted as the results have other uses, i.e. as the basis for recruitment advertising, the actual recruiting and interviewing later as a means of measuring the successful applicant's job performance and as the basis for a continuous sales training programme.

Robertson and Cooper* point out that personnel selection has two main elements. First there are individual differences between people and it therefore makes sense to attempt to match people with jobs. The second element is the proposition that it is possible to predict future job success on the basis of current or past behaviour. They point out that it is not possible to do this with absolute accuracy or that human behaviour is entirely predictable, but that it implies that systematic selection procedures can produce a more efficient workforce than a random matching of people with jobs. This is particularly true in the sales job area where mistaken selection judgements can prove very costly not only in the tangible cost areas of advertising, training, executive time remuneration etc., but also in the intangible costs of allowing the wrong man to project and sell company image, product and/or services; the results could be at best mediocre, at worst they could be disastrous for the company's future relationships with existing or potential customers. The reason why this is particularly applicable to sales management situations is that it can sometimes take a relatively long time to discover that the wrong appointment has been made because of the wide geographic spread of sales territories and also because the field sales person, mainly working alone, can cover up inadequacies, at least in the short term.

One danger in the use of the person profiles to evaluate applicants for sales jobs has been described as 'the halo error' i.e. where one personality trait overshadows and influences the effective evaluation of others.

In an adaptation of the halo error to the sales management situation, Strachan† points to the danger of sales managers employing men in their 'own image'. He terms this the 'halo' effect, and indicates that it emerges where sales managers knowingly or unknowingly follow the practice of looking for a large part of themselves in the men they recruit. He points out that when the 'halo effect' is pronounced, it blinds the sales manager to the faults or disadvantages of particular candidates and can be a serious danger to objective, fair and efficient selection. This again emphasises the need to carry out effective analysis of the job content, developing a good job description and identifying the qualities, traits, experience that the ideal person should bring to the job in the form of a person profile.

---

* I. Robertson and C. Cooper, *Human Behaviour in Organisations*. Macdonald & Evans, 1983, p. 109.
† I. Strachan, *The Training and Development of Salesmen*. Kogan Page, 1971, p. 56.

As sales personnel problems/difficulties arise or internal and/or external market situations change, the job analysis data can be updated, the job description re-specified and the person profile adjusted. There is always strong competition to discover and employ the best (potential) salesmen, and whether the sales manager achieves this depends on his ability not only to develop a system and identify the crucial elements necessary to perform a specific task but also on his (or his delegated managers') ability to apply it effectively and objectively.

Questions

1. What are the underlying differences between the many types of selling roles listed (e.g. differences of customer types, of service expectation by customers, of product knowledge etc.)?

2. Why is the activity of carrying out job analysis almost as important as the information it obtains for the sales manager?

3. Why is it important to have a job description and a person profile?

4. Why is it necessary to grade, rate and possibly weight the various elements of the person profile?

5. What are the tangible and intangible costs of appointing the wrong sales person?

6. What is the 'halo effect' and what are its dangers to the sales manager's recruitment plans?

CHAPTER 4

Selecting the right person

Objectives

This chapter is concerned with recruiting the right person for the particular sales job based on a job description and a person profile as described in the previous chapter. It will examine the main sources of recruitment and use of application forms. It will then consider the screening of applicants, the use of references, making telephone reference checks and compiling a short list. This will be followed by examining interviewing methods, the use of patterned interviewing, rating scheme and an interview record form, the use of tests, making the appointment decision and sending the letter of appointment.

Sources of recruitment

The methods of job analysis, job description and person profile developed in the previous chapter should form the basis of selecting the right sales person for a specific sales job.

Always commence the search for new sales personnel among existing staff unless the new role/task is so radically different or needs some specialised knowledge of a product/service/market new to the company or needs a totally fresh approach. Internal candidates should be divided into two categories, those already 'in sales' and all others; either may be seen as appropriate in certain circumstances. For example, persons dealing with telephone enquiries and orders in a sales office could be encouraged to see a field sales person's job as promotion, and such persons should be able to bring with them the sales/team work ethos of the company, as well as a knowledge of customers and 'the market'.

On the other hand, the recruitment of a person from another functional area of the company may be more appropriate. For example, in a highly technical engineering/electronics sales situation, an applicant from a production department could have the technical know-how needed but will, of course, need more training to acquire the right attitude to selling and customers, in addition to basic sales training. Certainly a policy of 'promotion from within' is always good for morale and motivation, offering opportunities in terms of career progression.

Existing sales or other staff can be involved by asking them for recommendations/referrals of people who could carry out the sales role/task. However, it is essential that they are aware of the details of the job and the type of person required. There are several main dangers with this method: the first is that a recommendation may be made on the basis of friendship rather than appropriateness of the person. Secondly, if on interview the sales manager does not appoint someone's 'friend', or appoints and later dismisses them, it could cause resentment from a person who before the recommendation was very happy in their present role but who now feels their judgement has been challenged.

Occasionally, recommendations from customers or potential customers are successful, particularly as there will be a psychological feeling that they need to support such a person if appointed. The disadvantages are similar to those in the previous paragraph.

One source often used is to attract competitors' sales personnel, but often there is the need to disproportionately increase salary and/or commission/bonus or benefits to make the move attractive which sometimes causes resentment with existing staff unless the increased benefits are universally applied. Also, some sales managers, although pleased with the potential new accounts that such a person could bring with them, are concerned with the loyalty factor, i.e. if a sales person can be 'bought' once it could happen again, the second time to the detriment of the company.

Although similar reservations are expressed about recruiting suppliers' sales representatives, some companies ask buyers in their own purchasing department to identify potential sales staff from those selling to them. The benefits are said to be that if they are good sales representatives they will know a lot about the company's business, its competitors and markets; also, their sales ability has been tested in a real-life selling situation.

Government and private employment agencies are another source of potential sales staff whose approaches range from the passive display of job opportunities to a high-activity recruitment drive for the right person. As the staff of such agencies are rarely specialised in the knowledge of a particular company, a highly detailed brief of the job and ideal person has to be given. The Professional Register operating at main government Job Centres is particularly useful when specialised/experienced sales personnel are required.

Polytechnics and universities are very useful sources of recruitment for sales personnel because of the many job-related diploma and degree courses that are offered. Particularly relevant are those which include periods of work experience in companies (sandwich courses), full-time courses that carry out assignments with companies and especially those in which marketing/marketing research/sales activities are studied. Also, some students will have had work experience before joining the course and, although they may view the sales job as further experience or as the next stage in their career progression, they can make a considerable contribution because of their high motivation and wide business appreciation.

When a sales manager feels in need of specialist professional help, or wishes to delegate the high initial administrative load of recruitment or is trying to fill a higher level sales job (e.g. executive salesman, area or regional manager, sales office manager), the specialist 'head-hunting' recruitment consultancy companies could be used. Although the costs of using this method may appear high, it depends on the perceived opportunity cost of the sales manager's time and how crucial the particular sales post happens to be, whether it is considered worth the fee; bearing in mind the cost of not finding the right man at the first attempt or of appointing the wrong man to a key post.

The sales manager should always be looking for new sales personnel either because of persons being promoted, leaving, retiring etc. or because of potential expansion, or simply so that he is aware of what is 'available in the market-place'. The sales manager should therefore keep and use a 'Potential Sales Persons' file where the names and addresses of likely future sales personnel are recorded and contacted when a post becomes available. These could include suitable people who write to the company on their own initiative, or simply call at the company for a sales job, or who the sales manager meets at business, professional associations or social functions.

Recruitment advertising

By far the most popular source of recruitment of sales personnel is that of advertising in national and/or local newspapers (paid for or free), trade and technical press and the journals of professional bodies. Less widely used because of its specialised nature is direct mail advertising based on lists of members of professional bodies. A high percentage of job advertisements either fail completely or attract insufficient or the wrong response, therefore a considerable amount of money can be wasted if it is not done effectively.

The question arises, therefore, whether recruitment advertising is best done by the sales manager, by the company's personnel function (which if not involved in sales personnel recruitment would advertise for all other personnel vacancies), by the company's advertising agency (which is often under-used in this area) or by specialist recruitment advertising agencies. It is a question of balancing the expertise within the company with the cost of buying outside services and the cost of making a wrong appointment or one that could have been filled more effectively.

Other key factors that affect the cost–benefit equation of recruitment advertising are:

(a) Does the advertising need to be national to get the right level of applicant, in which case particular national newspapers will be appropriate? If there are likely to be a large enough number of candidates of the right calibre at the geographic location of the sales post, then local, paid-for or free newspapers will be more economical. Where highly specialised sales personnel are required, journals of professional bodies, trade and technical press and direct mail advertising using professional body membership lists may prove more cost-effective; the response rate will be much lower but the quality tends to be higher. Care should be taken not to use overlapping media.

(b) The cost per column inch will vary between the press categories (national, local trade and technical and professional journal) and also within press categories (*Daily Telegraph, Sunday Times, Daily Mail*) and so it needs to be related to circulation and readership. Details of rates charged and circulation (i.e. number of copies sold) achieved can be found in the monthly publication *BRAD* (*British Rate and Data*) and comparisons made. Readership information is usually available from surveys sponsored by the particular medium. It must be remembered that the most popular medium will tend to have higher rates, will sometimes have longer delays before publication and, because of the number of advertisers, there will tend to be high competition for the attention of the reader in terms of type and size of advertisement.

(c) There is also a need to balance size and type of advertisement with the number of insertions. The size and type (classified or display) can have a considerable impact in getting the readers' attention but is it likely that all the potential applicants for a sales post will read the one advertisement on a particular occasion? Compare the overall impact and chance of one half-page advertisement being seen in one newspaper on one occasion with two quarter pages or four one-eighth pages either in one newspaper or several. The matter is complicated by the fact that publication frequency can be daily, weekly, monthly etc. and that various opinions exist regarding good and bad days to advertise and good and bad locations in newspapers and journals.

(d) Advertisements that use box numbers (i.e. not mentioning the name of the company), those that did not mention remuneration (salary, commission, bonus etc.) and those that do not mention the location of the sales territory do not receive such a high response rate as those that do. Clearly reasons must be exceptional for one of these factors to be left out of an advertisement.

After considering the above four points, a good approach to designing a recruitment advertisement therefore is:

(a) To decide whether it is to appear as a display or a classified advertisement; this will affect how the content is expressed.

(b) Next list everything that needs to be said in the advertisement and identify the objectives.

(c) List the major benefits of the job to readers.

(d) It pays to spend some time reading through other job advertisements of a similar nature in the medium chosen.

(e) Consider carefully the component parts of an effective job advertisement:

(1) A headline with impact to get attention. This may not be the job title, particularly if this would be misleading or may not be understood by the reader. A heading that arouses curiosity and is in the form of a question attracts attention.

(2) It is desirable to include in the advertisement something about the company as an employer of the particular job type being offered; this adds credibility.

(3) Based on the job description, details of the job, type of business, duties, responsibilities, location, scope and especially the attractive elements of the job should be given.

(4) Based on the person profile, a description of the type of person needed, age, experience, professional and/or academic qualifications needed/desired should be given; this enables readers to identify themselves 'into' or 'out of' the job.

(5) The rewards of the sales job should be clearly stated as this is one of the prime motivators to respond. Salary, commission, bonus, other financial inducements, pension, fringe benefits, use of car etc. should all be mentioned. If possible, job satisfaction should be highlighted.

(6) A statement of what action is required of an applicant and who should be contacted.

(f) It is not essential to have sub-headings but they do help to emphasise specific parts of the advertisement, as do 'bold' print and the underlining of key features.

(g) Always remember that you are 'selling' rather than 'announcing' a job vacancy; do not forget the Sex Discrimination Act and, to use the well-established advertising maxim, make sure your advertisement is legal, honest, decent and truthful.

The advertisement will suggest either that an interested reader should telephone a particular person for further information or write to a particular person. In both cases, the resulting telephone call or the application letter, in addition to making contact, should also be used as the first stage of the screening process. There is also a tendency of getting a higher response rate if there is an opportunity to discuss and obtain more information about the job on the telephone. The opposite effect will occur if applicants are asked for lengthy details (e.g. description of careers to date) at this stage.

If a telephone response is required, the sales manager should notify the telephone operator of an expected increase in the number of calls and give the name and extension number of the person who has been nominated to handle the enquiries. The smooth handling of applicants' calls helps to sell the company image and sets a level of efficiency expectation with applicants. Companies differ in their application of the telephone job enquiry approach. Some have a secretary handling the calls and merely recording such basic information as:

(a) Name.
(b) Telephone number(s) (with any time constraints) at which enquirer can be contacted.
(c) Address including postcode.
(d) Date and location of advertisement seen.
(e) Whether they have a current driving licence (if appropriate for post).
(f) Current employment, duration, salary, car, expenses etc.
(g) Previous experience.
(h) Brief description of education and qualifications.
(i) Salary requirements.
(j) Whether willing to move home (if appropriate).
(k) When applicant could be available.

Other companies have a sales executive/supervisor handling the telephone calls but, in addition to obtaining the basic information above, they probe more deeply as to attitudes, personal characteristics and job motivation. The information is written into an outline report on the applicant.

If a written response is required, there are again two approaches. First, the advertisement could say 'Write a letter of application to . . .' a named individual at a given address and applicants will then usually write giving some details about themselves; again, this could be used as a stage one screening device. While the response to those passing this screening will be to send them an application form, those rejected at this stage will need to be sent a sensitive letter thanking them for applying but pointing out that, although it recognises they have a lot to offer, it regrettably does not match up to the special needs of this particular sales post. The second approach is for the advertisement to say 'Please telephone or write for further details and application form to . . .' a named individual. This method will not produce the same amount of personal information as the first but does provide the opportunity to give applicants more information about the post and the company, and on receipt of this the applicant may or may not decide to proceed with the application, so a form of self-screening takes place.

At some stage in the selection process, whatever combination of sources of recruitment used, all applicants should be required to complete an application form. This will need to be carefully designed to obtain enough information on which to carry out the second stage of screening of applicants, but one which is not too long or blatantly personal (such information, if appropriate, is best obtained at an interview) that will deter applicants from responding.

Additionally, a personalised letter needs to be written (signed personally by the sales manager) to accompany the application form, thanking the applicant for responding, encouraging him/her to complete and return the form, explaining what will happen next and giving the deadline date for the receipt of application forms.

An information sheet giving additional details of the post, remuneration, deadline date for applications and the company may also be appropriate to send to applicants with the application form.

Application forms

The application form is crucial to the success of the sales person selection process because:

(a) It ensures that the basic information identified as necessary in the person profile (the quantitative factors, experience, qualitative elements and job motivation, see Chapter 2) is obtained in a concise, standardised manner and in a sequence that enables comparisons to be made between applicants.

(b) It enables a lot of the basic information about an applicant to be obtained more quickly than in an interview.

(c) Because of (a) it enables effective screening of applicants to take place, eliminating many unsuitable applicants, and results in a short list for interviewing.

(d) One of the abilities required from sales personnel is that they can 'sell the benefits' of a proposition, and application letters can reflect the emphasis of their own 'benefits' that applicants wish to highlight and can also play down weaknesses. The application form should be able to ascertain the unembroidered facts and eliminate emotive comment (except perhaps in the section 'Any other comments you wish to make, or information you wish to give, regarding your application').

(e) If it is well designed and on quality paper, it can project an efficient/quality image and 'sell' the company.

(f) It will form the basis of the successful applicant's personal file.

Application forms need to be designed to meet the special needs of particular companies and, ideally, within companies special versions of them should be developed for sales personnel.

The application form (Fig. 4.1) covers the applicant's factual details, education, early career, experience, present job information, names of referees. Some companies also require that a photograph of the applicant be sent with the completed form.

Name of company

Application form for the post of _____

To enable us to consider you for this post it would be helpful if you would answer every question fully. If you do not have enough space to answer fully or feel that an answer needs qualifying in any way, please continue the answer in the final section of the form.

Any information given will be treated confidentially and no enquiries will be made to past or present employers without prior consent from you.

Your contact with the company regarding this application is _____

Date _____ 19_____

1. Personal details

Name _____

(Surname in capitals please)

Present address _____

_____

_____ Post Code _____

How long have you lived there? _____ Nationality _____

Home telephone number _____ Business telephone No. _____

Date of birth _____ Place of birth _____ Age _____

Male ☐   Female ☐   Height _____ Weight _____

Are you a British Citizen? Yes ☐ No ☐

Present marital status:

Single ☐;   Married ☐;   Separated ☐;   Divorced ☐;

Widowed ☐;   Remarried ☐

Number of children ☐;   their ages _____

Number of dependants ☐;   their ages _____

Do you own a car? Yes ☐ No ☐;   Type, make, year _____

_____

Fig. 4.1 An example of an application form for a sales post

Have you a current driving licence? Yes ☐ No ☐

Are you physically handicapped in any way? Yes ☐ No ☐

If so, in what way(s) _____

_____

Date and nature of last illness, accident, operation etc. _____

_____

_____

Why are you applying to this company? _____

_____

_____

How did you learn of this post (advertisement, a friend, etc.)?

_____

Have you ever been employed by this company? Yes ☐ No ☐

If so, when? _____ and where? _____

Names of relatives/acquaintances employed by this company _____

_____

Education

Type of educational institution	Name of educational institution	Dates of attendance	Examinations passed	Nature of course taken
Primary				
Comprehensive				
Grammar				
Public				
Sixth Form				
Further Education				
Polytechnic				
University				
Postgraduate				
Other				

List any other educational experiences (correspondence courses, evening classes, Open University, day/evening release course whilst holding a job, etc.)

_____

_____

Training Courses attended

Dates from/to	Company or training scheme	Nature of course

What language(s) other than English do you speak? _____

_____

Employment Record

Start with MOST RECENT post and list below the names and addresses of employers; use additional pages if necessary.

Name _____

Address _____

_____

Type of business _____

          month   year   month   year

Employed from _____ to _____

Were you fidelity/surety bonded? _____ Job title _____

Salary _____ Commission _____ Bonus _____ Other incentives

_____

Describe duties _____

Why did you leave? _____

Can we contact this company? Yes ☐ No ☐; Name of person to contact

_____

When would you be available to commence work if appointed? _____

Name _____

Address _____

_____

Type of business _____

             month   year   month   year

Employed from _____ to _____

Were you fidelity/surety bonded? _____ Job title _____

Salary _____ Commission _____ Bonus _____ Other incentives

_____

Describe duties _____

Why did you leave? _____

Can we contact this company? Yes ☐ No ☐; Name of person to contact

_____

Name _____

Address _____

_____

Type of business _____

             month   year   month   year

Employed from _____ to _____

Were you fidelity/surety bonded? _____ Job title _____

Salary _____ Commission _____ Bonus _____ Other incentives

_____

Describe duties _____

Why did you leave? _____

Can we contact this company? Yes ☐ No ☐; Name of person to contact

_____

Name _____

Address _____

_____

Type of business _____

             month   year   month   year

Employed from _____ to _____

Were you fidelity/surety bonded? _____ Job title _____

Salary _____ Commission _____ Bonus _____ Other incentives

                                              _____

Describe duties _____

Why did you leave? _____

Can we contact this company? Yes ☐ No ☐; Name of person to contact

_____

Name _____

Address _____

_____

Type of business _____

             month   year   month   year

Employed from _____ to _____

Were you fidelity/surety bonded? _____ Job title _____

Salary _____ Commission _____ Bonus _____ Other incentives

                                              _____

Describe duties _____

Why did you leave? _____

Can we contact this company? Yes ☐ No ☐; Name of person to contact

_____

Name _____

Address _____

_____

Type of business _____

	month	year		month	year

Employed from _____ to _____

Were you fidelity/surety bonded? _____ Job title _____

Salary _____ Commission _____ Bonus _____ Other incentives

_____

Describe duties _____

Why did you leave? _____

Can we contact this company? Yes ☐ No ☐; Name of person to contact

_____

Which of the above jobs did you like best? _____

Why? _____

Please summarise any selling/product/industry/market job experience you have had in the above posts that you consider particularly relevant to this application.

_____

_____

Describe any supervisory/management aspects (including number of persons supervised) of the above posts relevant to this application

_____

Have you served in any branch of H.M. Forces?

Branch	Dates From To	Rank	Duties	Awards/Decorations

References (not relatives or former employers)

	Name	Address	Telephone No.
1.			
2.			
3.			

Social

What are your hobbies or special interests? _____

_____

Are you, or have you been, involved in any charity or social work?

Yes ☐   No ☐

If so, what sort? _____

Of what social clubs or organisations are you a member? _____

_____

Are you a member of any professional bodies?   Yes ☐   No ☐

If so, which _____

_____

Any other comments you wish to make, or information you wish to give regarding your application? For example, your ambitions, your long-term plans, your strengths, your attitude towards selling, what is the attraction of the post, etc.

Date _____   Signature _____

When application forms are sent out, they should be numbered and a record kept of the date they were sent, the date received back, who received the application, on what date and what action was recommended (arrange interview, telephone, reject etc.) and when it was taken.

Once the application deadline has passed, the next screening stage can take place by reviewing all the application forms. This is an elimination process carried out by comparing the information submitted against the job description and the person profile. The danger is that this process will become too subjective or that one factor on an application form may be given undue emphasis (a type of 'halo' effect) so that the elimination/selection list may be inconsistent in its make-up.

One useful method that gives this highly subjective process an objective approach is to use an application form rating scheme listing each applicant and rating specially identified factors on a 1 (poor) to 5 (excellent) scale. This method does allow for a qualitative approach as well as quantitative. For example, because of the number of past jobs held, an applicant could be rated as 4 against the experience factor, but because he was 'job hopping' without there being a consistency of job type perhaps he should be rated 3. On the other hand, an applicant with less experience and fewer jobs who could be rated 3 is perhaps rated as 4 because of the steady career progression and consistency shown although this may not be in the industry of the current post.

An example of an application form rating scheme is shown in Fig. 4.2.

Name of applicant	Age	Qualifications/ education	Relevance of qualifications/ education	Experience	Relevance of experience	Selling experience	Relevance of selling experience	Personal details	Social background	Motivations/ ambitions	Points scored	Comments
1.												
2.												
3.												
4.												
etc.												

Fig. 4.2 Application form rating scheme

Application forms, being concerned mainly with factual information, are rarely indicators of the nuances, the depth of attitudes and character traits (these are best probed at an interview) but they should show whether the basic requirements of the job description and the person profile are present. They help the sales manager to form an impression and will be useful later when interviewing to identify gaps in career continuity or areas of inconsistency. However, too many of these negative factors at the application form stage would suggest elimination unless there are exceptional reasons for giving an interview.

The application form rating scheme will produce a list of applicants in order of scores obtained; from these can be produced a 'long' short list. Different companies and consultants have different approaches to short-listing but for one vacancy only, a good method is to put together initially a 'long' short list of ten or eleven potential applicants, obtain references and, following the consideration of these, produce a short list of five or six. With more than one job vacancy, the numbers on the 'long' short list and the final short list will need to be adjusted.

References

These are of two types. The first is work-related (i.e. references obtained from previous and present employers) and the second is those personal references obtained from referees named by the applicant on the application form. However, if the applicant specifically states on the application form that he does not wish contact to be made with the present employer, this should be respected and only carried out later after a successful interview; most applicants do not object to contact being made with previous employers. It should be realised that the applicant would not have given the names of personal referees on the form unless fairly certain of a good reference. All the same, these are useful for noting how comments are expressed or what they leave out and certainly for comparison with the work-related references.

Work-related references can be obtained either in writing, by telephone or by personally meeting the referee. All three are used to verify and expand information on the application form and to obtain comments about the applicant. Consequently a broad, bland reference will be of little use and in any case will not cover all the information required. A patterned or structured form needs to be used to ensure all points are covered with every applicant. Many companies are very reticent about asking for references and even more so when it comes to checking the validity of information given. However, when the tangible and intangible costs of appointing the wrong person are realised, such investigation is more than justified.

An example of a work-related reference check is shown in Fig. 4.3.

If the form is sent through the post to be completed by the referee, more effective completion rates seem to be obtained by a telephone call beforehand so that the work-related reference check form is expected.

Sometimes persons contacted in organisations are reluctant to put into writing comments about former/present employees but might be prepared to comment on the telephone if assurances are given as to how the information will be used. Also, because some companies are concerned about passing personal information on the telephone in case the caller is not the person

Name of company
Work-related reference check   Date _____

Referee _____   Position held _____

Company _____   Telephone No. _____

Address _____

_____

Concerning: Applicant _____

              Address _____

I would appreciate your help and co-operation in verifying some information provided by

_____ who has applied for the post of _____
with our company and also to obtain your views and comments with regard to his/her
suitability for the sales post described in the details attached (these are the further details
which the company sent to the applicant with the application form).

1.   What type of work was he/she doing when he/she was with your company; at the
beginning, during and at the end?

2.   What were the dates of his/her employment with your company?

from _____ to _____

3.   Were you his/her immediate manager?

4.   If not what was your organisational relationship to him/her?

5.   Did he/she supervise anyone; if so, who and how many?

6.   How did he/she get on with people?
     (a) colleagues of equal status?
     (b) colleagues of lower status?
     (c) customers?
     (d) managers?

7.   Was he/she paid:
          Salary?   Commission?   Bonus?   Other incentives?

          These were _____
          Expenses?

8.   Was he/she provided with a car?

9.   Was he/she surety/fidelity bonded?

10.   What type of selling did he/she do?

11.   How did the applicant's results compare with others in a similar sales position?

12. Was the applicant a hard worker, self starter and does he have commitment?

13. What was the applicant's work pattern in terms of attendance, absenteeism, illness, etc.

14. How well did the applicant plan his/her work and respond to management guidance?

15. What was his/her response to training?

16. What were the applicant's:
    (a) Strengths?
    (b) Weaknesses?

17. What do you think of him/her?

18. Why did he/she leave your company?

19. Would you re-employ him/her again?   Yes ☐   No ☐

20. If not, why not?

21. Would your recommend him/her for this sales post?   Yes ☐   No ☐

22. Is there anything else you would like to say about the applicant that would help us to consider him/her for this sales post?

Thank you for your help and co-operation.

Signed _____

                Sales Manager.

Fig. 4.3 A work-related reference check form

he/she claims to be, it is often helpful to offer the caller's telephone number so that the referee can check and then call back.

Because of cost and time constraints, actually visiting referees is carried out only in exceptional circumstances. Using the reference check form as the basis for discussion, a face-to-face talk with a work-related referee is perhaps the most effective way of validating and extending information given by an applicant and obtaining an uninhibited opinion as to the acceptability of his/her personality and ability in selling.

The checking of application form information in general and the use of a reference check form in particular is a very effective approach but one that the sales manager may have to 'sell' to his superiors and also the persons contacted. However, it will help confirm or invalidate information, screen out some applicants, raise some topics for further discussion if the applicant is given an interview and, most important, enable a short list to be drawn up for interviewing.

Interviewing

An interview can be defined as meeting face-to-face specifically for the purpose of obtaining a statement and assessing the qualities of a candidate.

In the context of the needs of sales management, the interview and interviewing need to be more broadly defined to include the following, either singly or in combination:

(a) one-to-one interviews
(b) interview by panel of two or more
(c) group interviews
(d) role playing
(e) psychological testing/aptitude testing
(f) product/technical/process knowledge testing

Robertson and Cooper* state: 'An important and basic requirement of any selection device is that it should enable different selectors to come to the same conclusions about candidates they are assessing.'

However, in the sales management situation this may not strictly apply. The relationship of the sales manager to the sales person needs to be of a particular 'psychological fit'. This is not the 'halo effect' (i.e. to appoint someone like himself/herself) but the sales manager having the feeling that, even if all other factors are favourable, he/she also has a certain confidence in the person appointed. Confidence not only that they can 'get on well together' but that he/she can motivate, train and lead so that the sales person will be a 'self-starter' and work the same way when the sales manager is or is not directly supervising. This is particularly important with field sales staff who may be working a sales territory hundreds of miles away with relative little direct sales management supervision. On this basis, two different sales managers using the same methods in the same sales/company situation might well appoint a different person.

From the sales person's point of view, the relationship must 'feel right', that the sales manager will lead, inspire, keep him/her informed of developments, is interested in people, and will give constructive training and direction. Unless this is so, the applicant, depending on other pressures, may not accept the job even if it is offered; there should be an element of 'selling' the job, the sales manager and the company in any job interview.

Before any form of interviewing takes place, a programme needs to be arranged and the timetable for this will depend mainly on the number of candidates on the short list and which of the six 'interviewing' activities listed above, used singly or in combination, will take place. For example, a two-stage interview will take longer than a single one; a single interview in

* I. Robertson and C. Cooper, *Human Behaviour in Organisations*. Macdonald & Evans, 1983, p. 115.

combination with aptitude and/or psychological testing will need additional time.

Also, the programme will depend on where the interview will take place. If it has been a nation-wide search for a large number of sales representatives, the sales manager may find it more convenient to hold interviews in regional offices or in hotels in the regions and may even delegate the preliminary interviewing to area or regional managers. If they are to be carried out centrally, it is a good opportunity to 'sell' the company if they are carried out at Head Office or at a production facility rather than use a hotel as preferred by some companies.

So, assuming that an appropriate timetable has been arranged, that references have been obtained from named referees and previous employers, and that the short-listed candidates have been invited to attend, the actual process of interviewing can take place.

There are many opinions as to the most effective way of interviewing. There is the single interview on a one-to-one basis, or the preliminary interview followed by a final one later, both by the same person, or the 'second opinion' approach with two interviews carried out by two different people. There is the panel approach (i.e. the interviewing being carried out by two or more people), again with the alternatives of single or multiple interviews.

Whichever method is employed, the interview should have some pre-determined pattern or structure if pertinent information in line with the ideal person profile is to be obtained, or underlying attitudes are to be probed and drawn out and if comparisons between candidates are to be made. The most important thing to remember is that the sales manager is looking for the special type of person who can later control sales interviews with customers, guiding them in certain directions, and therefore the more effective the candidate is in selling, the more likely that the job interview will be controlled by him/her unless some objective, pre-determined pattern or structure is set up.

Ideally there are three aids to effective patterned interviewing:

(a) *The interview record form.* This should show the name of candidate, name of interviewer(s), date of interview, where it took place, title of sales job involved, objective of interview and a list of the areas to be probed, identified by examining the initial letter and the application form, i.e. discrepancies, areas that need expanding, omissions, peculiar wording of events or past activities and space for comment on these. It should also record length of the interview, assessment of the candidate's suitability for the job and any action promised or taken. Because of the problems of remembering particular individuals when later assessment and comparison of a large number of applicants take place, some companies use a camera to produce an instant photograph to be attached to the interview record form.

OBJECTIVE RATING SCHEME

Key factor/attributes	1	2	3	4	5
Ability to communicate	Has great difficulty in expressing himself/herself. Uses inappropriate words.	Below average in ability to communicate; is not clear and concise in expression.	Communication ability average.	Above average communication ability, good range of verbal expression.	Extremely fluent, communicates excellently. Interesting vocabulary.
Attitude to challenge and competitiveness	Highly competitive situations would cause stress and a sense of insecurity.	Would cope with various levels of competition but would not be at ease with the challenge.	Would be neither elated nor worried by highly competitive situation.	Various levels of competition would have only a marginal effect on improving performance.	Would thrive on challenge and competition and be stimulated to higher performance.
General appearance	Has that 'uncared' for look. Well below the acceptable level of personal hygiene and appearance.	Slightly below average personal appearance and neatness. Slightly inappropriately dressed.	Average acceptable level of personal appearance. Would not 'stand out' in a crowd.	Above average personal appearance and neatness; dressed appropriately.	Extremely well turned out, high level of personal impact. Presents a 'quality' image.

Fig. 4.4 Examples of rating key person profile factors

(b) *The patterned interview form.* This should list a series of opinion-type, open-ended questions to be asked of all candidates on specific areas to be tested, i.e. motivations and attitudes, likes and dislikes, work history, experience, education and qualifications, reconciliation of the demands of the particular post with candidates' present health, financial, domestic and social situation etc. By ensuring all candidates answer all questions, better comparison between applicants is possible. The purpose is also not to ask questions already covered by the application form.

(c) *An objective rating system.* This should take the form of listing key areas from the person profile (and possibly some from the job description) and, against each key area, shown on a 1 (poor) to 5 (excellent) scale, the level that could be expected from the candidate. Three examples of the key areas and their ratings are shown in Fig. 4.4, but some companies use as many as twenty-five areas to be rated.

Having set up the rating levels against which to assess all the short-listed applicants (it can also be filed and used again on future recruitment occasions), the second part of an objective rating scheme is to list all candidates horizontally on a single sheet of paper that also lists vertically the key factor/attributes shown in the rating scheme, so that against each name a rating value for the particular key factor/attribute can be given (see Fig. 4.5).

CANDIDATE RATING VALUE SCORES					
Key factor/attribute	Brown	Green	Smith	Jones	Baker
Ability to communicate	5	4	2	4	3
Attitude to challenge and competitiveness	4	5	3	3	3
General appearance	5	4	2	4	3
etc.					

Fig. 4.5

Although this may appear to be a rather mechanistic approach, it does enable a degree of objectivity to be introduced to what can be a highly subjective process. Also, if more than one person is involved in interviewing, the differences on such a points scale may develop constructive discussion as to the differences perceived.

Essentials of interviewing

Ensure that arrangements have been made to give a friendly welcome to candidates on arrival, that a comfortable waiting room is available and that coffee/tea is offered while they are waiting.

Ensure that the interview room is pleasant, airy and away from external noise, that the seating for interviewees and interviewer is comfortable and not opposite a window where either's attention can be distracted or where the sunlight or internal lighting can cause discomfort. A desk or table for papers etc. is helpful and, if there is a telephone, ensure that the telephonist has been told that there are to be no calls on this particular extension. In other words, an environment conducive to a relaxed interview where both the interviewee and interviewer can talk without interruptions or distractions.

A friendly greeting by the interviewer and a few moments of general comments are necessary to put the interviewee at ease. The questions/ discussion should centre around the requirements of the patterned interview form, the job description and the person profile. The interviewee should be encouraged to talk by the use of open-ended/opinion-type questions (usually involving the use of such words as what, why, how, where, who) and descriptive questions ('Would you tell me about . . .?' and 'To what extent do you think . . .?'). Give the candidate time to think of the answers, especially opinion-type questions. The interviewer needs to be a good listener, letting the candidate 'talk himself out' on a topic unless he deviates too far from the point, when the interviewer should interrupt with a question to regain control and direction of the interview. Interviewing must be about friendly, firm and fair questioning, listening, interpreting, probing, checking, assessing, accurately noting all relevant information; it is also about 'selling the company' to high-potential applicants.

There is little point in asking questions already answered on the application form unless an answer is oddly worded and/or unless there appears to be a discrepancy or contradiction either on the form or which arises during the course of the interview.

Avoid leading questions (those that indicate what answer the interviewer would like); ask one question at a time, phrasing them so they are neutral; don't take sides or challenge loyalties or moralise on the candidate's political, religious, social views or behaviour; it will only influence/inhibit later replies to questions.

Be observant and perceptive about what is said (whether it confirms the possession of knowledge, experience, skills claimed), how it is said (tone, manner, wording, emphasis and skill in expressing ideas) and the accompanying 'body language' (facial expression, posture, mannerisms, movement and/or agitation of hands and does the candidate look the interviewer in the eye when he/she makes a committing statement?).

Deal with any questions raised by the candidate as the interview progresses, but in any case give him/her the opportunity to ask them at the end and/or ask if there are any other factors the applicant feels should have been or would like discussed. The candidate should then be thanked for coming to the interview and told what action will now take place, e.g. 'I will let you know by telephone/letter after we have interviewed the other candidates'.

Even after the candidate has left the room, the interview is not complete until the notes have been summarised, the interview record card completed, the objective rating carried out and rating scores entered plus the noting of any additional/exceptional points.

Personal interviewing

This is the most popular recruitment method, but will only be effective if carried out efficiently, methodically and objectively. It may also be considered necessary to supplement it with the following activities which may be carried out before the interview (in which case it may have an effect on its content) or after (where they are often used as the final confirmation before an appointment is made).

Group interviewing

The purpose of group interviewing of candidates can range from briefing them on all aspects of the job and company instead of repeating the information to each individual, to using it to eliminate some of those on the 'long short list' (perhaps nine or ten), to produce a short list of five or six, to using it to choose the candidate that 'stands out' from the short-listed group.

One method is to set up a group discussion (on almost any appropriate topic, e.g. selling methods, the industry, the market situation etc.) to observe such factors as an individual's vocal expression, clarity of thought, attitudes, motivations, social skills, levels of knowledge, ability to take control of an 'interview' etc. This method needs a good chairman, and some companies also have one or two observers present also. Several companies introduce highly controversial matters for discussion so as to observe behaviour when feelings are aroused.

Another group interview method is, after initially briefing, to divide into smaller groups (two or three) to perform some task or exercise before reforming as a whole to discuss the findings. Several companies use small case studies appropriate to the company or sales situation to form the basis of the smaller group activity. These small group activity interviews are used to identify leadership qualities in candidates as well as those qualities mentioned for the discussion group method.

Role playing

The rationale for using role playing as a selection device for a sales position is that it tests in a practical way the validity of claims made in application forms, personal interviews and in references as to a candidate's ability in selling and social skills.

Ideally, the candidate, playing the role of a salesman, will be briefed (and given time to assimilate sufficient knowledge) as to the selling situations, benefits of the product/service, elementary market knowledge, objections usually made etc. The sales manager plays the role of 'buyer' and usually no one else is present, although several companies use video recordings for later analysis. Sometimes the role play approach is to ask the candidate to make a sales presentation of his present product/service.

The role play situation is obviously a false one and rarely does it result in a perfect sales interview, but it does give the sales manager an impression of the presence of social skills and how well a candidate can cope with the stress of a sales situation.

Psychological testing

Psychological tests can be divided into a number of broad categories including those that measure/assess personality, general intelligence, sensory perception, abilities and aptitudes, comparison and interpretation, reaction to stress and non-stress situations, verbal expression and mental dexterity.

They range from tests that can be purchased together with the answers, to those to which the answers need interpreting by a psychologist, to those that need administering and interpreting by psychologists or consultants.

The popularity of psychological tests seems to vary from time to time. There seems to be a sharp division between sales managers who consider them an extremely useful selection device and those who do not. With the recent advances made in behavioural sciences, sales managers have expectations that there should exist at least one type of test which has moderate validity with regard to the selection of sales personnel and which can provide data (regarding candidates) that cannot be obtained from other sources.

Personality is probably the most important single factor leading to sales success, yet it is the most difficult to evaluate.

Tests of ability are popular, particularly the ability to learn and assimilate new knowledge. Simple intelligence tests that measure the ability to think and reason, particularly those that measure the applicant's I.Q., have wide acceptance. Some companies use graphologists or handwriting experts who claim that from a minimum of 20 lines of a candidate's handwriting they can identify such characteristics as honesty, drive, ambition and can detect health, drink and other problems.

The danger with all these tests is for the sales manager to set a pass level that is beyond the needs of the particular sales post. This leads in some cases to over-endowed appointees quickly looking for more challenging sales roles or becoming frustrated with necessary routine work crucial to the sales job. Some companies now identify maximum as well as minimum standards necessary.

There are many such psychological tests available, but their 'track record' suggests they should only be used in conjunction with other selection methods, not as the sole indicator. The ideal time to use such tests is after the first selection interview and before the second.

Therefore the approach should be to determine the objective(s) of testing, identify the factors (e.g. personality, motivation, intelligence) that the sales manager wants to measure, find tests (and/or psychologists) that will measure these factors specifically, apply them as part of the selection procedure and later monitor the success of persons appointed. This way a bank of experience can be built up indicating which tests are useful in meeting the special needs of particular sales task/roles and sales managers.

Other selection tests

There is a wide variety of other tests that specifically measure the candidate's ability to cope with specialised aspects of particular sales jobs. These could include written competency tests with regard to product, technical, process and service knowledge, which are areas which are vital not only with regard to a candidate's ability to carry out the job but to his credibility with customers. Tests relating to dexterity and motor skills are particularly appropriate where physical sales demonstrations are necessary. Sales persons who need to run meetings with agents, distributors, franchises etc. need to be tested by making presentations or tested orally. This would also apply to applicants who would be required in the job situation to carry out rapid mental calculations with regard to machine performance, pay-back periods, discounted cash flow, profits, prices and discounts, stock turn and levels, profit per square foot of shelf space, insurance premium payments etc.

The selection decision

From previous employer contact, the selection interview(s) and the rating scheme supported, if appropriate, by various tests, a fairly clear indication of the best candidate on the short list should have emerged. Even so, the sales manager has to motivate, lead, train and rely on the appointee and should therefore be completely confident that the 'right' person has emerged from the process for him, the company and the customers. Picking the best of a 'poor bunch' should be avoided and if results of the selection process show the whole short list not to be of the desired quality to carry out the job effectively, the need to re-advertise the post in different media with or without changed job conditions should be seriously considered.

Following the final decision to appoint, a friendly letter of appointment should be sent to the successful applicant or a telephone call made, followed up by a letter of appointment inviting him/her to confirm acceptance and stating precisely what action should be taken. This should be done before the other short-listed candidates are told that they have been unsuccessful in case, after reflection on the interviews, the prime candidate decides to withdraw. In such circumstances, the other applicants should only be considered if they came close to the leading candidate. Unsuccessful candidates should be sent a letter that is sensitive to the disappointment that will be experienced by the receiver. To those in which the sales manager would have been interested if there had been more vacancies, the comment that he would like to keep the particular person's details on file for consultation in future vacancies is helpful.

Sales staff recruitment and the personnel function

A special case has been made for the sales manager to recruit/select his own sales staff. In companies where a personnel function exists, some involvement of it may be insisted upon, i.e. that it carries out the recruitment advertising or that it carries out the short-listing based on the sales manager's job specification and person profile. It may even be an accepted procedure that personnel staff be involved in initial interviewing. Even where the sales manager is not required to have the personnel function's involvement, it is helpful/useful to seek its specialist advice on recruitment matters, get it to check and discuss job descriptions, person profiles and recruitment advertisements, and to keep it generally informed. A second specialist opinion may avoid mistakes being made.

Summary

Having carried out job analysis, developed a job description and person profile, obtained information by means of application letters, application forms, references, contact with previous employers, carried out interviews using interview record forms, patterned interviewing and an objective rating scheme, supported if appropriate by other tests, the successful candidate has emerged and has been appointed. This process may appear somewhat protracted but such time is well spent when it is realised that a commitment is being made, possibly for a period of many years, to a person who will represent the company's interests. Also, the tangible and intangible costs of appointing the wrong person can be extremely high and the repercussions could be felt for many years.

Questions

  1. What are the advantages and disadvantages of the various sources of recruitment?
  2. What are the key considerations when using recruitment advertising?

3. Why are comprehensive application forms so essential to effective sales personnel recruitment and selection?

4. When recruiting sales personnel, why is it necessary to have previous employers' references and personal references and reference checks?

5. Why is a broader definition given to interviewing for sales posts and what are the advantages of the different types of activity involved?

CHAPTER 5

The training of sales personnel

Objectives

This chapter covers the scope of training in the sales function context, what training can and cannot do, and the multi-dimensional nature of training. It considers the partial delegation of the sales training function and where training should take place. It suggests an overall framework for sales personnel training to include induction/initial training, basic training, a continuous update/reinforcement training programme, and supervisory/management training. It considers training methods, aids to more effective training and examines the special situation regarding field sales training.

Scope of training in the sales management context

The rationale for initial and continuous training of sales personnel is to ensure they are fully equipped to perform their sales role/task at the optimum level. It recognises that even the most experienced sales person joining a company needs and should be given sales training and provided with knowledge about the company, its products/services/processes, the way it prefers its sales personnel to sell, the market and a whole range of applications and administrative knowledge. Training is necessary also because markets change, technology and products develop, and adjustments are made in company general and marketing policy. Also, it is necessary because sales personnel can get into passive, inflexible patterns of working and need to be motivated and revitalised in their approach to potential and existing customers and opportunities. Continuous training is justified also because sales personnel develop and change as time passes. Their change comes about as they learn from each other (bad as well as good working habits) and from experience as they integrate themselves into the changing organisation. Other change comes from their reaction (favourably or unfavourably) to the training programme.

Training has been defined as a short-cut to experience but although certain sales techniques might be acquired through 'trial and error' experience, certain types of knowledge (e.g. new technology) could not be obtained in this way. Even learned skills like sales techniques are a form of knowledge and the sales manager must identify and be aware of the acceptable levels of knowledge, skills and understanding. There are three such levels of knowledge:

(a) 'Must know' knowledge, skills and understanding are those without which the sales person would not be credible with customers and could not cope with the particular sales role/task.

(b) 'Should know' knowledge, skills and understanding are those which the sales person should know to make the 'deal' more attractive and to angle the sales presentation to the needs and problems of the customer.

(c) 'Could know' knowledge, skills and understanding are those that encompass relevant information beyond the specific company and/or industry/market, e.g. the business implications of the current state of the economy, new technological advances in customer industries etc. The latter almost requires training to become education and tends to be reflected in the sales person's 'total immersion' in his job.

What training can and cannot do

Effective training of sales personnel can ensure that the sales function of an organisation operates at its optimum performance levels. It can increase sales and/or profits, generate enthusiasm, job satisfaction and a sense of purpose and achievement with sales personnel, attract more and better quality of applicants to sales vacancies, increase credibility with customers and enhance customer goodwill. It can also decrease the need for intensive supervision and can reduce levels of sales staff labour turnover. More specifically, training can impart new knowledge, skills and attitudes, it can realign existing knowledge, it can improve and reinforce the quality of knowledge and skills, and can stimulate and revitalise sales activities.

However, training can improve, but not take, persons beyond their mental and physical capabilities, although it can give confidence and take them to levels of performance they personally would not have thought possible. However, it cannot convert a person who is fundamentally unsuitable/unfit for selling into a super sales person, and will not inspire sales personnel to sell a bad product or 'deal'.

Who needs training?

There is a danger that training will be thought necessary only for field sales staff, but anyone in contact with customers, potential customers or even customers' customers needs training and given knowledge at levels appropriate to their role. This means that the sales manager should provide training for:

(a) Salesmen, representatives and sales 'consultants'.
(b) Telephone sales staff.
(c) Sales engineers.
(d) Area, regional and national sales managers.
(e) Administration and office managers.
(f) Sales office staff in customer contact.
(g) Credit controllers.
(h) Telephone operators.
(i) Before-sales service staff (e.g. demonstrators).
(j) After-sales service staff (e.g. commissioning/installation engineers, service engineers).
(k) Manufacturers' agents or distributors' salesmen.
(l) Wholesalers'/retailers' sales staff.
(m) Transport and despatch staff (e.g. drivers, despatch clerks etc.).
(n) Anyone in customer contact.

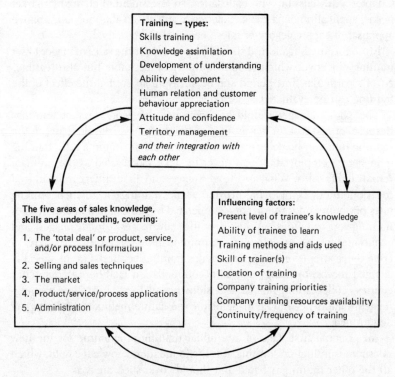

Fig. 5.1 A multi-dimensional approach to training for the organisation's sales function

It is important that the sales manager considers training in a multi-dimensional way, i.e. each dimension does not stand alone but influences the others. The three dimensions are shown in Fig. 5.1 and every sales job in every company in every industry requires a different intensity and combination of the factors shown in each of the dimensions if training is to provide the optimum level of sales performance.

The sales manager not only needs to state his philosophy on the training of sales personnel but ideally needs to set up a framework around which training programmes can be developed. An example of such a framework is shown in Fig. 5.2.

A framework for the training of sales personnel

The actual knowledge, skills, understanding content of each stage (preliminary, initial, basic, continuous, higher) shown in the framework in Fig. 5.2 should be determined by the sales manager investigating what is needed through a combination of job analysis (already carried out earlier, Chapter 3), discussion with colleagues, an assessment of changing market needs, application of past sales experience and an 'on-the-job' performance appraisal of each category of sales personnel to be trained.

From this investigation, it should be possible for the sales manager to set training objectives which should not only be desirable but also feasible, cover a particular time period and be 'measurable' so that the effect of the training can be evaluated.

The sales manager should also consider the economics of training. Because of its cost in terms of time and money, should part of the training function be delegated to area managers or should a sales training manager be employed? It can never be wholly delegated as the ultimate responsibility is his. What are the advantages and disadvantages (and indeed the economies) of employing an external sales training consultant or sending sales personnel on training courses operated by professional bodies or sales training organisations? What are the advantages, disadvantages and economies of using company accommodation for training (perhaps a conference room) or setting up a sales training centre (suite of specially adapted rooms) or using external accommodation facilities at conference centres, colleges and hotels? Decisions on all these and other training-related matters need to be made before the nature/methods of training are determined.

An essential first stage of any initial training programme for the new salesman is induction training; it is the foundation knowledge upon which all the other training is based and should cover such areas as:

(a) History of company.

(b) Present structure and organisation with names, titles and location of key personnel; these will be important either because of status (e.g. the managing director) or because of work relationships (e.g. the sales office manager) or because of customer relationship (i.e. past contacts).

(c) Information on associate/subsidiary companies if the company is part

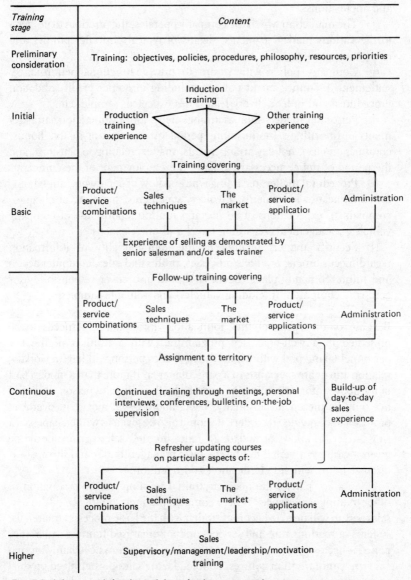

Fig. 5.2 A framework for the training of sales personnel

of a group and working arrangements with other companies if relevant, e.g. agencies, franchises, reciprocal trading etc.

(d) Company's marketing philosophy and sales policy, present and future, including its perception of salesmanship and the role of the sales force.

(e) The company's product/service range, sources of supply (where made or from whom purchased as components or as whole units), their operation and applications.

(f) The markets in which the company operates, the priorities to be given to the various market segments, details of typical customer profiles and competitor profiles.

(g) Company policy with regard to prices, functional/performance/ settlement discounts, credit policy (including customer credit validation procedures) and order/delivery lead times expected, samples etc.

(h) Personnel matters such as arrangements for remuneration, arrangements during illness (notification, period of payment of salary, bonus, commission etc.), holiday arrangements, matters relating to pensions, and the period of notice necessary to leave the employment of the company.

(i) Procedural matters regarding type and flow of paperwork (quotations, ordering, acknowledgements, invoices, statements, handling of cheques, complaints), expectations of *ad hoc* and routine reports, use of company vehicles, arrangements regarding travel and other expenses.

(j) Security matters relating to the confidentiality of information regarding customers, products/processes, profits and sales, computer access and future company plans. Security should also cover responsibility for company equipment (including vehicles) and valuable samples.

Because of the scope of this 'foundation' information, it needs to be presented in a well-organised programme, with a number of the key personnel taking part with whom the new sales person will have a working relationship or are specialists in a particular area. If more than a modest part of the above information is to be retained by the new sales person, it should not only be presented personally, using audio/visual aids (e.g. overhead projector and/or video recorder), it should also be given as written papers in a ring binder (to allow for updating). Later the new sales person should be given a written or verbal test by the sales manager/trainer and the answers discussed; this will aid clarification and retention.

Often a key part of the necessary initial training will be production or other training experience. Where complex products are involved, the new sales person will need to become familiar with the basic processes, materials, systems of manufacture and service, and an organised training experience period is necessary. For example, computer sales persons need hardware and software familiarisation courses, double-glazing sales persons need product and combination systems training, excavator sales persons need information on the hydraulic system contained within the machines etc. A member of the production staff should be responsible for the programme and the trainee(s), and frequent checks on progress need to be made. Even in companies employing only qualified engineers and technicians, some production familiarisation may be necessary to update or to identify key differences.

'Other training experience' relates to activities that help the new sales person to understand or more fully appreciate certain aspects of the job. For example, one petroleum company requires its new field sales force personnel to work for at least a month in a franchised garage. Another company manufacturing and marketing specialised computer office systems requires its new sales representatives to spend at least 3 months involved with the teams installing such systems. Yet another company processing food products requires its new sales representatives to work in its distribution centres and for part of the time to accompany drivers making deliveries to customers. As with production training experience, there should be a programme with a nominated responsible person controlling it and methods of monitoring progress. If a trainee has never sold before, 'other training experience' should mean accompanying a senior salesman on sales calls merely to give an understanding of what a particular sales job is like.

After initial training, the basic training stage should follow, based upon the five training information types essential for sales personnel: product/service and/or process information, selling and sales techniques, market knowledge, applications knowledge and administration knowledge.

Ideally, there should be a number of persons to be trained at the same time, enabling group working to take place and a specific in-company training programme to be developed. Such a company-specific programme could be run by the company (either sales manager, sales trainer or the training department) or a specialist consultant working in-company.

Alternatively, if only one or two trainees are involved, the choice is either individual training or sending them on one of the many sales training courses offered by professional bodies and specialist sales training companies. The main problem with these is that not being company-specific they will not be effective at product training and, by the nature of the broad spectrum of different companies and industries represented on such a course, the selling skills taught will tend to be general and may not always be relevant to the particular sales trainee's situation.

Product, service and/or process information or the 'total deal' being offered by the company

Rarely is a product sold without the need for some 'before', 'during' and/or 'after' sales service. Also, this area of training/knowledge does not simply apply to the technical understanding of the product, service or process but the ability of the sales person to translate technical features into customer 'benefits'. This is described in greater detail in the next chapter because customers buy what products will do for them, i.e. the benefit to them. Training in this area can relate to relatively long technical courses for complex products to one- or two-day product familiarisation courses. In every industry there is a need for courses that update existing product, technical, service knowledge. In complex product situations, the sales person with a production/technical background has a great advantage.

Selling and sales techniques skills and knowledge

In the widest sense, this area covers the practical understanding of interpersonal behaviour and more narrowly it is concerned with the professional application, in the sales situation context, of the use of social skills in the pursuit and achievement of specific sales goals. A large proportion of a sales person's time is concerned with human relations (rapport and 'getting on with others') and there is a whole range of techniques that can be used to influence/persuade persons in their buying patterns; these techniques are examined in detail in the next chapter. This also applies to methods of organising the sales person's time, territory planning, prospecting for new business etc. It is also concerned with training of sales personnel in the use of sales aids ranging from the development of simple visual sales plans and demonstration of samples/models to the use of audio/visual presentations using back projectors, tape/slide units and portable computers and video units. If appropriate, it would include the use of tape recorders to record customer stock levels and/or orders that can be fed into company computers using telephone lines for ordering and despatching activities, either direct or through office transcribing units. In situations of selling through retailers, sales personnel training may also need to cover the techniques of basic display or the more advanced methods of merchandising, i.e. psychological persuasion at the point of purchase without the aid of a retail sales person. In this case the sales person may be selling merchandising concepts to the retailer to allow him to use merchandising techniques to persuade the customer's customer.

Market knowledge

This relates to three specific areas: customers, their profile and why they buy from the company; potential customers, their profile and why they do not buy from the company; and competitors, their profiles, their product/service combinations, their policies, strategies and tactics etc. The broader issues relating to the industry and the economy generally, and the market environment and business procedures in particular, would be all included in this area.

Applications knowledge

This relates to the application of the company's product/service/'deal' to the specific needs of the customer, e.g. a computer systems company that needs to train sales personnel in the application of these systems to the banking, insurance or building society 'industries'. Another dimension of this is the application of the company's product/service/process 'deal' to the immediate customer, the intermediate customer and the 'end user'. For example, the sale of automatic landing equipment for aircraft will have applications knowledge implications for immediate customers (i.e. the aeroplane manufacturers), the intermediate customers (i.e. the airlines that operate the aircraft), and the end users (i.e. the tour operators and/or the passengers who travel in the aircraft). The sales person should be aware of the applications knowledge/information in all these areas.

Administrative knowledge

The training/information necessary in this category relates to:

(a) The broad administrative background of the organisation, structure (particularly if a subsidiary or part of a multi-national), persons, scope and functions, location of Head Office, production units, branch offices etc., sources of supply, other products/services sold but not by this particular sales person.

(b) Administrative rules/procedures/information related to the general running of the business, e.g. delivery dates and arrangements, creditworthiness requirements, credit arrangements and/or discounts, price list, terms of business, contractual obligations, installation and/or service procedures (if appropriate) etc.

(c) The personal administrative skills needed by the sales person in the planned use of time with customers, potential customers, prospecting for new customers and on administration. It also relates to control of expenses, samples, company equipment (especially company vehicles) and to the writing up of records (their analysis and interpretation), submission of relevant *ad hoc* and routine reports, and the feedback to sales management of market intelligence information. It covers techniques and knowledge for planning the operation and development of particular sales territories (territory management), routing procedures and of specific market segments.

The effective sales person is one who has been trained in the techniques, and has knowledge and understanding, of all five of the above areas. But perhaps of equal importance is that he/she should be trained to expect to need to continue acquiring and assimilating new knowledge, i.e. to develop the right attitude towards training and new knowledge.

The content of the basic training within each of the five areas mentioned should reflect the particular needs of a company in particular market segments. For example, although training in selling and sales techniques will have high priority in all basic training programmes, some sales jobs will demand that higher levels of product knowledge be included than in others (e.g. computer systems or hydraulics relating to excavators). In some cases there will be the need to give more emphasis to market knowledge. For example, a food manufacturer/processor sales representative may need to be highly knowledgeable about in-store merchandising and the economics of store management, e.g. being aware of, and able to use, such statistics as the profit per running metre of shelf space.

Ideally, basic training should be in three parts. The first, 'training centre' part with a programme developed using appropriate combinations of the training methods mentioned later. This should then be followed by a period of experience in the field where the sales person can observe the basic techniques being used by a senior sales person. The third part being a return to the original 'training centre' location to discuss/comment on his/her perceptions of the basic techniques used in the field and supplemented with a highly participative training programme integrating the five knowledge/skills areas and culminating in fairly realistic selling situations simulated through role-playing sessions. The use of a variety of combinations of the sales training methods mentioned later is needed to stimulate and motivate in these basic training sessions. Although reference has been made to field sales personnel, this basic training stage is also applicable to telephone sales and other categories of sales staff with the special aspects of their particular roles being catered for.

The continuous training stage takes place simultaneously with the sales representative or telephone sales person managing his/her assigned territory/customers, i.e. carrying out the designated selling role.

Continuous training should apply to all sales personnel, become a natural part of sales meetings, personal interviews, conferences, bulletins and newsletters and, particularly, during and after 'on-the-job' field supervision sessions with the sales manager. During these activities, weaknesses and special training needs may be identified, and these should form the basis of refresher courses on specific aspects of the five training information types.

The final stage referred to in the training framework (Fig. 5.2) is that of leadership, motivation, trainer, supervision and management techniques and knowledge for senior salesmen, sales supervisors, area managers, regional managers, sales trainers and sales office managers, and should reflect the five broad areas of management activity stated in Chapter 1. Set in the context of the particular company and with regard to the level/status of the person(s) being trained, sales supervisory and management training should cover:

(a) Developing policies, plans and procedures, and setting of objectives.

(b) Organising, co-ordinating and directing the sales unit (area, region, office, training centre/unit).

(c) Development of skills of communication and of motivating sales personnel.

(d) Supervision and controlling by monitoring performance, interpreting results and taking remedial action on time.

(e) Recruiting, training and developing appropriate staff.

By implication, these supervisory/management personnel will already be trained in the earlier five areas of knowledge/skills for sales personnel if they are to understand fully the sales tasks/roles they are supervising/managing.

Methods of training

The many methods of training available will be effective only if some pertinent aspects of the processes of understanding and learning are appreciated. Those that are particularly applicable in training related to the sales function of an organisation can be covered under main headings that can be remembered by using the mnemonic FRIDAES:

Frequency
Recency
Intensity
Development
Attitude
Effect
Sequence

Frequency of skills training and knowledge assimilation sessions will mean that they become second nature and will be habit forming. It will mean that bad selling habits can be eliminated by the substitution of good ones. But the number of points covered in one session needs to be limited and repetition should be made attractive by using a wide range of individual and group training methods if reinforcement of skills and knowledge by repetition is to take place.

Recency—the sales training programme must not allow too much time to elapse between teaching and doing. This may mean using role-playing soon after being taught in the 'classroom situations' and this experience applied very soon after in 'real-life' selling situations. 'On-the-job' training is very effective because of this **recency** factor; the method demonstrated or knowledge assimilated could be used in the next sales interview.

Intensity – again, the use of a variety of alternative training methods, especially those that are participative, are important as it is possible for trainees to hear and see but the information presented make no lasting impression. It is crucial that memory facilitation is built into the learning process and that monitoring/testing takes place often in the training programme. The best way to remember new knowledge is to scan through material first before concentrating on parts; quickly scan or summarise at the end.

New and experienced sales people need a **development** ladder and be developed step-by-step up to peak performance. The trainee and the trainer should be aware of the trainee's current level of knowledge and experience and know the next step after the present level of achievement. When peak performance has been reached, development must be maintained otherwise complacency and over-confidence will set in. Most sales people do not work to full capacity once a new level in their development has been reached and it has been mastered. Sales personnel need to be monitored individually otherwise what is perceived as an overall 'satisfactory' level of sales is accepted and the better/more experienced personnel do not reach maximum potential.

The right mental **attitude** to the training process in general and to the current sales programme and its content in particular are essential if training is to be effective. It is crucial that the person being trained can identify with the sales role/task as it is being projected through training. If a method being taught causes the person being trained to be uncomfortable or embarrassed, it will tend not to be used in 'real-life' selling situations.

The trainer's attitude, even if repressed, will 'come out' in training sessions; it is important that it is positive and indicate confidence in the content/methods being taught. Also, learning is greater when the person being trained has confidence in the trainer's knowledge and skills ability.

Effect – training in the sales context must be enjoyable as trainees of any sort like to do those things which bring pleasure, enjoyment and job satisfaction. Sales personnel are no different; in fact, there is a tendency for them to retain more of the basic skills/knowledge if such training is put over as a pleasant experience.

It must be recognised that people remember skills/knowledge better in patterns. A logical **sequence** from one point of knowledge to another will help the trainee to 'fix' the information in a pattern. It is often referred to as the 'association of ideas' so that one stage acts as a cue to the next set of knowledge. Thus in sales training it helps to develop techniques/knowledge based on the sequence of the sales interview (i.e. techniques for opening interview) followed by methods of getting interest, then the presentation of the main benefits of the 'deal' and, finally, 'closing the sale' by getting a decision and/or order.

Assuming that recognition is given to these basic aspects of learning, the next things to consider are the actual training methods. The effective combination of these will depend upon the needs of the three dimensions shown in Fig. 5.1. Also, it must be recognised that some will be more appropriate and effective through the personal approach in the 'training centre' atmosphere, others through the personal approach of 'on-the-job' training, others through the medium of sales meetings or conferences, and others through non-personal or distance learning (e.g. teaching machines or correspondence courses). Some of the many training methods available are now discussed.

Lectures

Useful for larger groups and to impart information when supported by visual aids.

Talks

A more informal method that can be used by trainers to impart information and by trainees so as to check knowledge and develop ability to communicate through effective speaking. One form of this is the spontaneous talk where the trainee, without warning, is asked to talk for 1 minute on a sales-related topic; or for a 5-minute talk which he/she is given time to prepare. In the first case, it develops the trainee's ability to respond to unexpected situations and, in the second, the confidence to address customer meetings.

Lessons and revision

Useful for imparting facts (e.g. product knowledge) where a series can be used to pass facts/knowledge linking each in a general progress with revision and testing of knowledge.

Demonstrations

Mainly useful to small- or medium-sized groups in product handling skills or in sales techniques.

Group discussions

Useful for developing a team approach, getting different angles/opinions on a basic problem/situation, reinforcing knowledge and identifying personal viewpoints.

Buzz groups

These are short-session, problem-centred, small group discussions often used to revitalise a training session when, of necessity, a lot of information is being imparted by the 'trainer'. It allows discussion on a small problem relevant to the main theme of the session.

Brainstorming

Useful for small group development of creativity, decision-making and identifying innovative ways of solving sales function problems through setting a theme and encouraging participants to produce individual ideas which cause others to enhance or develop them.

Seminars

Where individuals are encouraged to produce a 'paper' or give a talk about a particular topic (e.g. an aspect of product knowledge, the application of a sales technique etc.), followed by discussion of it by others in the group.

Syndicates

Where a larger group is divided into smaller groups (e.g. three or four trainees) to work on a problem/task and to later report their conclusions, usually in a plenary session with discussion of the findings by all the groups.

Tutorials

Usually training on a one-to-one basis, particularly useful for individuals or for correcting their particular problems.

Case study work

Particularly useful (individually or in groups) to develop an appreciation of apparent and real situations, solve problems and develop decision-making. It is a way of 'simulating' conditions of an industry/market, whether presented in written form or as a playlet showing the inter-relationships of a number of aspects of a market situation. The discussion and feedback of solutions are important parts of this learning process.

Panels

On a training course, panels of experts (perhaps of specialist executives of the company) can be set up so that trainees can put questions to them.

Alternatively, panels of trainees are set up and the remainder of the training group puts questions.

Quizzes and tests

Useful for monitoring the level, extent or quality of knowledge and understanding and can be interspersed throughout a training programme as a participative activity.

Role playing

This can involve two or three trainees usually playing the roles of buyer, salesman and (if three are involved) an accompanying sales manager or sales trainer. Best results are obtained by the actual role playing taking place in isolation rather than live in front of an audience. The audience-training side of role playing is through the use of behavioural analysis where aspects of the role playing (probing, answering objections, adequate knowledge etc.) are pre-listed for the audience who individually rate each activity and later discuss their assessments of the role playing. Video taping of role playing has tended to overtake audio tape recorders although this method is extensively used in training for 'selling by telephone'.

Job clinics

Based on the clinical psychology device of 'Quartets'. In the sales training role, it involves a sales person presenting his/her problems to another sales person playing the role of sales consultant; each have an observer who, after the presentation of the problem and the consultant's response, comment on the sales persons and consultants' performance. After discussion, the roles are then reversed; and later, observers change to become main role players as well. Individuals' selling problems are solved through the experience of their peers and it is therefore a very useful technique in arousing the interest in training of experienced and often reluctant 'older' sales people.

Projects

Useful either as an individual or small group activity which fosters the sales person's ability to find out/search for information, analyse and present it in a concise, meaningful way. Themes could be looking at potential/new market segments, specialised needs of certain types of existing customers, new applications knowledge etc.

Programmed interaction

Whether the programme is through the medium of a book, teaching machine, video recorder or microcomputer, it is a method that is useful for communicating facts, information (i.e. factual product/service knowledge, applications knowledge) and normally operates on a self-correcting answer process. It does not lend itself to training in selling skills because of the variety of possible, marginally different or qualified alternatives that arise when dealing with the behaviour of people.

Customer location visits

These should provide the trainee primarily with products/service application knowledge and real-life market-place situations. It is important that the objectives of the visit are made clear, that a briefing on the particular customer and any sensitive areas is given and that the level of knowledge gained is monitored after the visit.

Report writing

While it is acknowledged that most sales personnel are employed for their oral ability, training them to write clear and concise reports not only ensures adequate future communication (in-company and customer reports) but also helps to develop their ability to search out information, to marshal facts in a logical sequence and develop patterns of clear thinking.

Factory visits/courses

This method ranges from the occasional visit, where the product is not complex and has few changes, to a product knowledge course where rapid changes in technology or new products are being added to the product/ service range. Whether of short or long duration, it is essential that these visits are well organised, with a specific production manager/supervisor responsible for the sales person and for implementing the training programme, and a means of monitoring results.

Job rotation

The occasional change for several days to do a job which impinges on the sales person's own job gives an appreciation of the problems involved. For example, moving a field representative to a sales office job handling customer telephone complaints, a despatch job in the warehouse, a delivery job accompanying lorry drivers etc. Again, it must be organised with a briefing and debriefing to assess results.

Shopping

At one end of the scale there is the observation of another sales person's selling skills in a shopping situation for the purchase of a product/service not related to the sales person's job (e.g. observation of the selling skills of a retail sales person selling a shirt). This is followed by an analysis and discussion of the selling skills in the training group. At the other end of the scale, the shopping method is used by sending a sales person to another area where he is not known where he observes the selling skills of another sales person in the same line of business (e.g. a car showroom salesman going to a competitor's showroom in another area).

Sales meetings

All regular and *ad hoc* meetings of regional, area, district or branch sales personnel should contain an element of training. For example, one approach could be that the regular monthly sales meeting could hear short presentations, perhaps one on selling skills and one on product knowledge, from two different sales persons each month. At one meeting the presentation assignments are given to sales personnel for the next meeting. At the same time, the sales manager names a specific part of a topic area (e.g. overcoming price objections), saying that he will call on someone to make a presentation on this at the next meeting. This has the effect of causing all members of the group to prepare (and therefore revise) a presentation on the named topic. Thus at least three training revision topics will be covered at each meeting.

Sales conferences

All conferences, whether of a consultative or briefing nature, should contain a training element. In the former, methods of selling, applications and product knowledge can be discussed and developed. In the latter, for example, the launch of a new range of products, special methods of selling them, their special features and benefits should be suggested.

'On-the-job' training

This is one of the most important methods of training sales personnel; some sales managers would say the only effective way of training. The importance of training field sales forces by the sales manager accompanying individual sales people on sales calls is recognised and a special section dealing with this is covered later in this chapter. On-the-job training of telephone sales personnel is equally important and is done by monitoring calls.

Distance learning

This overall training area covers a variety of methods with the common characteristic that they are not person-to-person in their presentation and therefore errors and/or misunderstandings by the trainee cannot be immediately rectified or questioned on the basis of how the training information is received. The training information can be disseminated by such methods as letters and sales force bulletins, a sales manual, correspondence courses, audio and video tape recordings, and computer-aided learning through special software learning packages.

Developing a 'training centre' programme for sales personnel

Whether for basic/initial training or for later updating/reinforcement/refresher training, the following stages of training planning need to be adopted. Identify the need for training and set objectives, determine the skills/knowledge/understanding areas to be covered putting them into a logical sequence/programme using combinations of the training methods examined in the previous section, run the programme and finally monitor its effectiveness.

The duration will depend on the amount of training they need to contain, some companies find two or three 3-day programmes over a period of time more effective than other companies who prefer a 1–2 weeks' continuous programme.

Also, the content of the training programme will depend on whether it is to cover a mixture of product/service knowledge, sales techniques, applications and market knowledge etc., or whether it is to specialise on one aspect (e.g. selling and sales techniques); examples of both are shown as Figs. 5.3 and 5.4.

Day	Training topic	Training method
Week 1, Day 1		
a.m.	Welcome, course admin., briefing course objectives, relevant company background information	Talk and questions
	The market concept; cost, profit, breakeven and stock turn	Film and discussion
p.m.	Why does the company need to actively sell?	Buzz groups and discussion
	Market segments to be covered by product range, sources of market information	Lecture

Fig. 5.3 A 2-week basic training programme for field sales force personnel

Day		Training topic	Training method
evening		Private study on product knowledge	Programmed learning book
	Day 2		
a.m.		What makes a good salesman?	Group discussion
		The nature of salesmanship and the sales person's role	Lecture
		Basic sales techniques	Lecture and film
p.m.		Basic sales techniques	Lectures, film, discussion
evening		Case study on markets	Informal syndicates
	Day 3		
a.m		Report back on case study	Syndicate presentation and group discussion
		Basic sales techniques	Lectures, film, discussion
p.m.		Why am I in selling?	Buzz groups and general discussion
		Basic sales techniques	Lectures, film, discussion
evening		Free	
	Day 4		
a.m.		Product range A – features, applications, customer benefits and objectives	Lecture and video or tape slide presentation
		Product range A – markets and selling	Lecture and discussion
p.m.		Product range A – review	Group discussion
		Product range B – features, applications, customer benefits and objectives	Lecture and video or tape slide presentation
evening		Sales support activities	Talk by sales office manager
	Day 5		
a.m.		Product range B – markets and selling	Lecture and discussion
		Product range B – review	Group discussion
p.m.		Territory management planning Review of week	Briefing exercise, discussion
		Review of week	Knowledge test and discussion
Weekend preparation for 5-minute talks on sales topics later in programme			Private study
Week 2, Day 1			
a.m.		Reflections on last week	Discussion and revision
		Organise yourself	Lecture, film and discussion

Fig. 5.3 (cont.)

Day	Training topic	Training method
	Product range C – features, applications, customer benefits and objectives	Lecture and video or tape slide presentation
	Product range C – markets and selling	Lecture and discussion
	Product range C – review	Group discussion
evening	Advertising and PR support	Talk by advertising manager
Day 2		
a.m.	Product range D – features, applications, customer benefits and objectives	Lecture and video or tape slide presentation
	Product range D – markets and selling	Lecture and discussion
	Product range D – review	Group discussion
p.m. and evening	Effective sales communication	Five-minute talks by course members on sales topics – video taped, play back and discussion
Day 3		
a.m.	Sales contracts and other legal aspects of selling	Lecture and discussion
	Selling to large organisations	Case study and discussion
p.m.	Review of product ranges A to D	Quiz and summary
	Marketing intelligence and research	Lecture and syndicate
	Briefing for role playing	Talk
evening	Preparation for role playing	Work in pairs
Day 4		
a.m.	Simulated selling situations	Role playing
	Remuneration, salary, commission and expenses system	Lecture and discussion
p.m.	Simulated selling situations	Role playing
	Administration and admin. systems and correspondence	Lecture and discussion
evening	Course dinner with managing director and/or other directors	
Day 5		
a.m.	Simulated selling situations	Role playing
	Debriefing on role playing	Group discussion
p.m.	'Where do we go from here?' Setting personal objectives	Syndicates and report back
	Course review	Group discussion

Fig. 5.3 (cont.)

Day	Training topic	Training method
Day 1		
a.m.	Welcome, course admin., briefing course objectives, relevant company background, information	Talk and questions
	The marketing concept, cost, profit, breakeven and stock turn	Film and discussion
p.m.	Why does the company need to actively sell?	Buzz groups and discussion
	Selling is communication	Lecture, film, discussion
	Customer situation problems	Case study and discussion
evening	Preparation for 'benefits exercise'	Informal syndicate working
Day 2		
a.m.	What makes a good salesman?	Group discussion
	Selling yourself	Lecture and discussion
	Why do customers buy and what are we selling?	Lecture, film, discussion and syndicate exercise
p.m.	Previous session continued	Exercises continued followed by feedback and discussion
	'Prospecting' and sources of new business	Buzz groups, feedback and lecture
evening	Preparation for selling by telephone mini case studies	Informal syndicates
Day 3		
a.m.	Selling by telephone	Lecture, film, discussion, buzz groups with mini case studies
p.m.	Planning your time	Lecture, film, discussion, territory planning exercise
	Planning the sale and preparing interview structures	Lecture and syndicate exercise
evening	Preparation for role playing	Work in pairs
Day 4		
a.m.	Overcoming objections	Lecture, film and discussion
	Simulated selling situations	Role playing
p.m.	Getting the decision	Lecture, film and discussion
	Simulated selling situations	Role playing
evening	Course dinner with managing director and/or other directors	

Fig. 5.4 A 1-week basic 'effective selling course' programme

Day	Training topic	Training method
Day 5		
a.m.	Marketing intelligence	Lecture and discussion
	Simulated selling situations	Role playing
p.m.	Debriefing on role playing	Group discussion
	'Where do we go from here?' – setting personal objectives	Syndicates and report back
	Course review	Group discussion

Fig. 5.4 (cont.)

Both training programmes (Figs. 5.3 and 5.4) reflect the need to have a logical, progressive sequence of events, and the use of a variety of methods of presentation to gain and hold interest. Study notes with wide margins need to be handed out for each session to build up a course manual (in a ring binder) for future reference; also, they cut down the need for distracting continuous note-taking, although the wide margins permit the noting of aspects which specially interest the particular course member.

As far as possible, some form of group activity is necessary immediately after lunch to progress through the post-lunch drowsiness period. Coffee, lunch, tea should all be served outside the meeting room simply to allow course members to engage in movement and have a change of place and atmosphere; it is also to allow the meeting room to be tidied up (water replenished, glasses replaced etc.) and, if not air-conditioned, to be well ventilated.

It will be noticed that the penultimate session on each of the courses given as examples is entitled 'Where do we go from here?'. The purpose of such a session is for the individual to carry out a self-assessment of where they perceive themselves to be, what they perceive their aims and priorities to be, and to develop a plan of action as to how to achieve these. An example of a 'Where do we go from here?' exercise would be as shown in Fig. 5.5.

WHERE DO WE GO FROM HERE?

From the course, each individual will have obtained certain ideas and information that he/she will want to use. To help sort these into some order and some form of plan, a useful approach is to look at the major subject areas covered and to ask three basic questions:

1. Where am I now in relation to each of these subject areas?
   Self-assessment

2. What are my
   aims and priorities?

3. How can I get there?
   Plan of action

Fig. 5.5 An example of 'Where do we go from here?' exercise

To answer these questions, complete your own personal brief notes against the checklist below.

1. *Self-assessment*

How good is my knowledge of business practice and management?

    Assessment:
    Strengths:
    Weaknesses:

How good is my knowledge of marketing and selling principles?

    Assessment:
    Strengths:
    Weaknesses:

How good is my knowledge of own industry, my market segments and products/service 'deal'?

    Assessment:
    Strengths:
    Weaknesses:

How good is my knowledge and application of telephone skills?

    Assessment:
    Strengths:
    Weaknesses:

How good is my knowledge and application of planning and administrative skills?

    Assessment:
    Strengths:
    Weaknesses:

How good is my knowledge and application of selling skills?

    Assessment:
    Strengths:
    Weaknesses:

How good is my appreciation of other knowledge/skills areas in course, e.g. applications knowledge, competitor knowledge etc.

    Assessment:
    Strengths:
    Weaknesses:

2. *Aims and Priorities*

From your assessment, which areas do you choose as priorities? What are the objectives in those areas that you are determined to achieve?

(To help with your notes, supposing you choose the selling skills area. You might note the following:

'I want to improve my "Presentation", concentrating more upon *relevant benefits* to the customer. Also "*closing*" can be improved by trying out some of the suggested approaches – testing each in turn for effectiveness with my kind of customers'.)

Fig. 5.5 (cont.)

3. *Plan of Action*

Try to be as specific as possible although inevitably your notes will be more general in some areas than in others . . .

Continuing with the same example used under Aims and Priorities, your notes in this area might be:

'(a) To prepare for each major interview more carefully with regard to presentation and "closing" the sale.

(b) To review critically for at least two weeks immediately after each interview, the effectiveness of these two elements of the sale. To make notes of my self-criticism.

(c) To discuss with someone – a friend, colleague, manager – the interviews and what happened.

(d) To keep summaries of "better" presentations, of "decisions obtained" and to review at the end of the two weeks, what improvement has been made.'

Fig. 5.5 (cont.)

Course assessment forms asking course members to comment on the content, quality and presentation of each session need to be circulated at the beginning of the course and members encouraged to assess each session immediately it has taken place and while it is fresh in their minds. These are collected after the last session and analysed later by the sales manager, criticism and comments noted so that future training programmes are adjusted.

An example of a course assessment form related to the 1-week basic 'effective selling' course programme (Fig. 5.4) would be as shown in Fig. 5.6.

Sales training aids

Apart from the quality of the training, the skills of the trainer(s) and the ability of the trainee, the success of such programmes as those shown in Figs 5.3 and 5.4 will depend upon the general facilities available. The adequacy of the training room(s) in terms of size, lighting, heating, ventilation, layout, position of tables and chairs in relation to windows and door(s), comfort of chairs, availability of water, glasses and ashtrays, size and height of tables, carpeting and decoration, background music for pre-commencement and breaks, could be construed as sales training aids as any of these factors can affect the degree of knowledge obtained or skill acquired.

Non-course-related facilities such as comfort of residential accommodation; convenience of location and travel arrangements; timing, location, quality and quantity of meals and drinks; cloakrooms; facilities for telephoning out and receiving messages inwards; parking or taxi arrangements, all need to be considered in detail. All affect the general atmosphere of courses, the attitudes of the trainees and the company image projected to them.

Session	Was the subject matter relevant to your job?	Could the session have been longer/ shorter?	Suggestions to improve future courses
WHY SELL?			
WHY DO PEOPLE BUY?			
SELLING IS COMMUNICATION Film: Two-way communication			
SELLING YOURSELF			
WHAT MAKES A GOOD SALESMAN?			
WHAT ARE WE SELLING? Film: Reason to buy			
SOURCES OF NEW BUSINESS – PROSPECTING			
SELLING BY TELEPHONE			
PLANNING YOUR TIME Film: Time well spent			
PLANNING THE SALE			
THE INTERVIEW Film: Controlling the interview			
OVERCOMING OBJECTIONS Film: Challenge of objections			
GETTING THE DECISION Film: Getting the decision			
MARKET INTELLIGENCE			
SIMULATED SELLING SITUATION – ROLE PLAYING			

Fig. 5.6 Session appraisal sheet

The availability of effective presentation sales aids more directly affect the level and quality of instruction and learning, and underpin the various training methods listed earlier.

An effective sales manual
This should contain all the guidelines for the sales person covering all aspects of the job, its scope and functions, selling methods, relationships

with customers, competitors and with other parts of the company, administrative procedures, personal administration (i.e. expenses, hotels, cars etc.) etc. It should be divided into subject areas for easy reference and in a loose-leaf ring binder for ease of updating.

Trainee requirements

Place names, name badges, list of delegates, administrative background details of course, course programme, course study notes for each session, notepaper, binder or file for course notes, pens, pencils (and pencil sharpener), rulers, rubbers, etc.

Instructor's guide

This should cover company training policy and its implementation, training programmes, objectives for courses, course planning, preparation, training context, stages of instruction, selection of methods and training aids, presentation (introduction, development, recapitulation, conclusion), monitoring and evaluation of training, follow-up methods etc.

Visual selling aids

These are items that the sales person can use during a sales interview that will make the presentation more effective. It is part of the training task to make the trainee more familiar with the use and handling of these selling aids. They include sales literature, technical data/performance sheets, photographs, 'scratch pads' (for making calculations or, better still, getting the customer to make them), third-party testimony letters, samples and sample cases, flipcharts, portable video or back projectors, models, demonstration kits, portable/hand-held computers etc.

Instructional training aids

These are aids to communication and their use must depend on the criteria, what is to be communicated and how effectively will these instructional aids do it? They include overhead projectors (either with prepared 'acetates/ transparencies/slides' or a roll of acetate so that key parts of a lecture or talk can be written or drawn as the presentation proceeds); 16 mm film projectors together with films (of which there is a wide range that can either be purchased, or hired at a fee or free; the latter are usually 'sponsored' films often with a 'built-in' self-interest message); video equipment comprising a video recorder/player, camera, television monitor(s) and/or a video projector for large screen presentation; closed-circuit television system; 35 mm slide projector for either individual slide or tape/slide presentation; audio tape recorders; chalk board, flipchart, felt board (items to adhere to it need to be backed with felt); 'plastigraph' (board on which plastic characters are assembled); magnetic board (metal board on which are assembled characters that must be backed with small magnets); charts or diagrams; photographs, models; 'public address' system (only for large audiences); teaching machines and programmed learning texts; microcomputer and software for computer-aided learning; separate 'internal' telephone systems for 'selling by telephone' training, ranging from a single pair of telephones with recording and play-back facilities to a multi-pair unit with on-going monitoring facilities.

The individual company will, in the light of its training requirements, need to identify the best combination of the above sales training aids to give the greatest support to its training programmes.

'On-the-job' or field sales training

'Formal' initial, basic and refresher/update training are only part of the essential training package for sales personnel. The other part is 'on-the-job' or field sales training.

By making calls on customers and potential customers with sales representatives on a typical working day, the sales manager not only has the opportunity to foster good customer relations but also to effectively motivate, supervise, control and, most important, to train the sales representatives. By his very presence, the sales manager must realise that the occasion will not be a 'normal' interview but, by merely observing the interview, he should influence it as little as possible. The sales person should, after the initial introductions, take charge of the sales interview and not involve the sales manager. Likewise, the sales manager should not intervene in the sales interview other than in exceptional circumstances.

The particular characteristics of this form of training are that:

(a) as it is done 'on-the-job', it can be immediately applied in real-life situations;

(b) it is a very personal counselling, coaching, tutoring method so that the sales manager can concentrate on the individual's needs, identifying weaknesses and providing the means of correcting faults;

(c) it can be highly motivational; the sales manager's enthusiasm, confidence, determination and leadership can inspire a 'trainee' to achieve higher performance levels, to embark on a programme of 'self-training' and to accept that training must be continuous;

(d) it can be used to assess the effectiveness of earlier 'formal' initial and basic training, its deficiencies identified and its content and emphasis adjusted;

(e) it can develop the critical quality of self-analysis in the sales person so that a self-correcting mechanism is established, the performance being self-analysed and corrected on all sales calls not just those when the sales manager is present.

'On-the-job' training works by the sales manager analysing and assessing the sales person's performance in real-life interviews, discussing its strengths, weaknesses and perceived opportunities for improvement, the teaching and demonstration of the skills/knowledge needed for improvement and monitoring the sales person's application of them. However, before this can take place, a rapport must be established between the sales manager and the trainee. Also, the trainee must be 'sold' the idea that the sales manager is trying to help him and stifle the idea that he is being spied upon.

In the first stage of this process, the sales person's presentation must be assessed and evaluated systematically in relation to the marketing/sales objectives of the company but also against the job description and the identified and known (to both the sales manager and trainee) criteria and standards.

It is more effective if this assessment and evaluation is standardised and recorded so that comparisons can be made period-to-period to determine whether training and achievement progress is being made. It is useful therefore for the sales manager to develop an assessment and critique form as shown in Fig. 5.7.

Some companies using a sales person assessment form (it may have a different name) may assess fewer factors or have fewer grades than those shown in Fig. 5.7. Some use a matrix format so that (using fewer categories of grades) boxes are ticked rather than figures written in. Others use a weighting as well as a rating scheme, i.e. those factors that are considered more important than others are weighted accordingly. For example, if territory planning is considered very important, it may be weighted to a factor of 3 and any grade given for performance in that area is multiplied by that figure.

In some companies, the sales person assessment form is seen by the observer only and used by the sales manager as a means of identifying where training is necessary. In others, the sales manager gives a copy to the sales person being assessed; it then often forms the basis of discussion and mutually agreed training. But by far the most effective way is for the sales manager and the 'trainee' to each complete an assessment form. The advantage of this is threefold: first, it reflects how the sales person sees his/her performance, thus indicating a greater or lesser training problem. For example, if the trainee rates overcoming objections at 8 (very good) but the sales manager rates it as 3 (poor), it is obvious that the trainee does not think he/she has a problem in this area and it will be necessary to change attitudes as well as to instruct in the necessary skills. Secondly, the 'two views' approach gives the 'trainee' the opportunity to justify his/her higher or lower grading. Thirdly, it not only gives the sales manager an indication of areas of weakness on which to concentrate training, it also gives the 'trainee' a basis for his/her own self-adjustment.

Sales Person Assessment

Observer: _____

Sales person _____   Call location _____

Date of visit _____

Call pattern and result:

Customer group	Calls made	Enquiries	Orders
A (existing customers)			
(potential customers)			
B (existing customers)			
(potential customers)			
C (existing customers)			
(potential customers)			

Others (specify) _____

Time – Waiting _____

    Travelling _____

                         Time day started _____

    Meals and breaks _____

                         Time day finished _____

    Face to face _____

    Other (specify) _____

Assessment

Grade the following factors of the day's work according to assessment scale:

9 = Excellent	6 = Above average	3 = Poor
8 = Very good	5 = Average	2 = Appalling
7 = Good	4 = Below average	1 = Complete failure

0 = Not applicable or other factors prevent equitable grading

Attitude to selling	Pre-call preparation
Attitude to customers	Ability to get appointments
Attitude to company	Saw 'right' people
Attitude to products	Follows up leads
Determination of approach	Set selling objectives
Confidence	Overall knowledge of sales
Persistence	techniques
Poise	Presentation planning
Personal acceptability	Flexibility of presentation
Personality	Introduction and opening

Fig. 5.7 An assessment/critique form for use with field sales personnel

Ability to communicate	Use of sales aids
Shows enthusiasm	Gained interest
Lack of mannerisms	Sold product/service
Self-analysis	Sold self
Willingness to co-operate	Sold company
Willingness to learn	Sold benefits
Courtesy	Got customer participation
Customer service	Created desire to buy
Positiveness	Handled objections
Driving behaviour	Handled prices and calculations
Product/service knowledge (company)	Identified buying signals
	Use of trial close
Product/service knowledge (competitors)	Ability to get decisions
	Skill at closing sale
Applications knowledge	
Administrative knowledge	
Organised approach	
Territory planning	Total
Time planning	
Prospecting records	
Customer records	Overall rating
Sample/literature availability	(÷ 57)
Punctuality	
Personal appearance	
State of support materials	

Other comments:

Fig. 5.7 Sales person assessment form (cont.)

Although the assessment may indicate a number of weaknesses, it is important to concentrate on one aspect or group of related aspects at a time if the training is to be effective, moving to others on later occasions. The sales manager, having discussed in detail what needs to be done, must demonstrate to the trainee how to overcome the discovered problem; it is not enough just to tell the sales person what to do. This is not only to show the trainee how to do it but to demonstrate that the sales manager's advice is based on practical ability and knowledge.

The final stage is to get the 'trainee' to do it again, praising him for his improvement even though this may be only slight. However, if there is no improvement, it could be that either the sales manager's assessment of where the trainee was going wrong was incorrect or that the 'trainee' failed to understand the instruction/demonstration, or elements of both.

It is important not to criticise the sales person or comment on his/her performance in front of the customer or even comment on the interview anywhere on the customer's premises. The best place is in the sales person's car, away from the customer's view but immediately after the interview. The sales manager should foster self-analysis and give the trainee the opportunity to comment on/appraise his own performance before making his own. If the trainee is not very responsive, the sales manager should use open-ended/ opinion-type questions beginning with What, Why, How, Where, Who, When and the 'Yes . . . but . . .' sales technique described later. This should be delivered in such a way as to get the 'trainee's' co-operation. The sales manager should praise the good points as well as identifying the deficiencies, be friendly but firm, and should not make 'too much' of the post-interview conference which should in any case be relatively short. It is important not to criticise a sales person's actions without being able to suggest a better method and certainly never ridicule a sales person's work. The sales manager needs to make sure each comment is understood before leaving it; this is done by asking the 'trainee' to restate the problem and the solution. The basic rule should be to encourage initiatives but 'sell' standard procedures of selling.

Finally, at the end of the day, the sales manager should summarise the training points made during the day and identify those areas which need to be worked on before the next field training takes place. It is also important to leave the sales person with a project to complete (e.g. get some information, research an area, identify new outlets, etc.) before the next field training session

Summary

This chapter has broadly covered the principal training needs of sales personnel in organisations. However, the detailed scope, type and nature of the training will need to be adapted to the special needs of particular industries and selling situations. For example, contrast the training needs of sales personnel selling heavy equipment to the oil industry; a pharmaceutical representative selling to doctors and hospitals; a sales person selling fast-moving consumer goods to retailers; and a sales person employed in a retail store selling to the public.

Likewise, training of sales personnel as depicted will need to be modified/extended to meet the special needs of a 'selling by telephone' operation compared with the external field sales force; even though in both cases the sales person takes the initiative and contacts the customer or potential customer. Unlike the situation where the customer takes the initiative and telephones a company's sales office, or the trade customer approaches a sales person at the 'trade counter' of a wholesaler, or the consumer walks into a retail store. Sometimes, even the field sales person is in the 'customer initiative' situation when following up sales leads obtained by advertising or telephone.

Whatever the situation, the principles of effective training apply, assuming that the right person has been recruited, that existing personnel can be re-trained, that a basic customer need for the product/service exists and that training will change to meet the needs of the company, customers and sales personnel in the market-place. It assumes that all personnel will receive training but those in contact with customers in any way will receive some form of sales and/or customer relations training.

To be effective, the training of sales personnel needs to be organised around a progressive framework or pattern that covers the five areas of sales knowledge: skills and understanding (i.e. the 'total deal' of product/service), sales techniques, the market, applications of the 'deal', and administration.

The wide range of training methods and training aids available make it possible for the sales manager to develop continuous training programmes that are effective, flexible and interesting. Different combinations of methods and aids being used for induction, basic and follow-up, and supervisory training for both internal and external field sales personnel with a special emphasis on field sales/'on-the-job' training for the latter group.

Training for sales personnel will be only as good as the 'trainer', whether it is the sales manager or whether the training function has been partially (it should never be totally) delegated to a sales trainer, sales training manager, sales training consultant or external sales training course. Training for sales personnel is relatively costly in terms of time and money and therefore can only be justified if it enhances the effectiveness of an organisation's ability to sell.

Questions

1. Why should personnel in the sales function, in addition to the field sales force, need sales training?
2. What are the component parts of a framework for the training of sales personnel?
3. What are the five areas of knowledge, skills and understanding for effective selling; identify the training needs in these areas in a company of which you have knowledge?
4. Identify the methods of sales training appropriate in basic training for sales personnel in the context of a company of which you have knowledge.
5. Examine the programmes of the two training courses given in Figs. 5.3 and 5.4 and comment critically on their structure, content and continuity.

6. Identify ten aids you consider to be the most important to the effectiveness of sales training generally.

7. 'On-the-job' training has been shown to be crucial to the training of field sales force personnel. Consider how this concept can be applied to internal sales staff.

CHAPTER 6

Planned selling

Objectives

While most companies will differ considerably with regards to product/service, applications and administration, there will be a common theme with regards to selling and sales techniques. It will be the sales team's effectiveness in this area under the direction of the sales manager that will determine the level of sales and thereby affect profitability. Further, although this chapter is primarily about the techniques the sales person can use to influence buyer behaviour, it could also be seen as the techniques of how the sales manager sells training and sells himself to the sales team and customers. The chapter therefore covers planned selling and considers that selling is communication and persuasion. It also deals with the special case of selling by telephone, the importance of using a variety of types of questions to obtain information and the need for the sales person to sell himself/herself as well as the product/service. Sources and methods of obtaining new business are examined, why customers buy, what the company is selling and what the customer needs are considered through the use of benefits analysis. Methods of territory management, pre-call preparation and planning and the sales techniques appropriate to each stage of a selling interview are all examined.

Why planned selling?

In the last chapter it was emphasised that sales persons should be trained in five types of knowledge, skills and understanding, i.e. in product/service/process information; selling and sales techniques; market knowledge; applications; administration. All of these are highly company/industry specific and as such it would be difficult to cover them in a meaningful way in one book. Even selling and sales techniques need to be adapted to the particular needs of a company and its customers in particular market segments. However, it is possible to examine concepts, techniques and skills, the basic principles of which apply to all forms of selling. Although the subject is examined in the context of the field sales force, the basic principles apply to internal sales staff with only minor modifications.

Selling and sales techniques training could take the form that it simply gave the sales person a number of human relation techniques that could be brought into use in a selling interview with a customer as and when the sales person thought appropriate. The advantage with this method is that it is completely flexible and enables the sales person to develop the sales story in line with his own personality. The disadvantages are that parts of the sales story may be missed out or that some parts will be repeated unnecessarily or, because of the lack of structure, a customer with a dominant personality may take over control of the interview and direct the conversation away from the sales person's sales story.

The other extreme is to give a sales person a script of a sales story with everything written down and determined beforehand; in some cases, the sales story complete with diagrams etc. is used in front of the customer to take him/her through the sales story. The advantages of this method are said to be that there are no omissions as all the points are covered, there is no repetition and, by being prepared beforehand, it will be expressed more effectively. The disadvantages are that it is usually too rigid as no two sales interviews are alike and the customer often wants to deviate from the script to concentrate on specific points, whereas a script by its very nature must cover all the sales points. Further, one script cannot be written for all customer environments; and being written for another environment and by another individual, the sales person may be uncomfortable with the vocabulary used and may have difficulty in expressing it with conviction in the context of his/her own personality.

Therefore a middle way is needed which has as many advantages of the other methods as possible and few of their disadvantages. The answer is planned selling which has an element of structure but is flexible enough to allow for different or changed circumstances, encourages the total sales story to be told and yet permits it to be expressed in line with the sales person's own personality.

Planned selling is based on devising appropriate frameworks or sales plans on which to hang the given groups of knowledge/skills/understanding mentioned earlier. There could be frameworks or sales plans for different types of sales interviews and the method is versatile enough to allow for the same frameworks or sales plans to be used with persons of different status within customer companies, but the type of information would be changed to accommodate their particular interests. For example, a general framework could cover the stages illustrated in Fig. 6.1.

The customer or potential customer may raise various objections (a topic to be covered later in this chapter) throughout the sales interview and, while it may not be seen to be a stage of the sales interview, the answering of these may cause the sales person to deviate temporarily from his selling sequence.

The need to have a plan or sequence is to take the 'buyer' through the sale in a logical sequence. If things are said at the beginning of the interview that should come logically in the middle, or things are said at the end that should come logically at the beginning, the customer will become confused and usually acts safely by either saying 'No' or 'I would like to think about it'. For example, to try to 'Sell the benefits' in Fig. 6.1 before having identified the customer's needs could not only confuse the customer but may also cause the sales person to try to satisfy a need that does not exist.

Preparation and pre-planning	
Approach and open the sale	O
Create interest and identify customer needs	B
	J
Create confidence in the 'deal', the sales	E
person and the company	C
	T
Sell the benefits of the identified needs	I
Create desire to buy	O
	N
Get the decision and/or close the sale	S
Evaluation and follow-up	

Fig. 6.1

People remember more easily in patterns and the association of ideas one with another, so the framework or sales plan not only enables the sales person to be more effective by being able to remember the various groups of knowledge more easily, it is also an aid to better retention of the sales story by the 'buyer'.

Sales plans or frameworks should be flexible depending on circumstances, stages may be shortened/omitted or the interview terminated before all the stages have been completed if the objective of the sales interview has been achieved.

Sales personnel should be encouraged to develop sales plans or sequences so that in spite of interruptions in the sales interview and deliberate or unintentional deviations by the buyer, the sales person can get back to the theme without undue repetition and/or omission and thereby effectively control the sales interview.

Sales plans or sequences should be developed that are appropriate for the market situation in which the sales person is working. For example, in a 'creative' selling situation where the sales person has to sell the need before selling a product/service (e.g. a microcomputer to a small business), the following type of framework might be appropriate:

> Preparation and pre-planning
> Approach and open sales interview

> Establish the problems and needs of the customer
> Get customer's agreement he has these needs
> Prove this company's products/services can solve
>   the identified problems and satisfy the needs
> Summarise the buying benefits
> Close the sale of standard product or opportunity
>   to quote for a specially tailored 'deal'
> Evaluation and follow-up

Sometimes sales plans for a series of interviews, each with different objectives but with the overall objective of effecting an initial sale and a continuing supply relationship, may have to be developed such as:

(a) Make contact interview to discover the identities of the executive(s) who make buying decisions or can influence a purchase (i.e. the decision-making unit (DMU)).

(b) Fact-finding (problems and needs) interviews with individual members of DMU through the good offices of the 'nominal' buyer.

(c) Demonstration/presentation of proposals at which sales person tries to obtain order.

(d) Closing interview with the objective of actually getting an order or the signing of contract.

(e) Evaluation and follow-up interviews.

An example of the sales plan for the closing interview ((d) above) could be:

> Preparation and pre-planning
> Recapitulation of developments to date and
>   reposition company 'deal' offered
> Show how the company's product/service
>   combination can solve customer's problem or
>   satisfy his/her needs
> Motivate the customer by testimonial selling
> Create desire to purchase
> Close the sale and obtain order or contract
> Evaluation and follow-up

The stage of 'repositioning the deal offered' is done by the sales person stating the 'deal' (discussed at an earlier stage sales interview) as he/she sees it in case the customer situation has changed since the last interview. For example, the sales person understands that a machine of a certain capacity is needed but the customer has now decided that he/she wants two of a lower capacity; the sales person has either to reposition the deal to take account of the changed needs or to persuade the customer that the larger single machine is in his/her best interest to purchase.

Testimonial selling referred to in the fourth stage of the above sales plan takes the form of boosting customer confidence in the proposed deal, in the sales person and in the company by producing evidence (photographs, letters or simply stating performance data etc.) that show other customers have been satisfied by similar 'deals'.

In all cases, an 'Evaluation and follow-up' stage is important because if the sales person is to learn by experience, evaluation is necessary through self-analysis. Follow-up is important to ensure that the explicit and implicit promises made in the interview are actually kept; this makes for a satisfied customer and ensures a welcome on the next sales visit.

Sales plans and sequences are widely used in selling by telephone because of the lack of the physical presence of the sales person and because usually there is a lack of visual presentation; this must be compensated for in the selling framework and in the sales person's ability to paint 'word pictures'. A selling by telephone sales plan should include the following stages:

> Preparation and pre-planning
> Clear the customer's mind and give identity of
>   sales person and company
> Establish rapport and create interest
> Establish or confirm customer needs
> Deliver the sales message by stressing benefits
> Overcome customer objections
> Get a decision and close the sale
> Summarise the order
> Thank customer for order and his/her time
> Arrange for next call
> Evaluation and follow-up

Perhaps the most important stage is to clear the customer's mind of what is on it when the telephone rings. The telephone is an intrusive instrument; unlike a sales person on a face-to-face call, it does not wait to be announced and its insistent ringing demands action and always interrupts another customer activity. The customer therefore always has something else on his mind initially and to get his/her attention (particularly as the visual impact is missing) something needs to be said that will clear this and get concentration on the telephone conversation. As a general rule, it takes the first 15/20 seconds to get concentration and so the opening remarks must be able to be repeated if necessary without losing impact. The need to 'paint graphic word pictures' on the telephone is crucial because the visual presence of the sales person is lacking, although it is possible to send literature/samples by post and refer to them on the telephone.

Sometimes the telephone is used by the field sales force to get appointments, not to sell the tangible product, in which case a sales plan for 'selling' appointments could be:

Preparation and pre-planning
Clear the customer's mind and give the identity of
  sales person and company
Establish rapport and create interest
Justify an appointment by the need to show proof
Get appointment, say thank you and get off line
Evaluation and follow-up

The most important aspect in this sales plan is for the sales person not to get involved in selling a product/service (this will take place at the physical sales interview) but to return after each comment by the customer to selling the appointment. The techniques under each of these stage headings are dealt with later.

In some telesales situations, the sales plan/sequence is extended to a script, one that allows for the two-way nature and 'give-and-take' of conversation with opportunities for the sales person and the customer to ask and deal with questions. The argument for this approach is that every sales message that goes out is as near the same as is possible in form, sequence and content. This way it is possible to discover the sales messages that work (and those that don't) for a particular company; this makes it possible immediately to adjust the sales message.

Selling is communication and persuasion

There are almost as many definitions of selling as there are sales people, but one that is fairly comprehensive is: 'Selling is personal, two-way communication aimed at achieving specific objectives, notably profitable sales – it implies the need for particular knowledge, skills and understanding.' Compare this with the *Oxford Concise Dictionary* definition of *communicate* – 'Impart, transmit (heat, motion, feeling, news, a discovery, to); share (a thing) with; receive.'. . . 'hold intercourse with . . .' which could have been written by a sales trainer. Even the word 'heat' has implications of enthusiasm (an essential characteristic of a sales person) which has been defined as 'knowledge on fire!'. Also, the implications of the word 'motion' are significant in the selling context, suggesting that sales communication is not only the spoken word but also activity. For example, it could mean the sales person using a sales aid or it could be the customer actively participating in a demonstration or carrying out a price or performance calculation.

Likewise, the *Oxford Concise Dictionary* definition of the word *persuade* – 'Convince (person . . . of fact, that thing is so); induce (person to do, into action)' fits very appropriately into the selling context.

The need for the sales person to communicate and persuade effectively is appreciated if it is recognised that the basic aim is to continue an established relationship or to get agreement with the customer or to cause or change (purchasing) behaviour or to form or change attitudes or simply to extend, re-align or update existing knowledge. Problems arise at the sales person/customer interface when the customer:

(a) fails to hear, because of distractions, interruptions, his/her attention is elsewhere, or he/she genuinely fails to understand;

(b) doesn't want to understand because of personal or 'political' reasons or embarrassment or the fear of being proved wrong;

(c) hears correctly but is not convinced or is not interested, questions the basis or facts, disagrees, is hostile, or has not the mental capacity/know-how to comprehend (e.g. the situation of some commercial buyers in high-technology industries when confronted with new technology).

Sales communication is either explicit using words in face-to-face situations, telephones, letters, memos, reports etc., or implicit through the actions of sales personnel, i.e. whether the sales person is appropriately dressed, is punctual, can demonstrate effectively, does follow-up/progress customers' enquiries/orders. It follows therefore that the words used and the actions of sales personnel must be both appropriate and effective using as many of the five senses (hearing, sight, touch, taste and smell) as possible to support the presentation. Sometimes in the course of a series of sales interviews, the sales person does not confirm that the customer still remembers facts from earlier meetings and bases sales approaches on implied communication. Because of the lack of explicit information the customer, not wishing to appear stupid, can only say 'no' or give a 'delay' excuse.

Requirements of effective sales communication

There needs to be adequate planning, preparation and information. The sales person must research as much information as possible both before and during the sales interview to form the basis of an intelligent credible sales conversation. Has he/she contacted the right person(s) and got the right name(s), status and information about the customer's business, discovered what is the most convenient time to call and all the relevant data and support material? The sales person should be sure of what he/she wants to say; 'playing it by ear' or 'thinking on one's feet' are approaches that should be used only when there is no other alternative.

The sales person must be accepted by the customer as a credible person with adequate knowledge, ability and authority, and one who can act on behalf of his company.

The sales person needs to understand the customer's point of view. It may not be sympathy, which implies emotional involvement, but it must be empathy which is defined as the power of projecting one's personality into (and so fully comprehending) the customer. However, this means not only appreciating the customer's physical requirements (e.g. the product/service) but also the psychological and emotional needs (e.g. the satisfaction of ownership, the psychological need to take part in the selling process not just as a passive listener but as an active participant, and to be treated as a person not as an abstract customer who it is commercially convenient to know).

The sales message (including technical data) must be understood by the customer, but people do not understand if they are not fully conversant with technical jargon or the particular verbal shorthand used in many industries/markets, or if they do not concentrate on what is being said. Further, they do not concentrate unless they are interested in what is being said. The sales person must therefore create interest initially and throughout the sales interview. This will be done if the topic/theme is in the customer's interest, from the customer's point of view. The approach should always be initially, '*you* Mr Buyer, *your* business, *your* products . . .' etc.; if this is not possible, the approach should be '*we*' or '*our*' or 'let *us* look into it'. Only if advice is sought from the sales person should the approach be '*I* think'. To aid understanding, the sales message should be conveyed in the customer's own 'language'.

There needs to be an objective, to be achieved through the communication process, e.g. to give information, to realign customer's attitude, to an agreement, to get action etc. Further, the objective must be clear to the customer. With some people, you can tell them *what* action is required, others need additionally to be told *why* and others need additionally to be told *how* they should go about it, *where* it should be done, *when* it should be done and *who* should do it. The sales person must assess the level of intensity of communication needed by the other person to realise what action to take. The component parts of the conversation/sales interview should be put into a logical order (see earlier comment on sales plans and sequences) and common ground must be found between the two parties (e.g. the customer having a need/problem and the sales person the means of satisfying the need and/or solving the problem).

The sales person needs to draw upon his past experience with a particular customer or with persons doing the same type of job. Catching them at the right time and in a receptive/listening frame of mind and realising that too much sales communication is as bad as too little, are important.

The sales person also needs to realise that emotions mean as much as facts. The hidden psychological barriers of suspicion, fear, anger, antagonism, adverse attitudes, doubt and cynicism all get in the way of effective communication. Further, reticence to get too close to the sales person mentally or to give information may be due to the fear of how it will be used; in successful sales relationships, discretion plays an important part.

There needs to be an element of persuasion. The best approach is to show it is in the other person's own or company interest to take a decision favourable to the sales person. This can be done, having identified the customer's needs, by stressing the benefits that will ensue if they do what the sales person is suggesting and/or the losses that will result if they do not. It is often claimed that the sales person does not *sell* anything but merely helps the customer make a decision to buy.

Effective feedback from the other person(s) to determine whether the sales 'story' is understood and to assess reaction to what is proposed is essential. It is important, therefore, that the sales person is a good listener, stays 'tuned in' to what the other person is saying so as to interpret and evaluate it, and clarifies what is the feedback message if it is not clear. Sales personnel should be able to 'read' the atmosphere of a sales interview. Some sales people have psychological problems in admitting that they do not understand, so a simple method is for the sales person to restate the response from the customer ending with the question '. . . is that what you mean, Mr Brown?' The customer will either confirm that the restatement is correct or will disagree and explain what was meant.

Sales communication by telephone

To the customer/interviewee receiving the telesales/telemarketing telephone call, the caller is an image. The telesales person's voice, manner, attitude, friendliness and word power are the determining factors in the mental and psychological image formed in the receiver's mind.

Antagonism, opposition, anger, frustration, preconceived doubts of success, fear, all are negative emotional human factors which convey themselves over the telephone through the voice. Sometimes false impressions may be made that wreck and/or terminate telephone communication because there is not the 'visual' aid of the actual physical presence of the caller.

A more favourable attitude tends to develop if the telesales person is encouraged to imagine the physical make-up of the customer (even if it is incorrect), rather than addressing an inanimate instrument.

A series of guidelines can be laid down for developing and projecting a positive, pleasing telephone personality.

A relaxed conversational approach is best. A voice that is not relaxed tends to convey a certain tenseness, lack of patience and a lack of confidence. Proper breathing is often the key to a relaxed approach; lack of it often results in 'vanishing cadence', i.e. certain words fade and the ends of sentences become inaudible. Sometimes the same effect is obtained as speakers turn away from the telephone transmitter.

There should be no distractions during a telesales session; this may be difficult in a busy office but it can be reduced often by the exclusion of other personnel from a particular area.

A rapport should be developed and common ground found with the customer; especially with matters relating to *his/her* business, i.e. *your* needs. The words 'us' and 'we' are useful rapport words also; 'I', the sales person, should rarely be used.

It is important for the telesales person to smile and let his/her voice project warmth and the image of a smile. Voice warmth projects an aura of friendliness.

There is a need to keep an air of extra enthusiasm in the voice; almost the sense of urgency.

In the telesales situation it is important to clear the other person's mind and allow him/her to 'tune in', use his/her name and let them know early in the conversation the name of the caller and his/her company.

The telesales person should be direct in all that is said with an economy of well-chosen words. The customer should be helped to 'see' the product/service deal by using terms/phrases that are 'word pictures', e.g. brightness, luxurious, brilliant, considerably increased output, ease of operation, simple controls, first-class quality, superb performance, as smooth as velvet. Appropriate dynamic words such as impact, thrust, speed, rapid, drive control, and appropriately descriptive words such as ice-cool, delicate, fragrant, elegant, frail, fragile, tough, are all used to bring the spoken word into life and excite the listener's imagination.

Speech should be at an acceptable speed; not too slowly or the listener will be put mentally to sleep and not too quickly so that the listener keeps asking 'What was that you said?' It should be distinct with effective enunciation, saving valuable telephone time and inspiring confidence. When telephoning another part of the country, the telesales person should always commence slowly so that accents can be 'homed in on'; after a short time period, a gradual increase to normal speed will be necessary. Also, when presenting facts/figures/performance, delivery should be relatively slow and deliberate. An even output and rate of speech should be maintained.

The mouth should be free of obstructions to maintain clarity.

The voice should be animated and interesting. Pauses and emphasis enables the telesales person to express conviction through the voice. Inflections can help, i.e. by appropriately raising or lowering the pitch of the voice it is possible to inject qualities into the telesales person's vocal performance that will enhance the variety, meaning and colour of telephone sales presentations. Upward slides/inflections of the voice are useful in conveying feelings of anticipation, hesitation, astonishment, conflict, doubt. While downward slides/inflections imply certainty, confidence, affirmation and finality.

It is important to catch the customer in a listening frame of mind; if busy, he/she should be asked when it will be convenient to ring ('shall I ring back at 3 o'clock or 10 o'clock tomorrow morning?'). If it is to be a regular order-getting call (as with repeat sales to grocers etc.) a mutually convenient day and time should be agreed.

The sales person must be a good listener. By being prepared to listen to the customer, opinions, facts, needs, dislikes and objections will all come to the surface so that the telesales person can build a better sales presentation, developing strengths and avoiding weaknesses.

The telesales person needs to sell the benefits of the sales story, obtaining agreement at each stage throughout the presentation. There is a need to retain the customer's attention by making the 'deal/proposals' an exciting, interesting proposition based on his/her needs. Methods calculated to captivate the listener's imagination and hold his/her interest and attention should be used.

Interest must be shown in what the customer has to say: apart from obtaining vital information, it also promotes goodwill. Interest can be indicated by asking questions and really listening to the answer. The prospective customer should have ample chance to say what is on his/her mind. With a very talkative customer, control of the telesales interview can be recovered by interrupting with a question. The telesales person should be mentally observant of the customer's reactions and listen for 'buying signals'; and be prepared to deal with emotional prejudices or fears the customer may have.

A logical step-by-step sales presentation should be planned, specific and factual, and if possible vague claims and generalities avoided. In spite of interruptions and/or objections, the telesales person needs to keep to his/her presentations and return to the appropriate place in the sales story/script each time. Even so, there will be occasions when the telesales person judges that it would be appropriate to end the conversation.

Questions are a 'must' in sales communications

Questions have a special function in sales communication as they should be used not only to obtain information but to keep the customer's interest and participation in the selling process. The effective sales communicator uses the various types at different stages of the sales interview, commenting on and possibly discussing each reply so that the interview does not become an interrogation or a quiz.

Introduction/opening stage

Q. 1. The courtesy question, e.g. 'How are you Mr Brown?', which needs to be sincere and sound sincere; after all, the state of the buyer's health may determine his receptiveness and attitudes.

Q. 2. The curiosity question, e.g. 'How would you like to reduce your costs by 10 per cent?' Which, in the right circumstances, arouses the curiosity and interest of the buyer even before the sales person has announced who he/she is and his/her company.

Early stages of sales interview

In this part of the sales interview, the customer should be encouraged to give information and disclose his problems and needs. This enables the sales person, later in the sale, to put forward the most appropriate 'deal' or benefits of his/her product/service. To do this, the sales person can use:

Q.3. Opinion-type questions, e.g. 'What are your views on the new system of . . .?' or 'Why do you think most people in this industry are turning to . . .?' or 'How will you manage to continue production . . .?'

Q.4. Facts questions, e.g. 'Oh, by the way, how many people do you employ?' or 'By the way, what output do you get from your present machines?'. Notice how the directness of the question is softened by the prefix 'By the way'.

Q.5. The suggestive question, e.g. 'Have you considered . . .?' or 'What about tackling it from another angle, such as . . .?'. In this stage of the sales interview, the customer should be doing most of the talking as he/she answers the opinion and facts questions. If the customer deviates from the conversational direction desired by the sales person, the latter should interrupt with a further question to regain control.

Later stages of sales interview

With the information gathered from the earlier questions, the sales person can match up products/services or aspects of an individual product/service with the customer's needs. This is done by the sales person putting forward three, four or five major benefits (the composition of which is covered later in this chapter) that the customer will experience by doing business with him/her. Each is followed by an:

Q.6. Agreement question. For example, after stating the benefits in performance levels of a machine, the agreement question might be, 'You would like to achieve these levels of performance, wouldn't you Mr Smith?' If the sales person has correctly assessed the customer's needs and presented real benefits, the answer to this question is 'Yes'. The importance of the answer to the agreement question is that it not only keeps the customer involved in the selling process by obtaining a series of affirmations/agreements to a series of benefits, but the sales person is developing a positive/favourable attitude in the customer towards the sales proposals.

By implication, therefore, after any 'benefit' the customer should not be asked a negative question, e.g. after the benefits of performance levels of a machine the customer should not be asked 'I don't suppose you thought we could achieve those levels of performance, did you Mr Smith?' The answer to this is 'No' and a series of these tends to develop a negative attitude or at least uncertainty in a 'buyer' towards the sales proposals. The rule is to use negative questions only when, at the instigation of the customer, there is a need to discuss the benefits of competitors' products/services.

Of course, the customer will answer 'No' to a positive question if the sales person has wrongly assessed his needs/problems or suggested an inappropriate solution. However, the sales person can regain control by asking an:

Q.7. Explanation question. For example, after the benefits have been presented and the positive question 'You would like to achieve these levels of performance, wouldn't you Mr Smith?', should the customer answer 'No' then an explanation is required and a question such as 'Do you mind saying why?' is posed.

Although the answer 'No' may appear to be a setback for the sales person, by the use of the explanation question it can be turned to his/her advantage by obtaining further information and possibly 'drawing out' from the customer a latent objection that may never have surfaced and could have blocked the successful conclusion of the sales interview.

At the end of a series of benefits and affirmative answers to agreement questions (No. 5), the sales person may attempt to 'close the sale' by using one of the methods described later or, if he/she is not certain that the customer is 'sold', may think it appropriate to ask a:

Q.8. Summary opinion-type question, e.g. 'Well there you have the main benefits our product and/or service will bring you, what do you think Mr Brown?'

Alternatively, if the sales person thinks the customer is not completely 'sold', he can use the combination of two other questions:

Q.9. The direction-finding question. For example, 'I've mentioned five of the major advantages of our product/service, but I'm not sure which one most interests you . . . Is it the performance level benefit?' Customer: 'No, I'm quite happy about that . . .' Sales person: 'Is it the delivery benefit?' Customer: 'No, that's all right'. Sales person: Is it the mobility factor benefit?' Customer: 'Yes, perhaps that is the one which concerns me, if I could believe that . . .' The obstacle/doubt has been identified, but before dealing with it the sales person could use the other type of question:

Q.10. The committing statement question. For example, 'If I can prove the validity of the mobility factor, you would be prepared to place an order?' The answer to this should be 'Yes' unless it is not a sincere doubt but one hiding yet another obstacle, in which case another type of question should be used:

Q.11. The hidden objection question. For example, 'Isn't there some other reason Mr Brown?' The scope, type and answers to objections will be dealt with later in this chapter.

There are other types of question in the section on 'overcoming objections', also in methods for getting a decision or closing the sale, but the eleven question types mentioned above are crucial to information gathering and keeping the customer involved in the sale.

Actions speak louder than words

Every sales person has three things to sell: (a) the product and/or service (the 'total deal'); (b) the company; (c) himself/herself as a 'consultant', an adviser. Every sales person has an image (e.g. a happy, cheerful, reliable person with considerable expertise); if the image is acceptable, it will help the sales person sell himself/herself and establish credibility. If it is partially or not acceptable, it will be an additional barrier for the sales person to overcome.

There is therefore a need for the sales person to assess his/her personality and constantly seek to improve it. If everything else is equal between two competing sales propositions, the customer will buy from the sales person he/she likes the best. The acceptance of the sales person's communication will always stand or fall by the acceptability of their personality and the sincerity of their actions.

What is being considered is social interaction between two or more persons in the selling situation and as such it has both a physical and psychological dimension. One important aspect is that the sales person should not adopt a superior attitude even though he/she may be an expert. Talking down to 'buyers' or 'blinding them with science' or jargon merely makes customers defensive and/or suspicious. If technical points have to be made then, allowing for the technical competence of the customer, they should be prefaced with such phrases as 'As you know . . .' or 'As you are aware . . .'.

Even before the sales person speaks, communication will have taken place. The customer will have assessed the sales person's physical appearance, clothes, physique, hair, hands, shoes etc., the confident (or otherwise) way he/she walks, whether the expression on his/her face is tight with nervousness or conveys the friendliness of a smile, and the way he/she shakes hands. The sales person will be making the same sort of assessment of the customer and, additionally, must 'read' the implied communication of whether the customer stands up to greet and/or walks towards him, or appears to ignore him, whether he keeps him/her standing (the buyer is obviously telling the sales person that he/she will not be welcome to stay long) or whether he/she is invited to sit and where. Being invited to sit at the side of the buyer's desk (if there is room) is a much more friendly gesture than with the barrier of the desk between them.

The postures of both buyer and sales person (whether seated or standing), facial and gestural movements can indicate a number of attitudes, e.g. aloofness, defensiveness, suspicion, impatience, casualness, anger, self-satisfaction, sadness, resignation, questioning, doubtfulness etc.

Sometimes the actions of the sales person can be mis-read by the buyer, and this should be avoided by the former. For example, the sales person that is unable (perhaps through nervousness) to look the customer in the eye when making a committing statement may be interpreted by the buyer to be shifty or insincere, or as having a guilt complex about the sales proposition. Sometimes, into actions by the sales person may be read at least disrespect and at most complete disregard for the customer. For example, the sales person who is always late for appointments, who sits down without being invited, who spreads his sales aids, literature etc. across the buyer's desk without regard for other papers there, who smokes even after the customer has refused a cigarette, or who starts talking in a haphazard way which suggests that the customer isn't important enough to warrant advance preparation. The way in which the sales person listens to the customer's responses conveys many messages, and the amount of enthusiasm in the delivery of the sales presentation will indicate to the buyer the sales person's belief and confidence in the overall sales proposition.

Mannerisms are distracting and should be corrected/avoided if possible, but although they may be caused by nervousness they may signal (correctly or incorrectly) that the sales person lacks confidence and/or belief in the product/service or sales story. The sales person needs to ensure that any body movements, gestures or words are used for purposeful movements/conversations, not to distract the listener.

Reliability is a characteristic that the sales person needs to project, not only in meeting promises explicitly made during the sales conversation, but also by meeting the implied promises made every time a sales person accepts an enquiry and/or order. The acceptance of an order carries with it the implied promise that the products as discussed will be of 'merchantable quality' and do the task it was stated they would do, be in the quality and quantity stated and be delivered in the time agreed. This after-sales follow-through may not be as exciting as getting the new business but is important for continued business relationships in the future.

The most effective way to become an effective sales communicator through words, personality and actions is for the sales person to develop self-analysis and, through this, self-correction.

Planning and pre-call preparation

The sales person should be encouraged to be a territory manager; this implies that he/she will plan ahead, developing policies, and evolving strategies and tactics within the overall sales management plan. Organising and co-ordinating is essential to a territory manager; how much time should be spent on existing customers and how much should be spent on prospective customers and what is the percentage of time spent with both compared with the time spent on non-selling activities?

All this implies that information is available on which to plan and organise and, while some may come from the sales manager and/or sales office, the main source of information must be the sales person acting as a researcher, interpreting the data and acting accordingly.

Information must be obtained on market segments, the location of customers and on the potential and size of customer companies, business information, potential and actual customers moving out and those moving into the area, as well as information regarding competitors. It is with this information and his/her past experience that the sales person can manage his/her territory generally and prepare for individual sales calls in particular.

Sources and methods of obtaining new/additional business

In selling jargon, this is known as 'prospecting' and it follows logically that the customer is referred to as 'the prospect'. The continuous search for new business is imperative: in some cases simply to maintain the current level of business if there is a high 'customer mortality rate', in others to increase sales in line with the potential of the territory, the desired market share and the capacity of the supplying company.

There are a number of methods of finding new/additional business, including:

(a) Searching existing records to find latent/lost customers.

(b) Finding selected possibilities through research; either desk research or carrying out surveys.

(c) Finding potential customers who 'select themselves' through response to company advertising, i.e. sales leads.

(d) Cold canvassing, the selling jargon for working systematically through an area, in some cases calling on every company (e.g. office machinery market), in others on all those in a particular market segment (e.g food-processing industry).

(e) Contacts; everyone the sales person is in contact with during a day is a potential source of prospects.

(f) Customer recommendations; this ranges from simple suggestions as to who to contact, to introductions using the customer's name, to using the customer's name as a reference so that marginally undecided customers can contact for confirmation, to the 'endless chain' method. This latter method is where the sales person asks a satisfied customer for three new names; one or two become customers who in turn are asked for three new names etc.

(g) Personal observation: this can range from observing new businesses/ building sites, to features/news items in newspapers and trade press, to names and addresses on lorries and sometimes their contents.

(h) Centres of influences; some persons, because of their job or status, have detailed knowledge of particular parts of industry and commerce and are key sources of information on existing and new business, e.g. bank managers, professional and social club secretaries, controllers of research organisations, secretaries of planning boards etc.

(i) Product search to identify new applications/usages for new customers and new markets.

Sources of information regarding new business are also numerous, including:

(a) Enquiries to the company; even those that cannot be satisfied have potential for the development of new business in other fields.

(b) General enquiries to new businesses just setting up.

(c) Servicing personnel and other company staff, e.g. lorry drivers, telephonists etc.

(d) Other sales personnel in the same industry but not necessarily competitors.

(e) The national, regional and trade press, editorials, news items, features, advertisements, chairman's reports and financial statements.

(f) Trade catalogues and trade association publications.

(g) Industrial catalogues/trade directories (e.g. *Kompass, Stubbs, Dun and Bradstreet, Kelly's, Yellow Pages*, telephone directory, Roskil's *Who owns Whom, Industrial Market Location* etc.).

(h) Professional bodies in general, e.g. accountants, architects, Institute of Marketing, Market Research Society, British Institute of Management, and those applicable to the particular market/industry segment.

(i) Government departments and agencies, nationalised boards, train-ing boards etc., who often list not only their publications but also names, addresses and telephone numbers of whom to contact.

(j) Exhibitions and trade fairs.

(k) Customers' house magazines or newspapers.

(l) Government's Business Statistics Library, HM Stationery Office.

(m) Town planning registers and departments.

(n) Reference and commercial libraries.

(o) Chambers of commerce.

(p) Competitors (sometimes).

(q) Customers' customers.

(r) Local authorities and service authorities (e.g. gas, electricity, water etc.).

(s) Distributors and agencies.

(t)   Customers' personnel such as receptionists, telephonists, secretaries, commissionaires, buyers, sales personnel.

There are other methods and sources particular to individual industries/ businesses but the above list provides considerable material for basic research.

What do customers buy and what is the company selling?

As people make purchases to satisfy their needs and desires, their buying motives are fashioned by these requirements and they are motivated into buying action. Sometimes people live with situations/problems as part of their normal environment, completely unaware of, or unable to relate to, a solution that has been developed through a new product/service. It is the role of the sales person to be aware of customers' needs and desires and bring the latent needs/problems to the surface and then make proposals to satisfy the needs and solve the problems with his/her company's products/services.

Needs and, therefore, buying motives depend upon the person, the situation and the environment. Whether they are turned into buying action will depend on the intensity of the need, its priority listing in the range of customer's preferences, or in the individual's financial and other resources, and the ability of the sales person to show that his/her company's product/service will adequately satisfy the need or solve the problem. It must also be recognised that a satisfied need is no longer a motivation.

Buying motives can be logical, psychological and sometimes illogical; some examples are:

(a) *General buying motives* – thrift, saving, profit, approval of others, dependability, economy of operation, insurance, security, safety, convenience, prestige, ease, comfort, simplicity of operation, up-to-dateness, affection etc.

(b) *Industrial buying motives* – lower price, reduced labour required, cheaper labour required, faster working speeds, lower maintenance costs, better working conditions, reduced material stock-holding, safer operations, reduced space required, less machine down time etc.

It was said earlier that rarely is a product sold without some element of service involved. Therefore it is essential for the sales person to identify the:

(c) *Service buying motives* – risk reducing, applications advice, life prolonging, performance enhancing, expert advice availability, capital reducing, sales increasing, effort reducing, maintenance and repair needs, efficiency increasing etc.

People do not just buy products, they buy what products/services will do for them. Usually it is a combination of various buying motives, some with greater priorities than others, that cause people to buy.

Organisational buying is influenced by corporate, departmental and personal needs as perceived by certain individuals. But as purchasing is done through and by individuals on behalf of the organisation, the buying motives under each of the three headings must be appreciated. Most organisational purchases are made through a collective buying decision by a group of people, either when a purchasing policy is laid down or when each individual purchase is made. This group of people is known as the Decision-Making Unit (DMU) whose members must be identified by the sales person and their buying motives appreciated. These buying motives are affected by the role and status of a member of the DMU in the company. For example, motives for boards of directors are likely to be based on return on capital invested and quality, production managers on less machine down time and lower maintenance costs, research and design executives on compatibility with other components and performance, buying department on price, discounts, quality, delivery etc. Their motives will also depend on whether a purchase is a repeat one from an existing supplier, change in regular supplier or the purchase of product/service 'deal' new to the company.

The effect of product life-cycles is examined in detail later in the book (page 339) but it is necessary to recognise at this point that within each stage of the life of a product, the customer type, customer needs and, consequently, buying motives will change. Therefore the sales approach must be altered if the sales person is to continue to be effective. For example, in the early stages of the life of a generic product, the sales person's role is to gain acceptance of the product concept and to educate in its use. In later stages, when everyone understands the product concept, it is to prove that his brand/deal is better than that of competitors.

Customers' needs can be established by doing desk and field research, asking appropriate questions, observing inside and outside customer premises, carrying out 'surveys', contacting credible third parties, listening carefully, identifying problems/situation, and examining alternative uses for the same product/service with different customers.

Matching customer needs and buying motives with attributes and features of products/services, by converting the latter into customer benefits, is a vital part of the selling process. The presentation of these customer benefits is strengthened if supported by a reason why they are benefits. They are further strengthened if each benefit and reason is accompanied by the weakness of the customer's situation either without the product/service at all or if a competing product/service is purchased. From these weaknesses, potential losses to the customer can be identified in terms of money, time, space, efficiency, image etc. This 'product/service feature + benefit + reason + weakness of existing situation/competing product + loss experienced' approach is far more effective than the sales person merely listing the benefits of his/her proposals hoping that the customer is able to make a comparison between what the sales person is offering and his/her situation without it using a substitute product. Hence, in some companies it is referred to as comparison selling.

To demonstrate this approach, consider its application to a pocket calculator marketed by an international company. The special features/ attributes of this particular calculator are:

(a) Large green numerical display.
(b) Typewriter size keys.
(c) Angled operating surface.
(d) 'Clear last entry' key.
(e) Expandable memory.
(f) Mains adapter/recharger included in price.

and others . . .

It would be necessary for the sales person to apply the F + B + R + W + L approach to all these, as in Fig. 6.2. From this, key selling sentences, appropriate to the particular selling situation, comprised of various combinations of the above identified factors and each containing all five F + B + R + W + L components, can be developed.

Product: Pocket Calculator

Product feature: Large green numerical display

Benefits:	Reason:
Easy to read.	Large characters.
Less tiring on long sessions.	Green is a soft colour, easy on the eyes
Less liable to operator error.	Because of size and colour.

Weaknesses (of existing situation, supplier or product used):	Loss experienced:
Many other pocket calculators have characters ⅓rd the size.	Personal efficiency. Time.
By having to concentrate, because of the smallness of characters, with other makes it becomes more tiring and the mechanics of operating become more important than its use as an aid to make business decisions.	Image (because of increased chance of error.)
With many other makes a less portable desk calculator is necessary to get size and clarity of characters.	

Fig. 6.2

However, this approach should not only be applied to product/service combinations; it needs to be used for services and also for 'intangible' but nevertheless important parts of the 'total deal' that the sales person is selling. For example, continuing the above pocket calculator example, the service element of the 'deal' might include:

(a) A 1-year free replacement guarantee.
(b) A personal consultant in the form of the sales person.
(c) A UK dealer network.

and others . . .

The comparison selling F + B + R + W + L analysis applied to a service would be as shown in Fig. 6.3.

Service feature: A UK dealer network

Benefit:	Reason:
(a) Easily accessible before- and after-sales service.	(a) It covers the whole of the UK.
(b) Availability of trained experts, highly effective and efficient.	(b) Dealers can demonstrate, provide a repairs/spares service.
	(c) Has backing of comprehensive company service organisation.
Weakness (of existing situation, supplier, products):	**Loss experienced:**
(a) Many other companies sell through retailers with untrained staff.	(a) Time in obtaining service.
(b) With many other companies there is no UK repairs/spares service.	(b) Sometimes cost of returning product for service outside of the UK.
(c) With some companies products requiring service have to be sent out of the UK.	(c) Personal efficiency, i.e. while product is being serviced outside UK.

Fig. 6.3

Comparison selling F + B + R + W + L analysis applied to the 'intangible' features of the 'total deal' could refer to:

(a) Resources of multi-national company behind deal/product/service.
(b) Long experience of company in this particular industry.
(c) Large company programme of research and development.

and others . . .

The comparison selling F + B + R + W + L analysis applied to (c) could be as shown in Fig. 6.4.

Many sales persons concentrate on selling features/attributes/benefits but the full impact of the comparison selling, F + B + R + W + L, approach is obtained if analysis is carried out on service and intangible features as well. In fact, if competitors' products, prices, delivery times, service are the same

Intangible feature: Large company programme of research and development	
Benefits:	Reasons:
Develops new materials, processes and designs.	Anticipates customer future demands.
Improves existing designs.	Keeps customers supplied with more effective personal equipment.
Provides testing facilities.	Helps to bring/keep prices down.
	Helps to reduce the frequency of the need to replace power batteries.
Weaknesses (of existing situation, supplier, product/service):	Loss experienced:
	Time (operating outdated machines).
Tendency for other suppliers to lag behind our new developments.	Personal efficiency (because of lack of new feature provision).
Customer is purchasing outdated products.	Prestige (old-fashioned image).
	Space and convenience (because R & D causes development in miniaturisation).

Fig. 6.4

(or better), then the intangible features of the sales person and the company are all he/she has to sell.

Ideally, key selling sentences based on $F + B + R + W + L$ analysis should be developed around product, service and intangible features regarding which the sales person has the greatest possible advantage and the least possible disadvantage, i.e. a unique selling proposition. But even where, in response to a key selling sentence, a customer points out that the product he buys from his existing supplier has the same feature, this can be used to establish the fact that on this feature what the sales person is offering is at least as good as competitors.

When customers buy they put their trust in the sales person and company from whom they are purchasing. This confidence arises from the concern the sales person shows for his customers' needs/requirements and the understanding of their business and problems.

Territory management

This implies:
(a) Planning and the setting of objectives.
(b) Organising and co-ordinating.
(c) Motivating and communicating.
(d) Measuring and controlling.
(e) Development of territory and self.

Increased sales productivity implies more profitable sales per sales person achieved either by:

(a) Making more calls on more customers and potential customers.
(b) Making each call more effective.

The approach should be to:

(a) Analyse the way in which 'sales' time is spent.
(b) Analyse the causes of non-selling time.
(c) Consider the effectiveness of selling during the selling time.

One major factor in common between sales representatives is usually *time*, and its efficient use differentiates the successful sales person from his colleagues. In as much as job satisfaction in the sales representative's activity often stems from the very freedom to act on his/her own initiative and make decisions – or in other words 'to manage' – there is an obvious responsibility for the sales representative to plan and to continually analyse his/her activity.

Long-term time planning

(a) Market segmentation – the total sales opportunities are within certain product/service areas, within certain geographical limitations, and over a broad market area. All three aspects can be often segmented and a decision made on the time priorities and emphasis to be given to each. Which will be most profitable in the long, medium and short term? The sales person needs to identify growing, static and also declining segments and discover what changes in market segments are anticipated?

(b) Classification of customers – there is a need to:

(1) Discover and list both existing and potential customers.
(2) Categorise such a list, endeavouring to equalise workloads as appropriate in the light of a realistic sales call frequency, e.g.

High potential – Class A – Once a week
Good   – Class B – Once a fortnight
Moderate   – Class C – Once a month
Low   – Class D – Once a quarter

The actual frequency must be related to the sales representative's own market situation.

(3) Based on these categories, the sales person should decide the number of calls feasible over a time period (4/6 months), which implies considering the average number of calls per day, making the resulting list the long-term sales call target.

Remember, the normal tendency of sales representatives to obtain 80 per cent of their business from 20 per cent of their customers and spend 80 per cent of their time with 20 per cent of their customers.

Medium-term time planning

Sales 'campaigns' can be planned for individual or groups of customers and potential customers along the following lines:

(a) Define the situation – examine the major facts in the negotiating/selling/marketing situation and do research into the implications.

(b) Problems and opportunities – summarise the most important findings identified in the situation, pinpointing them as either problems which need to be overcome or opportunities on which the sales person can capitalise and assess potentials.

(c) Objectives – the sales person should detail as far as possible what he/she wishes to attain in the short and long term based on *What* and *Why*. The alternatives should be listed and objectives to be achieved written down, quantifying if possible and setting dates.

(d) Strategy (long-range) – the sales person should spell out in 'broad strokes' how the plan is to achieve the long-range objectives.

(e) Tactics (short-range) – these should be spelled out in detail how and by what methods the sales person intends to achieve the short-term objectives, where ideally they should take place and who will or should be involved.

(f) Monitor progress – the sales person in the context of his sales campaign should measure performance, interpret results, take corrective action if necessary.

Short-term time planning

There is a need to establish short-term priorities, e.g. where situations have arisen that are outside the medium- and long-term plans.

Can a series of sales interviews be grouped together geographically into a short-term, compact call system? Still using customer categories, where will the quickest results be achieved?

It is important for the sales person to write down a working schedule for the next day and/or the next week (the sales manager may need a copy anyway for contact and/or control) and to identify objectives to be achieved and quantify if possible within a time span.

Short-term time tactics could include arranging a nucleus of two of three fixed appointments each day supplemented by others which although not by appointment are based on information that indicates a high degree of success. A balance is required between flexibility and standard business procedure. An appointment indicates that the sales representative recognises the 'customer' is a busy person; it also implies that the sales representative is a busy, important person who needs to organise his time. Obviously a basic tool in arranging appointments is the telephone and a sales plan for doing this was shown earlier in this chapter.

Time management also implies the effective use of a diary and record cards, which not only control planned activity in the future but a careful study of past activity can reveal patterns of customers and the sales representative's call behaviour, which can help to decide what tactics should be used in the future.

A checklist for time management could include the questions, do you know, or have you got:

A detailed up-to-date map of the territory?
Addresses and telephone numbers of customers?
Details of hotels, telephone numbers etc.?
Best routes?
Alternative routes?
Industrial locations?
Own analysis of miles per call and average calls per day?
Time selling/time travelling/other non-selling activities?
The call conversion rate (how many calls are converted into sales)?
Total potential of area?
Competition in territory; its structure etc.?
Average value of order per call?
Cost per sale per £?
The miles per call factor (the number of miles covered in a period divided by number of calls made)?
etc. etc.

No one should know more about a sales area than the sales representative. Not all the information is immediately or continually applicable but it is often necessary as background material which assists in deciding objectives, strategy and tactics, and in feeding back information to the company as and when the market changes and, better still, before it changes.

The successful sales person is one that organises himself/herself to enable more effective use to be made of his/her other selling skills.

Planning the sales interview

In organisational selling, when individual companies have been identified, there is a need to carry out research; many 'buyers' say that only a minority of sales representatives seem to take the trouble to find out about the 'buyer's' company or the 'buyer' himself. Yet there are many sources of information provided for this kind of research, for example:

(a) financial, news and recruitment advertising pages of newspapers
(b) chairman's company report

(c) observation
(d) situations vacant columns
(e) trade directories (e.g. *Kompass*)
(f) chambers of commerce
(g) receptionists, telephonists, secretaries, commissionaires

What kind of information does the sales person need to enable him/her to make a sales presentation in the context of a particular company and its market situation?

(a) name of company
(b) affiliations in a group
(c) type of business
(d) number of employees
(e) names of key executives and personnel
(f) credit rating
(g) product/service range
(h) manufacturing methods
(i) testing procedures
(j) quality requirements
(k) purchasing procedures
(l) decision patterns
(m) stockholding policy
(n) need for technical advice
(o) investment plans
(p) product developing plans
(q) competitive situation of customers etc.

In selling goods/services direct to consumers, background information is still necessary but may be more difficult to research prior to sales interview. The electoral roll and/or telephone directory may be the only printed sources, but information will still be needed to pitch the product/service 'deal' at the right level. So, much information must be discovered during the sales interview, e.g. age, marital status, how many children, income group, occupation, car, resources, type of employment etc. Some purchasing decisions will be made by the husband, some by the wife, some by the children, some by reference to a third party and some jointly by any combination of those mentioned.

In industrial/commercial/business selling, a number of questions about the customer needs to be answered by the sales person (as far as possible) before the sales interview takes place, for example:

(a) the prospect – who is he/she?

(1) name
(2) position

     (3) peculiarities, attitudes, interests
     (4) problems, needs, desires
     (5) further contacts

There is a need to get to know something about him/her.
(b) What does he/she want?

     (1) unusual problems
     (2) resistances
     (3) objections
     (4) primary buying motives
     (5) secondary buying motives

There is a need to get to know something about his/her business.
(c) What can I offer?

     (1) product/service
     (2) order of presentation
     (3) what sales points
     (4) special advantages in his/her case

Link our service with his/her business.
(d) How should I offer?

     (1) co-ordination with previous interview
     (2) opening approach
     (3) sales points
     (4) what sort of proof
     (5) answers to objections
     (6) special points
     (7) co-ordination with subsequent interviews

(e) What do I hope to obtain? These are the objectives of the call and can be a combination of many possibilities, for example:

     (1) to sell at a profit
     (2) to identify/solve a customer's problem
     (3) to obtain a sympathetic hearing
     (4) to instruct in new knowledge
     (5) to re-align existing knowledge and attitudes
     (6) to improve/reinforce quality of knowledge
     (7) to stimulate and persuade
     (8) to find who are in the Decision-Making Unit (DMU)
     (9) to sell a works visit
     (10) to sell 'extended deliveries'
     (11) to update literature.

Objectives are needed not only to establish what should be done and as a target but also after a sales interview to measure performance, i.e. what actually happened against a standard set.

The sales interview

The need for planned selling and sequences for the selling interviews was examined at the beginning of this chapter by identifying the various stages needed in different circumstances in the sales interview. But there is a need to look at some of the stages in greater depth and an examination of the sales plan on page 150 is used to do this.

Having carried out all the pre-planning mentioned (pages 162–75), the sales person has arrived to meet the customer and carry out the sales interview. Initial courtesies are important so as to establish a friendly atmosphere and put customers at ease. A smile and a firm (not crushing) handshake, enquiry as to his/her health (if they have met before) and comment on any other personal items of which the sales person is aware, helps to set the scene. However, it is important that the time spent on courtesies is restricted otherwise, if the 'buyer's time is limited, he/she may terminate the sales interview before it can be fully developed.

Opening the sale and creating interest

The sales person has at his/her disposal a number of techniques for opening the sale, getting the customer's attention and creating interest:

(a) The specific product/service approach – a particular product/service that has special appeal (in consumer goods selling it may be the current 'promotional' line) is selected to create interest at the beginning.

(b) The new idea approach – where some new/novel aspect of a product/service, application, function, process, method, display can be used to gain attention.

(c) The curiosity approach – anything that arouses curiosity, so that more information is demanded by the 'buyer' or agreement is given or greater concentration by the customer takes place, will obviously help the interview. Curiosity kills a disinterested attitude in a customer, e.g. 'How would you like to reduce your costs by 10 per cent, Mr Brown?'

(d) The particular problem approach – where the sales person has been able to identify a particular problem that applies generally to a type of business or where it is one that specifically applies to this particular customer and the sales person is able to offer a solution through his/her own company's products/services, it makes a good opening to the interview.

(e) The major benefit approach – this is based on the aspect of the product/service 'deal' that will benefit the customer most.

(f) The 'news' approach – where some news about products and/or services is available, e.g. 'The reason I've called today is that we've made some changes in our servicing workshops which should speed-up repair work and I know a quick call out is important to you in the field.' Price decreases can be used in the 'news' opening approach but it is best to keep price increases until later in the sale, and before which the benefits of the 'deal' can be stressed.

(g) The facts approach – every buyer is interested/impressed with facts that are relevant to his/her business, especially if some third-party authority for them can be quoted.

(h) The question approach – enquiries as to health, 'How are you, Mr Brown?', are best used in the courtesies stage but curiosity questions ((c) above) and questions getting agreement are useful 'opening' tools, e.g. 'Which causes you more problems, machine breakdowns or weather conditions?' or 'How important is it for you to have a machine of this size?'

(i) The sincere compliment approach – as the name suggests, a compliment of some sort is paid to the buyer by the sales person either about the company, e.g. 'I must say that one cannot help but be impressed by such an up-to-date and modern production unit', or about the buyer personally, e.g. 'I've heard some pretty nice things about you in a business way and I have been looking forward to meeting you.'

(j) The reference approach – the sales person quotes the name of another company who is a satisfied customer or the name of a mutual/personal friend of the 'buyer'.

An important point is to avoid stunt approaches as they can go wrong, and always ensure that any approach which increases customers' expectations must not be followed by a sales interview which is an anti-climax or fails to deliver the high expectations of the opening.

Creating confidence

It was stated earlier in this chapter that in the first part of the sales interview the sales person must supplement the information obtained through pre-interview research by asking fact and opinion-type questions to fully understand the particular needs/problems of the customer and satisfy/solve them with the product/service 'deal' offered by his/her company by using buying 'benefits'. But this information may not be readily or fully given unless the customer has confidence in the sales person and his company. In fact, a salesman has three things to sell, his product/service, his company and himself/herself as an adviser/consultant.

The sales person must therefore prepare a number of examples so that he can impress the customer with convincing proof of his own and the company's credibility. Some of the types are:

(a) To make general claims, e.g. 'Many companies who have used our product/service are very pleased with it' or 'The demand for this product/service has increased considerably recently'.

(b) To quote expert opinion, e.g. 'Department of Health and Social Security research into factory fatigue has shown that . . .' or 'Professor Blank's research into production statistics shown in the Institute's Report indicates . . .'.

(c) To quote an anonymous case study, e.g. 'We solved this type of problem for a company in Exeter only last month . . .' or 'We have installed this type of machine recently in another company in the high technology field, and there we found . . .'.

(d) To quote a named case study – care must be taken in the choice because if the company named is not considered to be of the same standing as the customer it may not be seen as a recommendation. Examples of this type would be 'XYZ Ltd have these machines installed and are very satisfied with them' or even more powerful (provided the agreement of the man named has been previously obtained) 'Why don't you contact Mr Smith of XYZ Ltd and he can tell you how satisfied his company is'.

(e) To show visual proof – the previous methods would be greatly strengthened if visual proof in the form of photographs, drawings, brochures etc. can be used.

(f) There is only one thing better than visual proof and that is tangible proof, where the buyer can test or see the service for himself/herself. Examples of this would be demonstrations at the customer's premises, demonstrations at the premises of a satisfied customer or a free trial for a period.

Selling the benefits

Having created interest, 'sold' confidence in the product/service 'deal', in the company and himself/herself, and having added to his/her information by asking fact and opinion-type questions, the sales person must now show how the company's product/service can satisfy the customer's need and/or solve his/her problems by selling the appropriate benefits.

The basic method shown earlier in this chapter was for the sales person to prepare beforehand a number of key selling sentences based on $F + B + R + W + L$ statements (feature + benefit + weakness of customer's present situation either without the product/service or in obtaining it or a substitute product/service from another supplier + the loss which results from the weaknesses). These key selling sentences supported by positive agreement questions, e.g. 'You would like to achieve this level of performance, wouldn't you Mr Smith?' help to influence/cause purchasing action. However, it is realised that it would be impossible to prepare beforehand a key selling sentence based on $F + B + R + W + L$ statements for every possible situation. Perhaps two or three for each product/service, two or three for each aspect of service the company provides and two or three for intangible aspects of the company. By using the prepared F + B + R + W + L in key selling sentences, often the sales person will get into the habit of using statements based on the formula and will automatically develop these key selling sentences as the sales interview progresses.

Creating the desire to buy

Many sales managers would argue that if the customer's needs and problems have been correctly assessed in the early stages of a sales interview and the benefits of the correct product/service have then been stressed, the customer will want to buy and therefore the sales person can enter into the decision-making/closing stage of the sales interview.

Other sales managers would agree in principle but would point out that there is often a need to give the 'buyer' a feeling of security and assure him/her that he is doing the right thing by placing an order. This is particularly true when it will mean that the buyer's company is changing supplier, perhaps after many years with the present one, or this will be the first time his/her company has done business with the sales person's company, or the buyer's organisation is large and the buyer is responsible to one or several levels of authority for his actions, or if he/she still has some slight doubts about the proposed 'deal'.

Where such 'insecurity' exists, it is better to spend some time endeavouring to increase the buyer's desire to buy rather than face him/her with making an immediate decision situation where the safest one may appear to be to say 'No' or give a delay excuse (e.g. 'I'd like to think about it').

The methods to be used in 'Creating the desire to buy' are adaptations of those examined in 'Creating confidence' which would be summarised in this stage as 'testimonial selling'. Basically, it is giving assurance and a feeling of security by showing that other companies have acted on the sales person's advice and that they have been very satisfied with their purchase.

If there is some lingering doubt in the buyer's mind, it could be brought to the surface and dealt with by using a 'Direction-finding' question as shown on page 161 or questions such as 'Do you mind telling me why?' or 'Isn't there some other reason, Mr Smith?' Alternatively, after a delay excuse (e.g. 'I'd like to think about it') the sales person could say 'There is obviously something you are not happy about, Mr Brown, but let's think this through together then I will be able to help immediately with any points which need clarifying . . .'.

Overcoming customer objections

The customer may raise a number of objections at any time in the sales interview, although there is a tendency for more to be raised near the point where he/she must make a decision. The majority of objections are unknowingly planted in the minds of buyers by negative thoughts in the minds of sales personnel. A positive attitude of mind helps to create a climate favourable to closing a sale so that the buyer does not search for points upon which to base objections. Objections are often a request for information and must not be taken personally as a criticism of the sales person or his/her company.

The three principal things to remember about objections are:

(a) They have to be recognised by the sales person and confirmation given to the customer that the objection is understood.

(b) The sales person must realise why the objection is made.

(c) Objections can be turned to the sales person's advantage, particularly if following the answering of an objection, a related benefit is stressed.

There are four types of objections:

(a) sincere or genuine
(b) hidden or purposely concealed
(c) insincere or false
(d) unnecessary or self-inspired

Insincere or false objections usually appear early in the sales interview and often indicate that the prospect's interest has not been aroused sufficiently. The sales person needs to be a little deaf with false objections.

Unnecessary and self-inspired objections are those the sales person suggests either by drawing attention to past deficiencies of the product or service, by poor equipment handling, or a too technical sales presentation, or by deliberate misrepresentation; obviously all situations which need to be avoided.

Sincere and hidden objections:

(a) indicate that the buyer is paying attention
(b) indicate his/her sales 'temperature'
(c) identify his/her true area of interest
(d) reveal areas of competition
(e) often indicate that a buyer is 'sold'

When an objection is raised, a decision has to be made by the sales person whether to handle it immediately or defer it. The reasons for deferring objections are:

(a) to retain initiative
(b) if he/she does not know the answer
(c) it may be better to answer it later when it is more powerful in presentation
(d) to prevent breaking a trend of thought

The sales person should always defer when an element of prejudice is suspected in the objection. How are objections deferred? The sales person should:

(a) let the prospect know that he/she understands his point
(b) indicate that he/she has been clever to bring it up
(c) appear quite confident in receiving the objection and show it does not worry him/her
(d) suggest that he/she proposes to answer it later

What types of objections should be handled immediately?

(a) if the objection is crucial/pertinent to the discussion in hand
(b) if the sales person is unable to go on without dealing with it
(c) when the objection reveals the true area of the buyer's interest
(d) when it gives the sales person the opportunity to close the sale or obtain an order for one line before going on to the next.

Dealing with sincere objections means disagreeing agreeably. Some examples are: price or discount objections are usually raised because benefits have not been stressed sufficiently – if benefits are stressed first, price will look small by comparison. If buyer insists on knowing/discussing the price, then uses it as an objection, use the 'I agree . . . but . . .' approach.

Turn the objection into a question. After an objection is made, the sales person says 'Yes, I see your point Mr Smith, and it raises a very good question.' 'What you mean is . . . Is that the question?' The sales person is no longer in the position of having to prove a customer wrong but merely answer a question.

A combination of the previous two techniques can be used efficiently. The sales person should turn the objection into a question, then give the buyer a reason to purchase either by stressing a major benefit or by demonstrating or showing visual proof or by telling a verbal proof story.

Testimonial selling can be used after an objection has been raised. The sales person should show by photographs, illustration or calculations, or tell him/her what benefits have accrued to other customers in similar circumstances; visual and verbal proof stories deal effectively with objections.

Objections based on similarity – where products are similar to competitors, and prices, discounts, delivery etc. are the same or similar. 'Why should I buy from you?' or 'I am quite happy with my present supplier' objections are often raised. In such circumstances, the buyer will always buy from the sales person he likes best. The sales person must study human relations and improve his/her personal relationships with such customers, and then other salesmen will be asking how to deal with this problem.

Delay excuses are usually experienced when the sales person has made an imperfect job of selling. He/she has not 'sold' the benefits of the proposition in a way that appeals to this particular buyer. If the sales person meets the delay excuse often, he/she must improve his/her selling techniques and sell the benefits of placing an order and/or the disadvantages of delay.

If the sales person receives a blank refusal, then possibly the prospect is not in a position to place an order. He/she may not be the right 'MAN', i.e. the one with the Money, the Authority and the Need.

Hidden objections are often covered by apparently sincere objections, usually of the price or delay excuse type. They must be brought to the surface and dealt with using 'Why?' and 'Isn't there some other reason?' approaches.

The sales person should try the 'suppose' test – 'Suppose this difficulty did not exist, would you be interested?' If the answer is 'Yes', it is usually a genuine objection and this can be a disadvantage (in which case admit it and outweigh it) or it can be a misunderstanding (in which case the sales person should accept this as a fault in his/her presentation and, in the case of a demonstration, get the customer to correct it). On the other hand, if his/her answer is 'No', this is usually a false objection, in which case the sales representative should ignore excuses and create desire, find emotional satisfactions through psychological benefits, if possible use visual aids and/or verbal proof.

Objections indicate that the desire for the product has not reached a sufficiently high level. It is a sign to the observant sales person that his/her proposal and presentation have missed linking the customer's needs and requirements sufficiently to the features and benefits of his/her product/service. The objection itself may signpost the area omitted and it may need further probing to discover what this is.

Objections should be welcomed because they help to disclose the buyer's true area of interest; but not too many. The sales person should head off the buyer's objections by incorporating the answers in his/her sales presentation, so that they are answered before they can be raised.

The sales person should list all possible objections in the pre-interview planning stage together with their answers (see Fig. 6.5). There are usually several ways of answering each objection. New objections and answers should be added to the list as they occur so that a complete set is built up. There are answers to all objections and if a sales person has difficulty with

Product/Product Group			
Main sales features	*Main selling benefits*	*Objections usually met*	*Answers to objections*

Fig. 6.5 Objection analysis sheet

one particular objection, there should be discussions with colleagues as to how they answer it or the sales manager should be approached for advice.

Getting the decision and/or closing the sale

There are a variety of ways a sales interview can be brought to a successful conclusion by achieving the objective(s) of the call. This could be to obtain permission to submit a quotation, to get a purchasing decision or other objectives dealt with earlier in this chapter. To do this, the sales person should not resort to 'high-pressure' sales methods but rather 'naturally' lead the buyer to make a decision.

Objections occur throughout the selling interview, but particularly during the 'close'. Often 'buyers' need to be given a feeling of security before they are willing to act. The sales person should make it easy for the buyer to say 'yes' by converting his/her objections into a reason for buying, increasing his desire to buy, removing the doubts and asking for the order repeatedly.

By giving the buyer the complete sales sequence, it makes 'closing' less difficult as it gives the whole story and therefore makes a decision much easier. Scratch-pad calculations and illustrations, samples, display photographs and cut-away models, powerful eye-impact tests and demonstrations all help to close the sale. Also, during the benefits stage, the sales person can use special technical features if it can be shown what they mean in terms of benefits: 'Because of the . . . you get the benefit of . . .'. Sometimes the buyer has not indicated his major interest, so should be asked: 'I have mentioned four major benefits and I am wondering which you rate as most important; is it . . . or . . .?'

It is better to get agreement at each stage during a sales interview rather than expecting the customer to make one single, total decision at the end. There is no need to go through the complete sequence before trying to close if the customer signals he/she is willing to purchase.

The advantages of attempting a trial close are:

(a) It stops over-selling and talking oneself out of the order.
(b) It helps to uncover objections.
(c) It helps disclose the buyer's true area of interest.
(d) It helps speed the sale.

The sales person should watch for buying signals that indicate the customer is willing to purchase. For example:

(a) Physical signs such as facial expression, a shoulder shrug, a nod of the head etc.

(b) The raising of a sincere objection.

(c) A committing statement: 'If only I could be certain this line will sell in the way you say . . .'

(d) When the quotation or catalogue is studied carefully a second time.

(e) When the sample display piece is carefully examined again.

(f) When enquiries are made about delivery dates, or the number in a pack, or whether there are illustrated leaflets or display material, or the extent of advertising support.

(g) When the question is asked whether the product will do the job.

(h) When the buyer brings in another person for a second opinion.

　 . . . and many others.

There are many techniques of getting a decision and/or of closing the sale.

Natural close

This process can extend over months, and can have begun with an immediate 'rapport' between sales person and the customer. The whole negotiation has moved 'naturally' to business being placed. The survey carried out, the elements of technicalities, price and delivery have been agreed, problems established and recognition that the sales person's product/service is the optimum answer. This type of negotiation is characterised by the experienced sales person admitting that he/she 'felt it was right' and that the order would come to the company.

Assumptive close

This is virtually identical to the above. The two mould into one another with the sales person using such phrases as 'Well, we shan't have any trouble there . . .' or 'We can take a look at that after the first period run . . .'. There is no question of the business being placed, the sales person and customer are looking together at points which may arise after the purchase. Conversation is phrased in a way indicating that the sale has already taken place, i.e. an assumption.

The alternative or dual positive close

'Will you take six or twelve . . .?' or 'Shall I book it for this month or next?', both lead to an order. The advantage is that this method still leaves the sale open if the buyer has not yet made a decision and is therefore useful as a 'trial close' technique.

The leading close

'Will twelve be enough?' Whether the reply is 'Yes' or 'No', the answer means an order. Care must be taken in using this method as some very sensitive buyers interpret this as a verbal trap.

The progressive close

For a range of repeat selling lines, the sales person should begin writing as soon as possible in the interview. He should start with his/her promotional line or one with outstanding value and go through impulse lines to demand lines.

The concession close

A concession retained to the end will often give the extra incentive needed to get an order. Discount, free showcards, advertising support, better or special delivery or any extra service you can give. A concession should never be given without a return of some sort.

The summary close

The sales person should summarise all the benefits the buyer will experience when he/she places an order.

The visual and/or verbal proof story

The sales person retains a strong visual and/or verbal proof story referring to a customer who has experienced the benefits of purchase.

The fear close

Should be used with discretion as many buyers react unfavourably to it, e.g. 'If you don't place an order now we will be unable to deliver before the holiday period'. Nevertheless, it is widely used.

Major points close

'If I can prove the product/service will do . . . will you then be quite happy with my proposition?'

The minor point close

The sales person avoids the main issue of the product/service but gets customer's approval on a minor point – 'Do you want it delivered this month or next?' It is easier for the buyer to confirm a delivery date than to give an order. Advertising material, display material, service, method of payment etc. can also be used as the basis of a minor point(s) close.

The possession close

The sales person implies that the customer is going to buy long before he has arrived at a decision, e.g. 'When you have this model you will want it in a prominent position, won't you? What about over there?'

The physical close

Link the close with something physical, such as an actual delivery, trial order, demonstration, e.g. '. . . that is why I suggest you allow me to make arrangements for a demonstration'.

The impending event close

'Your new plant opens next month and you will want adequate service right from the start, won't you?' or 'With the extra shift and overtime working you will want to extend your catering services without disproportionately increasing costs, won't you?'

The 'pushing ahead of events' close
'When you see how well these drink machines work, I'm sure you will want to extend your automatic catering coverage to other types.'

The objection close
'From what you have said, you would be prepared to consider our product/service, if it weren't for this one objection, wouldn't you, Mr Brown?'

The ask-for-the-order close
When the other methods have failed, the sales person should ask for the order and ask for it repeatedly, e.g. 'May I have your order, Mr Brown?' or 'Let's give this purchase an order number straight away and you'll get the benefits more quickly'.

These techniques can be used individually or in combination.

Such 'closing' methods sometimes appear very artificial when viewed coldly in black and white, but when used appropriately in the sales conversation appear natural. There are others, but recognising the natural, assumptive and summary as being the most effective still allows room for the careful and considered use of such skills as the alternative and fear with the right situation and customer. In the last analysis there still remains the most simple and yet effective skill of merely asking for the order. If the rest of the negotiation has been correct, then this in turn becomes a 'natural'.

The last stage is to summarise the order, arrange date of next call and to thank the customer for the order and his/her time.

When the sales person has closed the sale, he/she should make sure it remains closed by regularly servicing the account and looking after the customer as a VIP. Customers appreciate being looked after and if trouble occurs it should be dealt with immediately, not passed to someone else, or for the sales person to disclaim all knowledge or responsibility. Long-standing business relationships depend upon reliability.

Evaluation and follow-up

After a sales interview, it is important for the sales person to evaluate it as soon as possible while all the facts and the 'atmosphere' of the call are still fresh in his/her mind. The analysis should be around whether the objective was achieved; the actual results; the buyers and the sales person's behaviour, attitude and reactions; and the interaction between the two parties. In other words, what did the sales person learn that can be applied to future sales interviews and to make himself/herself more effective.

The sales interview should be recorded giving date, person(s) interviewed, details of order placed/enquiry given, details of buyer and his office, details of his business etc. Details of any follow-up action to be taken, when, how and by whom, next call information such as when, how and by whom should all be recorded when updating the customer's record card.

The sales person should ensure that the order placed or enquiry made enters the company's administrative system as soon as possible, later checking its progress and finally ensuring that the customer has received it. A follow-up call to ensure that the customer is satisfied may be incorporated into the next 'regular' call or may form the basis for the reason for the next call to locate further business.

Summary

The planned selling approach brings a subtle combination of structure and flexibility to the sales interview. The sales plans that are developed not only allow the sales person to take the customer logically through the sales presentation but helps to fix the information in the sales person's mind. In some examples shown earlier, there may appear to be a lot of stages, but some may be dropped/shortened (if appropriate) as the sales interview progresses and, with use, the various stages together with other techniques in this chapter will become habit forming and after a while can be used with very little effort.

Two-way communication was shown as a crucial factor in the selling process and which, supported by persuasion, is used not only to discover the customer's needs/problems but to show how these could be satisfied and/or solved. This presumes the use of combinations of appropriate questions not only to obtain information but to hold the customer's interest and to enable him/her to participate in the sale. The effectiveness of the sales interview may depend on the sales person selling himself/herself as an adviser/consultant, thereby establishing credibility.

Skill at locating and gaining access to potential customers, as well as how well the sales interview develops, could depend on how well the pre-planning stage is carried out. Additionally, the successful development of a selling relationship may come from the sales person's ability to identify customer's needs/problems and buying motives and to match these with the product/service being offered and expressed as 'benefits'. Territory management linked with pre-call planning and time management are the ingredients for a systematic approach to developing the full potential of a sales person's territory.

Making a good approach, creating interest and confidence, and asking fact-finding and opinion-type questions are important early in the sales interview. These should be followed by appropriate benefits related to features of the total sales 'deal' that the sales person can offer, expressed in key selling sentences which should also include the weaknesses of the present situation without the product/service or an alternative product/service, and the losses which would arise from this. This may or may not be followed with the 'creating the desire to buy' stage; it all depends on the customer's level of intensity of desire to purchase.

Objections can be raised by customers at any time during the sales interview; they are basically of four types and familiarity with methods of handling them enables the sales person to overcome them and proceed to the final sales plan stage of 'Getting the decision and closing the sale'. Again there are a number of techniques for getting a decision and 'closing', and the sales person's skill in choosing the most appropriate one in a particular set of circumstances will be crucial to the successful conclusion of a sales interview.

Finally, the evaluation and follow-up stage needs to be based on self-analysis of the sales interview as the basis for future sales activity and the completion of necessary administration/paperwork together with 'progressing' the order/enquiry/quotation and later to check customer satisfaction with the outcome.

Questions

1. What are the advantages of planned selling and what are the alternatives?

2. What do you consider to be the ten most important aspects of sales communication?

3. Questions are crucial to effective sales communication. Identify those types that are most useful early in the sales presentation and those that are likely to be more effective if used later.

4. Identify ways in which customer's needs/problems and their buying motives can be matched to the product/service benefits being offered by a supplying company.

5. What do you consider to be the most important aspects of territory management?

6. Why is it necessary to create interest and confidence during the early stages of a sales interview?

7. Why does the customer raise 'objections' during the sales interview and how can these be handled?

8. Comment on the statement that 'a good sale closes itself' and that there is no need to employ methods for getting decisions and/or closing the sale.

CHAPTER 7

Motivating and communicating with sales personnel

Objectives

This chapter initially examines a variety of motivational approaches from a number of sources, i.e. concepts based on the research into motivating people which not only suggests a variety of alternatives but allow the sales manager to compare his/her current approach to motivation. This is followed by a case for having a motivational plan, and the key aims that such a plan should try to achieve, followed by the characteristics of the ideal sales team motivator. The actual process of motivation, together with the key elements, are established in a model and then examined. Finally, motivational methods are examined under the headings of intrinsic (contrived) and psychological (natural) rewards, the elimination of disincentives, the use of indirect reinforcement methods and disciplinary methods. The chapter recognises that sales people have a number of motives for behaviour and no two are alike. Also that individuals have different motives when they are organised in teams and can have different motives at different times and in different circumstances. A highly adaptive approach is suggested for the sales manager to accommodate human diversity.

Motivational approaches

In Chapter 1 (page 11), when examining general management principles, motivation was linked with leadership and communication. A motive can be defined as '. . . the inner driving force that dictates how great an effort will be made . . .' and motivation as '. . . identifying how to get the best out of subordinates by understanding why they behave the way they do, what their motives are, what makes them work well or badly, and using this information and a variety of techniques to motivate subordinates to higher level of performance'.

How does the sales manager ensure that the sales person making a sales call 200 miles away is selling the same way and with the same enthusiasm as he/she did when the sales manager last worked with him/her?

The key factor is motivation. Effective training will ensure that the sales person knows how to sell, but it is motivation by the sales manager and/or others acting in a managerial capacity that ensures that selling is done in the way and with the enthusiasm expected by the manager. Ultimately, motivation is what the sales person *wants* to do.

Robertson and Cooper comment* that

> . . . Problems and issues concerning motivation are frequently of central import-ance in organisational life. . . . Although many issues of this sort frequently have an individual motivational basis, it must be remembered that other factors such as inadequate training or job experience, personality characteristics, unsuitable organisation structure or inadequate supervision may also be involved. . . . One means of explaining the motivation to behave in certain ways is to propose the existence of certain internal, motivational states of drive or need. . . . Some theories of motivation focus on the content of motivation and attempt to uncover needs such as hunger, security, affiliation, self esteem, which underlie and control behaviour. Other process theories focus on the processes by which goals or needs exert their influence . . .

The nature of the selling job is such that an appreciation of both the content of motivation and the process by which it operates is important for the sales manager to appreciate when developing a motivation policy and plan.

A number of concepts/approaches exist and much research has been done in the area of the content of motivation, and the following approaches all contain practical indications for the sales manager in motivating the individual and/or the sales team.

The *economic* approach is that men and women reason out the consequences of their (selling) activities, that their needs and desires are essentially rational, and that they are motivated by money and economic cues and comparisons. It also suggests that any motivational activities of the sales manager are measured against economic calculations to determine whether the individual is to be motivated.

The *Maslow*† approach depicts men and women as not simply a product of their past experiences and learning, but forward-looking and self-directed, capable of shaping their own life and behaviour. Often referred to as the 'hierarchy of needs' approach, it claims that human needs can be hierarchically organised in the following order (starting with the lowest): physiological, safety and security, belongingness and love needs, self-esteem

* I. T. Robertson and C. L. Cooper, *Human Behaviour in Organisations*. Macdonald & Evans, 1983, p. 78.
† A. H. Maslow, *Motivation and Personality*. Harper, New York, 1954.

and the need for self-actualisation (realisation). When and only when a lower need has been satisfied, the next highest need becomes dominant and the individual's attention is turned to satisfying this higher need. This approach considers that only an unsatisfied need can motivate behaviour of any kind. It implies that the sales manager will need to know where individuals are on the Maslow scale to adopt appropriate motivational needs activity.

The *social–psychological* approach depicts men and women primarily as 'social animals' conforming to the general forms and norms of their larger culture (society generally) and to the more specific standards of the sub-cultures (e.g. religious sect or social group) and face-to-face groupings* (e.g. the family, the sales team) to which their lives are bound. Their wants and behaviour are largely moulded by their present group membership (e.g. sales person, mortgage holder) and their aspired group membership (e.g. millionaire class, jet set, sales manager etc.). The implications for the sales manager are that sales personnel can be motivated by social considerations such as social status, being socially acceptable and important, service to other parts of society etc. It has motivational implications for the team approach to sales management to create a spirit of togetherness, e.g. to be an 'in' member of the sales team, respected by himself and others outside the sales team (i.e. customers, family, friends etc.), respected and consulted by those in the sales team as a fully qualified member. Further, this approach has aspirational overtones as often individuals aspire to be like others, their behaviour emulating how they perceive their aspirational model would be likely to act. In these circumstances, the leadership qualities of the sales manager and 'setting an example' are likely to be strong motivators.

The *McGregor†* approach is based on two theories. In theory X, man is seen as inherently lazy and unambitious, prepared to work only when it is unavoidable and loth to seek or accept responsibility. According to this theory, direction, motivation and control must come from outside; thus the sales person is viewed as someone who must be driven by greed, fear and coercion if he/she is to work at all and must be under constant surveillance.

Alternatively, theory Y proposes that work is a natural human activity, capable of providing enjoyment and satisfaction; it implies that external control (i.e. the carrot and the stick) is not the only means of getting people to work. Further, it postulates that individuals can exercise self-control and self-direction if they are committed to the objectives to which they are working, and higher individual needs can be satisfied in the pursuit of organisational objectives. Individuals can learn to seek responsibility for decisions which further the ends of the organisation rather than merely comply with its rules.

* T. Veblen, *The Theory of the Leisure Class*. Macmillan, New York, 1899, and others.
† D. McGregor, *The Human Skill of Enterprise*. McGraw-Hill Book Co., New York, 1960. Reproduced with permission.

The implications of the McGregor approach to the sales manager are that of making the right decisions as to the time and place to use the right blend of theory X (e.g. fear, coercion, assignment of blame, reprimand where necessary, development of and authoritative consultant relationship etc.) and theory Y (enjoyment, job satisfaction, give responsibility, encourage self-direction etc.) as motivators of the sales team.

The *Herzberg** approach is based on the motivator (the sales manager) putting together the right combinations of two factors that contribute to satisfaction and dissatisfaction at work. Robertson and Cooper† explain this approach:

. . . Factors associated with good feelings about the job (motivators) are mostly derived from the job itself. The second set of factors (hygiene factors) are mostly external to the job and involve aspects of the physical or psychological environment (e.g. commission, company car, being called sales executive). Some of the most important implications of Herzberg's theory concern ideas about how satisfaction and motivation can be improved by restructuring or 'enriching' jobs so that they provide people with rewarding experiences . . .

. . . The core of Herzberg's proposal is that it will not be possible to motivate people by improving hygiene factors alone. Improvements in hygiene factors such as working conditions, interpersonal relationships, etc. will perhaps decrease dissatisfaction but will not improve motivation. True motivation, according to Herzberg, derives from factors associated with the job itself and relies on offering opportunities for achievement, recognition, responsibility, etc. . . .

This implies getting each sales person involved, giving credit and praise, encouraging the acceptance of responsibility.

The *McClelland* approach is based on a study of motive patterns and their effect on behaviour and personality. He identified an individual's need of achievement, application and power, most individuals being motivated to some extent by all three but one is usually dominant. He concentrated mainly on the motivation of achievement and found that a person with such a need has a strong desire for feedback, takes moderate risks, sets measurable goals, competes with himself rather than just with others (i.e. with some internal standards) and is always striving to improve.

Such a person is specifically concerned only with the desire to succeed but characteristically takes money as one measure of his/her success. Monetary incentives as such are ineffective in motivating the high '*n* Ach' personality unless directly tied to his/her performance. An individual having a high need for affiliation may respond better to social rewards, e.g. compliments and praise from others.

The recognition of motivation patterns should enable sales managers to

---

* F. Herzberg, *Work and the Nature of Man*. The World Publishing Company, Cleveland, 1966, p. 72.

† I. T. Robertson and C. L. Cooper, *Human Behaviour in Organisations*. Macdonald & Evans, 1983, p. 81

distinguish those who are self-motivated and those who require external motivation in terms of financial or social rewards.

The *transactional analysis* approach (originated by Berne, 1956) proposes that every person has three 'ego' states (child, parent and adult) and that behaviour (and therefore motivation) depends on which state is dominant at a particular time.

It is possible to recognise current dominant ego states in oneself and others by a variety of behavioural, postural and verbal clues. The child is perceived largely through the physical characteristics of some emotional display and by a variety of word uses, e.g. superlatives. The parent adopts expressive parental gestures and postures, and uses 'always', 'never', 'shouldn't' and a number of value-loaded words. The adult listens and responds with mobility of face and posture, uses question words and others such as 'probability' and 'unknown' indicative of the objective data processing, and prefixes opinions with, for example, 'I believe that . . .'

Transactional analysis can help sales managers to improve day-to-day interpersonal relationships, motivation and communication by enabling individuals to recognise their own and others' ego states and to respond appropriately so that communication can be usefully continued or successfully terminated without offence or anger.

The *Steers and Porter** approach was that management's role

. . . is to learn to identify . . . different kinds of basic motives or needs . . . able to fit the demands of a job to a pattern of behavior that will result from and provide satisfaction for the arousal of a given motive. The Manager can create this fit by the selection and appropriate placement of people with different motives by altering the demands of a given job, or by selectively arousing, satisfying and thereby reinforcing the kind of motivation that will lead to the most appropriate job behavior.

Often, much time and money is spent upon finding the right people for the sales force, training them, getting them the right equipment etc., but in some cases very little is done to motivate them continuously to achieve their optimum performance. The development of an overall motivational plan ensures that the company obtains the maximum return upon its investment in time and money in those other aspects of sales management.

The aims of such a *motivation plan* are simple to list but harder to achieve. The first aim should be to develop and stimulate, through dynamic leadership, a keen sense of loyalty towards the organisation as a whole. All individuals tend to have their short-term and long-term goals; likewise, companies have their short-term and long-term goals. If the sales person can be 'sold' on the importance of loyalty to the company, he will re-orientate his goal so that he is striving towards the same one as the company. If a deep sense of loyalty is developed in the sales person and he is 'sold on' his job, the

* R. M. Steers and L. W. Porter, *Motivation and Work Behavior*. McGraw-Hill Book Co., New York, 1975.

company and its products/services, not only will the company tend to experience a lower sales team labour turnover rate, but it will build in the mind of the sales person the perfect company image. Some companies spend large sums of money perfecting the company image in the minds of the consuming public, and the convinced sales person, as the ambassador of the company, can really 'sell' confidence in it to prospective customers. But if the sales person has a poor company image in his/her mind, it will not be possible to project convincingly a favourable image to everyone he meets.

Directly related to the first aim of the motivation plan is the second aim: to induce into the sales force the sense of prestige and of pride of belonging to the organisation and, in fact, of being partly responsible for the progress it is making, i.e. getting everyone involved. Everyone likes to be part of a successful venture whether it is in social affairs, sport, local affairs or business, and the sales person is no different in this respect. There is, therefore, a need to build pride in individual contributions. The individual will be motivated to greater things if he/she works for a company that is a leader in its own particular field, if it has a good public image or if its name is a household word.

Following logically is the third aim, to foster a team spirit of togetherness. Men and women are basically social animals and, in particular, the sales person, who is characteristically often an extrovert, will be more highly motivated if he/she feels a member of a team. The team spirit is a fine motivator, for in many cases an individual who on the odd occasion might be prepared to take things easy for his/her own sake, will not do so if it means letting down the team. The sense of satisfaction obtained in taking part, and helping individual colleagues, is a powerful motivator of sales personnel.

The fourth aim of the motivational plan is to foster the unqualified acceptance of the management of the company. Dynamic leadership comes about because the sales force accepts, trusts and relies upon the leader's ability to make sound judgements upon his/her ability and capacity to organise, upon the ability to show the sales person how to do the selling job, upon his/her sense of fairness and justice, upon the ability to apply just the right amount of discipline, and upon other necessary virtues. Rarely is the sales force better than the leadership qualities displayed by its leader and, in fact, the success of the sales force will often reflect the drive and enthusiasm of one man, the leader, the motivator, the sales manager.

The fifth aim is to inject into the sales team a friendly competitive spirit. As has been mentioned already, members of a team like to be held in high esteem by other members. Contests and competition throughout history have caused individuals to strive to become the winner, to achieve a better performance than the next person. Individuals always work more enthusiastically when they have something for which to work. However, it is essential that the competition remains upon a friendly basis, otherwise it may work as a demotivator, causing friction and antagonism within the sales force; obviously this result is not conducive to a high level of performance.

To the sales manager, getting the motivation plan accepted by the sales force is a challenge. It is similar to the basic selling job; in this case, with the sales person as the 'prospective customer', the sales manager must 'sell' the individual on the benefits he/she is receiving by working for the company at the present time and on the additional benefits that will be enjoyed through the acceptance of the motivational plan. The sales manager may have to create the need and then show how the motivation plan will satisfy it. Further, the sales manager must gain acceptance from the sales team in the image of a friend, consultant and a leader giving credit and praise to each sales person deserving it.

What are the characteristics of the ideal sales force motivator? First, he must have a genuine and sincere interest in the individual members of the sales team, showing confidence in each person and with the breadth of mind to treat all equally, with a friendly, fair and helpful (but always positive) attitude. The sales manager must provide the opportunities for individuals to improve themselves, and in this role should show by example that he is not only the senior sales person of the company but is also the senior sales worker of the sales force. If the sales executive has a reputation of 'living it up' in the company's time, it may act as an unwritten communication for the sales force to do the same, or at least it will supply them with a plausible reason for not working at peak performance. There must not be one law for the selling 'rich' and another for the selling 'poor'. The principle of example should be extended further into the work content of the sales person's job.

The level of motivation will be high if the sales manager can show that what he/she is asking of the sales person is not an impossible task. The ideal motivator is a 'doer' not just a 'watcher' and does it also by showing that he/she is in touch with real-life situations and problems arising in sales territories, not by running the sales force by remote control from behind a desk. This also implies that the sales manager is accessible and can be reached by the sales team; as upwards communication from the sales force is as important as downwards communication from the sales manager.

The sales manager can only get results through people, and the foundations for good relations are:

(a) based on good information, deciding on what is expected of a sales person
(b) pointing out ways in which the sales person can improve
(c) letting every sales person know how he is getting on
(d) looking for extra and/or unusual performance
(e) giving credit when due, as close to the event as possible
(f) getting people to accept change, telling them why change is necessary and telling them in advance how change will affect them

(g) making the best of each person's ability and looking for ability not being used

(h) always assisting in a sales person's advancement

(i) always 'sandwiching' criticism between two 'pieces' of praise.

The process of motivation

So far the theories examined tend to focus on the contents of motivation, but another dimension to its appreciation is to identify the stages that are involved in the process of motivation of individuals and/or a sales team. Robertson and Cooper* suggest that the most important process approaches to motivation make use of ideas about the expectations that people have about the consequences of their behaviour.

. . . Put simply, the theory suggests that the amount of effort people are prepared to invest in a task depends on three factors:

1. expectancy – whether the effort involved will produce better performance.
2. instrumentality – whether the performance will pay off in terms of outcomes, e.g. promotion.
3. valence – whether the possible outcomes are attractive for the individuals concerned. . . .

A number of such concepts of the cognitive process of motivation have been explored, modelled and modified by many researchers, as observed by Kast and Rosenzweig,† which can be adapted and/or extended to set up a motivational process model appropriate to the needs of sales management; such a model is depicted in Fig. 7.1.

It is as important for the sales manager to understand the stages and sequence of the process of motivation as it is to appreciate the previously examined approaches to motivational content. By being aware of the implications of each stage, he/she can influence the actual process shown in Fig. 7.1.

Motives

Motivation has already been defined at the beginning of the chapter, but put simply in the management context, it is the combination of the techniques used by the sales manager to use those inner driving forces (motives) of sales personnel to generate a level of effort which produces the performance necessary to achieve the stated objectives. Motivational methods are

---

* I. T. Robertson and C. L. Cooper, *Human Behaviour in Organisations*. Macdonald & Evans, 1983, p. 82.

† F. E. Cast and J. E. Rosenzweig, *Organisation and Management*. McGraw-Hill Book Co., USA, 1979, p. 246.

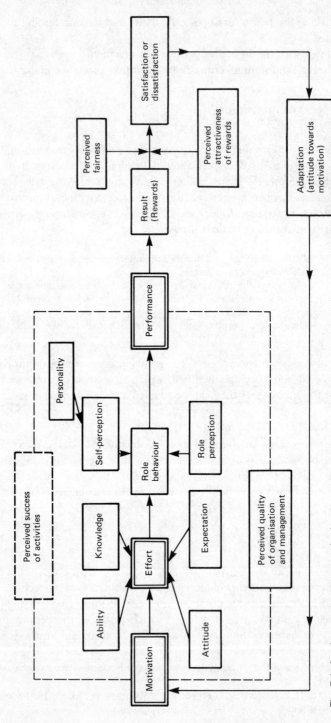

Fig. 7.1 A sales management motivational process model

examined later in this chapter. Some motives in isolation may be detrimentally too powerful. For example, ego drive makes the sales person want and need to make a sale as a personal achievement but taken too far becomes high-pressure selling, ignoring whether the customer wants the product or not. The sales person's feeling is that he/she has to make the sale, the customer is there to help the individual fulfil his/her personal psychological need. The sales manager may need to counter-balance ego drive by fostering empathy in the sales person. Empathy is the ability to feel as the prospective customer does in order to sell a product and/or service. It does not necessarily mean being sympathetic, as it is possible to know what the prospect feels without agreeing with that feeling.

Effective selling calls for a balance of these two factors; to need the sales intensely and yet allow the sales person to look closely at the customer and appreciate the customer's reactions and needs.

Effort

Motivation should lead to effort which has been defined as 'strenuous exertion', 'display of power' and 'something accomplished involving concentration or special activity'. Additionally, in the context of the individual in the sales team, it also implies the degree of application and commitment to selling and the company. Selling has been described as 'a way of life' rather than simply a job because it makes extra demands on the individual and requires a greater effort to be successful. Effort will be influenced by four factors that will affect its intensity:

(a) *Ability* – the power or capacity to sell, to 'get on with people', the level of cleverness or technical competence etc. It is important that the sales manager recruits sales personnel with the level of ability, mental capacity and intellect appropriate for the particular sales job. Effort will be diminished in proportion to the degree of inability of an individual.

(b) *Knowledge* – either derived from experience, education or training. The level and types of knowledge needed by the effective sales person were examined earlier in the chapters on training and selling. Lack of appropriate knowledge will constrain a sales person's effort both directly and indirectly because of lack of credibility with customers.

(c) *Attitude* – a state of potential behaviour indicating opinion towards an attribute of an object, service, activity, job, company, person, selling generally etc. Attitudes will affect the type and intensity of effort not only along a scale of right/wrong mental attitudes but also along a scale of positive/neutral/negative attitudes. In other words, a positive attitude in the sales person breeds confidence which encourages effort. Further, attitudes can be conveyed to customers by the subtleties of both verbal and non-verbal behaviour. Positive attitudes appear to be transferred to customers as if by telepathy, giving them confidence in the product/service combination, the company and the sales person as an adviser/consultant.

(d) *Expectations* – this influencing factor is the anticipation (expectation) concerning the amount and intensity of effort required to achieve a specific outcome and concerning the probability of the individual and/or the sales team being rewarded for achieving a desired outcome; it is also concerned with whether the effort involved will produce better performance. It is also the area in which the individual calculates, unconsciously or sub-consciously, whether the outcome is worth the necessary effort.

The sales manager may need to clarify the amount and intensity of effort required, hold out the possibility of some individual or team reward and build confidence in the individual and/or sales team that the required performance level is feasible and can be achieved.

Role behaviour

'. . . a role is commonly defined as a set of behaviors which is expected of everyone in a particular position, regardless of who he/she is. These behaviors are, of course, socially ordained: and the role therefore sets a kind of limit on the types of personality expression possible in any given situation. . . .'[*]

The concept of role describes the behaviour the sales person is expected to exhibit when occupying a particular job in the sales organisation, e.g. sales engineer, area sales person, area sales manager etc.

Taken literally, the role behaviours should reflect job descriptions for each job mentioned earlier but, additionally, it has implications for the manner and enthusiasm of the way the job is carried out.

Role behaviour acts as a filter for effort, and the sales manager will need to review frequently not only job descriptions but also the way they are interpreted and emerge as role behaviour by the sales person.

Role perception

The way that the role is perceived by the sales person will obviously directly affect the role behaviour. In the sales person, role perception will be fashioned by his past work experience (especially as a sales person), perceived ideas about the job perhaps obtained from external sources (e.g. television programmes or films) or internal sources (e.g. when working in production or in the sales office), training, other sales personnel etc. A man-about-town with an easy-going, if disorganised way, picking up considerable business by personal charm may not be the role behaviour that the sales manager

---

[*] J. M. Pfiffner and F. P. Sherwood, *Administrative Organisation*. Prentice Hall, Englewood Cliffs, New Jersey, USA, 1960, p. 39.

requires for a job that requires a dogged endurance, highly organised image with the sales person acting as a technical adviser/consultant over a period of time before an order can be expected.

Personality

. . . Personality theory . . . is concerned with the whole person in a total environment and it is of particular importance for organization theory and management practice. The personality of a human being is a complex combination of physical and mental attributes, values, attitudes, beliefs, tastes, ambitions, interests, habits and other characteristics that comprise a unique self. . . . From the point of view of personal growth and development, a deep, rich, integrated personality would seem optimal. However, these dimensions vary by degrees and many combinations are possible. It is important for [sales] managers to recognize differences in order to understand and predict individual behavior in organizational settings. . . .*

Self-perception

Out of personality comes self-perception which directly affects role behaviour. In the sales role context, a person's self-perception is his/her attempt to reconcile his personality with expected role behaviour. For example, a sales person may not want or only be partially enthusiastic for a changed sales role if his/her perception is that 'it's not me', i.e. the individual may feel that his/her personality is not right for, or cannot cope with, the new role. Alternatively, a person appointed to a sales post (e.g. promotion to area manager) may perceive that he/she has not the right personality but endeavours to 'act' out the new role perhaps for status reasons. In these circumstances, the sales manager needs constantly to build up the sales person's confidence to enable him/her to grow naturally into the expected role behaviour.

Performance

This relates to the execution, carrying out, putting into effect, doing the task, job, operation etc. But to view it objectively does imply that feasible, attainable, reachable objectives/targets have been set against which the level of the performance can be measured. Further, it does imply that the sales manager can be, and is specific about, precise behaviour/activity that constitutes a good level of performance. Establishing sales objectives were examined in Chapter 2 and the methods of measurement against these objectives are examined in the next chapter on control of the sales operation. No matter how well a sales manager operates, his/her effectiveness will

---

* F. E. Kast and J. E. Rosenzweig, *Organization and Management*. McGraw-Hill Book Co, New York, USA, p. 239. Reproduced with permission.

always be judged by the performance of the sales team; which means that performance needs to be monitored constantly and aligned to meet changing circumstances.

In Fig. 7.1 it will be seen that all the stages of the motivational process considered so far are framed with a dotted line. This is to depict symbolically that they take place within two sets of perceptions that affect these initial stages; they are:

(a) The individual's perceived success of his/her activities in the total and/or separate processes. For example, the individual may perceive that his/her efforts have been considerable but this may not coincide with the sales manager's 'reading' of what has happened. One method of identifying whether this situation exists is to get the field sales person to complete a sales call critique form and compare it with one completed by the person's field sales supervisor.

(b) The individual's perception of the quality of organisation and management will have a favourable or adverse effect on each stage of the motivational process. A well-run organisation can create confidence and pride of working for the company, which in turn could affect favourably effort and role behaviour. Similarly, perceived effective and fair management could affect attitude and the degree of effort expended.

Conversely, if organisation and management are not perceived to be supportive or cause the sales person embarrassment, this can produce an adverse effect on effort and performance. It is often reflected in a 'them and us' attitude, and the sales person 'distances' himself/herself mentally from the company by talking in terms of '. . . those people back at Head Office . . .' or '. . . you can never rely on promises they give you . . .' etc. In other words, it can affect the loyalty of the sales person to the company.

Results (rewards)

The result or outcome of performance to the individual can be viewed in the context of a return or recompense for work, service or merit, i.e. in the form of rewards. These are either intrinsic rewards that tend to be the natural result of the work itself and would include existing/challenging/enjoyable work, job satisfaction, sense of achievement, responsibility, self-esteem etc. Or, alternatively, they are extrinsic rewards such as salary, commission, bonuses, promotion, praise, recognition and esteem by others (especially family and members of the sales team) and may be necessary to satisfy some intrinsic need such as ego, survival, power and achievements.

Intrinsic rewards tend to have the greatest effect because they come from within the individual, but extrinsic ones may appear to have the greatest effect because they tend to be tangible and/or are observed by others.

Effectiveness of rewards depends on two factors:

(a) The perceived attractiveness of the reward. Although the absolute amount of a reward has a direct affect on satisfaction, it is a very individualistic matter and in the end all rewards will be judged/assessed by the value the sales person puts on them. What may be perceived as attractive by one individual may be seen to be only partially attractive or even irrelevant to others.

(b) The perceived fairness of rewards. The fairness/equitability factor can be affected by comparison with other individuals (another sales person) or a group (the rest of the sales team) where they are getting the same reward for less performance (e.g. the same salary) or more reward for the same performance (e.g. a larger or better quality company car). This factor is also affected by the actual content or size of the reward compared with performance (i.e. bonuses based on years of service and/or status) and on the method/machinery of determining the reward (e.g. sales commission schemes based on sales volume but which ignore widely differing sales territory potential).

Satisfaction or dissatisfaction

The result/outcome in the context of the perceived attractiveness of, and the perceived fairness of, the rewards will lead to satisfaction or dissatisfaction by the individual sales person. Satisfaction tends to be specific (e.g. winning the top sales person of the month award) or general (e.g. the overall feeling of being with a good team in the right job).

Dissatisfaction can be specific (e.g. the perceived inadequacies of a commission scheme) or it can be general which is usually the accumulation over a period of time of a number of small specific dissatisfactions; a situation that perhaps could have been avoided had it been dealt with early enough by the sales manager.

Adaption

The satisfaction or dissatisfaction the individual sales person experiences will result in the development of attitudes and reaction towards the motivation, effort, performance, rewards process. Therefore, as shown in Fig. 7.1, there will be a feedback loop to motivation. A satisfied individual will tend to have a feeling of elation/ego satisfaction and will be in a state of mind to be motivated at the same or a higher level. In order to restore the situation to one of perceived fairness, a dissatisfied individual will either:

(a) ask for more rewards
(b) change the object of his comparison
(c) reduce quality of performance or output
(d) reduce quantity of performance or output

(e) alter outcome (e.g. a sales person may increase sales in the short term by resorting to high-pressure selling which may not be in the individual's or the company's long-term interests)

(f) distort inputs/effort to influence outcome (e.g. a sales person may concentrate on a particular product or customer type to the detriment of others)

(g) start looking for other employment which in some cases could mean little or no sales effort being put into his/her present job

The wider influence of the dissatisfied individual on the remainder of the sales team should not be under-estimated and therefore needs to be dealt with or offset by activities of the sales manager.

Finally, the total process of motivation will only be effective if:

(a) the individual sales person can mentally link the motivation with effort, performance and reward

(b) the rewards are large enough to warrant effort expended

(c) certain aspects of the job do not conflict with the motivation process (e.g. a commission-only sales person being expected to spend 3 days' non-selling activity on an exhibition stand)

(d) the basic environment in which the motivation process takes place is fair (e.g. in a commission scheme, allowance has been made for differing territory potentials)

(e) the process and the rewards are in line or ahead of what is being offered by other companies in the same or similar industries/markets.

Motivational methods

The sales manager can only motivate or stimulate through specific or combinations of motivational methods. These tend to fall into five main categories:

(a) Methods that result in *physical rewards/incentives* (e.g. salary, commission, use of company car, sales competitions etc.). These have been referred to as contrived rewards as they are '. . . largely brought in from outside the natural work environment and generally involve costs for the organisation over and above the existing situation. . . . Although they can be used to positively reinforce behavior . . . they tend to lead to satiation rather quickly. . . .*

(b) Methods that result in *psychological rewards/incentives*, e.g. job satisfaction, security, more responsibility, public praise, status, being

---

* F. Luthans and R. Kreitner, *Organizational Behavior Modification*. Scott, Foresman and Company, Glenview, Illinois, USA, 1975, pp. 102 and 103. Copyright © 1975. Reprinted by permission.

consulted etc. These have been referred to as 'Natural rewards which exist in the natural occurrence of events. Social (motivational) reinforcers and existing procedures cost nothing extra . . . they do not generally lead to satiation (people seldom get tired of compliments, attention or recognition). . . .*

(c) *Elimination of disincentives*, e.g. unfair treatment and practices, favouritism, injustice, uneven sales territories etc.

(d) *Indirect reinforcement activities or methods*, e.g. using sales meetings and conferences, training, on-the-job supervision etc. as motivational tools in addition to their prime objective.

(e) *Disciplinary methods*, e.g. private reprimands, public admonition, notification of awareness of wrong doing, warnings, fear, loss of privileges, dismissal etc.

However, the sales manager will be constrained in the application of motivation methods by a number of factors:

(a) Will the particular motivation method produce behaviour or activities that result in the company and/or sales team objectives being achieved?

(b) Is the motivational method appropriate for the type of sales person involved (e.g. a sales achievement contest with the reward of a holiday for two in Paris may or may not motivate the family man with four children who prefers camping)?

(c) Will the motivational method stimulate in a particular work situation? For example, a sales person whose remuneration contains a large proportion of commission on new business will not be motivated into making effective service calls on existing customers.

(d) Is the time horizon of the operation of the motivational method appropriate? A once a year or Christmas bonus on annual sales will tend not to motivate in July.

(e) Can certain high potential sales persons dominate a particular sales competition? The knowledge that certain persons can or have dominated a particular sales competition tends to be a demotivator for others who may not make an effort for the rest of a sales period to have 'a good start' for the next sales period.

(f) Any commission earned should be paid as close to the event/activities from which it arose otherwise the impact of the cause-and-effect relationship is lost. Sales effort seems to be cumulative and once started can develop a momentum.

Using motivational methods to stimulate sales persons in the work

---

* F. Luthans and R. Kreitner, *Organizational Behavior Modification*. Scott, Foresman and Company, Glenview, Illinois, USA, 1975, pp. 102 and 103. Copyright © 1975. Reprinted by permission.

situation and in the context of the above constraints can be seen to be '. . . an intervention strategy designed to modify the behaviour concerned. . . . The purpose of the intervention strategy is to strengthen desirable behaviour and weaken undesirable behaviour. A major feature of human behaviour is the range and variety of rewards that might be used to provide reinforcement [i.e. to strengthen appropriate behaviour patterns]. 'Money provides an obvious example, but many other potential rewards can be identified. . . .' (Robertson and Cooper).* They then go on to instance the '. . . Possible Rewards for use in organisational behaviour modification' as suggested by Luthans and Kreitner.† These were classified in the categories of 'Contrived on-the-job rewards. . . Consumables, Manipulatives, Visual and Auditory and Tokens. . .' and 'Natural Rewards. . . Social and Premack. . .' which could be adapted to the sales management situation as in Fig. 7.2. They continue: '. . . It is worth noting that not all of the rewards involve the organisation in direct costs, such as friendly greetings and compliments. . . .'

Those rewards listed in the right-hand column in Fig. 7.2, i.e. under the heading 'Premack', originated from behaviour analysis research work carried out by Premack‡ and explained by Robertson and Cooper.§ '. . . Premack demonstrated by experiment that an event which serves as a reinforcer [to strengthen appropriate behaviour patterns] for some behaviour may not have a reinforcing effect on other, different behaviour . . .' Thus job rotation may motivate internal sales personnel on relatively mundane sales administrative work but may be a demotivator to a field sales person being paid by commission, as it may be seen as preventing him/her from earning money and keeping in touch with customers and the market place. Further, Premack has argued that there is, in effect, '. . . a hierarchy of reinforcement. The order of reinforcers in the hierarchy will change as circumstances change. . . .' For example, a sales person, after a period of being motivated by increased earnings through commission may, in the short term, be motivated by being given a job with more responsibility at the same basic pay if he or she sees this as a route to future promotion.

A special list of motivational methods/rewards appropriate to all sales personnel (especially the field sales force) needs to be developed. Using the 'Luthans and Kreitner' format, such a list could be developed to include those shown in Fig. 7.2.

* I. T. Robertson and C. L. Cooper, *Human Behaviour in Organisations*. Macdonald & Evans, 1983, pp. 231 and 232.
† F. Luthans and R. Kreitner, *Organizational Behavior Modification*. Scott, Foresman and Company, Glenview, Illinois, USA, 1975. Copyright © 1975. Reprinted by permission.
‡ D. Premack, 'Reinforcement theory' in D. Levine (ed.), *Nebraska Symposium on Motivation*. University of Nebraska Press, USA, 1965.
§ I. T. Robertson and C. L. Cooper, *Human Behaviour in Organisations*. Macdonald & Evans, 1983, pp. 225–6.

	Contrived on-the-job rewards				Natural rewards	
Consumables	Manipulatables	Visual and auditory	Tokens	Social	Premack
Expense account to cover travelling, own meals and entertaining customers	Company (prestige) car for business and agreed level of private use (e.g. on holiday)	Sales bulletins	Salary	Personal and annual appraisal interviews	Job satisfaction
Above-average hotel accommodation	Company briefcase, typewriter, equipment etc.	Monthly position lists	Commission	Public praise, i.e. recognition at sales conferences and meetings	Security
Payment of telephone bills	Other relevant gifts	Performance assessment against sales manual	Bonus and/or profit-sharing schemes		Opportunities to be creative
	Generous assistance with re-location expenses	Personal congratulatory letters	Payment with goods and/or services	Recognition through super sales person committees	Opportunities for further training and continued education
	Extra holiday time	Best sales person of the year award cup	Prizes from contests and competitions	Achievement in quota clubs	Opportunity for personal dignity
			Membership of golf and/or other social clubs	Act as consultant for new sales persons	Membership of a successful sales team
			Special pension plans	Being socially accepted	Status
			School fees	Being consulted	Awareness of a promotional ladder
			Private medical care plans		
			Mortgage loans or subsidies		
			First-class individual or group life assurance		

Fig. 7.2. Motivational agents/rewards particularly appropriate to the sales team

Some of the motivational agents/rewards appropriate to the sales team shown in Fig. 7.2 need further explanation, comment and examination.

The remuneration plan

No system of paying sales personnel can succeed as a motivator unless the underlying conditions of service on which it is based are fair and reasonable. Conditions of service refer not only to those company policies and procedures that directly affect the sales person's job (e.g. adequate expenses, adequately powered car, expectation of hours to be worked or number of calls to be made etc.) but also those that indirectly affect it. For example, product policy, pricing policy, quality control service to customers etc. need careful consideration before developing and using the various forms of remuneration as motivators. Thus motivation will be short-lived in a sales situation where commission rates are higher than normal in a particular market, if the product/service is wrongly 'positioned' in the market (i.e. a low-quality product/service marketed as 'high quality') or where the product is out-of-date, or where supporting service is bad, so that the extra effort involved in selling such a product/service far outweighs the extra commission and where the long-term reputation and credibility of the sales person is put at risk.

Further, the sales person will not be motivated if it is discovered that he/she is not receiving at least 'the rate for the job' in a particular industry. The differentials between industries reflect such factors as the degree of creative selling needed, the special nature or complexity of the product/service, the relative level of the market price, profit margins, the degree of innovativeness or novelty of the product/service, the position on and/or speed of the product/service life-cycle, and the current level of acceptability of the product/service by the consumer or user etc.

Appropriate territory planning is another important factor; for there is little point in offering high commission rates if the size or sales potential of a territory, or restrictions on the access to certain outlets, or the retention of certain large 'house' accounts by the sales manager or Head Office, make it impossible for the sales person to earn rewards from that sales territory that are considered fair and reasonable in the industry.

Similarly, the sales person will find it difficult to build up customer goodwill where quality is low relative to the claimed market position of the product/service and where before- and after-sales service is either poor or non-existent. In such circumstances, there will be a tendency for the sales person to receive progressively less repeat or recommended business, and to maintain his/her sales will have to spend a considerable proportion of available sales time locating new customers.

The remuneration plan operated by a company will influence considerably the sales manager's ability to obtain the optimum level of cost-effectiveness from the sales team.

Most remuneration plans are made up of one or a combination of four main elements:

(a) salary
(b) commission
(c) bonus
(d) payment with goods and/or services

The proportion of each of these elements to the total remuneration will depend upon company policy, the use of non-remuneration motivation agents, the present expected pattern of sales, and the degree of emphasis that the sales manager wishes to bring to bear upon the individual sales person. In other words, the best combinations of remuneration types that will bring optimum results for the company in a particular market. As the business scene is continually changing, it is in the individual company's interest to review annually the suitability of its existing remuneration plan, and the advantages and disadvantages of other methods.

Salary only

This is an equitable method of remuneration where the sales person spends a considerable proportion of time on tasks that are not of a direct selling nature. For example, time spent by sales engineers giving technical advice not only upon their product but upon systems applications generally; merchandising and display activities in retail stores; time spent at exhibitions and demonstrations that would not directly produce a sale. The effectiveness of such activities cannot be immediately measured by current sales and, therefore, tend not to be carried out efficiently by sales personnel whose selling time is linked with a commission scheme.

The salary-only method of payment is often found in industries where the product is either well-established or is exposed to a high degree of pre-selling by sales promotion and advertising so that the amount of creative selling by the sales person is relatively low and where there exists a high level of consumer demand.

Further, it is found in industries that experience wide fluctuations in sales volume due to seasonal or other repetitive factors, where the sales person, if paid by commission, would receive an extremely high reward during one period and nothing in the next.

It is an extremely useful system of payment where a high degree of mobility is expected of sales personnel, that is where members of the sales force are being continually moved, as with a company's sales task force, so that it is difficult for the individual sales person to build up a repetitive business connection. The salary-only method is often favoured where the various sales territories have widely differing sales potential, or are at different stages of development and where customer goodwill takes a long time to accumulate. Further, it is used when a relatively high level of personal security is an important factor to obtain the right sort of sales person and where sales areas are likely to require division or amalgamation in the near future.

It is also used where the sales person is part of a team whose joint efforts are what really sells the 'total deal', i.e. where estimators, design draughtsmen, technical advisers, commissioning engineers etc. are involved.

The salary-only method is often employed by companies who spend considerable sums of money upon training (especially technical training), and wish to keep their sales force intact and reduce labour turnover to a minimum. Payment by salary only is often considered an advantage as no commission disputes can arise, because of administrative savings as complex commission calculations and the keeping of commission records are avoided, and because of the ease of calculating forward the cost of the sales force.

On the other hand, the salary-only method is considered to suffer from the disadvantage that it does not give sales personnel the incentive to achieve a high and increasing level of sales. It has been said that this method of payment allows the sales person to get into a rut and lose enthusiasm, so that sales volume does not grow at the optimum rate. Also, some companies when using this method consider that they tend to lose the more ambitious sales persons who want to exploit their selling skill by linking their efforts to a payments by results system. Often the small or medium-sized company find the salary-only system impossible to operate in their early stages or when they are launching a new product because it becomes a fixed overhead without any guarantee of sales volume necessary for them to stay in business. Fixed salary scales are often linked with the cost of living generally so that the sales person's standard of living is maintained. Some companies introduce a slight incentive element by reviewing salaries annually so that on the basis of merit rating (i.e. what the sales person is worth to the company), or increased years of service, and/or selling record in the past year, the sales person will qualify for a higher salary.

Commission

A remuneration plan based upon payment by results, usually on a basis of a percentage of sales volume, can be of two main types: one where commission is paid in addition to a salary, and the other where commission only is paid. For any commission scheme to motivate, it must be finely balanced so as to be fair and reasonable to both the sales personnel and the company. Also, it must reflect individual efforts and not be dependent upon external unconnected factors (e.g. high promotional expenditure or supply shortages), and it must be easy for the sales person to calculate and understand.

In considering the first group, salary plus commission, the biggest problem is getting the correct balance between them both in the existing circumstances. If the salary element represents a large proportion of the remuneration and commission only a small part, then the latter will tend to lose its 'pull' as an incentive. On the other hand, if the salary element is too small and the commission element large, then the personal-security-minded sales person will tend to move away from the company, particularly when trade is slack. The middle way is best where the salary element is large enough to satisfy the need for basic security and yet insufficient in itself to support a high standard of living so that the sales person is motivated into action so as to earn more through commission. The different types of commission schemes are numerous; they range from commission at a set percentage rate upon all business from the sales person's territory, commission at a fixed rate upon all orders actually obtained by him/her, commission on all orders obtained from customers introduced by the particular sales person, to combinations of these methods where varying rates of commission are paid for business coming from these three sources. In some cases, it is paid on rising sale commission rates, so that as the sales volume being considered increases, the rate of commission increases, but in others the high rates paid upon the initial levels of sales are decreased at later levels. Thus in the latter case, the incentive is still there at the higher sales volume levels, but the sales person has to sell proportionately more to achieve an even higher reward. In some cases, companies pay different rates of commission upon different products and/or services so as to increase the turnover of slow-moving ones or to increase the turnover of product lines carrying high-profit margins. Thus the sales manager can influence the emphasis that the sales person is expected to make when selling the company's complete range of products/services, and the percentage commission carried by each item is obviously determined by the overall profitability of the optimum marketing mix in relation to market strategy.

In a number of cases, before a sales person can earn commission, he/she has to reach a certain quota or sales target. This is often calculated upon the basis of the fixed costs incurred by the sales person whether he/she obtained any business or not.

After the initial sales target figure has been achieved, commission is then paid either on a fixed percentage basis or upon a sliding, increasing or decreasing percentage scale. Alternatively, a small rate of commission is paid upon sales up to the quota figure and then the sales person again passes on to either the fixed or the sliding scale. There are many more sophisticated methods of paying commission. The majority are dependent upon awarding performance points for the achievement of sales (volume or value) of different types of products, others are dependent upon the award of performance points for other activities such as the number of new accounts opened, the number of displays obtained, the improvement of the ratio of successful calls to actual calls made etc. A set figure per performance point is paid; its value will depend upon the emphasis the sales manager places upon the various activities. Some companies operate multi-tier commission schemes based upon the performance point method so as to create an incentive in all the aspects of the sales person's task.

Salary plus commission is often considered to be the best method of remuneration to get the best work from sales personnel, as it combines the incentive factor with a reasonable basic salary. To get an above-average standard of living, sales personnel subject to such a scheme must sell a considerable volume of products. However, where the commission payment is based upon only those orders directly obtained by the sales person and not on others received from the territory, a certain amount of dissatisfaction arises. This is because the sales person often has to spend valuable commission-earning selling time servicing non-commission accounts, and therefore such accounts will tend to be ignored or treated indifferently. The same will apply to the situation where the company pays commission only upon the business obtained from accounts opened by the sales person; other accounts will receive little attention as they have no incentive interest, and the sales person will tend to spend a disproportionate amount of time searching for new accounts. It will be obvious that this method of paying commission is suited to new or under-worked territories.

A number of companies use the commission-only method of remuneration. This is either based upon a set or sliding scale percentage of total sales, or by fixed commission amounts upon different products within the company's product range, or by a set sum per performance point awarded for the various sales activities that can be measured.

Some ambitious sales people prefer to work on a commission-only basis so as to obtain high rewards and to exploit their selling skills to the full. This is particularly so where the product is high priced and where there is competition from cheaper, lower quality products.

Certain companies prefer the commission-only method of remuneration as it allows the forward budgeting of sales costs on a basis that is directly linked with the volume sold and therefore allows for the progressive building up of the business. Certainly it eliminates the fixed sales overhead of salary that may or may not be in direct proportion to sales and, because it reduces such financial risks, the commission-only method is often a popular method of payment by small and medium-sized companies.

Also, companies operating in the speciality goods field often favour this method of remuneration because it injects into the sales force that extra bit of keenness and enthusiasm so essential in speciality selling. The dual nature of the speciality sales person's job is such that if the sales person 'sells the need' and then does not sell the product, the potential customer is then wide open to persuasion the next time a competitor's sales person calls. The main disadvantage of the commission-only method of remuneration is that it tends not to foster strong ties between the sales person and the company; often loyalty being measured only by the level of commission paid, so that the attraction of high commission rates elsewhere will attract the sales person without the restraint of loyalty. Further, it is difficult to control the methods of working of sales staff and to get such sales personnel to take part in activities that are only indirectly linked with selling (merchandising, giving technical advice, exhibitions and demonstrations etc.) as they feel they are wasting valuable selling time and therefore losing commission.

When an element of commission is included in the remuneration plan, a feeling of discontent is often felt by some members of the sales force when it is paid only upon the volume of sales obtained. This is particularly so where territories differ widely in geographic and/or consumer industry population size and in territory customer potential, as the degree of skill and effort needed to obtain the same sales volume in different areas may not be comparable. Consider, for example, the situation in two adjacent territories; one where sales person X has worked systematically for a number of years and built up a good business connection, and the other that has either not been previously covered by the company's sales force or has been inadequately worked and is now covered by sales person Y. It is highly likely in such a situation that sales person X is obtaining quite a large sales volume with only half the effort put in by sales person Y. If the sales force is paid by commission related to sales volume only, and it is linked with a basic quota or target figure that must be reached before commission is paid, how strong will the incentive be to sales person Y who may have great difficulty initially in introducing the product and/or service into a new territory? Further, how strong will be the incentive to sales person X to increase his/her sales still further? If both sales persons are paid on the same commission basis for sales volume obtained, consider the difference in rewards in the following situation:

	Sales person X	Sales person Y
Calls per week	80	80
Calls made upon established customers	64	12
Calls made upon potential customers	16	68

As territories are developed, it often becomes necessary in the company's interest to divide them into smaller units so they may be worked more intensively. Such action often causes discontent in the sales force when sales people are rewarded only by a commission on a sales volume basis. Such division of territory often leads to real difficulties for the sales persons concerned, and often transition payment schemes (which in themselves often give rise to further anomalies) are introduced to offset the initial loss of earnings.

These problems in the payment of commission can be avoided by designing a remuneration plan that is based upon a territory potential figure and structured around a two-tier system of commission payment; one tier for the reward for sales volume and the other as a reward for sales effort. It is necessary to establish a sales potential figure for the territory (see also next chapter on control) and a lower figure that would determine the point at which commission for sales volume would begin to be paid, i.e. a basic sales quota. It is essential that agreement with the sales person can be reached on the size of the sales potential figure and upon the need for adjustment if potential customers move into or out of his/her territory. Further, many commission schemes suffer from widely fluctuating seasonal peaks and troughs in sales. Therefore, to remove these difficulties and to provide a basis for comparison, it is useful to use a moving annual total to calculate commission. Such a figure is arrived at by totalling the sales for the last 12 months at the end of each month. It is immaterial whether this is calculated January to December or July to June because where the last 12 months' sales totals are included, all seasonal fluctuations are allowed for. Supposing a sales person's total for 12 months ending in October was £70,000, and in November he/she sold goods to the value of £8000, this would be added to the previous figure (£70,000 + £8000 = £78,000) and then the previous November's sales figure (say £4000) would be taken away to keep it a 12 months' moving annual total. Therefore his/her current moving annual total would be £74,000. To see how such a two-tier commission scheme would work, consider the sales persons mentioned earlier – sales person X working an established territory and sales person Y who has just taken over a previously inadequately worked territory. They are paid on a salary plus commission basis and, for comparison purposes, it is assumed that their territories have the same potential, i.e. a moving annual total of £200,000. Further, sales person X has a current moving annual total of £146,000, sales person Y one of £74,000 and the basic sales quota to be achieved before sales volume commission is paid is £100,000.

The calculation of the sales volume commission (part A) would be:

	Sales person X	Sales person Y
Current moving annual total	£146,000	£74,000
Volume performance as a percentage of sales potential figure	73%	37%
Basic sales quota as a percentage of sales potential figure	50%	50%
Basic sales quota to be achieved	£100,000	£100,000
Sales volume commission @ £3 per 1% volume over basic quota	£69	Nil
	(i.e. 73% − 50% = 23% × £3)	

To calculate the second tier of this commission scheme (part B) which is payable for effort, it is necessary to calculate the percentage increase over the sales person's previous month's moving annual total; in this example, the moving annual total for the previous month of October:

	Sales person X	Sales person Y
Current moving annual total	£146,000	£74,000
Last month's moving annual total	£144,000	£70,000
Actual improvement	£2,000	£4,000
Percentage increase	1.3%	5.7%
Effort/increase commission at £8 per 1% increase	£10.40	£45.60

Therefore sales person X would receive a total of £79.40 (£69 + £10.40) and sales person Y a total of £45.60 for the month of October.

Obviously it is easier for X to earn more on the sales volume commission as he has an established business connection, but it will be difficult for him to earn large sums by means of the second-tier commission because of the difficulty in getting continued large percentage increases in sales. On the other hand Y, whose territory does not warrant the payment of a sales volume commission, can earn quite large commission by his increased efforts each month; it is possible for him to earn a higher total commission than his colleague. It will be appreciated, however, as Y's sales volume grows it will become increasingly difficult for him to achieve a large percentage increase, and it is at this point that the sales volume commission becomes operative.

Over a period of time, Y's remuneration for effort and volume could develop as in Fig. 7.3(a). Figure 7.3(b) highlights how it becomes more difficult to earn part B commission through additional effort. As the identified total potential for sales from the sales territory is approached, part A volume commission plays a larger part of the total commission paid.

Figure 7.4(b) shows a sales person building sales volume and commission over a period of time (along the horizontal axis). It is a territory that already has a small number of existing customers, reflected by the fact that the sales curve starts at a moving annual total of £70,000. In the early stages, reward comes from part B, effort commission, which being a percentage increase factor and not an absolute factor is shown falling away as it becomes more difficult for the sales person to achieve high rates of increase. The sales volume commission is calculated on the percentage increase over the basic quota achieved and begins immediately the latter has been passed. The main advantages of such a scheme is that both sales volume and effort are rewarded. Secondly, that it is highly flexible because the potential sales target, the basic sales quota figure, and the payments per performance point in both tiers can be adapted to suit the requirements of any company and

Sales period	Current moving annual total	Increase in moving annual total over last period	Part A volume commission as a percentage over basic quota	Part A commission £3 per 1% volume over basic quota	Part B percentage increase	Part B commission @ £8 per 1% increase	Total commission (part A + part B)
	£70,000	—	—	—	—	—	—
1	£74,000	£4,000	—	—	5.7%	£45.60	£45.60
2	£78,000	£4,000	—	—	5.4%	£43.20	£43.20
3	£84,000	£6,000	—	—	7.6%	£60.80	£60.80
4	£92,000	£8,000	—	—	9.5%	£76.00	£76.00
5	£100,000	£8,000	—	—	8.6%	£68.80	£68.80
6	£106,000	£6,000	6%	£18	6.0%	£48.00	£66.80
7	£112,000	£6,000	12%	£36	5.6%	£44.80	£80.80
8	£116,000	£4,000	16%	£48	3.5%	£28.00	£76.00
9	£120,000	£4,000	20%	£60	3.4%	£27.20	£87.20
10	£122,000	£2,000	22%	£66	1.6%	£12.80	£78.80

Fig. 7.3(a) An example of a two-tier commission scheme

later adjusted if necessary without great difficulty. It is, of course, possible to introduce other tiers to cover other aspects of the selling task which a company feels should be rewarded, and multi-stage schemes with five and six stages are not uncommon.

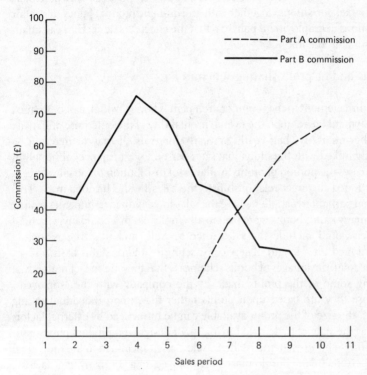

Fig. 7.3(b) A comparison of part A and part B commission relating to Fig. 7.4(a)

Criticism is often made of commission schemes claiming that they exploit the sales person, forcing him/her to take financial risks that are really the responsibility of the company. It is occasionally claimed that high-price, high-commission products sell at first because of initial enthusiasm on the part of the sales person and while he/she is exploiting the existing connection and/or 'friends'. But later, as he/she is unable to obtain an adequate income, the sales person is forced to find another job, leaving all the benefits of long-term customer goodwill accruing to the employer, who then repeats the process by employing another sales person.

There is no doubt that some commission schemes (and conditions of service) are weighted against the sales person, but they are not in a company's long-term interest as it becomes known as a bad employer and good sales persons will avoid joining it. Sales personnel that join the company knowing that their 'life' with it may be limited may seek to make it as merry a life as possible, with the attitude to sell at all costs, often resorting to high-pressure methods; which all adds up to a poor company image in the minds of customers and/or potential customers. Commission schemes are successful only if a true appreciation is made of selling costs, sales potentials and market conditions, together with an equitable product policy and a fair conditions of employment policy so that the effective sales person can attain a reasonable income.

Bonus and/or profit-sharing schemes

The third element in the remuneration plan is bonus, which can be defined as a payment based upon the overall profitability of the enterprise and made at either quarterly, half-yearly or yearly intervals. It may or may not be directly linked with the individual sales person's performance, although in some cases the portion of profits available for distribution to the sales force is apportioned in direct relationship to the sales he/she has obtained. This method particularly applies where the sales force is divided into sales teams.

In many cases, bonuses are paid to all employees in a company which, of course, would include the sales force as well, and this type is mainly apportioned on a length-of service or seniority and/or status basis.

The main advantages of bonus schemes is that they are in fact methods of sharing some of the profits made by the company with the employees. Because they are based upon profits rather than upon individual selling efforts, the size of the profits available can be influenced by external factors such as the state of trade, bad buying, poor design and product policy and, therefore, a bonus scheme is often useless as an incentive to the individual sales person. In an effort to make all employees of a company (e.g. factory, warehouse and office personnel – in addition to sales staff) sales conscious, some companies use the overall bonus method hoping to make employees realise that overall teamwork is necessary and that each department is inter-related. Unfortunately, from the sales motivation point of view, bonuses are often paid annually after the end of the company's financial year and therefore may not match the peaks or troughs of sales so that they are in fact too remote from the time of particular selling interviews to act as a day-to-day incentive.

In many cases in a period of fairly stable trading conditions, bonuses are paid regularly, are accepted and taken for granted as a part of basic pay and later, when trade and profits fall (and the bonus likewise), this is considered to be a pay decrease and in fact becomes a demotivator. Other criticisms of bonus schemes claim that as incentives they are paid at the wrong time. This is because they are paid from profits, so that when trade is booming bonuses are high, but when trade is bad and extra sales are required, profits are either low or non-existent, and the company is unable to pay a bonus just when an extra incentive is required. Some companies therefore pay commission and bonus to get around this difficulty. However, there are companies who favour bonus schemes in preference to commission arrangements, especially where the sales person is engaged in activities that are not directly related to individual orders, i.e. giving technical advice, merchandising, exhibition work etc. In industries where it takes a long time to build up customer goodwill, bonus schemes are favoured for sales persons opening new territories or taking over badly worked sales areas and are thought of, in these circumstances, as long-term investment.

Occasionally, bonus and/or profit-sharing schemes are paid out in the form of an issue of shares of the company, so as to foster the sense of part-ownership of the business, a common sense of purpose and to appeal to the self-interest instinct in the company's employees. The advantages and disadvantages of such schemes are in general little different to the ordinary bonus schemes; it is merely the method of payment that is different.

Payment during training

The training of sales personnel was dealt with in an early chapter but, of course, the problem does arise of how to pay sales people during an initial/basic training period. Obviously if the sales person is in basic training, he cannot be earning commission, and in many cases would not be earning a straight salary. A number of companies who pay their sales people on a salary plus commission basis normally pay only salary during the training period. This method would be impracticable where the salary element was so low as not to be a living wage. Remuneration of sales persons is particularly difficult where the period of technical training is long and, in such cases, some companies pay an 'average' commission, in others the payment of a fixed basic 'living' wage is found to be the answer. In other cases, the level of remuneration during training is determined by assessing the value of the trainee to the organisation, not in his/her present untrained state but his/her eventual potential worth to the company. Because of this factor, the level of pay necessary to obtain the right person for training may be influenced by their past experience, present salary, background, and any other factors for which the trainee may need to be compensated during the training period.

Variations in payment

The exact emphasis upon each of the three main elements of remuneration described, salary, commission and bonus, will be determined by what is best for the company in its own particular circumstance. But the attraction and retention of the best sales personnel will depend upon how up-to-date the company's remuneration plan is. Obviously it will be easier to design a payments system where the company is marketing a simple product and/or service range that is sold through one type of outlet, rather than where it is marketing a highly complex range with many prices, qualities, levels of profit margins and through many different types of outlets.

Further, in market situations where a high level of creative selling is necessary, as with speciality selling, rewards will obviously need to be higher upon each sale to compensate for the greater amount of prospecting for new customers needed, the fluctuating sales volume, and the lack of repeat business in the short period. Alternatively, selling staple goods or fast-moving consumer goods, the reward on each sale may be relatively low but this is compensated by the fact that if the sales person is working correctly he will obtain repeat business, this building up a less precarious but steadily growing income. There will tend to be higher commission rates on high-priced and/or high-quality product/service combinations.

The methods of payment of the sales force should be reviewed periodically, partly to ensure that such methods are as effective as possible, but also to ensure that the company is getting 'value for money'. The remuneration plan is a powerful incentive tool for the management of the sales force if used correctly, but its overall profitability to the company must be examined before it is put into operation to determine its effectiveness under all possible situations, and alternative plans made for use should the ever-changing market situation demand it.

Payment with goods and/or services

Some companies argue that the incentive power of the extra money earned through commission is short-lived as it is easily disposed of by spending. Also, because sales people get used to earning commission in good trading periods, the lack of it in bad times can have a disproportionate adverse effect, i.e. act as a demotivator. Such companies often turn to using commission schemes that produce performance and/or percentage increase points and these can be accumulated to 'purchase' a variety of goods and/or services. Such goods are a constant reminder to the sales person of the company, the benefits and his own efforts long after their money equivalent would be.

Schemes can be based on a range of items/services arranged by the company, e.g. watches, cars, glassware, cutlery, food and wine vouchers, calculators, home computers, gift tokens, Christmas hampers, family holidays, incentive travel etc.

Alternatively, specialist incentive companies are employed who produce a standard catalogue of a wide range of products (personal and household) rather like a mail-order catalogue but with relative performance points set against each item rather than prices. From such a catalogue, not only the sales person is appealed to but also his/her family.

Sales contests and competitions

These can be *ad hoc* (e.g. to generate sales to meet a particular market situation) or recurring (e.g. run annually at the time of an expected seasonal fall in sales) or as a changing series (e.g. a new type of competition every 3 to 4 months each with a different objective); the latter is often used in speciality selling where the variety is said to 'bring continued excitement to selling'.

Sales contests and competitions can be operated by the company or a specialist sales incentive company can be used to devise special schemes or operate their particular range of contests based on reward through a catalogue of products similar to a mail-order catalogue. As mentioned in the previous section, these indicate performance points against particular products and their major incentive appeal is that these points can be accumulated to 'purchase' really large prizes and that all sales persons are motivated as they can all obtain some prize, however small. Contests and competitions must give equal opportunities to all the sales team to win and must be fair if they are to act as motivators and not have the opposite effect.

Sales contests and competitions increase sales, if only temporarily, because they appeal to the competitive element in sales people. The prize will vary accordingly to the duration of the contest; if the period is too long, it may become a demotivator to the majority once a winner becomes obvious. The prize will also depend upon the amount of money available for the purpose which is, in turn, linked to the extra amount of sales the contest is expected to generate, the value of the company's individual products and the profit margins on them.

Such contests should be given a name to identify them (e.g. the Easter Competition, the November Handicap) and adopt a main theme, i.e. sell more of the new promotional line, to open more new accounts, lift sagging sales volume curves, obtain more exclusive dealership contracts etc. There should be a written set of rules, and judgement decisions should be made by a small group of executives to avoid any suggestion of bias.

Membership of social clubs (e.g. golf clubs, bridge clubs)

Often this is a combination of reward and ensuring that sales persons are in the right place, socially, to meet, entertain and mix with clients and potential clients. On the reward side, it is based on the sales person and his/her family finding access to club facilities and often to a higher social stratum, a physical and psychological benefit. On giving the sales person access to the right business location, it is based on three assumptions: that an effective proportion of customers or potential customers are interested in the basic objectives/activities of the club (tennis, golf, social, political etc.); that the sales person is physically (e.g. tennis) and mentally (e.g. bridge) able to adequately perform; and that client and sales person are prepared to use part of their private time to mix business with pleasure.

It is claimed in some markets that most of the business is 'done on the golf course', in others it is seen as a way of getting access to very busy people (e.g. pharmaceutical representatives getting access to busy doctors). In other markets, it is claimed that this method is grossly over-rated as a 'business-getter', especially if it requires increased expense accounts to enable sales people to adequately take part in club activities (or to receive lessons in the sport). As a motivating method, it is a condition of employment that people get used to a normal way of doing business; the social side, in some cases, takes over, and other 'non-club' clients or new market segments may not receive the appropriate amount of the sales person's time.

Peripheral token rewards

This involves a number of 'token' rewards that are either in money or can be measured in money, e.g. special contributory or non-contributory pension schemes, private health care and hospital plans, individual or group life insurance policies, children's school fees (especially where a sales person has had to move home), special interest loans or mortgage-subsidised schemes etc. All these may motivate sales people to join a company or accept them as part of basic 'pay', but tend not to influence the effort expended on specific sales missions or contracts, as do payments by results methods.

Visual and auditory rewards

Sales bulletin

The bulletin is an ideal method of maintaining enthusiasm and motivating a widely dispersed sales force on to greater performance, providing it emphasises the positive approach, i.e. it shows how things should be done rather than simply why they should be done. The sales bulletin should cater for an exchange of ideas and, because of this, members of the field sales force should be encouraged to provide articles and comments for publication, as well as those written by the management team. Its educational role in imparting knowledge regarding new products, new techniques and new market knowledge, as well as presenting new angles regarding existing material, should not be under-estimated, although it should not take the place of proper training courses but rather to supplement them.

To ensure that the bulletin is read, facts and opinions need to be presented in a highly interesting way, if possible from the angle of how it will benefit the sales force. To achieve this, the layout must be good, and the standard and presentation of the whole bulletin must be high. A careful balance must be made between telling the sales force how to do things and inspiring them to think for themselves. The sales bulletin should not be confused with the company newspaper or 'house organ' magazine; they both have different functions. The sales bulletin is usually most successful on a weekly/monthly frequency, and should be used to keep contact and communication with the sales force, teaching, exchanging ideas between sales personnel with similar problems, inspiring and motivating them. The company 'house organ' magazine is more successful on a monthly or quarterly frequency and, as such, is too remote from the day-to-day problems and motivation of the sales team. In any case, such a 'house organ' is more often required for wider circulation either in the public or trade relations field, or to build up the company image, or to foster a feeling of 'togetherness' between all employees in large organisations.

Personal letter

The personal letter as a means of motivating sales personnel has its limitations, the main one being the size of the sales force. The sales manager with a sales force of up to twenty will find this method extremely useful. On the other hand, a company with 200 sales persons would have great difficulty in personally motivating them through the medium of the personal letter and, although this function may be delegated to regional, area or branch level, some of the impact of being written to by the company's 'senior sales person' will have been lost.

Properly worded personal (especially congratulatory) letters do motivate; the sales person receiving one is impressed by the personal touch, the fact that the sales manager is interested enough in him/her as an individual to write a personal letter. The personal approach must adopt the form of a consultant or friend trying to help the sales person, tactfully pointing out omissions, or making a constructive suggestion, rather than the popular image of the sales manager wielding the whip and trying to catch out the sales person on the slightest pretext. In the case of the very large sales force, the 'personal' letter becomes a highly impersonal, duplicated document that not only fails to motivate but is sometimes not even read. However, it is possible to use the personal letter quite successfully even in large organisations by using the principle of management by exception. For example, the sales manager of a field force of 200 sales people could write personally to a particular one in exceptional circumstances; i.e. to the top sales person in each area every sales period, or to a sales person who has just obtained a large contract for the company, or (as some companies do) a personal letter to the sales person on his/her birthday thanking him/her for their efforts in the past year and wishing him/her success in the coming year.

Monthly positions lists

Sometimes referred to as sales force league tables, these show every member of the sales force on a list in the context of sales achieved as a percentage of the sales target set, which allows for a comparative list to be prepared irrespective of territory potential.

This list may be published in sales bulletins or sent with other correspondence and, while it is gratifying for the leaders, it is very demotivating for the last few sales people on the list; and someone is bound to be last.

Best sales person of the year award/cup

Again this is a coveted award and only one person can win. Should one person take the lead early on in the time period, it may become a demotivator for others.

Company (prestige) cars

In most cases a car is essential for members of the field sales force whether it is owned or hired by the company or owned by the sales person with mileage allowance and/or expenses paid by the company. In some cases, a contributory leased car is involved. It becomes a motivational device when a so-called 'prestige' car is involved, i.e. the size or make is more 'up-market' than others in the sales force. The difficulty is when a sales person fails to perform adequately and the car should be 'down-graded' again. With the sales person's own car, disproportionately high expenses may be refunded for its use. In some companies, the incentive may come through allowing the sales person's wife or husband to drive the car or permission is given for it to be driven for private use, especially on holiday and/or abroad.

Expense account to cover travelling and other expenses

Acceptable levels of expenses must be made clear to the sales force; if these are particularly generous, then they might well motivate. On the other hand there is then a temptation to 'make pocket money on expenses' (i.e. to not take meals or stay at low-grade hotels) or to adopt an extravagant life-style which is difficult to maintain. Further, there is the use of this kind of expenses to entertain customers and potential customers which may be necessary in some cases but can become widely mis-used by a sales person and/or customer. In some companies, the use of 'above-average' hotel accommodation and also the total or part payment of telephone bills may be used as a reward, but its mis-use in some cases and the disadvantages of that also applied to generous expenses make these two motivational methods unattractive for some companies.

Additional methods

The additional methods of motivation that result in psychological rewards/incentives and shown in Fig. 7.3 under the heading of natural rewards can be very powerful and yet may not incur much direct cost.

In the social reward group, the *personal interview* is a strong motivational method if it is approached from the angle of the sales manager being a consultant, a friend, someone who is helping the sales person to achieve greater performance. With a large sales force, the personal interview may have to be delegated and carried out at lower management (field) level. However, this method can still be used by the senior sales executive of a large sales force on the basis of management by exception. For example, where a sales person has achieved a high level of success; or where a sales person, who until recently has been a good volume sales producer, seems to have hit rock bottom, i.e. in exceptional circumstances. In both cases, there is need for personal motivation. In the first case, the success of the sales person is recognised and obviously appreciated by someone of importance in the company and it is likely that the sales person will be motivated to even greater levels of performance. In the latter case, the reasons for the sales person's current poor performance can be determined. If possible, the problem is resolved on the spot or some agreed action identified with the ultimate goal of the sales person being motivated to return to his/her former position of a high-volume sales producer.

In the same category is the sales person's annual *appraisal interview*. The object of this is to review the individual's past year's activities and performance against the aims and objectives set at the previous annual appraisal interview and to identify an agreed direction, aims and objectives for the sales person for the coming 12 months. It is helpful if these are written down and a copy retained by both the sales manager and the sales person.

Being consulted by management and being socially accepted by key members in the sales team and by management are all motivators in this social reward area. For example, *public praise* and/or *recognition* at sales meetings and conferences. In some companies there are 'super sales person committees' whose members receive special treatment at conferences and sales meetings and who are consulted by management regarding matters of sales policy and everyday sales problems. Membership of such committees is attained, for example, by reaching certain pre-determined sales level or other sales activity (e.g. opening X number of new accounts), or a combination of a number of these.

Such committees are similar to '*quota clubs*' operated in some companies where members of the sales team automatically become members when they have passed their basic sales quota (see pages 212–14). In some companies, a version of this is operated known as a '150 club' where an elite group of sales persons is formed by those achieving 150 per cent of their half-yearly sales target in the first 6 months of a year. Again, quota club members usually receive special and preferential treatment at conferences and sales meetings. They often have a special club tie or distinguishing button to wear and run their own special social events etc. Obviously, super sales person committees and quota clubs are used as motivators with medium/large sales forces.

The final group listed in Fig. 7.3 under the heading of natural rewards are the 'Premack' type; this term was referred to on page 204. This is concerned with activities which, although not direct motivators, nevertheless are important as they tend to reinforce other more direct motivators.

The third of the five categories of motivational methods identified on page 203 is that of the elimination of disincentives. Unfair treatment and practices sometimes take place unintentionally but more often through deliberate bias on the part of a manager. It can occur from a single reaction to some infringement of the company rules or a perceived personal affront or emerges over a period of time through a series of situations. Favouritism is a basic human failing: different personality types result in some people being able to 'get on' better with one person than another. There is a danger in the case of the sales manager that the apparent ease of some relationships can lead to certain members of the sales team being favoured in some way (not necessarily related to sales performance) and others not. To the latter group, this may be a large psychological demotivator, however trivial the favouritism. An even greater demotivator is blatant or arbitrary injustice; this may not only act as a demotivator but may cause certain types of person to undermine or take adverse action against the sales manager to prove him/her wrong.

There are many other examples of disincentives, and sales managers need to take conscious action to eliminate them. It needs a special type of motivation and firmness of action to eliminate them from subordinates (i.e. regional and area managers, sales supervisors and sales trainers) and the use of behaviour checklists and advice from others for the sales manager to eliminate them from his/her behaviour and attitudes.

The fourth of the five categories of motivational methods identified on page 203 is that of indirect reinforcement activities or methods whose prime objective is something other than motivation but carries with its operation the chance to motivate.

Sales conferences fit into this category; their basic role is either to consult the sales force (e.g. on sales or marketing problems) or brief it on some particular event that is about to happen (e.g. the launch of a new product range, advertising/promotional support in the coming year, a change in company policy that will affect the sales force) or simply may be a regular event that reviews past performance of the sales force and indicates the direction for the future. Some conferences divide into smaller working party or discussion groups for part of the time, dealing with the same or different topics; a synopsis is then fed back into the main conference in a plenary session.

There is obviously the opportunity for an element of training to be subtly incorporated into sales conferences (as mentioned earlier in Chapter 4) but also it is an opportunity to motivate. The presence of senior directors of a company, the giving of a keynote speech by one of them, even their socialising with the sales team, all adds to the perceived importance of the occasion. All working sessions should have a motivational theme, i.e. how they will help the individual and the sales team. The sales conference is an opportunity to 'sell' the company, its products and/or services to the sales team and motivate it to higher performance.

It was stated earlier (Chapter 5) that all regular and *ad hoc* meetings of regional, area, district or branch personnel should be seen as an opportunity to motivate the sales team. The life of the individual member of a field sales team is relatively 'isolated' in the sense that although working with people (customers), he/she is representing the company alone, there is no immediate 'back-up' support available, there is no immediate communication with other colleagues in the same situation and facing the same problems. The sales meeting, therefore, is an important motivational tool because it brings individuals working alone into a team situation, where information can be given to, and received from, management and two-way communication can take place in discussing and, hopefully, solving mutually experienced selling and allied problems.

Whether in a training 'centre' environment or 'on-the-job' training, there is an opportunity to motivate and lend support to any sales person involved in training activity; which means everyone, as training for the sales person must be continuous if it is to be effective. The very nature of training (i.e. making the sales person more knowledgeable, more skilful in the use of techniques and more confident as a person) should be motivating. But it is how the training is carried out, as much as its content, that makes the sales person want to achieve higher levels of performance.

There is an obvious link between 'on-the-job' training and 'on-the-job' supervision and it is very difficult to identify a demarcation line. A uniting factor is motivation. Although an aspect of 'on-the-job' supervision, making 'double' sales calls with sales persons, is engendering customer goodwill and maintaining customer contact, it is mainly concerned with monitoring the sales person's methods, attitudes and behaviour with the objectives of identifying problems and needs, so that he/she can be helped. It therefore should be a supportive and a motivating activity.

The fifth category of motivational methods are those that relate to disciplinary methods.

Any organisation needs a set of rules, guidelines, 'standing orders' that are acknowledged either formally (e.g in the written contract and conditions of employment, the job description, standing orders with regard to the use of company property) or informally (e.g. the normally acceptable social levels of truthfulness, regard for others in the sales team, punctuality, avoidance of insubordination etc.). Infringement of any of these 'rules' requires a response from sales management otherwise it may be repeated and become a new standard of behaviour not only for the initial 'wrongdoer' but also for certain other members of the sales team who may not be slow to follow the example.

It is important that the formal and informal 'rules' are clear to the sales team, that the sales manager has a monitoring system that can identify when they are broken, that he/she assigns the blame to the right person and 'punishes the offender'.

The reaction by the sales manager may take many forms depending on the seriousness of the infringement, e.g. a private reprimand, a public admonition, notification of awareness of wrong with or without demanding a written explanation, warning with or without the promise of more serious repercussions if the infringement is repeated, loss of privileges, an appearance before a company disciplinary board, dismissal etc. The problem is finding the 'appropriate' punishment for the infringement. The general rule is that the response should be as soon as possible after the infringement, but not before any temporary emotional bias that may cloud the sales manager's objectivity has subsided. Further, it is important that all infringements, the responses and the result are recorded and kept on file. This can be used for control purposes (i.e. to monitor the improvement with an individual) or for assembling a case for ultimate dismissal. The latter is also important in case a dismissed sales person makes a complaint to an external industrial tribunal for wrongful dismissal. The problem with all these disciplinary activities is that if not handled properly by the sales manager they can become demotivators.

Summary

A lot of research has been carried out into motivational approaches, styles and postures by managers, i.e. into the elements of the process of motivation and into what methods/activities actually motivate any way. The diversity of motivational approaches appears to indicate that there is no one style or posture that will cover every situation or person or moment in time. The sales manager needs to examine all the approaches researched and practised by others to be able to put together an approach appropriate to his/her situation.

As with any other managerial activity, a plan is necessary in this key area of motivation together with recognition of the essential characteristics of the ideal motivator.

Understanding the basic process of motivation and the key elements of it will not only help the sales manager to build effective motivation but will also help to identify weak spots in motivational activities if circumstances change and/or things go wrong. For example, the fact that ability, knowledge, attitude and expectation of the sales person combine to determine effort. Further, the fact that the role behaviour of the individual will not only be affected by his/her perception of the role of a sales person but also by personality and self-perception.

Motivation methods need to be used that not only provide some physical reward, although the power of financial incentives should not be under-rated, but provide psychological rewards that arise from the nature of the work itself. Conversely, the elimination of disincentives/demotivators and the use of indirect methods that help to reinforce both the intrinsic and psychological rewards are crucial to effective motivation. All organisations need to have ground rules, formal and/or informal, which need to be enforced by disciplinary methods if infringed. Applied with skill, these can be powerful motivators; applied incorrectly or insensitively, they can become demotivators.

Questions

1. A number of researchers have suggested a variety of motivational approaches. Identify three that you consider to be the most important, indicating their main proposals and say why you consider them to be the most important.

2. One such approach has been described as the 'carrot and stick' approach. Explain what is meant and give examples of how the concept can be applied to sales management.

3. What are the main stages of the process of motivation and how can each one be affected by the sales manager?

4. Identify the five broad categories of motivational methods that are available to the sales manager, explain in what ways they are inter-related and comment on which you consider to be the most powerful motivational category.

5. Money is acknowledged to be a key motivator if appropriately used; comment on the advantages and disadvantages of salary, commission, bonus, profit-sharing and indicate situations where they may or may not be appropriate.

6. Identify what you consider to be the essential key features of a motivational plan for a sales manager with an internal telephone selling operation as well as a field sales force.

CHAPTER 8

Supervision and control of the sales team

Objectives

This chapter examines the need for supervision and control of sales personnel if the objectives set in the sales management plan (Chapter 2) are to be achieved. Motivation (Chapter 7) should produce the will to act, but in this chapter methods of supervision (direct contact) are considered that ensure the sales operations are proceeding in the manner expected and according to plan. Further, control is examined in the context that it develops systems to obtain the optimum feedback of information, effective ways of measuring performance, compares actual performance with standards, norms and predictions, and interprets the trends and results in the context of the individual sales person and the market situation. Finally, aspects of effective control are considered that will ensure that remedial action is taken to adjust sales activity (if necessary) and later an evaluation of the effectiveness of the sales plan. This chapter is the culmination of the sales planning activity and its results.

Supervision

Good sales team supervision and control is that which interferes least with the sales person's freedom of initiative; it should lead to greater performance and achievement with the minimum amount of 'bossing'. It suggests rather than dictates and harnesses the pride and ambition of the sales team in such a way as to stimulate an all-out effort which in turn develops a particular momentum, each success building on the previous one. It appreciates the definite objectives for sales personnel to work towards as considered in the sales plan, and helps the team generally, and individuals in particular, achieve it. The essence of good supervision can be stated in seven points:

(a) *Know* – the individual sales person and the real situation in which he/she operates.

(b) *Plan* – identify what you expect him/her to do.

(c) *Inform* – clearly define to the sales person what you want done and check that he/she understands.

(d) *Motivate* action.

(e) *Monitor* – by supervision, know that he/she has done it.

(f) *Acknowledge* – let the individual know that you are aware that he/she has done it.

(g) *Show appreciation* – privately or publicly let the sales person know that you appreciate what he/she has done and if possible reward in some way.

Supervision does not mean domination but 'people' management, the ability to lead and not drive, to inspire and not to threaten. It is more effective when sales personnel know they are being monitored. Where possible, 'sandwich' one item of criticism between two items of praise.

'On-the-job' supervision has already been examined in the context of training (Chapter 5) and motivation (Chapter 7) and in this chapter it is considered from the angle of the contribution it makes to control. Supervision can be seen as personal or 'direct contact control' which complements the indirect or remote control process in which the sales manager takes action based on information provided by others, e.g. in reports or by the analysis of data.

Supervision is necessary for all types of sales personnel, e.g. sales office, internal sales staff, telephone sales persons, field sales personnel, sales trainers and regional/area managers and sales supervisors. The supervision of field sales personnel by working with, and observing them, can be divided into:

(a) Supervision of the new/developing sales person, i.e. of ensuring the continuation and application of initial/basic training in real-life sales situations, building up confidence, showing that the selling course techniques really do work. This is additional to those contained in (b) and (c).

(b) Supervision of the established sales person, i.e. ensuring that time is effectively used, that company equipment and resources are properly applied, that expenses incurred are justified, that company policy, instructions and methods are observed, that bad selling/organisation habits are eradicated and that new, more appropriate methods are established. Supervision, therefore, can be defined as to '. . . direct or watch with authority the work in progress'.

(c) Supervision of regional and area managers as well as sales supervisors and trainers in the context of their particular role and objectives.

Control

In Chapter 1 (page 15), control was defined as a management activity concerned with checking performance against pre-determined objectives set in plans to ensure progress and performance. It means:

(a) having the optimum information feedback systems
(b) having an effective system of measuring performance
(c) comparing and verifying results with objectives and past performance and meaningfully interpreting trends and results
(d) knowing where, how and when to take remedial action

Sales management information feedback systems

Putting this in the context of sales management, the sales manager will need to set up systems that will provide sales order entry and other information that can be measured, assessed and evaluated against pre-determined yardsticks or standards. This will enable the sales executive to identify the progress or otherwise of the sales management plan, so that operations in progress can be monitored and remedial action taken if necessary.

The sales management plan needs to be monitored as it is operating and regularly reviewed at appropriate intervals. If certain pre-designated situations occur, contingency plans should be substituted. Alternatively, if in the light of radically different economic, market or company conditions prevailing during a particular sales period, it may have to be re-written.

The most immediate source of control information is obtained when working with field sales personnel making routine calls on customers or potential customers or physically monitoring the telephone selling operation. An example of this type of control was examined earlier on pages 143–4 using a sales person's assessment form as part of 'on-the-job training' but with the dual purpose of providing general control information.

The next most immediate source is information from regular sales meetings and the occasional conference. This is followed closely by daily, weekly, monthly (as appropriate) reports that are pre-formatted written accounts of activities that relate to operations, goals, objectives, procedures, standards or simply describe what happened in a sales person's day and are provided by the sales person and/or a sales supervisor/manager.

Some companies provide small tape recorders so that sales persons can record details of orders obtained and information to be reported; the latter application could also be used by sales supervisors. The tape is sent to the sales office where it is transcribed into a printed report and/or customer orders. A variation of this is where the sales person telephones his/her orders and report at a pre-arranged time and which is recorded in the sales office and later transcribed into a printed report.

To make call reporting and order entry more efficient, especially where the sales person sells a wide product/service range containing several thousand items and can take orders for several hundred product lines each day, some companies use computers. Hand-held computer terminals and electronic mail are two of the computer applications being used. These can reduce clerical work for the sales person and the sales office and allow faster deliveries to customers and faster reporting of control information to the sales manager.

The hand-held computers are battery operated, can store order and other details, and at the end of the day the terminal transmits the data over normal telephone lines to the company's computer. More powerful terminals are available which allow the computer to send information to the sales person; these often store updated product prices and delivery dates, carry out calculations etc. so that sales persons can answer questions on the spot, take and place orders and provide control information.

The electronic mail application is the use of computer-based 'mail boxes' accessed through a telephone by computer terminals. The sales person can call up his/her mail box to collect messages, to input orders, to leave messages requesting information or providing required control information, or simply to obtain instructions.

In recent years, some companies have abolished the use of sales persons' reports or adopted the attitude of '. . . report only when there is something to report or some action is required'. This has been done mainly on the grounds of saving the sales person's time in writing them and the sales manager's time in reading them, especially when they report a static situation. But even negative information may be useful in control situations and, allowing for the 'fiction' in some sales reports, it is still generally considered to be an effective way of gathering control data; it has the added advantage of forcing sales personnel to reflect on what has happened.

The sales person's report would be the outcome of the administrative side of his/her job and would be based upon the maintenance of individual customer or potential customer record cards and a call plan.

Record cards
These should cover information appropriate to the market, the type of business and the company, but for each customer or prospective customer include at least the following basic headings:

(a) Name, addresses (several if manufacturing, operations, accounts departments are at a different location to the purchasing office) and telephone number(s).

(b) Account or reference number, category of account or call frequency, any special discount or pricing arrangements.

(c) Type of business, industry, size of business or number employed.

(d) Names and status of contacts, particularly identifying decision-maker(s), best day/time to call for each.

(e) Type of product/service normally purchased and some estimate of potential.

(f) Record of visits or telephone contact, i.e. date, who was seen and the result.

Although record cards should be kept and, more importantly, used by the sales person, an examination of them by the sales manager can be requested on each field sales visit, or on particular monitoring days with a telephone sales operation.

Call plan

As the name suggests, this identifies the customers or prospective customers the sales person intends to call upon or, in some cases, the company decides he should call upon. It is usually based upon a weekly routing pattern but could be longer or shorter depending on the type of business. So a weekly call plan would indicate:

(a) A list of calls by days of the week.

(b) Name of customer and brief location on particular days.

(c) Whether by appointment, regular call, *ad hoc* call, call requested by customers.

(d) Purpose/objective (i.e. obtain enquiry and/or order, open account, closing interview for 'long' negotiated 'deal', demonstration, deal with complaint, collect outstanding debt etc.).

Report form

This would be designed to cover the needs of the particular company and should contain information to show which customers were in fact called upon compared with the call plan; it needs to cover at least:

(a) Day and date of call and approximate time.

(b) Name and address of company.

(c) Objective/aim of call.

(d) Who was seen.

(e) Results.

(f) Other issues, enquiries, complaints etc. raised.

(g) Action to be taken by sales person.

(h) Action to be taken by company (who, when, how).

(i) Other information obtained by observation or discussion (i.e. relevant changes in customer company, competitor activity, apparent changes in creditworthiness etc.).

(j) Proposed date and objective of next call.

When received by the sales manager, it is important not only that the sales person's report is read, but is commented upon (i.e. criticism or praise, questions of fact etc.) to indicate the reports are being read and the sales person is being supervised.

Sales managers'/supervisors' field or monitoring reports

Whether the sales manager personally works with the individual field sales person or personally monitors the individual telephone sales person or delegates such work to regional, area or sales supervisors or trainers, it is important to record the facts/impressions gained of such supervision to provide control information and for later comparison/reference.

In some companies, regional/area managers, sales supervisors or trainers are required to provide the sales manager with a field visit plan. This indicates field visit patterns over the next 3–6 months, giving names of sales personnel and the dates on which the 'supervisor' intends working with them. Examination of such a plan ensures fair and appropriate coverage of supervision and highlights if the 'supervisor' is spending disproportionately more time with those sales persons who are easy to supervise rather than with those who badly need supervision and help.

One type of sales supervisor 'field' or 'monitoring' report, the sales person assessment form, was examined in the earlier chapter (Chapter 5, pages 143–4) to assess training needs but, additionally, it provides control information and reports on the individual.

However, the regional/area manager or sales supervisor also needs to produce a weekly or monthly report on the geographical area for which he/she is responsible. Such a report would be designed to cover the particular needs of a company and its sales teams and would normally include the following basic information:

(a) Name, location, status of the particular 'supervisor'.

(b) The time span of the report (from . . . to . . .) and date completed.

(c) Agreed sales potential of area, sales targeted/sales realistically forecasted, actual sales achieved, justification of any difference.

(d) Summary of all field sales visits made with individual sales persons, their names, dates, location of territories. Names of customers or potential customers called upon, type of call (e.g. arrange demonstration, 'cold' call, lapsed customer etc.), standard of sales aids, general attitude etc.

(e) Brief assessment of each sales person, their training and personal needs, particular problem(s), any action recommended they should take and the action sales 'supervisor' promised/intends to take.

(f) Broad assessment of trading conditions, expansion or decline of demand, effects of external factors (e.g. competitor activity, effect of economic conditions, technological developments, needs of customers and potential customers, legal factors etc.), internal factors (e.g. basic appeal of current product/service combinations being offered by the company, appeal of present pricing, discount, delivery policy and operations etc.).

(g) What specific action(s) the sales 'supervisor' intends to take either to improve performance or to bring sales/profit performance up to required level.

(h) What specific actions and/or support the sales supervisor expects of the company and of specific executives or departments.

In fact, the regional/area manager or sales supervisor's report should give the sales manager both a quantitative and qualitative assessment of the sales activity in that area within the time period indicated. With a small sales force where there is no delegated level of field sales management, it would be appropriate for the sales manager to compile his own report of this type. This is because it permits comparison from one period to the next and between individuals and territories, and the mere activity of putting together the required information causes an objective assessment to take place rather than a subjective feeling to develop.

When systems are developed or methods adopted to enable standards to be established to achieve objectives, the levels at which these are set become methods of control, e.g. calculating territory sales potential; classifying/categorising customers according to size, potential, past sales to determine the frequency of making sales calls, the determination of the length of journey cycles and the priorities set for each cycle (see Chapter 2, pages 33–5). Comparison of the standards set and the performance achieved in each of the above levels produces a variance which needs to be explained and/or interpreted.

Other sales management control information can be obtained from company and/or industry data, published and specifically purchased marketing research and observation etc.

Performance appraisals by means of periodic checks of operations to determine the levels of performance being achieved in specific areas such as work output and quality, response to complaints, evidence of adherence to budgets, are further ways of obtaining sales management control information. A variation of this method is to use the sales person's/sales 'supervisor's' job description (i.e. pre-determined details of the tasks, responsibilities, authority and relationships to supervisors, subordinates and others in the organisation) to compare what is taking place in practice.

So far it has been assumed that the sales manager will set/devise systems for obtaining control information, but there are a number of systems companies who produce 'ready-made' and well-tried systems designed to extract a wide variety of sales control data. An example of one such company would be Kalamazoo Ltd Business Systems who provide ready-made systems that allow greater control by the manager. These are:

(a) Sales personnel – performance records: history, training, sickness, promotions, salary etc.

(b) Display ideas – transparent pockets in loose-leaf binders protect and transform leaflets, photographs, products, documents etc.; build sales by better presentation of products.

(c) Hire purchase – hirer's card, collector's record written simultaneously. Increased protection; less work, more calls.

(d) Sales analysis – daily analysis, without copying work, gives salesmen's area and national totals within minutes. No laborious lists or extracts.

(e) Customers' pre-printed orders – save salesmen's valuable time. Reduce error and improve clarity. Increase 'drops' or calls per day.

(f) Stocks – know stock position daily. Use daily sales totals as basic figures.

(g) Loading schedules – establish complete accuracy on loadings and balance returns with sales and issues.

(h) Production schedules – accurate analysis of sales and stock balances provides overnight production basis. Used extensively in food industry.

(i) Price lists – reprint as often as required, however many alterations. New process cuts re-rewriting, slashes costs of printing copies.

(j) Salesmen's daily reports – combine daily report and customer's history records. More accuracy and less 'homework'.

(k) Index of customers and prospects – vital for increasing sales. Never requires re-writing. Always up-to-date.

(l) Cash collection – done by salesmen in half the time, including Bank Slip. Greater protection; prevent defalcations; avoids errors.

Measuring sales team performance

Having set up the 'machinery' for, and obtained sales management control information, the next stage in the control process is the measurement of performance (although in some cases obtaining the control information will involve measurement anyway).

One such method is through ratio analysis which can be used to establish relationship values between key performance and administrative factors. Some of these were shown as part of the cost analysis example on page 47; other ratios relevant for the sales manager would be:

Enquiries/invitations : Discussion/interviews
Tenders : Enquiries
Opportunities to quote : Calls made
Orders : Demonstrations
Contracts : Enquiries
Contracts : Tenders
New clients : Old clients

Specific examples of ratio analysis are as follows:

(a)

	Existing customers	Prospective customers
Ratio: calls to enquiries	2 to 1	4 to 1
Ratio: enquiries to orders	3 to 1	6 to 1
Number of calls to obtain one order	6	24

In a hypothetical situation, the order-getting potential of two salesmen could be:

Salesman	Calls made	Calls on existing customers	Calls on prospective customers
A	90	72	18
B	90	18	72

Salesman A order-getting potential from

(1) existing customers – 12 orders (72 ÷ 6)
(2) prospective customers – 3 orders every 4 weeks (18 ÷ 24 = ¾)

Salesman B order-getting potential from

(1) existing customers – 3 orders (18 ÷ 6)
(2) prospective customers – 3 orders (72 ÷ 24)

(b) Cost per call made in a particular sales period:

$$\frac{\text{Sales person's remuneration} + \text{All relevant expenses}}{\text{Number of calls made}}$$

$$= \frac{£14,000 + £4,500}{1600} = £11.56 \text{ per call}$$

(c) The orders/calls ratio:

$$\frac{\text{Total number of orders}}{\text{Total number of calls}} \times \% \text{ ratio}$$

$$\frac{1050}{1490} \times \frac{100}{1} = 70.4\%$$

(d) Average value of order by salesman:

$$\frac{\text{Value of orders}}{\text{No. of orders}} = \frac{£90,150}{1050} = £85.85\text{p}$$

(e) Average value of order by customers:

$$\frac{\text{Value of order}}{\text{No. of customers}} = \frac{£90,150}{184} = £489.94\text{p}$$

(f) Average cost per order obtained

$$\frac{\text{Sales person's total cost}}{\text{No. of orders}} = \frac{£18,500}{1050} = £17.61\text{p}$$

(g) Territory share:

$$\frac{\text{Sales revenue}}{\text{Territory potential}} \times \frac{100}{1} = \frac{£90,150}{£890,000} = 10.1\%$$

(h) Sales administration cost per order:

$$\frac{\text{Sales admin. costs}}{\text{No. of orders}} = \frac{£13,125}{1050} = £12.50 \text{ per order}$$

Other control performance indicators are used either by comparing the performance between sales personnel or by comparing the same sales person's performance in different sales periods or by comparing the individual sales person's performance with his target. These include:

(a) Total sales per area compared with national sales.
(b) Sales made per sales period compared with target.
(c) Number of customers and/or potential customers per sales area.
(d) Time taken to cover territory (length of journey cycle).
(e) Marketing costs needed to support a sales area.
(f) Number of working days of individual sales persons per sales period.
(g) Number of training, meeting or conference days per sales person.
(h) Percentage of call quota achieved.
(i) Ratio of face-to-face selling time to total time in sales period.
(j) Ratio of calls made on potential customers compared with existing customers.
(k) Number of demonstrations obtained compared with orders received.
(l) Miles travelled per sale value and/or calls made.
(m) Selling cost to territory turnover.
(n) Cost per call.
(o) Average calls per day.
(p) Cost of opening new accounts.
(q) Bad debts to sales ratio.
(r) Number of new accounts opened compared with existing accounts.
(s) Number of accounts closed compared with existing accounts.

An elementary example relating to a small (or part of a large) field sales force of assembling control information, measuring and analysing it is shown in Figs. 8.1(a) and (b). A further example, this time relating to a telephone selling operation, is shown in Fig. 8.2.

A simple sales analysis of product and/or service sales by sales person or sales area compared with budget forecasts will identify where under- or

Sales area/ sales person	Total sales calls made	Total orders obtained	Total sales revenue	Total existing customers	Total potential customers in area	Sales Person Cost			
						Salary + commission	Direct expenses (car, hotel, entertaining etc.)	Indirect expenses (sales trainer/ management time, courses etc.)	Total
1	2,010	1,420	£151,000	215	480	£17,000	£10,200	£2,000	£29,200
2	1,600	1,150	£147,000	174	415	£15,800	£11,000	£2,000	£28,800
3	1,450	980	£110,000	162	420	£14,700	£10,000	£2,000	£26,700
4	1,210	617	£74,000	125	300	£12,600	£9,600	£2,000	£24,200
5	940	245	£46,000	74	402	£12,100	£10,500	£2,000	£24,600
6	780	148	£24,000	42	340	£12,000	£10,200	£2,000	£23,200
TOTAL	7,990	4,560	£552,000	792	2,357	£84,200	£61,500	£12,000	£156,700

Fig. 8.1(a) An example, relating to a small (or part of a large) field sales force, of assembling and measuring control information

Sales area/ sales person	Orders/ calls ratio	Value of average order	Market share by number of customers	Total cost/ sales ratio	Total expense/ sales revenue	Cost per order obtained
1	70%	£131.30	44.8%	19%	8%	£20.56
2	71%	£127.82	42.0%	19.5%	8.8%	£25.04
3	67%	£112.24	38.5%	24.2%	10.9%	£27.24
4	51%	£119.93	41.6%	32.7%	15.6%	£39.22
5	26%	£187.75	18.4%	53.4%	27.1%	£100.40
6	18%	£119.40	12.3%	96.6%	50.8%	£156.70
TOTAL	50.5%	£133.05	32.9%	35.45%	20.2%	£61.52

Fig. 8.1(b) An example of the measurement and analysis of control data shown in Fig. 8.1(a)

Telephone Selling Assessment

Date . . . .

Name of sales person . . . . Industry/market . . . .

	Month 1	Month 2	Month 3

Data
   Number of customers
   Number of calls made
   Number of orders received
   Number of enquiries received
   Value of orders received
   Sales person's salary and commission
   Supervisory/training on-cost
   Cost of telephone calls

Analysis
   Order : call ratio
   Enquiries : call ratio
   Average value of order per call
   Average value of order per customer called
   Average cost of each call
   Cost per £1 of each order

Fig. 8.2 The assembly and analysis of control information relating to a telephone selling operation

Product/service combination	Sales area 1	Sales area 2	Sales area 3	Sales area 4	Performance totals	Budget forecast
Total						
Budget forecast						

Fig. 8.3 Performance/Budget comparison forecast

over-achievement has taken place (see Fig. 8.3). A variation on this theme giving progressive information on a monthly basis could be as in Fig. 8.4.

From this wide variety of ways of measuring performance from control data, the individual sales manager needs to put together the combination of measures most appropriate to his company/sales force/market situations and which give most effective control. With the additional availability of computer capacity, a far greater number of control-measuring devices can be used/calculated than if the measuring process is carried out manually.

Budgets are very effective ways of monitoring and controlling the sales management plan. They are expressions of the objectives of various aspects of an organisation and provide a means whereby business (including the sales function) can be directed in relation to an objective. Closely linked with budgeting is the use of standard costs which are unit costs set in advance of production and selling. Budgets and standard costs are useful where sales management control is complicated during a sales period by changes in sales by units, price changes, sterling value changes and perhaps changes in the product/service sales mix. For example, the sales budget and forecast of a particular product group for the month of April 19X5:

	Product X		Product Y		Product Z		
Sales unit forecast	4,000		7,000		10,000		
	each		each		each		Total
Sales at standard selling prices	£2.00	£8,000	£1.00	£7,000	£0.50	£5,000	£20,000
Standard cost of sales	£1.20	£4,800	£0.70	£4,900	£0.40	£4,000	£13,700
Standard profit on forecasted sales	£0.80	£3,200	£0.30	£2,100	£0.10	£1,000	£ 6,300

SALES BUDGET CHECK

Month ending..........

Product/service combination (lines)	This month			Year to date			Sales last year to date	Increase/ decrease over last year (%)	Action to be taken
	Actual sales	Budget	% realised	Actual sales	Budget	% realised			
1									
2									
3									
4									
5									
6									
7									
8									
etc.									
Totals									

Fig. 8.4 Sales Budget check

Actual sales made during April 19X5 were:

> Product X 3000 units sold for £6500
> Product Y 7500 units sold for £7200
> Product Z 9400 units sold for £4200

It will be seen that a true assessment must take into account three possible variances: price, volume and product mix.

(a) Sales price variance – comparing budget price and actual price obtained:

Product	Budget price	Actual unit sales	Actual sales at standard price	Revenue obtained	Variance
X	£2.00	3000	£6000	£6500	+£500
Y	£1.00	7500	£7500	£7200	−£300
Z	£0.50	9400	£4700	£4200	−£500
				Overall sales price variance	−£300

This indicates the effect of changes in price made during the period, perhaps the result of special deals, increased discounts etc.

(b) Sales volume variance – relating the volume of sales to profit or loss:

Product	Budgeted sales volume	Actual sales at standard prices	Variance	Profit margin	Profit margin × variance
X	£8000	£6000	−£2000	40%	−£800
Y	£7000	£7500	+£ 500	30%	+£150
Z	£5000	£4700	−£ 300	20%	−£ 60
				Overall volume variance	−£710

(c) Product mix variance – comparing the budgeted pattern or mix of products within the total budgeted sales with the actual pattern during the period:

Actual sales	Product	Units sold	Budgeted price	Actual sales at standard prices
	X	3000 @	£2.00	£6000
	Y	7500 @	£1.00	£7500
	Z	9400 @	£0.50	£4700
	Total actual sales @ standard price			£18,200

The mix or pattern of sales in the budget is £8000 of X, to £7000 of Y, to £5000 of Z; i.e. 40, 35 and 25 per cent respectively of total budgeted sales at standard prices (£20,000). If actual sales had been made on this pattern, the sales mix variance related to profit or loss would be:

Product	Budget pattern	Total actual sales at budget prices	Actual sales on budget pattern	Actual sales @ SP	Variance	Profit margin	Profit or loss
X	40% of £18,200		£7280	£6000	−£1280 ×	40% =	−£512
Y	35% of £18,200		£6370	£7500	+£1130 ×	30% =	+£339
Z	25% of £18,200		£4550	£4700	+£ 150 ×	20% =	+£ 30
					Total variance		−£143

Thus the above table shows how sales of individual products deviated from the pattern or mix laid down in the budget and the consequent effect on profits. However, within the pattern laid down in the budget, it is possible for variance to occur within the sales mix; this can be seen by comparing budgeted sales with actual sales on the budget pattern:

Product	Budgeted sales volume	Actual sales on budget pattern	Variance (2−3)	Profit margin	Profit variance (4×5)
1	2	3	4	5	6
X	£8000	£7280	−£720	40%	−£288
Y	£7000	£6370	−£630	30%	−£189
Z	£5000	£4550	−£450	20%	−£ 90
				Quantity	−£567
				Sales mix	−£143
		Overall volume variance as (b) above			−£710

This type of analysis clearly indicates where actual sales, revenue and profit are not according to budget and therefore where action should be taken.

A further important part of the monitoring and control process of the sales plan relates to costs incurred by its operation. It is therefore necessary to compare actual with budgeted costs to identify if any deviation has occurred and to discover why, so that remedial action can be taken; the format in Fig. 8.5 would be useful to do this.

Interpreting trends and results

Having obtained sales management control information through a feedback system, and having measured performance by persons and areas, the next stage in the control process is for the sales manager to compare the results with stated objectives and with past performance and then to meaningfully interpret trends and results.

Comparing results with stated objectives will usually cause differences or variations to emerge and these need to be investigated and reasons sought rather than being merely rationalised away. To compare present with past performance may indicate apparent progress or apparent decline. The

Analysis of sales, selling and related costs

Cost area	Actual costs this period	Budgeted cost	Percentage ± realised
Direct cost of field sales force:			
Salaries			
Commission			
Bonus			
Car operating expenses			
Travel/entertaining			
Direct cost of selling by telephone:			
Salaries			
Commission			
Bonus			
Telephone costs			
Direct cost of supporting activities:			
Salaries of internal sales staff			
Support literature			
Sales aids			
Advertising			
Sales promotion			
Samples			
Exhibitions etc.			
Sales office and administration			
Sales training:			
By own staff to own staff			
By consultants, external courses			
By own staff to customer's staff			
Cost of operating branch offices and warehouses (if appropriate)			
Cost of physical distribution if part of branch or warehouse operation			
Cost of agents/distributors:			
Commission			
Retainer			
Expenses			
Consignment stocks			
Cost of marketing research activities directly related to sales operations			
Cost of stockholding of finished products			
Bad debts			
Sales management cost or overhead			
Contingency funds			
Total			

Fig. 8.5 Format for Actual/Budgeted comparison

interpretation of trends and results needs to be carried out in the context of the conditions/situations in the company or the 'market-place'. For example, an under-achievement against a sales target may in fact be a better than could be expected result in the context of market conditions. In the following illustration by Bolt, * the 'Product group' categories could be seen also as sales regions or individual sales persons etc. in a comparison of forecast and achieved sales.

Product group	Company sales forecast	Actual sales achieved
A	£800,000	£900,000
B	£600,000	£560,000

From the data shown it would appear that a better marketing [sales management] job has been carried out on Product Group A [or in sales region A or by sales person A] by increasing sales by £100,000, than with Product Group B where sales were £40,000 down on forecast. But if the size of the market involved and the company's share of the individual market or industry are considered, a totally different picture is revealed.

Forecast

Product group	Industry or market forecast	Company sales forecast	Forecast share of market
A	£10,000,000	£800,000	8%
B	£12,000,000	£600,000	5%

Achieved

Product group	Industry or market sales	Company's actual sales	Actual market share
A	£15,000,000	£900,000	6%
B	£ 8,000,000	£560,000	7%

. . . the former assessment of the marketing [sales management] performance with these two Product Groups [or sales regions or individual sales persons] will be reversed. In the case of A the fullest advantage has not been taken of a tremendously expanding market and the company's market share has dropped from 8% to 6%. On the other hand, the initial assessment of a poor marketing [selling] performance for group B must be reconsidered because this market has in fact contracted, and although the product group is down on forecast, the market share has increased from 5% to 7%. It is therefore very important . . . to consider (a) whether the market upon which the forecast [target set for area or sales person] was based has expanded or contracted, and (b) what was the size of the market share?

Other factors beyond the control of the individual sales person or area managers (e.g. strikes, fire at own or customer's or competitor's facilities, abnormal weather conditions, major change in competitor's 'total deal' or the setting up of a new competitor facility in a particular area, a major customer leaving or coming to a particular area etc.) need to be taken into account when interpreting trends and results.

* G. J. Bolt, *Market and Sales Forecasting—a Total Approach.* Kogan Page, 1981, p. 80.

The interpretation of trends and results obtained from analysing control information requires the sales manager to seek causes rather than excuses for results. Consider the individual sales person's control data and its analysis in Figs. 8.1(a) and (b) in the context of an actual company.

There seems to be an obvious link in making calls to doing business (sales person 1) Although sales person 2 is marginally better in converting calls to orders, it was discovered on investigation that he had a rather different method of closing a sale. The conversion rate of sales persons 5 and 6 are not acceptable in the light of the conversion rate of the others. There appears to be no apparent excuse for either, although sales person 5 did take over this rather run-down area a year ago. Notice the anomaly of sales person 5's abnormally high 'value of average order' figure, i.e. £187.75; on investigation, it was found that he was concentrating on, and spending a lot of time with, certain types of customers whose purchasing potential was only in the high-quality, high-priced items in the product range and none of the other qualities. The sales manager was not misled by the £133.05 average order; if it had not been for sales person 5 the average would have been £122. Sales person 6 did not have a bad 'value of average order' figure but was simply not getting enough orders. It was discovered that sales person 3 was not trying to sell the higher priced products in the range and this gave him the lowest value per order.

Again, the market share by customer indicates poor performance by sales persons 5 and 6; in the case of 5, it was found that he was spending 82 per cent of his time with existing customers and avoiding visiting potential customers. The sales manager decided that he had to specially tutor sales person 5 in 'Prospecting for new sources of business/sales opportunities'; he also intended observing sales person 3 in this particular activity.

The company's remuneration plan was based on salary plus commission, hence sales person 6 was not justifying the £12,000 basic salary (and was certainly not receiving commission), but the huge difference in sales revenue between sales persons 6 and 1 caused the sales manager to investigate other incentive payments for the latter. He immediately investigated the fact that the expenses incurred by the highest volume earner and the lowest were the same, i.e. £10,200. Especially as sales person 6 had a 96.6 per cent total cost/sales revenue ratio and the fact that he was therefore only producing £800 more in sales revenue than he was costing. The significant fact also is that sales person 6's cost per order obtained was £156.70 for an average order of £119.40. The sales manager immediately investigated whether 6 should be completely retrained or should be moved from the field sales force.

The total cost/sales ratio and the cost per order obtained was investigated for sales persons 3 and 4 and, after discussions, a new approach to journey planning was agreed with them to reduce expenses and increase the opportunity to make extra sales calls.

Additionally, the analysis in Fig. 8.2 must be seen in the context of the length of time a sales person has been working a territory, whether the company has played its part in developing goodwill, the economic conditions in the area/industry, whether customers are coming into or leaving a particular area etc.

Taking remedial action

Finally, in the control process there is the stage of knowing where, how and when to take remedial action. Knowing where to take action will be made clear by the analysis of data geographically. For example, an individual sales person may be identified who is not reaching his/her sales target for a particular customer/product group, or an overall drop in sales and morale in the sales force may take place if a competitor has a technological breakthrough with a particular product. As to how to take action, this will need to be appropriate for particular company situations. For example, in the two examples mentioned above, the 'how' of dealing with the individual sales person's problem could be immediate on-the-job training; with the overall drop in sales and morale, a sales conference may be more appropriate. As to when the remedial action should take place, it should be immediately as far as the individual is concerned but a sales conference might be better delayed until R & D and/or production can produce a matching or new technological breakthrough in the particular product/service area or the sales manager can develop a new strategy to offset the effects of the technological breakthrough by a competitor.

In some companies, 'management by exception' is practised in this stage of the control process, i.e. on each of the measures of performance a minimum level of performance is identified and as long as the results are above this level no remedial action need be taken. Often maximum levels are identified also because results above these levels indicate either exceptional effort on the part of the sales person, in which case he/she should be congratulated, or that some basic criteria in setting performance levels has changed. For example, an abnormally high level of sales revenue may indicate the arrival in a particular sales territory of a new, large customer, thus territory potential will have increased. The most economic use of the sales manager's time is made through the use of management by 'management by exception' as he/she can concentrate on the 'exceptional' situations indicated.

Evaluation

After monitoring and control comes the evaluation of the results. Evaluation is the essence of good sales management planning. It indicates whether the sales plan is working to the optimum level and signals to the sales manager any unforeseen problems and basic changes in the market-place which may necessitate a change in the sales plan. It also permits the sales manager to measure overall sectional and individual performance in terms of accomplishing the set objectives and can form the basis of future sales planning activity.

Each sales manager needs to set up an evaluation checklist appropriate to his market/industry/company, asking (and answering) such questions as:

(a) Were the corporate objectives, policies and strategies feasible/realistic in practice?

(b) Were the broad marketing/sales objectives, policies and strategies feasible/realistic in practice?

(c) Was the broad sales 'mission' correct in the light of ensuing events in the market-place?

(d) Had the company's strengths and weaknesses together with problems, opportunities and threats been comprehensively and realistically assessed?

(e) Were the profit objectives realistic and to what degree were they achieved?

(f) Were the marketing and sales strategies and tactics appropriate and should they be continued or modified for the future?

(g) Were the assumptions made regarding market share, market position and competitors' activities and reactions correct?

(h) Were the most effective market segments selected?

(i) In what areas was the sales plan at fault and was it implemented correctly?

(j) Were monitoring activities and performance measures and analyses effective?

(k) Do we need to retrain, modify or re-write the long-term sales plan? Etc. etc.

The evaluation process not only helps the sales manager to improve sales operations/plans in progress but also enables improved future sales planning to be carried out, making the company and the sales team more effective in the market place.

Summary

Supervision and control are closely linked activities ensuring that the objectives set in the sales plan are being worked towards and ultimately achieved. Supervision was defined as '. . . direct or watch with authority the work in progress . . .' and should normally involve seven activities, i.e. know, plan, inform, motivate, monitor, acknowledge, show appreciation. 'On-the-job' supervision has a training and motivation aspect as well as the contribution it makes to control activity. Supervisory activity can be usefully grouped into that with new/developing sales persons, established sales persons and those managerial supervisory levels in the sales team.

Control involves having information feedback systems, measurement and comparison of performance with objectives, interpreting trends and taking remedial action. If fundamental changes take place in market/company situations, contingency plans or even a re-written sales plan may need to be substituted. The various sources/systems of information are such that sales managers can put together a number of methods that monitor and control every type of sales team activity, but this still requires the sales manager's expertise in deciding how to interpret trends and results and to decide on the appropriateness of remedial action. What is the solution to the problem that has been identified by the analysis of control information? The sales manager's action will be judged by others in the sales team as a measure of his/her effectiveness as a manager.

The assessment of the sales plan will more effectively take place if the sales manager develops his own evaluation checklist, appropriate to the particular market/industry/company needs. From the process of evaluation of the effectiveness of the sales management plan, the sales manager should receive valuable indications for future planning.

Questions

1. Distinguish between motivation, supervision and control and describe why they are crucial to effective sales management.

2. What are the sources of control information that are available to the sales manager?

3. There are a number of methods of measuring performance; identify four you consider to be most important to a sales manager and give your reasons.

4. Why is it necessary for the sales manager to interpret trends and results instead of accepting the implications of statistical analysis at face value?

5. Knowing where, how and when to take remedial action is one of the final, but equally crucial, parts of the control process. Consider the situation of the six sales persons whose performances were analysed in Figs. 8.1(a) and (b). Where, how and when would you take remedial action in these examples?

6. Evaluation is the last stage of the control process. Which *three* of the evaluation questions do you consider to be the most important? Give your reasons.

Administration and support activities

SECTION 6.2

Administration and support
activities

CHAPTER 9

Sales management and administration

Objectives

This chapter initially examines the role of the sales manager in administration and the principle that it should be delegated in a variety of ways to specialist staff and as far down the organisation as possible. In doing this, it covers the various administrative functions appropriate in the sales management area. It then reviews the operation of the sales office and, by examining the various recognised approaches, identifies the activities that make up effective sales administration. Finally, it considers the need and the strategy for updating and/or re-organising existing sales office arrangements for introducing new systems.

The sales manager as an administrator

Just as the sales person's job is a blend of actual selling (including 'flair') and organisation/administration, depending on the selling job, so the sales manager's job is a blend of sales management operations (planning, analysis, decision-making, problem-solving, recruitment, training, motivation, supervision, control and selling) and organisation/administration. In the latter case, it means not only the organisation/administration of the resources of people, machines, money and time, but also the setting up and operation of administrative systems that service, support and make more effective the sales function operation.

Depending on the actual sales role in a particular company and market, the sales person may have relatively a lot of administration to carry out (e.g. arranging demonstrations or factory visits, making appointments, developing designs, proposals, estimates) or relatively little (e.g. where even the sales person's route and calling sequence is determined by a sales controller). The sales personnel in both cases would still need to organise their time, territory and themselves. The sales manager's aim should be to reduce non-selling administrative time as far as possible (e.g. time spent in the sales office doing administrative tasks) to release sales personnel to do the job for which they

are employed – selling. A number of non-selling activities may be economically pulled back into a central location (i.e. a sales office) to be dealt with
more cost effectively.

The same is true of the sales manager's job; by the nature of the role it will
always contain proportionately more administration (in level and content)
than that of the sales person. The type, level and content of the
administrative element will vary from company to company but even so,
depending on the size of, and the 'mission' of, the sales management
operations, there will be administrative tasks that can be delegated:

(a) functionally to specialist office staff
(b) centrally to a specialist administration manager
(c) territorially to field sales personnel
(d) geographically to regional/area/district managers
(e) organisationally to branch offices, warehouse or distribution centres;
showroom and/or demonstration centres, service centres etc.
(f) by combinations of the first five.

Those functions that are delegated should be better performed as they
will/should be carried out by specialists in special support areas (area
managers, secretaries, sales correspondents, credit controllers etc.). Those
retained by the sales manager should be better performed as he/she will have
more time to really manage the selling operation, e.g. carry out strategic
planning; lead, motivate and control the sales team; negotiate large contracts
etc.

There will, of course, be some administrative activities that the sales
manager should not/cannot/would not want to delegate, depending on the
company/market situations. However, whether administrative functions are
retained or delegated, the ultimate responsibility and accountability will be
that of the sales manager.

The size of the sales management operation was mentioned as a factor of
how much administration the sales manager would have to deal with. For
example, the administration and support activities necessary for a highly
specialised national field sales force of ten for a chemical engineering or
'high-tech' company would require far less administration (although they
may need more technical support) than a field sales force of 150+ for a
fast-moving consumer-goods company.

The 'mission' of the sales management operation (and therefore of the
sales function) was also mentioned as a factor of how much administration
should/could be delegated. The sales management mission in this context
not only refers to the objectives stated in the company, marketing and sales
management plans but also in its relationship to the current stage of the
company development life-cycle.

In the early stages of the life of a new company or new venture, there will
be sales management 'setting up activities' that are almost entirely

administrative. In the first operating stage, the role of the sales manager is likely to be concentrated on developing systems for field sales operations, fighting for a toe-hold for the company and its product/services in the market-place. There will tend not to be a high volume of business or administration but, whatever there is of the latter, it needs to be delegated as far down the organisation as it will go, to release the sales manager to exercise his innovativeness and flair in identifying sales opportunities and to expand markets.

In the next stage of company/venture development, administration increases considerably as new, exploitable market segments are identified and at a time when the sales manager needs to be concentrating on increased market penetration, market share and dealing with competition. At this stage, administration increases not only because of *ad hoc* activities (e.g. recruitment and training of sales personnel to increase the size of the sales force) but also because of the need to set up more detailed information feedback systems and methods of measuring performance (see the previous chapter). Often there are also internal administrative problems directly related to the success of the sales manager's sales operations but in functional areas not under his/her control. For example, the rapid identification, development and exploitation of market segments may cause problems related to production capacity and the continuity of supplies, problems related to delivery and distribution, and financial administrative problems related to financing of strategic stocks at various geographic locations and the financing of customer credit. These latter activities may not always be within the direct control of the sales manager, but it will be his sales team who will have to deal with customer problems and complaints arising from them and this increases administration considerably.

In the third stage, where the company has become mature, the high growth rate has slackened (although sales volumes may be higher), initial and secondary markets are becoming saturated and the company position in them may need defending, but the company tends to maintain its market position because of its reputation. While encouraging and welcoming new developments, the accent is on effective management of the *status quo* and administration through careful planning, motivation of the sales force to sell the present range of company products/services with conviction. This will need to be aided by good administrative and support systems, effective control over costs, and the development and retention of soundly based policies that are necessary to maintain continuous, steady and short/long-term success. Administration will tend to dominate the sales manager's life in this stage or at least encourage effective ways of delegating it to others.

Provided the sales manager (and others) cope with the mature stage effectively, taking advantage of every sales opportunity that arises, this stage can last for many years. But unless the company can identify new product/service opportunities in existing or new market segments, it will tend to decline. Even so, the sales manager must obtain the maximum/ optimum sales revenue and/or profit from the company situation as it exists by reducing costs in many areas, by improving sales team productivity and/or performance, considering radical solutions, by abandoning non-profitable or least profitable market segments, and putting sales resources into more profitable areas, changing channels of distribution and/or franchising to meet the company's reduced investment situation etc. All these activities put a high emphasis on administration which in some areas the sales manager will find difficult to delegate.

Also there will obviously be more administration needed if the support activities provided are more than to service a field sales force. For example, the sales manager's responsibility may cover:

(a) finished stock warehouses (centrally or in geographically spread branch offices)

(b) distribution from branch warehouses

(c) showrooms and trade/public sales counters

(d) a telephone sales operation

(e) customer service, which can be before-sale such as demonstrations, special product design, technical advice, packaging design, planning (e.g. kitchens), estimating and measuring; also, after-sales service such as quick delivery, installation, servicing, availability of spares, maintenance contracts, merchandising, safety/insurance inspection visits, etc.

(f) a product support operation

(g) a credit control operation

(h) operating a merchandising service in retail outlets

The size of the administrative job and the impact of the 'mission' of the sales management operations have been examined in relation to the balance between administration and sales operations in the sales manager's job, but delegation of administration to ease the load on the sales manager or to make operations more effective was suggested earlier in six ways.

Delegation functionally to specialist office staff

Specialist, routine, and some supervisory/control administrative activities will be better performed by persons specially trained to do them. Functionally specialised activities would include shorthand/audio typewriting skills, word processing, operating computers, credit control etc. Routine activities would include handling enquiries and quotations, order recording, computing prices, keeping records, checking, confirming, sorting, copying, filing, indexing, retrieval of information.

Supervisory activities would include supervising others, administrative activities, liaison between sales force, production, accounts etc.; operating sub-budgets, e.g. petty cash, stationery, stocks etc.

Control activities could include a continuing analysis of field sales personnel activities (sales, targets, quotas, call/quotation/order analysis), credit control, centralised finished stock control, sales persons' call report analysis, weekly itinerary control, vehicle report and expense control etc.

It would be impossible for the sales manager to be an expert in all of the specialist areas but he/she must understand their capabilities.

Delegation centrally to a specialist administration manager

This would relieve the sales manager of the management aspects of the administrative role of his job, though not the responsibility to top management for its effective operation. This is an ideal solution where the administrative load is considerable; the alternative would be for the sales manager to retain all the administrative management functions and to appoint a field sales manager to carry out the selling operation functions. In a large organisation, both may be appointed.

The extent to which the delegation of administration can be carried out by the appointment of a sales administration manager can be seen from the following job description example:

JOB SPECIFICATION: SALES ADMINISTRATION MANAGER*

Job specification for: Sales Administration Manager
Reporting to: National Sales Manager
Responsible for: Planning, implementing and controlling sales administration, i.e.:

1. Establishing the administrative requirements of the sales organisation and its customers.
2. Submitting budgets corresponding to 1, for approval.
3. Implementing the approved budget by establishing and maintaining the internal sales staff, and the procedures which meet these requirements, with particular reference to:
   (a) Nominating the groups of salesmen and/or customers to be looked after by each internal sales person and ensuring their names are known to both.
   (b) Ensuring that all communications to and from customers come through to them.
   (c) Ensuring that systems exist and work for providing customer requirements on time (e.g. correspondence, literature, samples, quotations, goods etc.), and advising the sales manager when these are in danger of becoming overdue.
   (d) Ensuring that all statistical analyses are provided as and when required.
   (e) Ensuring that sales personnel receive copy correspondence and invoices.
   (f) Ensuring that the administrative responsibilities of sales personnel are minimised.

* From *Overhauling Marketing Operations*, a specially commissioned Institute of Marketing publication by Paul Weiner, Managing Director, Management Consultants Limited.

(g) Ensuring that requests for designs and/or quotations are accompanied by all necessary information.

4. Defining the jobs of each member of the internal sales staff in such a way that standards can be set, performance measured against these, and training directed at systematically improving this performance.

5. Formally reviewing the performance of internal sales staff every six months in the presence of the sales manager.

6. Recommending the hiring and firing of internal sales staff.

7. Contributing to company policy by submitting written reports on any aspect of this thought to need attention, these to be discussed at monthly meetings chaired by the sales manager (copies to be forwarded to the marketing director).

Attended meetings: Monthly with the National and Regional Sales Managers

Expenditure limits: Not to exceed budgeted costs without authority

Delegation territorially to field sales personnel

While there are many routine activities in which individual sales persons get involved that more economically could be done by sales office personnel, most companies want their sales personnel to actively manage their territories which implies a type of administration. In doing so, sales personnel need to plan, set objectives, organise their time and journeys, co-ordinate activities (e.g. the balance of sales calls on existing customers to those on potential customers), motivate and communicate with customers, monitor their own performance and take remedial action. By practising 'management by exception' (i.e. where the sales manager sets personal minimum and maximum performance 'norms'), the individual sales person is allowed to 'manage' his/her own territory unless performance results are lower (or higher as this would indicate the need for praise or a reappraisal of the performance norms) than the 'norms'. Such a situation would 'flag' the need for the sales manager's attention.

Delegation geographically to regional, area, district managers

The possible extent of geographical delegation of administration can be seen by identifying the administrative content in the following job description of a district (regional) manager for a particular company.

DUTIES OF A DISTRICT (REGIONAL) MANAGER

He is responsible for establishing and maintaining the distribution of all the Company's products in his district, and for developing sales to the maximum potential in his district. In the discharge of this responsibility, he performs the following duties:

A. Analyses and organises his district territories, office, policies and procedures.

B. Plans all activities.

C. Supervises the following personnel:
1. All sales personnel in his district.
2. District Office personnel.

D. Selects, hires, trains and checks training of all personnel under his supervision.
1. Interviews, screens, and hires sales applicants and office personnel in his district. Requests check on applicants' occupational and personal references and approval by Head Office.
2. Instructs new sales people in company organisation, company policy, products and procedures, benefits and future possibilities. Coaches and trains older sales personnel.
3. Instructs or delegates responsibility to show new sales personnel how to make out the following:

(a) Orders of all types.
(b) Daily reports.
(c) Expense reports.
(d) Advertising requisitions.
(e) Special reports to District Manager.
(f) Customers' record sheets.

4. Instructs new sales people regarding the application of their time, territorial coverage, routing, classification of accounts, development of the Company's merchandising plan and other duties.
5. Trains new personnel in actual selling and methods of distribution of Company's products. Gives examples of how to make basic (company's) presentations to all types of accounts.
6. Works with all sales personnel.
7. Makes evaluation of each sales person.
8. Analyses and makes recommendations for territory changes and sales person's promotions and pay.
9. Supervises all accounts.
10. Concentrates on active list of volume accounts who produce and are responsible for the greater percentage of the district's volume. Personally visits each once a month.
11. Checks the following reports:

(a) Daily reports and orders
(b) Expense reports.
(c) Route lists to determine complete territorial coverage.

12. Interprets credit policy and information.
13. Makes comparative territorial sales and expense analysis.
14. Checks customers' record books to ascertain if being kept up to date. Analyses accounts with sales people.
15. Attempts to make amicable settlement of customer complaints if sales person is unable to accomplish satisfactory results.
16. Approves all transfers of merchandise, when advisable.
17. Approves merchandise returns from dealer's stock to factory, if substantial quantities are involved.
18. Assign sales personnel for checking window display installations and also for assisting in special market research activities in the test cities.

E Holds district sales meetings or conferences:
1. For instructing sales persons in general activities on sales promotion.
2. To adjust territorial sales effort to combat competitive sales offers.
3. To realign sales efforts to compensate for market changes.

F. Holds customer sales meetings with wholesalers and chain stores for the purpose of:
  1. Obtaining greater distribution or concentration.
  2. Developing distribution:
     (a) Supervises reserve expenditure on sales drives.
     (b) Directs all sales persons to frequently attend customer sales meetings to develop and improve their technique in holding sales meetings.
     (c) Enlists interest of major customers' sales management and personnel in benefits of specific sales promotion activities and drives developed on their behalf and develops customer sales meetings through district sales personnel for all other accounts.

G. Makes all allocations to territories and examines territorial allocations to customers.

H. Maintains, staffs and trains personnel in district offices wherever established by management. Organises and supervises office procedure.

I. Confers with sales persons on prospective customers and recommends to Sales Manager all new accounts to be added to the company's customer list. Forwards to Sales Manager for final approval.

J. Represents the company at various local association meetings and conferences.

K. Reports in sufficient detail weekly to the Sales Manager at Head Office on general conditions within the district including comments, suggestions and recommendations, e.g. on new accounts; customer notes; competition activities; sales staff activities; specific requests; any other pertinent information.

Delegation organisationally

This would include delegation to:

(a) *Branch offices* that would act as control, administrative and support centres for the field sales force and provide a 'local' service to customers.

(b) *Warehouse and/or distribution centres.* In some cases the sales function is responsible at regional (and sometimes national) levels for controlling adequate 'strategic' stocks of products and for the 'localised' transport (or use of the public transport system) to provide customers with a high level of delivering service. These activities need to be properly managed and administered so that someone is administratively responsible locally.

(c) *Showroom and/or demonstration centres.* Where a range of products needs to be 'shown' to appeal to customer choice (e.g. builders' supplies, office equipment, consumer capital items etc.) or products need to be demonstrated (e.g. computers, video players, cars, machinery, TV receivers etc.), showroom and/or demonstration facilities need to be arranged as near as possible to the 'centres of demand'. Because of the strong case for these facilities to reflect local/industry demand, they are best administered locally although the ultimate national responsibility may be that of the sales manager. The alternative to 'own' showroom and/or demonstration centres is to use those of distribution channels (i.e. retailers, wholesalers), but direct control is then lost.

(d) *Service centres*; where products need installation and after-sales services such as repairs or maintenance, these can be provided through 'own' centres, or 'franchised' out to specialist, company-trained, service firms (e.g. Hotpoint, Hoover do this). Whichever course is chosen, both systems need administration and control.

It will be seen that this form of delegation of administration could be closely linked with the previous category (geographically) as they are often linked (unless a specialised national network is necessary) with regional, area, district managers.

Delegation by combination of the previous five categories

As each company has different internal considerations and faces different external situations, combinations of these five categories need to be considered by the sales manager both initially and at 6-monthly intervals to ensure that the sales organisation changes to accommodate changing circumstances.

The sales manager may or may not like his role as an administrator but the effectiveness of a sales team may reflect how well it is being administered.

Sales administration and the dynamic sales office

Every office in a company should be a 'sales' office; personnel in customer contact such as in a telephone selling operation, or in a field sales support activity, and even in accounts offices have an obvious sales role. Effectiveness in the sales role means not only selling products and/or services but also promoting the company image.

But even in those offices that never have, or only occasionally have, customer contact there should exist a 'sales' or 'market' orientated attitude, i.e. to do what is best for the company in the 'market-place'. There is also a need to internally 'sell' the image of efficiency between departments within a company if only through the effectiveness of their operations.

The sales office has not only a sales administrative role but also a very definite selling role, whether it is direct (a telephone selling operation) or indirect (obtaining sales leads, running training facilities or carrying out field sales support).

In many companies, the sales office plays a passive role compared with the sales force. It would be competitively more powerful if this could be changed into a dynamic, highly motivated, pro-active and efficient series of activities providing not only the necessary sympathetic and supportive administrative role for the field sales force but also an additional selling interface in the market.

The dynamic changes that take place in markets and the needs of customers should be reflected in the activities of the sales office.

The area, district, regional or national sales office should be the focal point/nerve centre for the sales activities appropriate to its level of operation in the organisation.

Approaches to the operation of the sales office

An office should not be an end in itself but a means of making a particular function of a business more effective administratively. The operation of the dynamic sales office should be the sum total of all office functions and activities that help the sales team of a company achieve its objectives and/or its optimum performance.

The operations of the sales office can be viewed in a number of different ways:

(a) the functional approach
(b) the activity approach
(c) the systems approach
(d) the behavioural approach
(e) the environmental approach
(f) the organisation approach
(g) the management approach
(h) the decision-making approach
(i) the automated sales office approach

These need to be expanded to indicate their true potential to the sales manager seeking administrative effectiveness.

The functional approach

The sales office can be organised to operate a variety of different functions. The individual company can put together its own series of functional modules to suit its own market and organisational needs, which will be reflected in branch and/or central sales office operations, and which can be changed or rearranged when its needs change. The range of functional services that the sales office could provide would include the following.

Basic sales administration
This involves:

(a) Handling correspondence/enquiries/orders/complaints from customers; enquiries/reports/requests from field sales personnel; enquiries/reports from other parts of the company, from suppliers and others.

(b) Keeping records (customer and sales personnel) and information regarding prices, discounts, stock availability, technical data etc.

(c) Progressing enquiries, quotations, estimates, orders, deliveries, service etc.

(d) Assembling and/or analysing data (reports, comparisons, technical performance etc.).

(e) Safeguarding assets (payments, stock, equipment, contracts etc.).

Acting as an information/communication centre

As communication is a two-way process, this implies that it will be an information-receiving centre as well as an information-giving centre. It will be an information centre to top management, other departments, marketing or sales executives, the sales force and, most important of all, to the *customer*; it should collect, classify, store and send out information on all aspects of the sales operation. Sales information can be divided into two main types:

(a) Intelligence data – concerning sales activities for deciding what to do and how to do it.

(b) Control data – for evaluating how effectively sales activities are being done; this also provides the opportunity for feedback so that the operations in progress can be improved.

The sales manager will need to use both types of data to manage the sales team and to provide dynamic sales presence in the market place.

To perform its information/communication centre function competently, the sales office (and the sales team) need to be appropriately equipped so that each aspect of the information provision (processing, retrieval, communication, copying etc.) is adequately covered. The equipment/systems shown under those information headings in Fig. 9.1 need to be considered by the sales manager and appropriate combinations chosen, installed and operated. From time to time their effectiveness should be reviewed because of rapid developments in technology in these areas. To perform its information centre role competently the objectives, tasks to be done and services required should be considered and assessed on a cost/benefit basis in the five information categories of processing, retrieval, communicating, copying and protection; a periodic review of these is necessary to keep the sales office at peak efficiency.

The scope and potential operation of a number of the individual items/systems shown in Fig. 9.1 are described in Chapter 10 when considering information technology services/systems as an area of special support for the sales function.

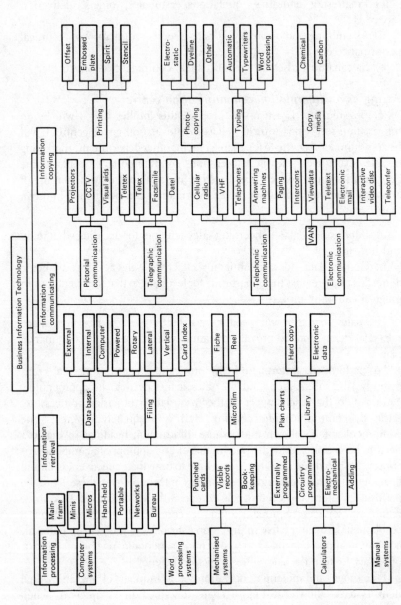

Fig. 9.1 The component parts of business information technology

Sales and product support

The sales office can provide support to the field sales force by keeping sales personnel supplied with sales literature or sending it to customers on request and letting the sales person concerned know that a request has been made. It should also keep the sales force supplied with other stationery (order forms, calling cards, report forms etc.) with appropriate display material, visual aids for selling, current catalogues and price lists etc.

As the field sales person is very mobile, the sales office should act as the 'fixed letter box' so that the sales person can be contacted. Customers should be encouraged to contact the sales office for information needed rather than waiting for the sales person to call. Sales personnel should be able to 'name' a person in the sales office whom the customer can contact; in fact, in some large companies 'sales correspondents' are appointed to look after the internal administration and the customers of a number of sales persons.

These 'sales correspondents' or other designated persons in the sales office should be responsible for keeping the sales person informed with regard to stock availability, delivery times, monitoring the progress of orders and contacting the sales person if unexpected delays are likely or if problems have arisen.

Product support can range from providing product information, supplying technical data sheets and answering customers' product/technical enquiries that can be done by specialist sales office staff to operating a complete product support unit; the latter is dealt with in detail in the next chapter. Product demonstrations, installation, maintenance, spares and repairs service may be included in this particular function based on the local sales office.

Acting as a market intelligence/research centre

The sales office can perform this function by obtaining information from internal records, trade journals, financial pages of newspapers, sales personnel field reports, telephone and postal surveys, enquiries, orders, invoices and payments, economic/industrial data, covering similar subjects and markets etc.

The relationship of the sales function with that of marketing research is examined in detail in Chapter 11. But, additionally, the sales office could, if required, make useful contributions covering the following areas of marketing research: product, pricing, packaging, market, competitor, consumer/use, sales, distribution, communication (PR, advertising, sales promotion), environmental, and research involving combinations of these; sales research is particularly pertinent for sales personnel and the sales manager.

The continuous analysis of sales should be a normal everyday activity of any sales office and there are a number of basic performance indicators that can be obtained. Facts discovered by such analysis often provide the solutions to many sales problems, much of the data being found within company files. It is merely a matter of the sales office extracting them and processing them into a usable form.

There are many basic performance indicators that can be obtained:

(a) sales volume by broad and/or product group
(b) area sales volume and potential
(c) time period sales volume, in units and value
(d) price/sales volume
(e) channels of distribution
(f) order size statistics
(g) cost data
(h) sales potential
(i) stock control data
(j) analysis of product mix
(k) analysis of buying habits by key accounts

These examples do not exhaust the range of possible headings under which past and proposed future data can be obtained from within a company. Other basic control indicators can be seen in the previous chapter (Chapter 8).

Market and sales forecasting unit

'Market and sales forecasting concerns the potential and prospective sales volume/value for the individual product (company), and sets a sales goal in an anticipated market within the overall economy.'*

Its importance is emphasised because a market/sales forecast should form the basis of all financial budgets in a company as ultimately all budgets depend to a certain extent on an estimate of the number of products/services the company is likely to sell. The amount of overhead costs per unit will depend on the spread of fixed costs over the predicted sales volume/value, and the setting of expected sales against expected costs will affect profit forecasts.

To the sales manager, market and sales forecasting will be particularly important and this relationship will be dealt with in depth in a later chapter.

But as a function of the sales office, the forecasting of sales potential nationally and by geographic region will help the sales manager to identify market share in specific market segments and to design feasible-sized sales territories for sales personnel. Actual sales forecasts for particular sales territories can be calculated objectively using a series of appropriate statistical/mathematical methods and these can be compared with the subjective forecasts of individual sales personnel.

The sales office can therefore produce a short/medium/long-term forecast

---

* G. J. Bolt, *Market and Sales Forecasting—a Total Approach.* Kogan Page Ltd, 1981, p. 26.

for the sales manager using a number of techniques to make comparison, so that forecasts for forthcoming sales periods or re-forecasts for the present period are constantly available.

Acting as a selling by telephone unit

All sales offices have the potential for this function to a greater or lesser extent simply by having a telephone. There is a sales opportunity when the customer takes the initiative and telephones to either obtain information, or place an order, or make a complaint. There is a planned sales opportunity when the telesales person takes the initiative and telephones customers and potential customers with the objective of carrying out a variety of tasks, e.g. to sell a product and/or service, to obtain a sales appointment, to obtain or give information, to handle or sell on a complaint.

The telephone is a powerful sales method that can be operated as a function of the sales office, and the general approach and specific techniques are dealt with in a special section of the next chapter.

Adopting a direct marketing role

Sometimes a company may identify a widespread segment of a market, the consumer/users in which buy in very small quantities or buy infrequently or once only, that would not warrant the cost of a sales person calling. In total, the sales turnover may be substantial and very profitable.

The sales approach may be made through direct marketing which means through advertising either in the national or trade press or through the mail. In the former case (provided the 'deal' offered is right), success will depend on whether the national newspaper or trade journal reaches the right people and in the latter case (mail) it will depend on how good is the mailing list.

The sales office can be used to place advertisements (suitably key coded to assess the success and timing of them), receive, progress and despatch orders. The attraction of this type of selling/marketing is that only interested customers respond, sending a cheque with the order. By using an 'allow 28 days for delivery' message, the activity can be easily integrated with other sales office functions.

Recruitment and training of sales personnel

The recruitment and training of sales personnel was dealt with in depth in Chapter 4. The role of the sales office in this process will depend on the size of the sales force and the needs of the company.

With a small sales force, the recruitment will be done by the sales manager using the secretarial services of the sales office to place advertisements, make appointments etc. In these circumstances, formal training will tend to be done on external courses with on-the-job training done by the sales manager.

With a large sales force, the recruitment may be done either centrally or delegated down to regional or area managers with the administration aspects being covered by their regional or area offices. The initial and formal training aspect may be carried out at a central training unit; alternatively, this function may be delegated to areas or regions with sales trainers based at these offices.

The sales office can be seen as a focal point for training, maintaining and updating sales training manuals, arranging courses for sales personnel internally and externally, hosting or arranging for sales meetings, being the base for sales trainers and possibly providing space for a training room.

Adopting a public/consumer relations role

Public relations (PR) is about favourably projecting a corporate image or dealing with adverse publicity detrimental to the company name, image, products, brands, services etc. While the company Head Office may have a PR officer/manager/department to deal with it countrywide, at regional, area or district level it will be the local sales office who will have to project the national PR policy and deal with local public problems. In Chapter 6 (page 161), it was said that the sales person has three things to sell, the product/service combination, himself/herself as a consultant, and the company; it is in the latter area that the local sales office needs to 'cover' the PR activity so that the sales person has a 'company image' to sell.

Consumer relations/services can range from the sales offices listening to customers, dealing with their enquiries/complaints to a fully developed customer services department (dealt with in detail in the next chapter) that covers before- and after-sales service and customer information.

Adopting a physical distribution role

In many companies, products are delivered from factories and/or central or regional warehouses direct to customers. In others, goods are distributed in bulk from central locations to area/district sales offices/warehouses acting as strategic stock centres so that goods for orders obtained by the sales force based on a particular local sales office can be supplied without delay so as to meet or beat competitors' delivery services. Sometimes this will involve showroom/display facilities, stock planning and control, and even the operation of delivery lorries or vans for the local sales office to perform this function.

Adopting a credit control role

Most sales personnel will be told in their training that a sale is not complete until the product/service combination has been delivered and payment for it received by the company. The credit control role of the sales office can range from checking financial references obtained from the customer by the sales person when an account is opened and reminding sales personnel of payments due, to a fully developed credit control unit (described in detail in the next chapter) in which 'credit controllers' contact customers, reminding or pressing for payment monies due to the company. Some companies perceive the customer/sales person relationship as one of close working/ friendship/mutual trust, not to be 'soured' in any way (even temporarily) by the latter having to ask/press for payment. The problems of having to ask/press for money is therefore passed to a third party, the sales controller, leaving the customer/sales person relationship intact.

The activity approach

Depending on the particular needs of a company, the sales office may be required to carry out special activities, but the basic ones would include:

(a) order recording

(b) order processing (preparation of paper work and control)

(c) entering data into customer records

(d) scrutinising and recording individual sales persons' activities, routes, expenses, commissions, bonuses etc.

(e) computing estimates, quotations, prices, discounts, tax etc.

(f) handling customer and general enquiries, progressing quotations, setting up contracts

(g) keeping statistical records, making returns and providing reports

(h) handling sales persons' itineraries, in some cases routing field sales personnel

(i) passing on sales leads to the appropriate sales person

(j) arranging telephone sales call schedules

(k) making appointments for field sales personnel

(l) recording territory data, journeys, group work

(m) keeping a sales office diary and reminder system

(n) scrutinising and processing reports from sales persons and sales supervisors and identifying the need for action

(o) carrying out liaison between the sales team and production (or suppliers), the accounts section, management and customers

(p) operating sales budgets

(q) keeping and updating files of sales personnel etc.

In a number of companies, a dynamic approach to these activities has been adopted. The basic feature of this approach is that the sales office operations should not be viewed as a passive enquiry-to-order process; it should be a process by which sales office staff are allowed to show initiative, and one in which the results can be seen and appreciated by all those involved.

The sales office should play an active part in selling as well as in administration. The relationship between sales office and customers can be seen in the following activities.

Customer identification

Sales office staff should be concerned with the tactical identification and development of individual customers after the overall market has been calculated and defined (perhaps by marketing research). This tactical function can be carried out through desk research to establish possible sales contacts. This ensures that the fullest sales involvement is achieved, that the expertise and experience of the sales activity is brought to bear on appropriate contacts, and also that the field sales force is given service in the most acceptable manner. Such a sales activity can ensure that the first field call on a new contact is effective. It will also help to eliminate wasted sales calls.

Enquiries and quotations

This activity is concerned with the receipt and analysis of enquiries from various sources, and the transmission of these into meaningful and attractive offers. For example, when a request for sales literature/technical data sheets is received, it shows potential customer interest and is an opportunity to sell/elicit a quotation (obtain an order). In the passive office, the literature is sent usually with an anonymous compliments slip. In the dynamic sales office, the sales opportunity is seized by suggesting one or more of a number of positive actions. The sales office person can suggest that the named receiver of the literature takes one of the following specific actions:

(a) order immediately (to avoid disappointment, to obtain benefits, to obtain quick delivery)
(b) ask for a quote
(c) send for a sample
(d) send an order
(e) file for future reference
(f) replace an older out-of-date leaflet (i.e. update the customer's 'library')
(g) read and act in certain ways
(h) pass a copy to R & D, a technical department etc.
(i) include details in their own catalogues, sales literature etc.
(j) put a copy into their 'library'
(k) tell us how many extra copies they need for other executives, branch offices or departments
(l) pass to a colleague
(m) give copies to all their sales force
(n) look at, read and act in a certain way
(o) say that a sales person will follow up this request for literature

With regard to formal quotations, some form of presentation is necessary. Rarely does this form of submission to a customer receive the same thought and attention as is given to the sales person's presentation. The formal offer is frequently the first intimation of price and of the full potential benefits to reach the customer, but is often worded, e.g. 'One off–Cat. No. –C49/978–Broaching machine with various attachments–£950–delivery . . . a.s.a.p.'. The transformation of this jargon into something carrying a sales message is not difficult. The benefits offered by the product should be built into the quotation so that anyone about to criticise the price cannot avoid reading of the advantages that will arise from buying the product in question.

It is also necessary to indicate quotations that require special follow-up activity by the sales force. It may be known, for example, whether or not a customer has an order to place, or whether he is among seven other sub-contractors submitting a price for a project at the planning stage that is already being adequately followed up with the main contractors.

Order, appraisal and analysis

The responsibility here is to ensure that orders are compatible with items on offer and, additionally, that the potential for ancillary or supplementary equipment or other company products is not ignored. Most orders are an indication of demand for other items in addition to the one on the order itself, and the sales office receiving it should be alert to the possibility of obtaining further business. Frequently, after effort has been spent in achieving a sale of an item of capital plant, the purchaser is willing to supplement his order with a quantity of maintenance spares or even a maintenance contract. The pursuit of an order for spares (if appropriate) or related items should be, therefore, a normal activity of the sales office.

Order progressing

The aim of this activity must be to avoid delayed deliveries or at least convert a failure to provide delivery on time into a relative success by the manner in which a customer is told of the impending delay. This is one of the most difficult areas in which to maintain morale in the sales office, and the difficulty is compounded if the company continually breaks its promises. Customers are usually prepared to accept rational explanations, rather than the conventional 'it will be another two weeks, and I am afraid I don't know any more about it'.

Order follow-up

This function is to follow and exploit orders after delivery when there is likely to be a need for servicing and ancillary equipment. Repeat orders may be possible following the successful completion of the first transaction and continued contact will ensure the development of a favourable customer relationship.

Each member of the sales office should be given the satisfaction of actually winning an order or at least have played an identifiable part in it. Obviously, there are difficulties in this approach, because it means that each member of the department must be trained in a much wider range of skills.

However, this should be regarded as an advantage in the sense that the existence of a body of highly trained and motivated personnel must be an asset to any company as a source of future field sales personnel and management potential.

The systems approach

The identification of a need for, and the setting up of, a series of processes performed in a prescribed sequence forming a complex or unitary whole, which transforms an input into an output.

Such sales office systems can be passive (i.e. one that merely administers sales) or dynamic (i.e. one that actively solicits sales or follows up sales or actually tries to extend the business, or that causes other parts of the sales function to be more effective in developing sales). The latter could incorporate a lead-getting component for sales personnel or have a direct selling role, e.g. by telephone selling. An elementary example of a dynamic sales office system is shown in Fig. 9.2.

The behavioural approach

This approach considers the sales office as a human and sociological system, i.e. it recognises the levels and types of persons in the system, their relationships within the groupings, with other departments, and with customers. Such systems must be designed to minimise conflict and maximise co-operation and co-ordination. This type of system must have in-built motivations, job satisfactions, job development, and financial and non-financial incentives.

All effective systems work through well-motivated people.

The organisation approach

Just as planning (by setting objectives and establishing policies and procedures) is the basis of effective sales office administration, so organisation is its framework. This approach to the sales office operations is through its organisational framework.

Organisation is concerned with the definition of:

(a) the responsibilities of managers and other personnel employed in an organisation; and

(b) the inter-relationships established because of these responsibilities.

Whenever more than one person is involved in any aspect of a business, organisational problems arise, and the sales office is no exception.

For effective organisation of the sales office, there must be clearly defined areas of responsibility for individuals and groups, and for the relationships

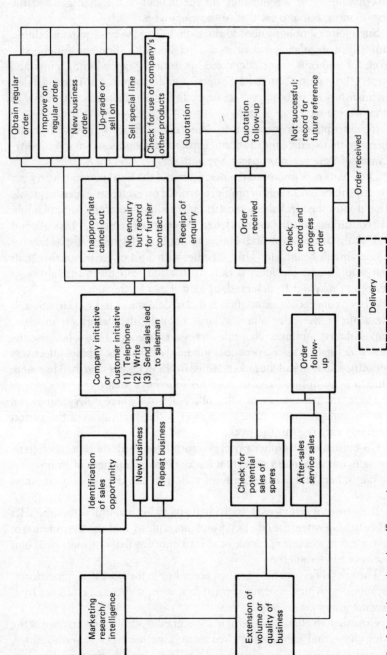

Fig. 9.2 A dynamic sales office system

between them. These areas are best defined through the medium of job descriptions; these are not only for the benefit of the manager and the organisation, but also for that of the employee.

Such job descriptions need to show the title of the post, responsibilities, duties (key, regular and occasional), relationships (line and functional), scope of authority (over operations, personnel, expenditure, terms and prices), limitations, immediate superior and subordinates (if applicable), membership of committees, remuneration and other benefits, terms of employment etc.

Job descriptions are necessary to clearly define the work and also to ensure there is no overlapping and no gaps in organisational responsibility. Examples were given on pages 257 and 258.

Organisation is improved if a description of the ideal person to carry out the sales office task (a person profile) is evolved for each post. A person profile should show the ideal characteristics and qualifications for a particular job, i.e. education, vocational knowledge, experience necessary, physical effort and skill, adaptability and concentration, intelligence, disposition or temperament, health etc. This, together with a list of the personality traits that would make the ideal person for the job, will mean that although perfection may not be achieved, at least it can be the aim.

A basic concept of organisation is that of delegation and specialisation. If the scale of the sales office is large enough, the delegation of tasks, responsibility, authority etc. will increase efficiency. This is because the duties delegated to a specialist subordinate will be more effectively performed, and so will the tasks retained by the delegator who then has more time to perform them and manage his functional area.

There are some areas in sales office activity where delegation is not feasible and, in such a case, the answer is the duplication of the person currently carrying out the work.

Co-ordination is another aspect of organisation and is the process whereby the sales office manager or section leader develops a pattern of group effort among others and secures unity of action in the pursuit of a common purpose.

It also means getting each individual and individual unit within the sales office to understand the other's job and motivations, and also the fostering of co-operation wherever possible or at least ensuring that one individual unit does not hinder another.

The sales office can be organised according to the work type, procedures, locations, activities, systems, support functions, sequences, customer type, product group etc.

Organisation charts are useful to show graphically the organisation of the sales office, and can also be used to indicate the types of relationships. Examples were given on pages 7 and 54. These include direct relationships (i.e. that of superior and subordinate), functional relationships (i.e. certain advisory or specialised relationships, perhaps that of a credit controller, under an established arrangement, advising a despatch clerk to hold back delivery and where the despatch clerk is responsible to his own section head). These relationships can be lateral (i.e. between persons of fairly equal status in the organisation but performing different functions) and they can be of a staff relationship (i.e. the personal assistant to the sales office manager has no authority of his own but derives it through carrying out work on behalf of the manager).

To summarise, the function of organisation in the sales office is that of balancing and keeping together the team, developing authoritative procedures, ensuring the suitable allocation of tasks to the various members, and seeing that these are performed with due harmony.

The management approach

Another way of looking at the operations of the sales office is through the scope of the sales office manager's job and his particular management style.

The Institute of Administrative Management defines office management or administrative management as '. . . that branch of management which is concerned with the services of obtaining, recording and analysing information, of planning, and of communicating, by means of which the management of a business safeguards its assets, promotes its affairs, and achieves its objectives'.

By implication, the effective management of the sales office is carried out by:

(a) Planning – by setting objectives, evolving policies and developing procedures.

(b) Organising and co-ordinating resources ('Men, machines, methods, and money' etc.).

(c) Communicating, motivating and supervising.

(d) Measuring performance, interpreting results and controlling, by taking corrective or remedial action on time.

(e) Development of staff and *self*.

To examine the operations of the sales office through the role of the manager presumes knowledge of the objectives of the role, a description of the job and a profile of the person most likely to succeed in that job.

The decision-making approach

Historically, the sales office has been concerned with 'housekeeping' and routine matters, but in recent years in many cases the nature of the sales office has changed in the sense that it has become increasingly involved with the capture, storage, retrieval and manipulation of data on which sales management decisions are made. In the past, such decisions were subjective/intuitive rather than objective, corporate and based on good data.

The basic functions/activities of such a decision-making office approach was examined and outlined* as follows.

Every office concerned with management decision-making carries out the same set of functions, although the relative importance of any single function and the time spent on it, will vary from office to office and project to project. These activities can be summarised under the following headings.

Data search – the collection of relevant information. In a manual system, hard copy is the normal source. The amount of time spent in this activity is a key indicator to the technology required.

Data input – the transfer of gathered information to a working document, such as a work sheet, report or set of notes.

Data validation – the review and verification of gathered information.

Data presentation – the conversion of gathered information into reports, tables or graphic presentations, for use by management in decision-making.

Data distribution – the dissemination of the information to personnel concerned.

These five functions are all areas in which technology can be used to improve performance. To these must be added two essentially human activities.

Thinking – productive or creative thinking is one thing that an office automation system cannot accomplish, but the use of office automation can release valuable time by freeing executives from mundane or routine tasks.

Administration – managing, counselling and planning are essential organisational activities, which office automation can assist but not replace.

. . . The long term solution is undoubtedly a totally integrated system which will, with equal facility, handle the routine structured chores of the office and the less structured processes of decision-making, plus the interchange of information between them.

Although the above comments are in the main in the context of manual systems, another dimension is added when information technology is added; see first part of the next chapter.

The automated sales office approach

The term automation originally defined as '. . . automatic control of the manufacture of a product through successive stages . . .' has been latterly extended to cover the use of machinery to save mental and manual labour in all areas of company activity. In the context of the sales office and the present state of high technology, it implies an electronically perceived, logical, systematic and pre-determined sequence of actions, automatically followed through from initiation to completion and including, if necessary, the identification and correction of errors.

The automated sales office is particularly relevant to the needs of the sales manager and the sales/marketing aspects of a company. The variety of activities described earlier in this chapter translated into the context of the

---

* 'The aims of office automation'. International Data Corporation in the special supplement 'The wired workplace', *Management Today*, December 1983.

automated office are reflected in a multitude of equipment functions. Some of these are computing, word processing, electronic typewriters and printers, mailing list, management, microcomputers, spread sheet budgeting, electronic mail, graphics, voice mail, electronic calendars, person and company electronic filing, electronic telephone systems and telex, information retrieval, colour reprographics, fax (facsimile) transmission, database access, videotex (e.g. teletext or viewdata).

The key to the automated sales office, however, is the function of comprehensive in-company information sharing and the answer to providing this are integrated systems which interconnect the functions and technologies mentioned above. Integrated systems jump the gap between the single function, dedicated single function, stand-alone or cluster activity and integrated, inter-related, communicating systems, although they may, in fact, be operated through comprehensive work stations working on a network.

Larger companies tend to be closely linked to central data-processing systems as all mainframe manufacturers now offer software capable of providing a high degree of integration and automated sales office potential. For the medium-sized companies, the minicomputer manufacturers have also seized the opportunity of offering integrated office systems. The intense competitive pressures in the microcomputer sector have caused both hardware and software companies to develop systems that enable the smallest companies to realise at least some of the benefits of the automated/integrated office concepts.

With so much new technology already available and beginning to be exploited, much of what will happen in the development of the automated sales office will depend on economic circumstances and the degree to which society and business accepts changes in employment, social and work patterns. But three factors seem certain for the future. First, the spread of the automated sales office will enhance rather than detract from the opportunity for creative office work. Second, automation will not be achieved without planning and organisational change. Third, greater management/organisational expertise, more technical knowledge and better planning will be needed to cope with the growing quantity of office information systems and complexity of the automated sales office.

Adapting sales office systems

Sales office administration must support the overall objectives of the sales/marketing plan and the activities of the company's sales function. Sales managers must therefore be prepared to update and/or re-organise existing arrangements or introduce new systems. Before it is possible to do this, the existing organisation/administration/system needs to be analysed in relation to the company's own and market needs on the basis of its strengths that can be retained or built upon and its weaknesses/faults that need correcting or eliminating.

Weaknesses/faults in particular need to be identified, e.g. bad, poor, slow information systems and communication, unreasonable delays in handling customer enquiries, quotations, orders, complaints; slow information processing and retrieval, inadequate management information, lack of clear lines of responsibility, authority and accountability, poor organisation and inadequate co-ordination and other appropriate criteria.

Often it will be found that the present systems do not support current system objectives, and future objective setting can be simplified by looking at the underlying reasons for changing and/or automating. Some examples are shown in Fig. 9.3. *

Slogan	Basis	Typical habitat	Typical focus	Aim	Typical targets
Cheaper	Office as overhead	Manufacturing and extractive industries	Clerical and junior staff	Cost control	1. Labour costs 2. Bought-in services 3. Space
Better	Office as production area	Large service organisation (bank, insurance company)	Staff up to supervisor or junior manager levels	Efficiency	1. Turn-around time 2. Level of service 3. Speed of decision
New	Office as strategic resource	Small to medium service organisation (research unit, designers)	Entire office population	Effectiveness	1. Type of product 2. Market served 3. Working arrangements
Policy	Office as display area	Any (but especially IT suppliers, advertising)	Anywhere in the organisation	Image improvement	1. Staff morale 2. Corporate image 3. Response to external pressure

Fig. 9.3. Office automation reasons, and their habitats

Having identified the problems/clear aims/objectives, then guidelines need to be set, the total volume of present and future administrative work assessed, alternatives examined with regard to the balance between machines, systems and human resources; decisions made as to the optimum solution in the light of cost–benefit analysis and the cost in human terms (work satisfaction, rewards, quality of life, over-specialisation, work

* Roger Whitehead, 'Getting IT right', *Administration*, the Journal of the Institute of Company Secretaries and Administrators, May 1985, p. 7.

monotony etc.). From all this, the general sales manager, in conjunction with the sales administration manager or supervisor, should be able to produce a new sales administration plan and organisation with a built-in monitoring and evaluation system.

Summary

Good administration can enhance the effectiveness of the sales function and its operations; poor administration can adversely affect the performance of the sales team which, in turn, could affect sales volume, cash flow and, ultimately, profitability. Realisation of this should cause the sales manager to give a high priority to effective administration and yet take action to ensure that administrative activities are delegated to specialist personnel and as far down the organisation as possible. This will ensure that those administrative functions retained will be better performed and that the sales manager has more time to develop policies and strategies appropriate to the changing needs of the company and the market-place. It will also give the sales manager more time to lead and inspire the sales team.

Examples were given of how the sales manager can delegate administrative tasks functionally, centrally, geographically, organisationally, territorially and combinations of these.

The amount of administration to be done, the amount that can be delegated and the actual administrative role is affected by the current stage of the company development life-cycle. The amount of sales administration will also depend upon the size of the company, the size of the sales function and its scope of operations, and the number of support activities for which the sales manager is responsible, e.g. a telephone sales operation, merchandising in retail outlets, customer service.

The sales office selling role as well as its administrative role and whether its approach is passive or dynamic will all affect its ability to support selling operations and the sales manager. The actual activities and operations of sales administration were reflected in the chapter by an examination of eight different approaches to sales administration. These approaches covered functions, activities, systems, behaviour, organisation, management, decision-making and automation which all have their part to play depending on the role of the sales function and the needs of the company, internally and in the market-place.

Finally, consideration was given to updating and/or re-organising existing administrative arrangements and introducing new systems. The method is to identify strengths and weaknesses, set new objectives in the context of existing and future sales administration expectations, examine alternative ways of achieving the objectives, develop strategies and the organisation structure necessary together with a monitoring and evaluation system.

Questions

1. What are the six ways in which the sales manager can delegate administrative tasks?

2. What are the various factors that determine the amount of administration to be carried out or delegated by the sales manager during the various stages in the life of a company?

3. Identify the differences between a passive and a dynamic sales office.

4. What are the eight different approaches to sales office operation? Indicate the importance of five of them in relation to the needs of a sales manager in an industry of your choice.

5. What are the likely future developments of the automated sales office in the light of developments in current information technology?

6. What are the stages that should be followed in adapting sales office systems?

CHAPTER 10

Sales support activities

Objectives

This is a composite chapter made up of six areas of activity. The only common factor that links them to sales management is the fact that they can all play an important support role to the sales function of a company. The chapter covers:

(a) *Information technology services* which examine the help and support the sales manager can derive from communications, information and computing systems and equipment.

(b) *Selling by telephone* and/or *telemarketing* which can be viewed as a self-contained sales/marketing activity or as a sales support activity to the field sales force.

(c) *Credit control*–this is based on decisions of an organisation as to the amount of credit and the credit period it will allow its customers. This is often influenced by past custom, the accepted practice in an industry, the amount of credit competitors are willing to give, as well as by the credit assessment and monitoring of individual customers. Credit control affects cash flow and discount/pricing structure but favourable credit terms are also a sales promotional tool.

(d) *Customer service*–is examined in the context of it being all the benefits of value to a company's customers, additional or ancillary to the main product or service contained in the 'total deal' sold by an organisation.

(e) *Merchandising*–is dealt with in relation to selling product/service combinations through middle men and/or retailers and around the definition of it being psychological persuasion at the point of purchase without the aid of a sales person.

(f) *Product support facilities* are particularly important sales support activities in the selling/marketing of industrial, scientific and technical products and consumer durables.

Because of the diverse nature of these six areas of sales support activity, summaries are given at the end of each.

Information technology services/systems

Like their counterparts in other functions of a business, sales managers need a substantial amount of information at the right time in a usable form. Without it they could not hope to plan, forecast, organise and co-ordinate, supervise and control, their current and future sales activities and profitability. However, unlike the more structured world of production, design, finance and accounting, the information required in the sales/ market area is more varied, complicated and often more difficult to obtain.

Sales/marketing, in dealing with the problems of identification and satisfaction of ever-changing consumer and organisation user demands, cannot resolve the information issue from a set of static procedures based only on past history and naive extrapolations. The successful sales manager must solve problems that include those that are highly subjective, are difficult to analyse, are imperfectly understood, are continually evolving, of differing priorities and are of varying magnitude.

To deal with such situations, the sales manager needs to develop information systems, the main aims of which should be to provide more accurate and up-to-date market/sales information, to increase the productivity of the sales force, to improve customer services and to reduce administrative costs, that in turn lead to increased sales, improved market share and greater profitability.

Information technology (IT) has developed and can be used by the sales manager to achieve these aims. IT has been defined as '. . . the transmission, processing and display of information to those who need it. . . .' Also, '. . . as the acquisition, processing, storage, dissemination of vocal, pictorial, textural and numerical information by microelectronics based combinations of computing and telecommunications. . . .' It has been further defined as '. . . any communication, information, computing system or equipment that enables the sales manager to achieve the optimum level of performance of the sales team. . . .' If these definitions are analysed, most sales managers will recognise they carry out the activities implied already; it is simply that IT helps them do it more extensively, efficiently, quickly and in far greater depth and breadth.

Obviously computing, information and communications systems and/or equipment operating anywhere within the sales function of a company will impinge on the activities of the sales office. Integrated systems were mentioned in the previous chapter when considering the 'automated office approach', but it needs to be recognised that truly integrated sales management systems need to include systems/equipment used outside the sales office, e.g. hand-held or portable computers operated by field sales persons. Also they need to support communications, information and computing in five forms: data, text, graphics, image and voice.

Practical information support

The areas in which types of information systems can help the sales manager are:

(a) Sales and market history, performance, analysis by region, product, individual sales person, sales type etc. against target, recording of new sales.
(b) Market and sales forecasts.
(c) Competitor history, performance, analysis and projections.
(d) Market share, history performance and analysis.
(e) Pricing history and analysis.
(f) The various budgets and expenses.
(g) Sales/market modelling.
(h) Sales force control.
(i) Territory planning, journey cycle and sales force routing.
(j) Source of enquiry, replies, quotations, analysis and conversions.
(k) Customer and prospects records.
(l) Sending and receiving communications.
(m) Mail-shot printing, addressing.
(n) Advertising response monitoring.
(o) Monitoring of leads.
(p) Sales accounting.
(q) Order processing, invoicing and statements.
(r) Access to internal and external data bases
      and many others.

In fact, information systems and technology can help the sales manager with most of the planning, operating, supervising, monitoring and control activities mentioned in earlier chapters.

Relevant IT systems and equipment

There is a wide variety of IT systems/equipment that is already available and becoming available from which the sales manager can choose. Technology is developing so rapidly in the information, communication and computing areas that almost any comment on available equipment/systems tends to be out-of-date very quickly. However, a list of such systems would include the following.

Computers

Mainframe equipment
This is usually found in medium/large companies, forming the basis of the

central data-processing system; the sales manager could access it by a remote terminal.

Minicomputers

These are usually found in medium-sized companies either operating singly or forming part of a network of area sales offices or integrated office systems of which the sales office would be a part.

Microcomputers

These are often found in small companies or networking in medium-sized companies. Where found in large companies, they are either used in a 'stand-alone' interactive mode or can be used to interface with a mainframe computer as one of its terminals when not being used 'independently'.

Hand-held or portable computers

These are often given to sales personnel to improve their performance. For example, an application of the hand-held computer in the area of fast-moving consumer goods is for the direct input of orders, calculating terms, or as a two-way communications facility with the sales office, e.g. routing, product and price updating, call-backs and details of daily work sheets; they can also be used to prompt sales personnel to ask the right questions. In the life insurance industry, they are used by sales personnel to demonstrate to prospective clients the way life insurance/pension schemes work and provide on-the-spot quotations and comparisons. In the industrial equipment area, they can be used for calculating/estimating quotations of various alternative product/service combinations, emphasising financial package options, demonstrating various pay-back and discounted cash flow options, tax implications, examining different time-scale implications, trade-in values of old equipment etc.

Software packages

There are standard software programs designed to handle functions such as word processing, sales force control, sales forecasting etc. However, very few businesses have 'standard' requirements and software has to be adjusted to fit the needs of a particular business and a particular sales team, or the operation of the business has to be adjusted to fit the software, or special software has to be 'tailor-made' for the business. Software packages appropriate for the sales manager and sales office cover:

    (a) Word processing.
    (b) Mailing list management.
    (c) Graphics (for presenting data diagrammatically).
    (d) Spreadsheets – figures are shown horizontally and vertically; adjust one figure and all the others are adjusted automatically. They can be useful for budgeting, forecasting, 'what if' questions, determining the size of sales

force, allocating territories, designing remuneration plans, evaluating sales persons etc.

(e) Personal and company filing.
(f) Databases (for storing, sorting and finding information).
(g) Communications.
(h) Electronic mail
(i) Scheduling.

A number of software packages specifically designed for the sales/ marketing area are available and three that are particularly appropriate were reviewed by David Bailey.*

'Sales Generator' from Kalamazoo-Gilbert

. . . has been designed in modular form and provides four main elements: management information, territory account management, control of enquiries and quotations and a marketing data base for customers and prospects. All four modules can be used, integrated or on a stand alone basis, and can be linked to word-processing, graphics or spreadsheets. . . .

'Salesfacts' by Q Mark Systems is a package

. . . designed for high value industries such as electronics, computer service, telecommunications, defence and financial and professional services. A common feature will be a lengthy sales cycle, a tradition of a managed sales force with clearly identifiable products and prospects, and a definite requirement for tight control over sales activity, involving regular monthly reviews.

The Salesfacts cycle commences with the issue of prospect documentation produced by the system for all sales personnel. Armed with this information on the potential customer, the sales person makes his/her call and records the results, which are then fed back into the system. An important factor of this package is that the sales person is required to estimate the probability of success in obtaining an order, and to identify the buying/selling status of the prospect.

These assessments will be considered by the area or field Sales Manager and their review with the salesmen/women and can be amended as necessary. In addition, they can draw on on-demand reports from the system to assist with the review. At the end of this stage the system produces revised sales forecasts, tracks key dates and produces month-end reports, covering territories and prospects, that give an overview of trends and opportunities, thus enabling management to review the progress of the sales and marketing function. . . .

'Sales Director' from Beck Systems has the aim of providing

. . . better control over the sales force and to give management more information on customers, contacts and enquiries. On receiving an enquiry which is defined as 'an interest in the company's products expressed by a customer or potential customer', an enquiry number is allocated by the system, which goes on to produce a letter or quotation, as appropriate. The enquiry number and action taken are held within the system until the final outcome of the enquiry.

A 'shuttle report' is then produced, which gives full details of the enquiring company, plus a history of all other live enquiries from the same source. These

* David Bailey, 'Disks with extra byte', *Marketing*, 9 January 1986, pp. 34–5.

details are printed out and sent to the sales person. When he/she visits the potential customer, the results of his/her call are entered on the duplicate of the 'shuttle report', giving details of products the prospect might order, quantities, price and expected date of order. The sales person also enters a confidence rating anticipating the probable outcome of the order.

The new information is fed into the system; it produces an up-dated 'shuttle report', which goes back to the sales person, and the up-dated enquiry now forms the basis of hot list and order forecast reports. . . .

Systems/devices

(a) Operating systems control the basic functions of the computer, and software has to be written (or adapted) for a particular operating system (e.g. CPM or MSDOS are two popular systems).

(b) The mouse is a relatively simple hardware device enabling the user to move the cursor rapidly to any part of the visual display screen by manipulating a 'rolling ball'. Software developed to work with the mouse means that by moving the cursor to a display point on the screen that indicates an action to be taken, such as filing or printing, and then pressing an appropriate key, a whole series of activities can be initiated which would otherwise require many keystrokes.

(c) Windowing; this permits the sales manager or sales office to refer to other pieces of work when working on a current job; in effect, 'opening a window' on to any information contained in the computer, while working on one set of data information from elsewhere, can be used to check results.

(d) Multi-user facility allows work on the same project to be shared out between members of the sales office team at different computer terminals.

(e) Concurrency is a system that allows the sales office person (or sales manager) to switch easily from one job to another without having to save one aspect of a job and then call up another.

(f) Networking is a system that allows the linking up of one computer to another. This allows for the sharing of peripheral devices such as printers and plotters in different offices at one location and/or the sharing of information at one or a number of geographically spread locations (e.g. area sales offices).

(g) A modem is a device that allows one computer unit to communicate with another through the medium of the ordinary telephone system and is particularly useful for the passing of data between sales units at different geographical locations.

(h) Plotters are devices that allow computers to produce line drawing printouts of data that has been assembled and processed and stored.

In practical terms, information computing systems that are appropriate for sales managers fall into three main categories that are determined not only by their nature (i.e. whether they are passive or dynamic), but also by their 'question-answering' power.

At the passive level there are database, data storage and retrieval systems which enable data to be accumulated internally by the company or externally by specialists (e.g. Magic, Harvest etc.) that can be easily accessed and instantly obtained when needed. These make it easier for the sales manager to bring relevant accumulated data to bear on special questions and problems, and on general decision-making.

At a slightly more dynamic level are monitoring/tracking systems which provide on a continuous basis or at discrete time periods (e.g. daily, weekly, monthly) control-type information that indicates whether operations in progress are going according to plan (e.g. an individual sales person's sales figures or total sales/profits in a particular product or geographic area).

At the most dynamic level are the analytical/interactive information systems which not only provide data and monitoring information but are interactive in the sense that they can indicate what will happen to a number of the aspects of a business if one factor is changed. For example, what will happen to demand, profit, stock levels etc. if price is increased by 5 per cent? These systems are designed to supply answers to such questions as what factor(s) caused the changed situation, why did a particular event happen, what actions could offset an adverse event etc. They range from combinations of simple comparisons and cross-tabulations to complex sales/market modelling that evaluate alternative outcomes of business/sales management.

Word processing systems

Equipment which processes and edits text and information by use of a typewriter keyboard (with alphanumeric characters and a number of control keys), display screen, a high-speed printer and a computer memory facility. Some systems have 'full screens' (VDUs) but some have 'window' screens showing only one or a few lines of text. These will allow the operator to see what is being typed and to correct errors or format before printing or input into the memory. There will be varying facilities for inserting and deleting material from the texts and automatic re-alignment of pages, moving blocks of typing from one page to another, and information can be re-organised and printed in different ways. The larger, 'shared logic' systems have a central memory to which several workstations can be attached.

Word processing and word processor/systems are an important aid to the efficiency of the sales office and the sales manager because of their versatility.

There is a choice with regard to the type of equipment available on which to carry out this activity:

(a) The electronic typewriter is the cheapest option but is considered to be only a replacement for the conventional typewriter.

(b) A single-line display system which offers basic editing storage and retrieval functions but has limited interactive capability.

(c) A dedicated word processor with full-screen display that can offer the most complete range of facilities. This type of machine is appropriate if the work involved is heavily document-orientated and involves considerable amounts of correspondence, reports, tenders for orders, quotations, contracts, manuals and other paperwork that may need updating and/or revision, e.g. a paper-intensive sales office.

(d) A word processing software package for use with a personal computer or a mainframe computer terminal. This is appropriate where typewriting is not the main requirement, i.e. as in the case of the sales manager where word processing would be useful for drafting reports but where interactive capability, enquiry, presentation of data, budgeting and forecasting etc. is also required.

Telex

The telex service provides a fast means of printed communication, a copy of the message being produced on teleprinters at both the sending and receiving locations. As a fully-automatic system, immediate connection is made by direct dialling to other subscribers in the UK or worldwide. Messages can be sent or received by a subscriber through an unattended teleprinter which is a particular advantage when sent outside normal business hours or overseas where there may be time differences or differences in working hours.

A telex machine can have its own repeat dialling and word processing facilities, plus a memory for stored messages; it can also be set to send the same message to several addresses automatically.

A development has been that of teletex which is a standard system that links electronic typewriters, office to office. A letter is typed in the normal way, the teletex number is keyed in and a typewriter at the destination types out an exact replica of the original letter.

Low-cost telex systems enable existing microcomputer, word processor or electronic terminals to be transferred into a two-way national or international telex facility.

Photocopiers

Although this type of image copier continues to become more sophisticated (i.e. colour, improved definition and increased speeds), its real breakthrough into the new type of information technology comes with the development of the intelligent copier. This is a device which is a combination of a non-impact printer and a copier that will print output direct from computers and word processors with no hard copy required, but will still be able to make image copies of documents.

Microfilm and microfiche

This is a method of filing, especially useful to sales functions that generate large quantities of written material, and is largely used to provide company 'library' facilities with long-term, relatively cheap storage while occupying a minimum of space. However, it can also be used to provide a sales office/customer/distributor service in the form of technical diagrams and drawings of complex machines, equipment, sub-assemblies and spare parts, in the form of easily accessed and regularly updated information.

Interactive video disc technology

Unlike traditional video systems which simply carry out a one-way communications function, computer-controlled interactive video disc equipment can be used by the sales manager to provide a two-way communications facility for customers and sales personnel. It provides not only the capability and capacity for textual and tabular information but also for graphics, including half-tone pictures; it has the additional advantage of massive storage capacity.

It is useful for two-way communication at exhibitions and trade fairs, point of purchase locations, in electronic retailing of products and/or services, in disseminating public or special group information, for reference by agents/distributors/area sales offices and for a variety of sales staff training applications.

Depending on the degree of sophistication required, some video disc equipment can ask questions, respond to questions and/or answers, analyse individual customer requirements, demonstrate and explain product/ services, help customers make buying and other decisions, and it can provide information (performance, technical data, applications, availability etc.) on any one of hundreds of product/service combinations.

Fax

Facsimile communication equipment permits the transmission (electronically) of messages and/or the reproduction to remote locations of original documents in writing, drawing/graphics, typed or printed form. Improvements in performance and unattended operation for both reception and transmission together with its specialised role of transmitting and receiving in any alphabet (e.g. Arabic, Japanese, Chinese etc.) will make this method of communication very attractive for many sales managers involved in international selling/marketing.

Telephone

A wide range of compact and flexible office telephone systems have been developed to suit every type and size of business; many of these have been linked with desk-top automation.

Private Automatic Branch Exchange (PABX) systems have an automatic internal service as well as an outside line on one telephone. On each extension connected to a PABX it is possible to dial other extensions; and each extension can be given a different status, i.e. all calls must go through the operator, local calls do not need to go through operators, or national calls can be directly dialled, or all calls including international ones can be dialled direct at each extension. Also, the PABX has evolved from a voice-only system to a general communications switch capable of handling voice, video and electronic data for both internal and external communication.

Private digital switching exchanges use electronic systems instead of the mechanical switching of the PABX systems. This means, theoretically, that dependent on the number of circuits installed, each board has the capacity to handle an infinite number of outside lines and extensions and also internal extensions. Information on the status of each extension is shown on a screen (e.g. extension ringing, engaged etc.) and incoming and cleared lines are also indicated by flashing buttons. Incoming or transferred calls can be either automatic or monitored, and additional facilities exist for conference calls, direct dialling on outgoing and internal calls.

With manual, automatic or electronic switchboards, it is possible for sales office tape-recording facilities to be linked into systems so that sales persons, agents, freelance negotiators can feed in orders/enquiries at prescribed times during the day and/or evening that can be later transcribed into 'hard copy' and processed.

However, with a highly mobile sales force and the need for mobility and flexibility of operation of sales executives, there is an obvious need for mobile telephones. Because of the shortage of radio wavebands, the demands of emergency and public services, car telephones have been limited in number and are very expensive.

Cellular radio system

The resolution of the above problems has emerged with the cellular radio system. A relatively small geographic area is divided into a number of discrete cells, each with a transmitter using the higher UHF waveband and transmitting weak signals. The telephone user is detected as he/she moves into a cell and allocated a radio frequency through which it is possible to speak to the exchange or to a called party. As the user's car crosses the boundary to another cell, he/she is automatically allocated another frequency without any interruption of service. The same combination of frequencies will be used in other cells too far away to interfere with the caller's signal.

Such cellular radio systems will be seen as an affordable convenience by many sales executives. Apart from the primary market for voice conversation, there is an important secondary market for the transmission of low-speed data, such as sales orders. These systems will be attractive to any company with highly mobile sales executives and/or a substantial field force of sales personnel, maintenance engineers, merchandisers or delivery vehicles as they can provide higher productivity, more efficient working, improved management and tighter control.

Videotex

This is the generic term to describe two television text systems, teletext and viewdata. Teletext is a one-way, interactive system which uses the television broadcasting system. It exists in the UK as Ceefax (BBC) and Oracle (ITV), is essentially a 'free' service and gives immediate access to commercial data such as exchange rates, stock prices and other useful business information in addition to other information such as weather reports, sports results and other useful social information.

Viewdata is a two-way system using communication land lines (public or private) and a computer/terminal/TV configuration. This type of videotex is best known in the form of the public Prestel service (which offers a wide variety of business-orientated data) although there are many private systems in operation. Viewdata systems provide selective access to a variety of business and other data, some paid for and obtained through special access code numbers and some 'free', although there is still the overhead cost of the service and the cost (where appropriate) in a public system of the telephone call. A useful business development has been the introduction of Gateway systems which allow authorised users to access private viewdata systems.

This system enables sales personnel, through the use of the television set in their own home, to connect with the company's head office computer via the Prestel Gateway system. It is therefore possible for members of a field sales team to enter details of customer's orders at the end of each day, to submit his/her sales activity report, obtain information on stock levels, price changes, promotional offers and discounts.

A variation on this theme is to install a viewdata terminal in the homes of each sales person so that they can enter details of a customer's order. The link mainframe computer confirms that the items are in stock (or indicates the expected delivery delay), initiates sales ledger routines, indicates a picking list for the warehouse and confirms that the customer is creditworthy.

Private viewdata systems are used in providing the sales networks of companies and/or their distributors/agents with information regarding the stock availability and location of models (car manufacturers), plant and equipment, spare parts etc. They are also widely used in the travel and tourism industry to provide travel agents with tour operator information and in the life insurance business to provide sales branches, sales personnel and brokers with information regarding insurance options and rates.

Viewdata systems are beneficial to the sales person and the sales manager as they give access to a large database which can be automatically updated; they reduce the need for, and cost of, data-type newsletters/information sheets; they reduce telephone enquiries and are cheaper and more flexible than a conventional computer terminal network. Also, because such systems are interactive, the sales person can not only obtain information but can react to it by asking other questions and can also give the computer information to act upon.

Electronic mail

This is the delivery of messages by electronic rather than physical means. There are systems that can provide a simple electronic messaging facility between a sales manager and his field sales team. For example, a sales manager enters a customer enquiry, new contact names, updated listings of products or services, or other instructions at any time to await collection. Each evening, the sales person 'accesses' the electronic mail box through a terminal to collect the messages. In the same way, the sales person can enter messages to the sales manager, e.g. new orders, new contact names, enquiries, request for technical data back-up, weekly sales figures, refer to files and data at Head Office etc. Thus electronic mail promotes more effective two-way communications resulting in less time and money spent on telephone calls, fewer visits to head and/or area offices, a quicker response rate etc. It should therefore mean less non-selling time and more time calling on potential and existing customers.

Teleconferencing or videoconferencing systems

These bring together businessmen/women (executives, sales personnel, distributors/agents) in different parts of the country or the world, without the time and expense of travel. Relatively cost-effective systems which carry special video and high- and low-speed data permit communications between two or more centres nationally and/or internationally. It makes for a 'personalised' type of briefing and consultation with colleagues, faster decision-making, greater productivity, and lower travel and other related costs for operating a large but dispersed sales force.

Answering and paging machines

There is a wide range of equipment that can be used to respond to telephone calls to the sales manager and individual members of the sales teams at any time of the day or night. Some are sophisticated to the extent that, without wires or switches, messages can be collected and left for others, and can be repeatedly played back if necessary, and appropriate greetings recorded for callers.

Operating independently or linked with answering machines are the range of radio paging machines that can indicate either that a central point should be contacted or can pass actual messages.

Personal information centres

Basically, this is the bringing together in one unit of a number of the information, communications and computing devices already mentioned. They can range from units that include a high-speed executive telephone with built-in autodialler, directory, memory, call reminder, electronic notepad, electronic diary, clock and four function calculator; to units that include all those features plus telex facility, Prestel screen, messaging terminal with 'automatic send' and 'unattended receipt' facilities, a computer terminal with mainframe access and external services, a 'stand-alone' business computer with business applications packages, concurrency features and instant screen print facility. The degree of sophistication required will depend on the needs of particular sales managers but, where appropriate, the features available in personal information centre units can increase the sales manager's effectiveness.

IT assessment factors

The sales manager needs to audit his/her present information systems and their effectiveness with current needs and those to be catered for in the future. Assumptions may have to be made, uncertainties identified and constraints applied. The sales manager needs to list priorities for the overall information system and/or appropriate sub-systems related to the objectives to be met, develop project timetables and outline specifications, identify decisions to be made and the resources needed. Additionally, the impact on individual sales persons on the sales team and on the organisation needs to be assessed and also the degree of management and other support actions needed. Each alternative sales management IT proposal should be supported by an evaluation of the capital, on-going and maintenance costs, expenditures and expected benefits at each stage, together with an appraisal of likely risks and consequences.

Summary

Introducing or updating information systems and technology within the sales function of a company introduces change. The nature and extent of that change depends not just upon what kind of system or technology is introduced but also upon who introduces it, why, when and how. The kind of information system/technology that may be desirable may not be feasible in practice as it can vary enormously in cost, complexity and the area of application. However, the sales manager needs to develop information systems that provide more accurate and up-to-date market/sales information, that increase the productivity of the sales force, that improve customer services and that reduce administrative costs relatively; all this within the context of increased sales, improved market share and greater profitability.

IT in the form of communication, information and computing systems and equipment can help the sales manager to be more effective in planning, operating, supervising, monitoring and controlling the total sales function; improved quality and quantity of information, more quickly and readily available, makes the opportunity for speedier and more effective decision-making.

There is available a wide range of information technology equipment/systems that can help the sales manager; these include computers of various types (mainframe, mini, micro, hand-held, portable, operating with a variety of software packages and with numerous devices/systems), word processors, telex, fax, telephones, cellular radio, videotex (teletext and viewdata), electronic mail, teleconferences and personal information centres.

Before embarking on any communication, information and computing system project, the sales manager needs to audit the present systems, list priorities for present and future, and make comparative assessments of various options in terms of real and opportunity costs (time and money), and in management and human terms.

Questions

1. Why does the sales manager need effective information systems and what sorts of information should they provide?
2. What is information technology in the context of sales management?
3. What are the potential sales management uses of the various types of equipment/systems available and their advantages and disadvantages?
4. What does the sales manager need to do before adopting new communications, information and computing systems/equipment?

Selling by telephone and/or telemarketing

Earlier (page 267) selling by telephone was mentioned as a sales office activity, identifying two different approaches, i.e. where the customer takes the initiative and telephones the company, and where the 'company' takes the initiative and telephones the customer. This activity can vary from being a small part of a sales office person's day ('answering the 'phone') to being the full-time job of a number of 'telesales' operators with their own supervisor/manager; this section is mainly about activities towards the latter end of this range.

Sales depend on contact with the customer. There are three areas that produce close customer contact: the field sales force, direct mail and telephone selling. However, only in certain types of situations is it possible to 'clinch' a sale over the telephone (telesales), but it has many other roles that can help to make the company more effective in the market-place (e.g. telemarketing).

The telesales operation should be seen as complementing the activities of the field sales force. The obvious value of telephone selling is that it is flexible, rapid and a call can be made in a fraction of the time and at less cost than the field sales person's visit. Further, communication by telephone achieves greater penetration and response than direct mail. It also permits economic repeat calling and call backs. Telephone selling can relieve a company's sales force of time-wasting routine work and enable it to spend more time 'prospecting', concentrating on volume accounts, merchandising etc. In fact, in some segments of a market it may make more economic sense to cover them entirely by selling by telephone. For example, 'telesales' comes into its own in dealing with low unit value products whose potential is very large, highly fragmented and widely dispersed geographically.

Telesales/telemarketing can, in appropriate company/market situations, carry out a wide range of activities; some of these are shown in Fig. 10.1.

As with any system of selling, telesales/telemarketing does not suit every industry, product or service. There are many occasions when it will not work, for instance when goods/services are sophisticated/complex and need to be seen or demonstrated; although in these cases the telesales unit may be used to obtain appointments for a personal call.

Further, with the telephone it is impossible to use the impact of the personal appearance or the subtleties of 'body' language, e.g. facial and gestural movements and the appeal to the other senses of sight, touch, smell and taste. Although in the latter cases it may be possible to link the telesales/telemarketing telephone call to material/samples sent previously by direct mail. Also, it is very easy for the buyer reached by telephone to terminate the conversation by replacing the receiver.

Another disadvantage of the telesales/telemarketing call is that (unlike on

For the company it can	For business relationships it can	For customer relations it can
Optimise field sales staff time for selling, by qualifying prospects and making appointments	Obtain a regular order	Carry out selective sampling
Keep out competition	Sell more than the regular order	Be used to carry out research into customer needs
Service an existing market efficiently by selling to existing customers and handling enquiries	Obtain a 'new business' order	Sell certain types of products/services
Improve goodwill	Up-grade (e.g. increase quality) or enhance an order to 'sell on'	Cause order stimulation/interest
Economically obtain sales leads	Build customer lists	Sell some types of product/services or obtain leads for the field sales force
Achieve better market coverage by re-activating old accounts, introducing new product/services, and opening new accounts	Screen sales leads	Deal with and/or sell on a complaint
Initiate new sales markets	Obtain new contacts and details of buyers	Where appropriate, encourage subscription renewal
Conserve letter-writing by planned telephoning	Sell 'disposables'	Give a quick response to enquiries
Accelerate cash flow by collecting overdue accounts and selling on a complaint call	More easily fit sales call timing to the convenience of buyer's purchasing cycle rather than the sales person's sales calling cycle	Tactfully deal with credit problems and/or overdue accounts
Obtain customer reaction to a new product/service	Ensures retail stocking of products and 'loading up'	Effect 'cross' selling
Obtain useful market research information	Re-activate past and latent accounts	Promote and sell special lines appropriate to customer needs
Generate traffic	Reduce cancellations and returns	Up-grade or enhance an order or enable telesales persons to 'sell on'
Maintain contact with field sales/service personnel	Increase seminar/symposia attendance	Give or obtain information
Enable quick sales/marketing decisions to be made regarding new opportunities, e.g. seasons, weather, new business opportunities etc.	Be used to service marginal or otherwise uneconomic accounts	Where appropriate, encourage membership re-activation
	Act as a direct mail follow-up	Give a personalised approach to customer service
	Act as a credit 'jog'	
	Act as coupon follow-up	

Fig. 10.1 What telesales/telemarketing activities can do

a personal call) the sales person cannot assess the customer by the size and state of his premises, his business potential and stability, and through observation identify his present suppliers.

It is sometimes thought that product/technical knowledge can be a problem for telesales staff. In fact, because telesales persons can be given product/service/technical training or be briefed for special sales drives, or can readily refer to documents/data sheets etc. or a supervisor, or have available computer-aided data input and retrieval system/terminal, in some cases they have a distinct advantage over field sales persons.

Selling by telephone/telemarketing, when properly planned, operated and co-ordinated with other methods of customer contact, is probably the most controllable medium a company can use. Even personal selling by a field sales force is not as susceptible to control; for example, the sales manager cannot be certain that the field sales person will be where he/she is wanted at the time most appropriate to deliver a particular sales message.

The sales manager cannot know exactly how many customers and potential customers have seen a particular TV commercial or poster, or read the press advertisement or direct mail leaflet and perhaps, what is more important, know what the reaction really was.

With the telephone it is possible to ensure that the exact desired message is being communicated, when it needs to be communicated and in the form the sales manager knows works best. Further, it is possible to monitor how it is being delivered, how many messages are reaching their target, what the reaction is and what the results are.

Operational considerations

The adoption of selling by telephone/telemarketing must be preceded by the well-tried management formula of identifying company needs/problems, determining broadly how needs can be satisfied and/or problems solved, the setting of objectives, evolution of strategies and tactics as to how these objectives can be achieved.

Having decided to operate selling by telephone/telemarketing, the sales manager has two alternatives, either to set up his/her own telesales/ telemarketing unit or to employ one of the many external specialist organisations/consultants to conduct the whole operation on behalf of the company.

Generally, an external specialist organisation is most appropriate and economical in situations where a company wishes to make occasional intensive use of the telephone, e.g. for canvassing, a special sales drive or market research purposes, or for obtaining maximum intensive market coverage and impact in a short space of time when launching a new product.

Where the use for such a telesales/telemarketing facility is continuous or where a direct sale, involving a wide range of product/service outlets, is to be made over the telephone, and where it is to be highly integrated with activities of the field sales force or direct mail, it is usually more appropriate that the company should be set up, operate and control the telesales/telemarketing unit itself. For example, in addition to advertising and exhibitions, one large industrial products company uses personal visits by directors and regional managers for large contract users; sales people and direct mail for large users; sales persons for opening medium accounts which are then maintained by direct mail and telesales; for small users, telesales, direct mail, using sales people only to deal with complaints.

This unit can be centrally located and/or divided into sections to handle on a national scale particular product/service combinations, particular customer types (by activity or size) or specific channels of distribution etc. Alternatively, units can be located in sales regions, areas, districts around the country each handling all the appropriate telesales/telemarketing activities in a geographic area.

Personnel for these units are normally mainly female, especially in the fast-moving consumer-goods area. This is because many companies consider that they are better able to get through to the buyer/interviewee, they seem to have a more suitable temperament for telephone work and, once having made contact, they are better able to keep the prospect's interest and have a better chance of 'closing a sale' or getting agreement.

Whether male or female, telesales/telemarketing personnel need to be carefully chosen on the basis of adaptability, intelligence, ability to establish 'support', quality of voice, empathy, personality, ability to get on with people and resilience, in addition to all the other qualities necessary for a sales person as mentioned earlier in Chapter 4.

Also crucial to the effectiveness of a telesales/telemarketing unit is the training of personnel in the art of establishing a friendly, informal and helpful telephone link with the customer/interviewee. Much of the training activity covered in Chapter 4 will apply to telesales personnel.

It is essential that telesales/telemarketing personnel work as sales persons in their own right with clear terms of reference and under properly planned conditions.

To promote team work and competition, telesales personnel normally work altogether in a single room at separate desks planned for the various operations of telephoning, note-taking, data input and retrieval, customer record card reference work etc.

In order to obtain maximum productivity in terms of effective calls and optimum sales, it is essential that the telesales workstation is subjected to work study and environmental considerations, for example:

(a) Desks of the correct height.
(b) Comfortable but supporting chairs (static, mobile, rotating) as appropriate.

(c) Lightweight personal telephone headsets that leave both hands free.

(d) Adequate catalogue, price list, delivery information, technical data, space.

(e) If possible/appropriate, computer-aided data input and retrieval, e.g. facility to 'type' orders into computer; automatic presentation of customer's buying record, credit status, payment situation; access to data bank regarding stock availability, part numbers and/or geographic location; automatic 'question prompts' regarding product/service/technical detail; automatic order format.

(f) If computerised, visual display units (VDUs) are used; colour-intensity adjustment and strategic siting to avoid window or artificial light reflection/glare is essential.

(g) Adequate lighting (daylight and/or artificial).

(h) Adequate ventilation and heating.

(i) A rest/refreshments area away from desks.

(j) Soft colour decor.

(k) Carpeted floor to aid noise suppression.

(l) A 'vanity' mirror which some practitioners claim enables telesales personnel to 'look good and therefore feel good' while others claim it is a reminder of what they are taught on their training course, i.e. 'to put warmth into their voice by smiling when they speak on the telephone'.

(m) Be part of a telephone system whereby the telesales/telemarketing supervisor/manager can unobtrusively listen in to any of the sales conversations being held; in training, talk to any of the trainees; and also be able to record selected parts of the conversation in progress.

In the selling by telephone situation, all the techniques mentioned in Chapter 6 will apply, e.g. preparation, opening the sale, creating interest, selling benefits (with the benefits plus reason plus weakness plus loss, B + R + W + L formula), closing the sale, overcoming objections; all will be relevant and appropriate depending on the product/service combination, the market/customer situation etc. Particularly important are the sales plans/sequences mentioned on pages 152–3 and guidelines to effective telephone communication on page 156.

The telesales/telemarketing unit can also be used in receiving telephone calls, i.e. when it is used in conjunction with press or TV advertising which suggests to the customer that he/she should contact the company by telephone. This is done usually with a British Telecom 'Freephone' telephone number arrangement so there is no cost to the caller. Such an arrangement means that immediate response is given following the advertisement, i.e. take orders, give information, deal with credit card purchase, despatch brochures or other promotional material etc. The problem with this type of operation is that customers may see the company's advertisement at any time in a newspaper and up to midnight or early morning on TV which would mean running what could be a highly uneconomic answering service. The answer to this problem is for the company to use the Telecom TAN 24 hours' service provided by British Telecom but using the company's name. The operator has all the answers, available through a computer link, to all relevant information from the company's data file. There are a number of other specialist companies who also operate this type of service.

Summary

Selling by telephone and/or telemarketing can be viewed as a sales/ marketing operation in its own right or as a support activity to the field sales team. It can range from taking only a small proportion of the time the individual internal sales person takes to being the only activity of a number of specialist sales persons operating under a specialist supervisor. Also, activities can differ depending on whether the operation is based on the customer taking the initiative and telephoning or whether the company takes the initiative and systematically contacts existing and potential customers.

Telephone selling and telemarketing (where appropriate) offers a wide range of benefits to the sales manager and can make the sales function of a company more effective. In this chapter, what selling by telephone and telemarketing can do was examined in depth, being conveniently divided into what it can do for the company, for business relationships and for enhancing customer relationships.

Selling by telephone and/or telemarketing, while not always suitable/ applicable to all market/company situations/needs, is very controllable and has certain advantages over personal visits. These include the sales manager being able to determine the exact message, the most suitable timing and form; it is easy to monitor what is being said; allows instant supervision of the telesales person, how many effective calls are being made, customer reaction and what the results are.

If a telesales operation is to be used, policy decisions need to be made as to whether it should be one set up and operated by the company as part of the sales function or whether to use the services of external specialist organisations. Either approach can be operated nationally/centrally or dispersed geographically.

Internally run telesales operations need to be staffed by persons with particularly 'open' personality attributes, highly trained (initially and continuously), working with a high level of team spirit, in a well and appropriately equipped environment. Planned selling techniques developed in early chapters are particularly important in selling by telephone.

An incoming call telephone sales operation can also be run to cater for responses to press and TV advertisements for the purpose of taking orders, giving information etc. Specialist organisations are often used to provide such a service because of the need for a 24 hours/weekend service.

Questions

1. What are the advantages and disadvantages of using a telesales/ telemarketing operation?
2. What are the activities that telesales/telemarketing can do better or more effectively than personal visits?
3. In what circumstances would it be more advantageous for the sales manager to use external organisations for telephone selling rather than set up his/her own?
4. What are the key operational considerations in setting up an internal telesales unit?
5. In what circumstances would a company consider setting up a telesales unit for incoming calls?

Credit control

The wise sales manager will instil in sales personnel the fact that any sale is not complete until the account has been paid. Linked with this axiom should be the policy that sales should not be obtained at any cost, i.e. the opening of accounts without due regard to risks (e.g. slow payers or bad debts) or the giving away of large discounts so that the eventual revenue adversely affects cash flow which in turn may indicate that normal credit periods need to be reduced to produce adequate cash flow.

There are two areas of sales-support financing, the magnitude of which the sales manager should be acutely aware. One is that of financing strategically placed stocks of finished goods to provide customer service. The other is that of financing trade credit, i.e. giving customers time to pay for goods/services purchased. Both are assets in as much as they are money tied up, one in goods, the other in debts. The risk in the former case is that products will become obsolete, damaged in storage or pilfered; in the latter case, the risk is that the debt will not be paid or paid at a later than expected date. The former provides the service of availability/good delivery, the latter provides the service of financing the customer's business based on the accepted pay-back/credit periods normally expected in a particular industry. They need to be kept in balance and both have an opportunity cost, i.e. if money is tied up in either it cannot be used for other purposes. Profit flows not only from the effective investment of capital but also from its velocity, i.e. number of times working capital is turned into goods and back again into cash.

Credit policy

This is formed by decisions of an organisation as to the amount of credit it will allow its customers; it may be directly linked with its debit policy. Credit policy can range from 'cash with order', 'payment at time of ordering or purchase', 'cash on delivery', 'payment before next order', 'payment on presentation of a pro-forma invoice', and various specific times permitted for payment. In some businesses, this latter group is often associated with a discount on price, e.g. '3¾ per cent cash within 7 days', '2½ per cent cash on monthly account'.

The amount of credit time (and discount) allowed is often determined by past customs and accepted practice in a particular industry as well as by the amount of credit competitors are willing to give. Giving credit is obviously a commercial risk and organisations try to reduce this by asking customers to prove their creditworthiness by presenting bank or other references or investigating them. Also, it is normal for organisations to set aside contingency funds to cover possible bad debts. This is ordinary commercial credit practice.

Obviously the result of credit policy decisions will affect the organisation's cash flow and discount/pricing structure and this must be allowed for in any financial planning. Credit policy may be also considered a sales promotional tool: if an organisation can offer better credit facilities than competitors, it is likely to attract more business, especially in times of high interest rates affecting other forms of credit. The converse situation is also true. In some cases, purchasers will attempt to finance their stocks or work in progress by extended credit.

Difficulties arise, however, because of 'conflicts' of interest between different parts of a company. For example, the finance view could be one of full financial disclosure by customers while the preferred sales/marketing approach might be characteristically one of minimum credit examination of customers. Again low credit risks and tough credit terms will be preferred by the finance section while medium credit risks and easy credit terms will be preferred by sales/marketing. Likewise with collection procedures, charac-teristically finance will want these to be tough and sales/marketing will want them to be easy.

It could be fatal if the extreme views of either party dominate. A tough credit management policy will tend to mean good cash flow but low sales. A weak credit policy will mean that cash flow/liquidity will be poor but sales will tend to be high; in this case, the longer credit has become a leading aspect of the company's sales/marketing mix. Also in the latter case, there will be increased debt recovery costs, in time and money, costs of unnoticed bad debts, and increased interest charges or money borrowed to meet cash flow needs. What is needed is a firm but fair credit management strategy where customers and the company know exactly where they stand.

Credit control can be operated through:

(a) The sales force.
(b) The setting up of a credit control office with credit controllers.
(c) A combination of (a) and (b).
(d) Factoring – this is where the supplying company transfers its debts to a third party (a factor) who advances (usually in two stages) their invoice value and makes a factoring charge ($\frac{1}{2}$–$2\frac{1}{2}$/3 per cent).

The process of credit management

The whole process of credit management needs to be based on a carefully defined and well thought out credit policy, with aims and objectives, how the company's credit management will operate and how it will be monitored. The basic conditions of sale, matters related to the passing of title of goods, the rights, limitations and responsibilities of the seller and the buyer etc., as well as the terms of doing business, credit levels, cash and (if appropriate) monthly discounts and methods of payment all need to be identified and publicised in catalogues, price lists and on order acceptances, invoices and statements. All these factors need to be considered and developed in the context of the special market circumstances in which the company finds itself.

The outcome of such a policy and details should be the development of procedures and guidelines to be given to internal and external sales personnel and credit controllers. These should cover the handling of potential new credit accounts and the methods of assessing and checking potential and existing customers' current creditworthiness through observation, reputation, bank/trade/trade association references and enquiries by credit enquiry agencies and the sanctioning of credit for specific customers.

The credit system should allow for the speedy notification of these credit levels and limits to customers, sales personnel and credit controllers at the beginning and during a business relationship. Procedures also need to be established in relation to disputes, 'stoppage in transitu' (i.e. stopping the delivery of goods in transit), when and how to engage in legal action and what action to be taken with regards to bad debts and customer insolvency. The procedures for monitoring of trading results, the establishment of a credit management system that 'flags' deviations from agreed norms/standards/limits, speedy invoicing and the despatch of statements, and the sending of reminders if necessary, all need to be developed.

Credit insurance needs to be considered not only for markets overseas through the Export Credits Guarantee Department of the Department of

Trade but also for home markets. Insurance companies exist (e.g. Credit and Guarantee Insurance Co. Ltd, Trade Indemnity plc) who will provide this cover. The premiums will obviously reflect the risk involved and whether the whole turnover is to be covered or only part, and will need to be balanced against the possible cost of not having cover. Because of the conditions necessarily imposed by such insurance companies, the value of credit insurance is that not only does it cover (partially or wholly) financial loss but ensures that a company's credit policy and procedures are adequate for the risks involved.

Procedures for account collection need to be established. These will be either routine collection such as automatic payment by customer, collection by sales persons, reminders and/or collection by credit controllers. Alternatively, account collection methods will be exceptional, i.e. debt collection using mercantile agencies, professional debt collectors, County Court action (under £5000), specialist solicitor firms and High Court action.

Companies need to identify the situations, levels and time periods of debts that will lead to the stoppage of supplies to a customer and the withdrawal of credit. Also the actions to take place and conditions that need to exist before a resumption of supplies and credit can take place.

Throughout the year, a company needs to operate a collection timetable and at the end of every credit period its effectiveness needs to be assessed and adjusted if necessary.

Credit management in operation

Whether a company's sales team takes the initiative and obtains an order from a customer or the customer takes the initiative and sends an order, any request for credit needs to be agreed/sanctioned only after creditworthiness investigation. The problem does not arise if the trade is cash with order or payment against a pro-forma invoice, and these methods may allow the business relationship to continue even if bank/trade/credit enquiry agency references are not favourable. The alternative, and a situation of last resort, is to refuse to do business with the other company.

A senior person in each company should carry the responsibility of credit sanctioning, operating the pre-determined company credit guidelines. After investigative credit is agreed, sales and accounting offices need to be notified and the customer sent written confirmation which sets out the basic arrangement. If credit is to be refused, the customer (and the sales person) should be told why in a way that does not cause offence.

Sales persons, internal and external, should be taught to be vigilant with regards to credit and customer behaviour. For example, a prospective customer who has resisted the attempts by a sales person to do business for a long period, suddenly and with or without approach from the sales person, sends or gives an order to the company, may be extending his credit base.

This could be after his existing suppliers have stopped supplies because of credit infringement or non-payment; he may be having significant cash flow problems and may at this time be a bad risk. Also, existing customers who are already taking full or extended credit and are also increasing the numbers of supplying companies need to be identified by the sales team, reported back to the sales manager and their credit situation investigated.

The collection of outstanding debts can be established as a normal part of the sales person's job, requiring him/her to collect monies if they are still outstanding after the usual invoices and statements have been sent. Alternatively, the sales person can be required to obtain cash with order or the payment for the previous order when calling to obtain the next one.

Alternatively a credit control office can be set up with a specialist credit controller(s) who cover the accounts of various sales persons. If customers do not pay at the required time, the credit controller(s) either write to, telephone, or ultimately call on the late-paying customer. This is an important sales force support service as the sales person can still enjoy a good rapport with customers without having to become involved with the collection process.

It is essential that such a credit control office works closely with the sales team (internal and external), the area managers and the sales manager and be able to work on the fullest information available both internally from the accounting department, sales office, sales personnel, area managers, the sales manager but also externally from credit enquiry agencies and subscription computerised databases. Organisations operating such databases provide corporate members with rapid access and search facilities on credit information and receive data from them. Such data consists mainly of the payment histories of individual consumers and companies experiencing current payment difficulties.

Because non-payment of accounts is a highly sensitive customer relationship area, credit controllers need to have natural ability in 'getting on' with others and/or receive training in this area. This getting on with others needs not only to be expressed and reflected in their telephone skills but also in their writing of clear, concise and persuasive letters. The telephone is often preferred as the main credit control/customer contact tool because of its immediacy, economy (sixty to seventy calls per day is often achieved) and because it achieves an immediate response, i.e. promise of payment or non-payment, reason for delay etc.

The credit controller, using all the human relations and selling skills mentioned earlier in the chapter on planned selling, needs to find out the name of and contact the person who is the decision-maker with regard to payments. He/she also needs to identify what is the problem, probing if the answers received are not credible, sell/persuade on a course of action and finally extract a promise to pay and note the date of the promised action. If the ideal person is not available for a telephone conversation, the credit controller should ask for a date and a time that he/she will be and leave a message that he/she will be contacted then.

Letters, on the other hand, are invaluable for reinforcing telephone contact, for communicating with persons who avoid telephone contact and/or are evasive regarding appropriate action. They are widely used to ask about credit rating and in taking up bank/trade references as some persons will not discuss these matters over the telephone. When letters are used for outstanding account collection, they should be addressed to the person who is the 'decision-maker' with regards to payment and, if this approach fails, the final letter should be to the chief executive of the customer company. This latter course of action should be used sparingly as it tends not to foster good relations with useful lower-level credit contacts.

Letters should be clear, concise, to the point, and polite but firm. They should be sent first-class post with the ultimate letter being sent 'recorded delivery' or even 'registered' to ensure maximum impact.

Personal visits for the purpose of outstanding account collection by credit controllers are not usual but, where the amount involved warrants it and where the personal touch is needed, the exceptional method may succeed where the others have failed.

Credit is a two-edged instrument, to be given and to be taken, and in some companies credit controllers are responsible not only for collecting outstanding accounts on time but also for obtaining/extending the credit and the credit period enjoyed by the company from its own suppliers by telephone and letter or dealing with creditors' sales persons. The increased cash flow and avoidance of bad debts by collection and the extension of credit from suppliers obviously reduces a company's need to borrow from other institutions for working capital. However, where these two activities are carried out by credit controllers there is less likelihood of their activities being controlled by the sales manager and more likelihood of it being run by the financial function.

Whether the 'collector' is the sales person or a specialised credit controller, there are certain guidelines to observe. The first is the need to practise empathy, i.e. the need to appreciate the customer's point of view and situation. To keep the collection of outstanding accounts in its proper perspective, it is essential that the sales person/credit controller is not over-conscientious or aggressive or, alternatively, not embarrassed or over-conscious about asking for a settlement of the account. After all, the money does belong to the supplying company and its payment is part of the contract between it and the customer. There is a need to have the right mental attitude towards the collection of outstanding debts.

Often, sales persons/credit controllers have problems caused by pre-conceived or anticipated customer reaction to requests for payment, e.g. they may expect resentment or aggression. If this expectation is reflected in the credit controller's approach, relationships may suffer if, for example, the customer has forgotten or he/she is taking as much credit as possible until asked for payment.

There is therefore the need for the right mental attitude on the part of credit controllers; the collection of outstanding accounts must not antagonise, neither must it be impersonal or routine.

There are many methods/approaches open to credit controllers, some of which are:

(a) A straightforward request for the sum outstanding.

(b) Shift the onus for payment on to a third party. The sales person can shift it on to the credit controller and still retain his special friendly relationship with the customer. When dealing direct with the customer, the credit controller can shift the onus on to the company's own creditors who need to be paid.

(c) Assume that the customer wants to be reminded about payment.

(d) Assume that he/she has forgotten to pay.

(e) Ask for his/her co-operation.

(f) Assume that the invoice/statement has been lost in the post.

(g) Assume that something must be wrong with the product and/or service and that this is holding up payment.

(h) Recapitulate the whole transaction(s).

(i) Assume that the customer is not taking/accepting his/her proper responsibilities.

(j) Threaten the cutting of supplies unless the account is paid, say, in 48 hours etc.

(k) Assume there is only one other course of action.

(l) Set a firm date for the stopping of supplies or the withdrawal of consignment stocks.

Throughout, the aim is to lose as little goodwill as possible with a sound human and reasonable, but firm, approach.

Factoring was defined earlier as where a supplying company transfers its debts to a third party (a factor), who advances (usually in two stages, 80 per cent immediately and the remainder when the account is paid) their invoice value and makes a factoring charge ($\frac{1}{2}$–$2\frac{1}{2}$/3 per cent).

Factoring is widely used in overseas business because of transport and other delays normally experienced but is also used in the home market, especially by companies who sell on short-term credit to a number of customers and/or who need money for expansion (especially of working capital) and/or have tight cash flow working limits where a high 'velocity' of working capital is crucial.

The usual arrangement is that the factor will maintain a detailed sales ledger and the company debits the customer on the factor's invoice stationery, copies of which are sent to the factor immediately to enable the detailed sales ledger to be properly maintained and fully up-to-date. The factor sends out statements at the end of credit/sales periods and in fact operates the company's credit management process. To transfer such a sensitive customer relations activity to a third party requires a very close working relationship between the company and the factor. It also requires the latter to operate sensitively with the company's customers and that prior consultation takes place before drastic action (i.e. legal proceedings) is taken. Factoring, used properly, is a useful credit control and sales force support method.

Summary

A sale is not complete until the products/services involved have been paid for; prices, discounts, profitability are all affected by slow payers and bad debts. As there are peaks and troughs in sales through seasonal and other factors, revenue will often not flow into a company at the same rate as it is paid out, i.e. on wages, raw materials and components, overheads etc. In the interests of budgeting control, companies may have to purchase short-term loan/overdraft options from their bankers or others to cover expected cash flow deficiencies at certain forecasted points in the financial year. These options need to be based on good market and sales forecasting and will be affected by credit policy.

Strategically placed finished stocks and trade credit both represent money tied up, and both can be affected favourably or unfavourably by the activities of the sales team.

Methods of credit and payment need to be related to a company's own and market circumstances. Internally by attitudes of functional areas and capital funding, and externally by the expectations of customers and activities of competitors.

Credit control was seen to operate through the sales team, credit controllers and factors. The process of credit was perceived to be based upon a credit policy with wide-ranging considerations. From this policy came a series of developments and guidelines for the sales team and credit controllers, and the system included not only new but also existing customers. Credit insurance, especially in overseas markets, was considered and the recourse to legal proceedings and other methods mentioned.

Credit management in operation covered the following up of references and credit sanctioning or refusal. Monitoring existing credit arrangements was seen to be a crucial activity upon which to base the collection of outstanding debts.

The operation of a credit control office was seen as a sales support activity as it enabled the sales force to 'off load' the problems of collection, removing it as a difficulty towards maintaining a friendly relationship between the sales person and the customer. Various methods of non-paying customer contact were examined: telephone, letter, personal visits and, as a last resort, recourse to more persuasive legal action.

Certain guidelines and approaches to customers with outstanding debts were examined based on getting the best response and by losing as little goodwill as possible with a sound, human, reasonable but firm approach.

Factoring as a credit management device was defined and examined, and recommended in some overseas business deals and in the UK market. Particularly in situations where companies sell on short-term credit to a number of customers and where companies need urgent money for working capital and expansion, tight cash flow working limits and where a high 'velocity' of working capital is crucial.

Credit policy, management, procedures were all seen as supporting the sales function.

Questions

1. Why is credit control important to the company as a whole and to the sales manager in particular?
2. Why does credit control cause conflict between various functions of a business? Give examples of potential conflict and indicate how they might be resolved.
3. What are the stages and/or component parts of an ideal credit management plan?
4. What are the accepted methods of credit collection?
5. Factoring is an external method of credit control. How does it work, what types of circumstances are appropriate for its use and what are its benefits to the sales manager?

Customer service

There are very few products sold that do not have some form of service associated with them so, as was mentioned earlier (in Chapter 6), the sales person sells a product/service combination – a total deal. Where competing products perform in similar ways, where prices/discounts are similar and where delivery times are broadly the same, the service element is often what attracts a customer to one 'deal' as opposed to another. The quality and extent of customer service can be a crucial sales support activity.

When a product is involved, customer service can be viewed either as:

(a) *Before sale*: demonstrations (equipment), trial periods, special product design, technical advice, extraction of quantities needed (e.g. building materials from housing plans), tastings (wine and food), tester samples (perfumery), design service (e.g. packaging), quotations and estimates, measuring (e.g. carpets), planning (e.g. kitchens), sale or return arrangements (for middlemen and/or retailers), freephone arrangements for ordering, presentation of product/service 'deal' options.

(b) *After sale*: quick delivery, installation, servicing, availability of spares, contract maintenance, repairs, merchandising activities (e.g. for retailers), provision of display units, safety/insurance inspection visits, insurance cover, accounting systems for small customers, specialised computer software items, special financing arrangements.

These services are additional/ancillary to the product offered, but in some cases service is the main 'product', e.g. financing the purchase of a product (hire purchase for consumers or providing loans for industrial customers) is an ancillary service for the equipment supplier but finance is the main 'product' for a finance house or bank. Thus the suppliers of main 'product' services will need to supply ancillary/associated services. For example, hotels may provide a special reservation service, laundries/dry cleaners may provide a collection/delivery service, travel agents may provide insurance services etc.

It will be seen, therefore, that customer service in the widest sense can be described as all the benefits of value to a company's customers, additional or ancillary to the main product or service contained in the 'total deal'.

Although the customer may never have occasion to use all or any of the services available, their very existence, in relation to competitors' product/service deals', should attract new customers and give existing ones a sense of security and confidence in the supplier. In this context, the range of services to be offered by a company should be planned to attract as well as serve customers.

Thus identifying what customers want before purchase is important in the provision of before-sales services and the package of services offered will influence potential customers. On the other hand, many of the after-sales services may only be used and assessed some time after the initial purchase. Therefore it is important to identify what customers want after purchase, particularly as some services (repairs and maintenance) will be used nearer to a replacement purchase. Therefore, after-sales services are important influences of customers about to make replacement decisions. They are also powerful originators of favourable/adverse 'word of mouth' advertising.

Customer service activities are also powerful sales tools as they give the sales person additional benefits with which he/she can persuade potential and existing customers to view the 'total deal' offered and buy.

Customers expect that quality product/service combinations that include an enhanced service element will cost more, and higher prices will be accepted and paid provided the services are relevant to needs. In fact, the higher initial price of a high-quality product/service combination may be divided by the longer period of expected usage the customer will experience (perhaps showing it is cheaper per year), provided that longevity of product is a benefit the customer wants. For example, the customer may prefer less service, a lower price and a shorter life if, as in the case of some 'high tech' products, it will become outdated or obsolete in a relatively short space of time.

Profits that are earned because of a range of customer services (much like that of an advertising programme) will not often be 'in phase' with the expenditures made to provide the services, i.e. they often emerge long after the setting-up expenditure was incurred. There is a building up of corporate image related to the provision of customer services. Often there will be 'hidden' profits; these may take the form of not having to resort to price competition because the services offered offset the lower price element contained in competitors' deals. This will either prevent or reduce the loss of business to competitors or at least match service offerings of competitors. Again, customer services can provide the sales force with a means of offsetting price, advertising and sales force competition.

Customer service effects should be viewed as a sales support activity by identifying the various miscellaneous indirect benefits. For example, one gain from increased customer service offerings might be that the supplier's employees pay more frequent visits to the customer's premises, raising a higher visual profile and presence. Further, the provision of certain customer services may make customers more receptive to operating instructions, or advice on the provision of an optimum environment for the operation of a product/service combination or even provide the sales force with an opportunity to sell further specialised support equipment and/or services. Effective customer service may even promote a more tolerant attitude by customers towards occasional imperfections or breakdowns that do occur even with the most efficient company and its product/service combinations. In fact, relevant effective customer service activities can enhance the reputation and corporate image of a supplier or simply make it easier and more pleasant to do business with them.

Companies, and particularly sales managers, need to identify relevant 'packages' of customer services that are appropriate to the needs of the particular company in the market-place; it must also be a package that is feasible for the company to provide in terms of scope, resources and opportunity costs.

The provision of customer services can be costed into the price of the main product/service combination, in which case they are often described as 'free'. In such situations it is sometimes possible to give large customers special discounts where particular services are not required.

Customer services can be costed as a separate charge that can either break even, make a profit or make an apparent loss, the effect of which is to subsidise the particular service from the product itself or other product/

service combinations. In each case, customer attitude to the method of charging is as important as a mechanistic method of covering costs.

A useful approach is for the sales manager to identify needed customer services by asking what should be provided in terms of the type of benefit/value they provide for the customer. The list might include:

(a) Performance-enhancing services.
(b) Life-prolonging services.
(c) Risk-reducing services.

These would include services that provide economy of operation, prolong life of equipment, simplify operation, ease financing, reduce risks, improve reliability, increase efficiency, improve flexibility, increase sales, ensure safer operations, etc.

Most types of customer services fall into these value type categories and the sales manager/marketing manager/managing director needs to consider, under each heading and others, the customer service that must, should or could be included in the product/service or service/ancillary service combinations (i.e. the 'total deal') in the context of potential needs of customers, the service(s) provided by competitors and the 'cost/benefit' to the company.

Summary

There are very few products sold that do not have some form of service associated with them and these can be usefully examined as activities that take place either before or after the sale. However, in some cases a service is the 'main product' (e.g. finance provided by a finance house), but such service suppliers will need to consider what ancillary/associated services they could or should offer to make their 'deal' attractive to customers (e.g. the finance house may offer 'free' insurance cover).

Customer service can be described as all those benefits of value to a company's customers, additional or ancillary to the main product or service contained in the 'total deal'.

Some services offered may never need to be used by customers but their existence will attract as well as serve them and as such should be planned with both aspects in mind as service is a powerful sales tool. The spin-off to companies in providing customer services may be reflected in an increase in sales or may not be immediate but may take time to build up, before obtaining the 'hidden' profits of an enhanced corporate service image.

A quality service, as with a quality product, will tend to cost more to the customer. The cost of customer services to the supplier can be built into the price of the total deal, or charged as a separate price that can be set to make a profit, break even or make a loss possibly subsidised from the product itself or other product/service combinations.

Finally, it is useful to consider the provision of services under value-type headings to determine what customer services must, should or could be offered in the context of customer needs, competition and the benefits to the company.

Questions

1. What does 'customer service' mean in terms of before- and after-sales facilities and in cases where a company's main 'product' is in fact a service?
2. What are the hidden benefits to a supplier of customer service?
3. How are customer services paid for?
4. Customer services can be categorised by type of value they provide: identify and describe the three main types.

Merchandising

This sales force support activity is extremely important when selling consumer goods through wholesalers and/or retailers, especially fast-moving consumer goods. Merchandising can be defined as psychological persuasion at the point of sale/purchase without the aid of a sales person. Alternatively, it has been described simply as activities that ensure goods 'sold in' are 'sold out' by retailers at the anticipated rate. It can therefore be seen as a specialised part of sales promotion but one that is normally under the influence/control of the sales manager.

Many manufacturers and marketing organisations realise that to maximise sales they cannot afford to leave merchandising activities in the hands of the retailer and that they must accept much of the responsibility for originating and advising on merchandising policies and strategies. Further, they need to ensure the success of such policies by implementing them in retail stores through the medium of merchandising activities of the sales person or by a specialised merchandising team with the aid of sales promotional and display material, a variety of techniques and the retailer's co-operation.

If merchandising in retail stores is part of the sales person's job, it is essential that it appears in the job description. Further, clear instructions should be given and priorities established as to the types of stores, types of merchandising and the amount of time to be spent on these activities. Indications of these activities would need to appear in the sales person's activity report.

If merchandising/display activities are to be carried out by a specialist team of merchandisers, a supervisor/manager will need to be appointed, reporting directly to the sales manager, to plan, organise, supervise, train and control its activities.

The sales person or specialised merchandiser needs to have certain personal characteristics in addition to the basic sales person characteristics listed in the earlier chapter on selection of sales staff. These additional characteristics should ideally include an element of artistic/creative flair for display/colour/shape/ability to sell (initially) intangible ideas, ability to think up unusual angles and new approaches, and a spatial ability to perceive his/her merchandising ideas in the context of the total store.

Training both in basic merchandising skills and to update merchandiser/sales people in an ever-changing retail scene is vital to the continued success of any merchandising operation. Also, close liaison with both the company's advertising and sales promotion departments and advertising agency is essential.

In the context of merchandising, the sales manager should ask the question, 'Do my sales team sell to or through retailers?' Or perhaps it would be better to ask, 'What percentage of a sales person's selling interview is spent on helping the retailer to sell more of our products or giving him/her ideas that will pull more goods through the retailer's store?' The greater the advertising support for a particular line, the smaller should be the percentage of the sales person's time spent on 'selling in' and the greater should be the 'selling out' activities.

However, it is obvious that in order to be able to merchandise the goods in the retail store, the sales person must sell them in first. So the techniques shown in Chapter 6 are essential to 'selling in'. In fact, 'selling in' appropriate amounts of goods effectively blocks competitors where a retailer has a perceived volume of a particular product type in mind and also causes 'stock pressure' or the need for turnover/cash flow that causes the retailer to be more receptive to ideas on increasing stock turn and/or 'pulling' more goods through the store.

Even members of a merchandising support team will find it necessary to use the planned selling techniques in Chapter 6 to persuade the retailer to allow him/her to merchandise part of the store, or to give adequate/more space to merchandise/display the company's product range. The sales manager will find it necessary to evolve a suitable merchandising/sales sequence in the same way as the ordinary sales person. To combat retailer inertia towards a company and/or its products, the merchandiser/sales person must keep the retailer conscious not only of the company's products but also of the market/sales/profit opportunity month after month.

Any merchandising activities in the retail store should be aimed at increasing profits for the retailer as well as for the supplier. If a retailer is faced with two propositions for similar products, with similar prices and delivery dates, the choice will tend to be that of the company whose sales personnel/merchandisers have helped in the past and who are likely to help to make more profits in the future.

Whether the company operates a policy of selected outlets or one of mass distribution and display, its success will depend to a great extent upon its ability to seize market opportunities and to take advantage of trends in consumer habits, fashions and tastes. A supplier's merchandiser/sales person should be trained to help retailers develop their business on the supplier's range of products, thinking of the retailers' problems as though they were their own. Sometimes the retailer is blamed for inactivity and accused of indifference, but before adopting this attitude the sales manager should analyse the actions of his sales team/merchandisers in the light of the competitors' co-operation with the same retailer.

Merchandising activity in retail stores can increase sales/profits in three main ways. It can increase the number of customers, it can sell more to existing customers and it can increase sales and/or lower costs. There are a number of merchandising activities the merchandiser/sales person can carry out under these three main headings that can obtain higher profits for the retailer and also increase sales and profits for the sales person's own company. Some of these are indicated in Fig. 10.2

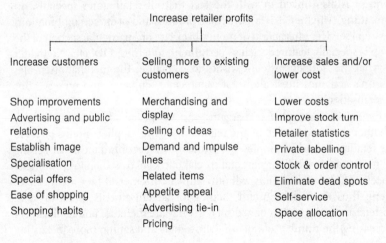

Fig. 10.2 Increasing retailer profits

In the first category, 'Increase customers', the shop improvements item reflects the approach that the whole store should be merchandised to customers; which means the whole shop should be used as a display case to passing consumers. It means removing the backs of closed windows and high displays, in which case the interior must be attractive enough to act as a magnet to draw in potential customers. It could also mean rearranging shop layouts, changing from counter service to self-selection or self-service, or updating fixtures and fittings, especially lighting, air-conditioning, refrigeration or cooling units, measuring and weighing points, and cash payment points. Because merchandising/sales people build up expertise through training and experience, they are often able to give retailers advice and can often name specialist companies who can advise or give an opinion on and/or carry out shop improvements or provide new technology.

Advertising and public relations can be used to increase customers. The former by giving information as to location of stores, products offered, special promotional lines, bargains, price reductions etc. The latter by building up corporate/shop image, community contribution and involvement. The choice of an appropriate theme and media will be dealt with in a later chapter. It is sufficient here to mention that suppliers and retailers can become involved in co-operative advertising, and merchandisers/sales people should be able to advise on co-operative/promotional themes.

Every retail shop has a store image, either favourable or adverse, e.g. value for money, quality, low prices, pleasant store personnel etc. This image needs to be taken into account when merchandising a store, with merchandisers/sales persons adapting their own company's contribution to meet the overall theme/atmosphere/ethos of the particular store. This image concept is also linked in with the fact that all retail stores specialise in something, whether it is a particular product and/or price combination, personal service, satisfaction or money back etc. or a particular section of the shop is specially featured such as perfumery, toiletries, DIY etc. No matter in what the store/department wishes to specialise, the merchandiser/sales person's activities must allow for, appreciate, enhance and preserve this specialisation.

Everyone is attracted to bargains and to special offers to customers, whether these are funded by the retailer or by the supplier. Bonus offers to the retailer are trade examples of this and are in fact only a means of 'selling in' more, unless these bargains and special offers are passed on to consumers. Special offers to consumers will only attract customers if they are aware of them; thus they make useful themes for advertisements (press or store posters) and point of purchase displays. They are therefore powerful ways of increasing the number of potential customers and selling more to existing customers.

All store layouts and displays should be designed/located to make it easy for shoppers to buy, with clear-cut lines of customer traffic flow, signposting and a logical sequence and grouping of product types. If aisles between display shelves or cabinets are narrow or displays or 'dump bins' congest normal traffic lanes, the store gains a reputation of being difficult to shop. A further aspect of ease of shopping is the height of shelves, ease of reading prices and identification of brands. If displays of products from which consumers are expected to select are too uniform, too tightly packed (a 'starter gap' should be left) or form a special pattern, customers will tend to avoid touching them. This partly accounts for the popularity and justification of 'dump bins' or 'tumble' displays in supermarkets.

Merchandisers/sales persons should be aware of the shopping habits of the purchasers of their type of products. For example, it is generally accepted that the type of shopping carried out at the beginning and middle of the week is different from that carried out in the latter part. This is particularly so if the product needs a buying decision of both husband and wife, as in the case of a consumer-durable item such as a refrigerator or television receiver. At the beginning of the week, the shopping traffic is relatively light; and even in the case of food products where some are purchased throughout the week, the purchasing patterns are different in the latter part, especially where this is emphasised by late-night shopping. The growth of freezer centres, supermarkets, hypermarkets and out-of-town shopping centres has meant that some consumers carry out food and household product purchasing on a once monthly (or even longer) basis.

Further, research indicates that fewer housewife shoppers are taking shopping lists to the shops and therefore this is the merchandiser's opportunity to suggest the company's product/service to the potential purchaser. The purchase of some goods follows a particular order and therefore the sequence of displays in relation to traffic flow should reflect this if possible. For example, in supermarket operation it is recognised that the housewife often makes a buying decision about the type of meat before purchasing the other items that make up the meal. In the case of clothing, a decision is made about a dress before decisions are made about handbag, gloves and hat.

The merchandiser/sales person should be aware of research findings for a particular area regarding the percentage of buying decisions for his/her product type that are premeditated, made at point of purchase, and bought on impulse, as it should influence the merchandising approach. For example, in many urban areas research suggests that 70 per cent of food-buying decisions (product type or brand), 80 per cent of chocolate and confectionery decisions, and 90 per cent of cake-buying decisions are made at the point of purchase. With consumer-durable goods (e.g. washing machines, TV, car etc.), a greater length of time for consumer assessment needs to be allowed, occasionally resulting in several visits to a retail store. A study of consumer habits is essential for effective merchandising by merchandiser/sales persons who can then anticipate customer behaviour.

In the second category, 'Selling more to existing customers', the first item, merchandising and display, covers the basic principles involved in these activities.

Some supplier companies define merchandising simply as moving goods into a selling position. They feel it is no measure of their selling success to have large quantities of their products sold into the store room at the rear of the retail outlet. Moving the products into a selling position implies the use of effective display techniques, and the mnemonic AIDA can be applied. Displays must attract *attention*, create and sustain *interest*, foster the *desire* to possess, and motivate buying *action* by the consumer.

There are a number of factors upon which the success of a point of purchase display depends. One of the most important is *profitability*; displays must not only sell, but must achieve maximum profit opportunity. They can do this by using 'hot-spots' in the store to display products that are both high profit and fast-moving. If this is not possible, a decision must be made to display either fast-moving, high-demand items with lower profit margins, possibly made fast-moving by price cuts, or high-profit lines that move relatively more slowly.

The *position* or siting of a display is also important and if the merchandiser/sales person can show the retailer that his company's products and his display will increase profits, then he will be able to obtain the best sites in a store. The display site may not only increase the sales of the merchandiser's products but may also attract customers into the less well-shopped parts of the store selling other products as well. Obviously the aim will be to position displays in places where prospective customers are likely to be passing, or are looking, or to where they can be attracted. That the display must be visible is obvious, but some people look without really seeing, and one factor that will make them see and appreciate a display is that of sheer *size*. In most fields of retailing, the maxim 'The larger the display the larger the sales' holds good. This is, of course, difficult in small retail outlets where space is at a premium and also with products that have a limited shelf or display life (bakery goods, meat etc.).

Design and *pattern* at the point of purchase will also cause the display to be noticed. A display from which the merchandiser intends customers to take or handle the product should not be too uniform. Therefore a compromise can be effected by displaying the products in two parts; one part attracts the potential consumer by its startling pattern or layout, and the other can be a tumble or a uniform display, but with a starter gap. This is really going back to the consideration of *availability* for, if the displayed product is inaccessible, too tightly packed, forms part of a neat pyramid etc., the shopper is discouraged from selecting for himself/herself. Size and pattern are part of the overall display factor of *impact*, and the merchandiser should ask himself/herself, 'Is my display a "shopper stopper"?'

A further element of impact is the use of *colour* in displays. Where the merchandiser/sales person is merely placing printed display pieces, he has little choice with regard to the colours used although, presumably, point of sale advertising material tests will have been carried out by the company's advertising department or its advertising agency. Even so, the merchandiser should carefully consider the display's setting and background. Will the colours clash with surrounding displays or interior decorations? If so, it may discourage the potential consumer from looking at it. On the other hand, if the printed display piece is mainly red and yellow (both of which psychologically 'demand action') and the background is also made up mainly of these colours, the display will simply merge into the background and be 'lost'.

Another colour-related concept that is important to the merchandiser/ sales person is 'after image'. In certain display situations, the colour can either enhance or deter the appeal of a product, particularly if the product is white in colour or has adjacent white walls. For example, if a potential customer stares hard at a green/blue display piece placed on or near a white fridge-freezer, the shopper will perceive a red (denoting warmth) hue on the white equipment. This is the effect of 'after image' which is a quirk of human vision to see the colour on the opposite side of the colour spectrum when the gaze is transferred to a plain white surface. Conversely, a red/orange display piece on or near a white heater or cooker can give an after image of green/blue coldness.

If the merchandiser has to create displays, he/she should indeed be colour conscious and be aware of the effectiveness of various colours and their psychological associations. He/she should of course, as far as possible, continue to use the colours (and type of lettering) used by the company in its advertising, to aid product recognition at the point of purchase. The use of black at the point of sale will project a dramatic effect, but point of sale display must be made exciting and therefore black must be used carefully. White projects cleanliness, authority, clinical atmosphere, newness. Red is associated with heat, fire, gaiety, excitement, passion, festivity and demands action. Yellow is a warm colour and is associated with summer and sunshine, brightness, spring, holiday atmosphere, gaiety etc. and is another 'action' colour. Blue is a colour that projects coolness, stability, dignity, restraint, and is associated with the sea and the sky. Green is another cool colour, projecting freshness, nature appeal, lushness, growth. Purple and violet project the image of royalty, formality, solemnity, regal occasions, dignity etc. Depending upon the type of market, brighter hues of these colours will have greater impact than more subdued tints. The effective use of colours is a subtle merchandising tool because many people are unaware of the psychological influences they have on them.

Another element of impact is *motion*, either real or apparent. Animated display, whether it is a working model powered by a small electric motor or a mobile hanging from the ceiling 'powered' by the air flow in the store, attracts attention by its movement. Apparent movement can be effected by a silk-screen printed animation which incorporates a small electrical flasher unit so that as it is automatically switched on and off, the changing angles of light give the impression of movement. Apparent movement can also be projected by simple electric signs and display material that presents a different message from a different angle. There is a wide range of continuous video display and message machines/devices that can bring movement (and in some cases sound) to point of purchase display.

Appearance is another vital display factor; the appearance of the point of purchase display should reflect the brand or product image (i.e. quality, value for money) or the use of colour to emphasise a particular benefit, such as pink for the softness of paper tissues, white for cleanliness, brown and yellow for suntan lotion etc.

The display factor of *inducement* is a vital one when immediate consumer action is required; the inducement, incentive or benefit need not be one of financial gain as there is a wide range of non-financial inducements that can be offered to the potential purchaser at the point of purchase (e.g. information leaflets, entry forms for competitions, recipes etc.). A vital display factor is that of *freshness*; the display should look freshly dressed the whole time, should never look faded or dirty, and when it is no longer fresh it should be replaced. A member of the retailer's staff should be 'appointed' (if possible) to keep the display clean and tidy, and to keep the fixture full of the product, between the merchandiser's visits.

The retailer should be reminded of the well-known retail fact that full fixtures sell more than those that are partially full. This is due to a number of factors: the 'out of stock' position is avoided, mass display sell more, full displays attract the impulse buyer and they create the atmosphere of fast-selling stock. Also, special displays away from normal positions sell more because they attract attention, break up 'shopping monotony', create a low-price impression, highlight new products and create impulse sales.

There are many types of retail display; some are based on the use of manufactured units that merely have to be assembled, others on units made up on the spot by the creativeness and often the ingenuity of merchandiser/ sales person. There is a third, i.e. that of a combination of the two groups mentioned.

Other than the strategic placing of manufactured units, the merchandisers of some companies are more concerned with the second type of display. Especially in fast-moving consumer goods, ingenuity in merchandising display has fostered a technique known as cut-case display, which is carried out by cutting the 'shipping' or fibre-board packaging cases in a variety of ways which, in different combinations, can produce a range of differently shaped displays. Case-cutting techniques have the advantages of reducing the handling of the displayed goods and the need for other display material, and they are are easy to erect; all that is needed is a sharp knife, a rule and a stapling gun. These techniques have been so successful in the grocery, household, hardware and other fields that manufacturers are having dotted lines printed upon shipment cases to indicate where to cut. The basic rule is that the side of the case the merchandiser is cutting should be uppermost so that the products fall away from the knife blade which, in any case, should not be too deeply inserted.

By using either manufactured display units or made-up units, or a combination of both, displays can be erected in the windows, on the floor, among shelving, on counters etc. Floor displays can be the simple 'dump bin', special floor unit or the self-standing wire basket type complete with centre rod for fixing a 'talking' sign, or it can be a tumble display in a specially ticketed shopper's trolley or a series of shoppers' wire baskets. Special end of gondola (fitment) displays can be set up using related-item techniques and demand and impulse items in a variety of ways. End island mass displays are very effective because of sheer size. The 'spectacular' type of display, perhaps 15–20 feet long by 5–6 feet high, are particularly effective if they have a theme.

Displays on counters are, in the main, restricted because of space. But displays appropriately placed (if possible, near to cash registers or check-outs, weighing and wrapping points) are most effective.

Under the heading of 'Selling ideas', the point of purchase display that suggests new ways of doing things, new applications, new recipes, new menus, new angles, always attracts attention. While competing products may be capable of doing these things, goodwill accrues to the company whose retail displays sell new ideas for new or existing products and will tend to be reflected in high sales figures.

Products in any type of retail store can be divided into demand and impulse lines. The demand lines are those that people must have and which bring them into the retail store in the first place; the impulse lines are those about which customers need reminding or which they can be persuaded they need at the point of purchase. Strategic placing of the manufacturers' impulse lines near the retailer's demand lines will increase the manufacturer's sales; also, the supplying company's demand lines should be used as magnets to draw attention to its own impulse lines. Demand lines such as meat, butter, bread, tea, sugar, detergent etc. are used to great advantage in supermarket operation to cause the customer to shop the whole store. In the retail chemist shop, the location of the prescription counter at the rear of the store has the same effect; but in any section of retailing, demand products or services can be used in this way. In fact, the strategic placing of demand lines within the retail store can be used to eliminate the 'dead spots' that still claim their proportion of the retailer's overheads. When considering the position of demand and impulse lines it should be remembered that customers will bend down or reach upwards for demand items but they will tend not to do so for impulse lines, and therefore the latter should be positioned between waist and eye level.

Another technique that can be used in counter display or self-service is that of related-item display, i.e. where two items are linked together by usage or time. It may be two or more goods items such as cheese and biscuits (one at a reduced price and one at the normal price) or it may be a food and a non-food item such as tins of fruit displayed with sundae dishes or baking ingredients and baking tins, clothing items such as dresses, handbags, gloves etc., or it could be a reminder or suggestion display linking two items, e.g. torches and camping equipment or sun glasses and suntan lotions. When buying one of these items, it is visually suggested to the shopper to purchase the other.

One very important factor in merchandising display activities in the retail store can be called mental-appetite appeal. Most consumers have ideas, and fantasies, and possibly see themselves at times as perfection in certain fields: the perfect housewife, the perfect mother or father, having a slim figure, or having other desirable attributes. This part of human behaviour makes the consumer susceptible to suggestion at the point of purchase. The inclusion of a mental-appetite appeal element in retail display can create the right atmosphere – the perfection atmosphere. The projection of healthy happy families by merchandisers of vitamin or health preparations, the man-about-town image created by manufacturers of hair preparations and other toilet preparations for men, or the simple model of a perfectly shaped pair of legs displaying nylon stockings, all create mental-appetite appeal when observed by the members of the appropriate market segment.

There is a need for 'advertising tie-in' at the point of purchase either with the company's or the retailer's current advertising trends. The theme of any merchandising/display should be, if possible, that projected by all the other forms of a company's advertising and sales promotion if full value from expenditure on these media is to be achieved. There must be continuity of theme at the point where the final buying decision is made so that the potential consumer, already predisposed towards the product by advertising, recognises it, makes the mental link and identifies the selling proposition. Advertising without merchandising does not maximise its market opportunity and loses a large part of its effectiveness. The advertising theme carried through to the point of purchase display can cash in on the advertising slogan and message, which is basically 'Buy our product because . . .', and offers the consumer rational or emotional buying benefits and reasons for doing so.

The use of tactical pricing as a merchandising and display factor has considerable possibilities if used carefully. Thus if price cuts are used as magnets, the regular price, the special price and the saving should be indicated at the point of purchase. This is because the average shopper knows relatively few of the wide range of prices that faces him/her in retail shops. Further, there is a need to limit the range of special offers to a small proportion of a company's products to ensure overall profitability. Price reductions on particular products should be for limited periods only; otherwise the customer becomes conditioned to expect the lower new price and accepts it as 'normal'. In this case, not only is the original reduction no longer an additional incentive to purchase, but when the price returns to its proper level the consumers consider that it has been increased with no extra value added and this can cause them to substitute other brands.

With some products, the level of price is an indicator of quality to the consumer (e.g. cosmetics): therefore, care must be taken in using pricing as a merchandising device. However, even with high-priced/high-quality products, introductory price offers appeal. With fast-moving consumer-goods, introductory or sales revitalisation offers of 'two for the price of one' are attractive to the customer and yet still maintain the higher price image. Understanding psychological price levels (e.g. with some product prices under £1, under £10 or £100 resulting in customer-attractive prices of 99p, £9.99p and £99) will help the success of some merchandising themes.

In the third category, that to increase sales and/or lower costs, the actual direct lowering of costs may not be possible for the sales person/merchandiser; but the indirect method, that of spreading existing overheads/on costs over a higher level of sales, has this effect. When merchandising activities increase cost in any way, it must be outweighed by the additional increase in sales and profits. One way of reducing the retailer's costs should be resisted, i.e. the use of the merchandiser/sales person as an unpaid 'shelf filler'.

Profit per each product sold (profit margin or mark-up) is naturally of interest to both the retailer and the merchandiser/sales person, but often the overall profitability of a retail operation with any product is of greater consequence and this involves the concept of increased stock turn and may mean reducing profits per item and prices to achieve it. For example, consider the following situation:

Situation	Capital invested in stock	Profit mark-up	Annual stock turn	Gross profit
A	£100	15%	1	£15
B	£100	15%	12	£180
C	£100	10%	20	£200

Situation A merely illustrates how stock turn works; £100 invested in stock that sells only once each year at a 15 per cent profit margin will produce £15 gross profit. In situation B, the annual stock turn is 12 and therefore the profit is increased to £180 (12 × £15). Situation C shows that when a reduction in price by cutting the profit mark-up per item by one-third is made, the retailer will make £20 more gross profit than in situation B. In fact, the retailer could cut his profit margin to 9 per cent with a stock turn of 20 and still get the same gross profit as in situation B, £100 (9 × 50), but there would be no incentive for him to do this as he will have to handle more goods to achieve the same results. On the other hand, the retailer may be able to enjoy extra bulk discounts that may make it worth his while. Obviously there will be a point between situation B and C where the extra gross profit caused by increased stock turn and reduced profit margin will outweigh the extra cost of handling the extra goods.

An appreciation of retailer statistics in particular geographic areas is crucial to the credibility of merchandising suggestions. For example, the possibility of a relatively large display using proportionally more space may be more acceptable in areas where rents/rates are low than in others where the cost per running metre of shelf space is high. Other important retail statistics are sales by product or product group or department or floor area, sales over a time period, the ratio of capital turnover (by dividing net sales by total assets less current liabilities), profit per square metre, profit per running metre of shelf space etc. Wage rates, seasonal patterns, accepted profit norms (profit mark-up or margin), expected market share, type of shopping and type of customer are just some of the many retailer statistics of which the merchandiser/sales person should be aware if he/she is to have empathy with a retailer.

The supplier's merchandiser will be welcomed by retailers if he/she arrives with the right mental attitude, i.e. that his/her activities will result in the retailer selling more products and increasing profits. To do this, the merchandiser must appreciate the retailer's overall problems and not just those relating to the merchandiser's product group. For example, the merchandiser must be aware of the retailer's problems of stock and order control, of the ideal minimum and maximum stock levels, the balancing of appropriate stock levels with bulk-buying discounts and special offers. Obviously stock will have to be increased if a product is to be specially promoted. For example, studies carried out in the retail food trade indicate that, on average, three times more stock is needed if products are specially displayed but sold at the usual prices, and five times more stock is needed if the product is specially displayed and is being promoted at an incentive price. Stock levels must be related to sales, the delivery cycles of suppliers and the value of using store space for one product with a certain volume and gross margin as opposed to another product. To appreciate fully the retailer's position, the merchandiser must be aware of the fact that true profitability in retailing (as in any other type of business) is based not upon net or gross profit, but upon net return on capital invested.

Private labelling (i.e. having goods supplied with the retailer's own name) can increase retail sales and lower cost because it promotes the retailer's name and image and because, as the retailer will be required to place large orders to warrant the production of products with his/her name on them, lower prices and/or advantageous terms can be negotiated. Private labelling will affect the merchandiser as there is yet another 'brand' to fight and especially if his/her company are the suppliers. If the latter is the case, the sales person may be expected to 'merchandise' his own company brand and that of the private label of the retailer; or at least do nothing that will adversely affect the sales of the retailer's private label brand. With 'private labels', the retailer competes by locating his lower-price brand next to the higher-priced brand leader.

Self-service as a shopping system is generally recognised to lower retailers' costs and extend sales compared with the counter service and self-selection methods. The merchandiser/sales person's approach and the merchandising technique employed will need to be appropriate for the type of system being used in the particular retail outlet. Products merchandised in self-service situations need to 'sell themselves' as opposed to counter service stores where shopping advice is readily available.

The merchandiser/sales person who can help the retailer eliminate 'dead spots' in a store is always welcome. Dead spots arise because of the shape and/or layout of a store or the sequence of stock or direction of 'traffic'. Often because of his/her wide experience in a variety of stores, the merchandiser can give advice or, by creating a 'selling' display, create shopping interest that can turn the dead spot into a profit-earning area.

The final important aspect of merchandising is that of space allocation. How much space should a merchandiser/sales person endeavour to obtain for his products and showcards? Not storage space in the retailer's store room, but selling space on the counter, in the window, or stocking and selling space upon shelves, and special display space, all within sight of the potential consumer. There is a correct share of space the merchandiser should obtain, not only from his company's point of view but also from the retailer's viewpoint. If the merchandiser does not get the correct space allocation, he will not maximise his company's marketing opportunity in each retail outlet, and the retailer will not maximise his profits. It is often a question of selling the retailer on the level of the profit factor that the merchandiser's product will achieve against those of competitors'.

The retail store owner or manager in any product field will be motivated by such statistics as the anticipated profit per linear metre or cubic metre of space and the percentage the product contributes to total gross profit in relation to the percentage of total floor space that the product display will occupy. These and others need to be related to feasible anticipated sales volume, net/gross profit margins, pack size, shelf or counter depth etc.

Whether the product is small or bulky, if advantages can be shown to the retailer, the merchandiser can get more space for his products, displays or showcards and, what is more important, space at recognised selling 'hot spots' in the store by indicating profit optimisation in these places. In the case of a brand leader, it is possible to 'sell' the retailer that space for particular lines should be allocated on a basis of the share of the market that the product achieves.

The advantages to the merchandiser of space allocation by market share is obvious and to the retailer the advantages have been identified as follows:

- It avoids out-of-stock situations.
- Avoids wasting space on small brands.
- Avoids too frequent refilling of shelves of small amounts of major brands.
- Logical grouping makes customer selection quick and simple.

– It is the best presentation of products that will give extra selling power to the shelf.
– It means that less frequent and easy shelf-filling reduces labour costs

If the merchandiser's product is not a brand leader, he must discover its particular advantages in the five main space-allocation measurement areas mentioned earlier. By getting at least his product's correct space allocation, the merchandiser is blocking competitors' efforts to obtain a greater share.

Shelves in self-service stores and supermarkets should be stocked with regard to economy of the retailer's labour and the appearance of the packaging of the product. For example, at least one-and-a-half cases of each size of the product should be on the shelves if possible, so that when the shelf stock drops to half a case, the shelf-filler can replace with a whole case. This eliminates the extra labour of returning partially full cases to the store room, avoids loose packages being damaged, removes the temptation to pilfer and makes stock checks easier.

There exists a difference of opinion as to where the big demand item in each product group should be located. Some merchandisers say that the product with the largest market share should be placed in the first section of the gondola or island; first in this case meaning the one the shopper sees first in relation to traffic flow. Others claim that the big demand item should be at the far end of the gondola so that the shopper has to shop the whole 'island' (fitment) (that may contain some impulse items) to reach the next section of the store. In any case, the first section of a display unit is often masked or its impact lowered by an 'end island' mass display. Also, if the merchandiser wishes to promote a particular line, the best place is next to the high demand items. In most cases, the vertical dressing of shelves has more impact and is more convenient for the shopper. A complete vertical section of a gondola starting with the large, heavy sizes on the bottom shelf (because it has larger stocking capacity) rising to the small sizes on the top shelf, with the fastest moving size between waist and eye level. On the other hand, the horizontal dressing of shelves is effective where there are demand and impulse items in adjacent product groups. For example, if the high demand white sliced bread is placed along the bottom shelf, speciality breads on the next, and the high profit margin and high impulse item cakes are placed between waist and eye level, high profit optimisation will take place. If possible, the merchandiser should try to establish his own company's 'department' within the retail store. This is often possible if the products have a sufficiently large turnover, or if the company is willing to provide a special fitment and if there is room for it; although today it is possible to 'rent' space in certain types of retail shops.

The basis of effective merchandising is the ability of the merchandiser to assess a retail situation, determine the problem, weigh and decide the best strategy, and take action seizing the most appropriate merchandising opportunity. He/she must endeavour to increase the company's selling area within each store, increase the number of displays, ensure stocks are in a selling position, make it easy for customers to buy, and to use all the techniques of merchandising to show the potential customers the benefits of buying his/her company's product here and now. Further, the merchandiser must be prepared to check the results of his/her merchandising activities. The merchandiser must be primarily a sales person but with a creative flair for new ideas, unusual approaches, new angles, and have the ability to create displays that motivate consumers into buying action. The merchandiser will always be welcome if he/she can give the retailer new merchandising ideas, because he/she is helping to move stocks out rather than simply selling them in.

To combat retailer inertia, the merchandiser/sales person and the company must keep the retailer aware of the market and profit opportunity month after month. The key to this is commitment by the sales person if he/she is responsible for merchandising or by the member of specialist merchandising teams.

Summary

Merchandising, defined as psychological persuasion at the point of purchase without the aid of a sales person, is important to any manufacturer, processor, importer, distributor, wholesaler whose product/service combination is sold through retailers. Although it can be seen as part of the activity of sales promotion, it is normally implemented through the sales team or a team of specialist merchandisers. If the latter is not under the direct control of the sales manager, there must be very strong liaison because goods must be sold into the retail store before merchandising can take place.

Many manufacturers originate and advise on merchandising policies and strategies together with supplying sales promotional and display material and require their sales team/merchandisers to take the greatest advantage at the point of purchase.

Personnel involved need to be trained in the specialised skills of merchandising and need to be continually updated as to what is currently motivating consumers. Persuasion of retailers by means of planned selling techniques to accept what will be initially intangible merchandising concepts that sell more goods profitably is fundamental to the success of merchandisers/sales persons in the retail situation.

Merchandising activity in retail stores can increase sales/profits in three main ways. It can increase the number of customers by shop improvements, advertising and public relations, improving and establishing a particular store image, by specialisation, by the use of special offers, by making the retail store easy to shop and by appreciating and allowing for consumers' shopping habits. It can sell more to existing customers by effective merchandising and display, by the selling ideas of products usage, by skilful joint merchandising of demand and impulse lines, by related-item display, by appealing to consumers' mental appetite, by tying-in point of purchase merchandising with the company's (manufacturer or retailer) current advertising theme(s) and the appropriate use of tactical pricing.

Finally, merchandising activity in retail stores can increase sales/profits by a combination of increasing sales and lowering costs. This can be done by improving stock turn, appreciating and using all available retailer statistics, by the appropriate use of private labelling, by effective stock and order control, by eliminating 'dead spots' in a store, by the adoption and enhancement of self-service techniques and also the skilful use of space allocation.

Merchandising is about seizing opportunities at the point of purchase in the context of the current market situation, monitoring results and taking remedial action that produces an improved profit situation for both supplier and retailer.

Questions

1. What is merchandising and why is it important to a company and its sales function when selling product/service combinations through middlemen and/or retailers?

2. Merchandising requires special personal attributes in the sales person; what are they and what is the case for having a special team of merchandisers?

3. What are the merchandising activities that tend to increase the number of customers in retail outlets and how do they operate?

4. What are the merchandising activities that tend to sell more to existing customers and what personal qualities do they demand of a sales person/merchandiser?

5. Some merchandising activities have a direct effect on sales and costs in retail outlets; identify these, indicating how they affect the retailer and the sales person/merchandiser.

Product support

Product support is an activity that enhances the effectiveness of the sales team, and is particularly important in the area of selling/marketing industrial, scientific and technical products and consumer durables.

In the marketing organisation of a company, brand or product managers are often appointed who are responsible for the overall profitability of a particular group of brands or products. They are responsible for everything related to the brand or product group, e.g. marketing research, pricing, liaison with production/finance/distribution, forecasting, advertising and sales promotion etc. The sales function and particularly the field sales force should be given and can obtain from the brand and product manager information regarding the product (e.g. technical data) that can then be used in sales presentations.

There are some situations where the products are being sold to/through highly qualified professionals (e.g. doctors and pharmaceutical products) or are particularly complex (e.g. 'high-tech', computers etc.), are based on particular technical concepts (e.g. excavators based on hydraulics, printing presses using pneumatics) or on some specialised scientific process (e.g. the industrial applications of precious metals, particularly platinum, as catalyst materials in chemical processes), where an active product support group needs to be set up.

Such a group will not only supply data to customers, enabling/licensing authorities (e.g. local authorities, health regulating bodies, weights and measures inspectorate etc.) and the sales team, but members would be available to technically brief the sales team at meetings or conferences and make 'double calls' with individual sales persons to customers where particular technical problems exist or technical advice is required.

The product support group may or may not be under the direct control of the sales manager, but as a sales support/back-up organisation he/she should have a part in the planning and operation of such a group in view of its importance to the sales team. The product support group/section functions to co-ordinate the collection, processing, distribution of data and information on products, processes and techniques at a central source. Naturally the type of support needed/given will depend on the type of product/service the industry/market and the particular company needs, but the scope of such support can be seen from the example of one company. The product support group/section activities are divided into two areas:

(a) Services:
    Specialised sales training (for own and distributor's staff)
    Service training (for own, distributor's, end user staff)
    Product appreciation, knowledge, utilisation, training
    Technical enquiries
    Visitors' reception
    Demonstrations
    Conference/symposia facilities
    Technical services (including collection and processing of technical
      data)
(b) Publications:
    Training material (sales and service)
    Service information

Service bulletins
Parts change bulletins
Parts manuals
Microfilm parts slides for microfilm readers in sales offices or at
  distributors' trade counters
Operator/maintenance handbooks
Workshop manuals
Proprietary parts literature
Comparative competitive data
Technical sale presentations

The flow plan of these areas is shown in Fig. 10.3.

In some companies, product support activity is extended to contract maintenance of plant and equipment, safety inspections, and the evaluation of plant and processes for insurance and renewal purposes.

The product support group will need to reflect the particular needs of the product type, the science or technology on which it is based, the market segment for which it is intended and the company organisation. Thus with pharmaceuticals, product support could take the form of a medical services unit led by the medical director (usually a doctor) and including such specialists as pharmacologists and others to provide data sheets and products related to medical conditions, advice on the application and efficiency of new/changed product formulations and advice to the sales team.

In situations where a service is the 'main product', technical support is often needed, e.g. large accounting firms may have taxation specialists, insurance companies may have group pension scheme specialists, banks may have specialists in small businesses, shares, securities, overseas transactions etc.

Product support activities are also crucial to the installation, operation, maintenance of consumer-durable products such as cars, washing machines, vacuum cleaners, television receivers, video recorders etc. These are important customer service activities and their technical nature requires them to be performed by personnel who are trained and have up-to-date product and technical data, the latter being provided by the product support team. This is essential whether the service is provided directly by the company, its retailer, agents/distributors or specifically franchised repair companies.

Effective product support is a very saleable service ranging from being an added sales benefit that the sales person can use to sell the basic product/service combination or a revenue earner in its own right through the sale of supplementary/additional technical and training manuals to charges for contract maintenance, safety inspections etc.

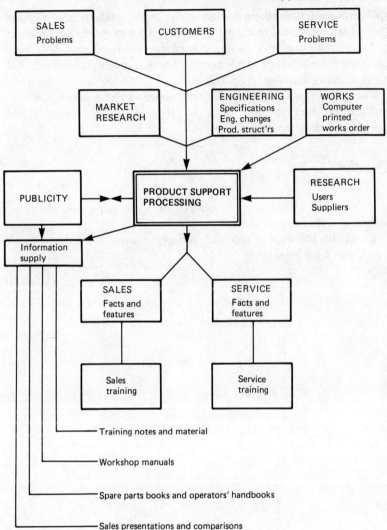

Fig. 10.3 Product support group flow plan

Summary

Product support is necessary where the product/service combination is complex, based upon a technical concept, involves a highly specialised process, or where the customers are professional and/or technical users. Product knowledge is a basic requirement for any member of the sales team and can be injected into the selling process by either employing technical specialists and training them as sales persons, or giving sales persons (perhaps trained or experienced in another product group area) product knowledge. In less complex product areas, brand or product managers can often supply adequate product/technical information, but in complex product/technical areas specialised product support is essential.

Product support can be given through advice and information, services, publications and, in some cases, is extended into maintenance and insurance vetting/monitoring activities.

Questions

1. Why is product support needed for some industrial, scientific, technical and consumer-durable products?

2. Identify the scope of potential product support in two industries with which you have knowledge.

The impact of the various environments in which sales management operates

Sales management operates within a number of environments/ constraints/relationships: broadly, they can be classified as internal to a business which, by implication, can be considered at least partially controllable; and those external to a business which, by implication, are non-controllable.

The figure on page 334 shows the main factors involved, all of which can affect the role/activities of sales management.

The external factors determine the broad environmental limits within which a business in general and the sales function in particular will operate. The majority of these factors cannot be changed to any great extent by individual company action but they need to be recognised and appropriate allowance made for them in sales management decision-making and operations. Some, however, can be influenced and therefore could be seen as partially controllable, e.g. a company could develop products, processes or services that could affect technology or adopt policies that affect the activities of competitors/consumers/trade channel behaviour.

Changes in, and the impact of, internal factors will need to be anticipated and evaluated and should be reflected in the system and operation of the sales function.

The interface between sales management and other major functions of a company (i.e. production, purchasing, finance, accounting, personnel, research and development etc.) were examined in Chapter 1.

Chapter 11 covers some internal factors by examining the sales interface with certain general practices/concepts in marketing, together with the activities that make up the fact-finding, analytical and strategy-determining activities of marketing.

Chapter 12 examines the sales interface with the communications, service and tactical aspects of marketing and the special relationship with brand and product management.

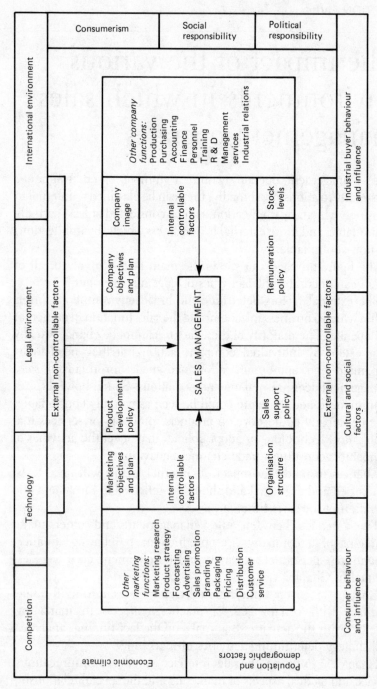

Factors internal and external to the company that affect Sales Management

Chapter 13 examines selected external factors/environments that particularly affect the activities of the sales function and sales management.

Chapter 14 examines changes/trends that are emerging or are expected to emerge in the future to the various environments in which sales management operates and how they are expected to affect sales management thinking, its role objectives, strategies and organisational structures.

Companies (and, by implication, sales management) cannot operate in a vacuum. Management's success will depend not only on its ability to accommodate the present and future internal and external environments/constraints/relationships but also on its ability to identify them or changes in them, in the first place.

CHAPTER 11

The sales interface with marketing (1)

Objectives

The aim of this chapter is to examine the relationship/interface between the sales function and various basic marketing practices/ concepts and the fact-finding, analytical, strategy-determining activities of marketing. It considers what the sales function can expect to get from them and what sales and sales management could be expected to contribute to them. The basic marketing concepts include the marketing concept, consumer/user satisfactions, environmental pressures, product/service life-cycle, market segmentation, market position, market opportunity, marketing mix, and the optimum profit product/service mix. The fact-finding, analytical activities considered include marketing research, product/service planning (to encompass new product/ service policy and development, and policies relating to factors that cannot be 'divorced' from the product/service itself, i.e. branding, packaging, pricing), and market and sales forecasting. As part of a company team effort, the sales function and, consequently, sales management is very much involved in integrating effort, avoiding duplication and conflict at the interface with marketing (and for that matter with any other part of the business) and working towards the common aims – the company policy and plan.

Basic marketing concepts and their relevance to the sales function

It is obvious that the sales plan and the marketing plan should be compatible with each other and both with the overall company plan. The closeness of their nature and function will cause, inevitably, some overlap of marketing and sales activity in some companies. In fact, in some small/medium companies the sales manager will be the marketing executive in all but name, while in some larger companies the sales manager and the sales function will come under the marketing manager/director, and in others marketing and sales have distanced themselves from each other. The ideal situation is for both the sales and marketing functions to be highly integrated, highly interdependent with each other and with other functions in the company. By understanding/appreciating the implication of marketing for sales management, the sales manager and his team can be more effective in the market place.

There is a distinct difference between the *marketing concept* and *marketing*. The *marketing concept* is a philosophy, an attitude or a course of business thinking, while *marketing* is a process or a course of business action. Naturally, the way of thinking determines the course of action.

To be effective, the marketing concept must permeate the entire company from top to bottom. Executives in production, finance etc. should all adopt the marketing concept in their thinking and yet not necessarily be involved directly in marketing activities. The sales manager and the sales function are no exceptions to this approach.

The *marketing concept* is a philosophy, not a system of marketing or an organisation structure. Basically, it is about marketing decisions in all functional areas of a company in terms of what is good for the company in the 'market-place', which should of course be reflected in all sales management and sales function activities.

Marketing, on the other hand, is the 'umbrella' process of integrating and co-ordinating all the functions which serve to identify and anticipate needs, communicate these needs to research and development and to production, create and stimulate demand, and transfer the products and services from the supplier to the customer. It will be seen that the sales team's approach to identifying customer needs and satisfying them is very close to some of the aspects of marketing; each can contribute to the other.

The extent to which an organisation can orientate itself towards its market depends on the nature of its business and the peculiarities of those markets. The more advanced technically and scientifically an industry, the more will the 'customer's' needs be influenced by the results of the supplier's own research. In fact, the customer in such 'industries' is often best served by being persuaded (often by sales personnel) to modify his ideas, method, approaches, so that his needs are more economically or effectively satisfied than by those which he may originally specify. The sales team has a crucial role in this as well as the other methods of customer communications (advertising, sales promotion etc.).

Customers do not buy products/services but *bundles of consumer/user satisfactions*, i.e. what the product/service will do for them rather than what it is or its physical make-up. These satisfactions, which are the basis of buying motives, can be logical (e.g. price) or psychological (e.g. status) and can be experienced before, during and after purchase. Every individual (personal or corporate buyer) has certain needs, some of which are latent inasmuch as the individual having lived with a problem or set of circumstances may not be aware that a solution is available.

Needs vary from one time period to another. Also priorities change, e.g. if the objective of a purchase is to replace a worn-out machine, the replacement order will not be followed immediately by another but, if the priority suddenly becomes one of expansion, many more will be needed. Further, needs can have different status levels, i.e. there are those that must be satisfied (e.g. food), those that should be satisfied, and those that could be satisfied; three different sales opportunities.

Marketing men and/or marketing researchers will tend to search for *buying motives* of groups of customers or market segments and should be able to advise the sales function where the most likely customers are for the company's product/service combinations. The individual sales person will need to identify the potential customers in his/her geographical sales area and then, through research and discussion in sales interviews, identify a particular customer's corporate, sectional and personal needs and then 'tailor' a sales presentation suggesting product/service combinations that will meet those needs.

Another influencing factor is that of *environmental pressure*. All companies operate in, and are therefore affected by, the situations and problems of four independent environments: those of the international economy (terms of trade, labour costs, exchange rates etc.), the national economy (booms/slumps, government policies etc.), the more broadly defined customer satisfaction market (e.g. electricity, gas, coal, all compete with oil-fired central heating) and the immediate market (e.g. other competing manufacturers of oil-fired boilers). By asking the question 'What business are we in?' and coming to the conclusion, for example, that the company is in the home central heating business, rather than the business of the manufacture of oil-fired boilers, both the marketing and the sales approaches are more likely to be successful because of their customer-need orientation.

The effects/pressures of the four environments on a company's business must be anticipated and reflected in the planning of both marketing and sales operations/approaches.

An additional aspect of environmental pressures on marketing and sales is that they are affected by certain *non-controllable external factors*, including:

    (a) consumer/user attitudes and habits
    (b) competition
    (c) trade attitude and habits
    (d) government controls
    (e) technological factors
    (f) cultural and social factors
    (g) economic factors

(h) the legal system
etc.

Marketing and sales plans and personnel need to identify and allow for the problems and take advantages of the opportunities that the above environmental pressures cause (see also Chapter 13).

Concept of the life-cycle

All products, processes and services have life-cycles. There is a life-cycle for the individual company's product and there is also one on an industry-wide basis, which is really the sum total of all individual company life-cycles for a grouping of products that are physically very similar or offer similar customer satisfactions.

Successful marketing depends on the reconciliation of the different stages of the main life-cycles, i.e. the company product/service and overall industry life-cycles. The characteristics of the various stages of product life-cycles can be readily recognised, tending to be the same in most markets although their duration may differ considerably. The market situation changes in each stage of the life-cycle indicating the need for different strategies and tactics. These marketing strategies are effected through the marketing mix (see later). It is life-cycle-stage recognition in combination with effective strategies, tactics and the correct marketing mix that enables a company to achieve optimum profitability and growth.

A hypothetical product life-cycle applicable to an individual brand or a whole product category is shown in Fig. 11.1; the characteristics of each stage and the appropriate effective responses are shown beneath each stage.

Just as the marketing strategies and tactics need to change as each stage of the life-cycle emerges, so do the strategies and tactics of the sales team need to change to deal effectively with the changing market situation. In fact, it may require a different type of sales person to deal with the different selling/communication role in each life-cycle stage.

In the initial stages of the life-cycle of a new generic product, the sales team's approach needs to be one of educating potential customers as to what the new product concept can do for them. It is an approach of 'selling' the need or bringing it to the customer's level of awareness, proving that the new product/service concept can satisfy the need.

In the middle and later stages of such a life-cycle, the sales approach needs to be that of selling brand versus brand. The majority of consumers understand the basic product/service concept and therefore the sales person needs to sell the particular benefits of his 'bundle of satisfactions' against those offered by competitors. The skills needed are not only in the actual selling process but also in the sales person's ability to identify particular

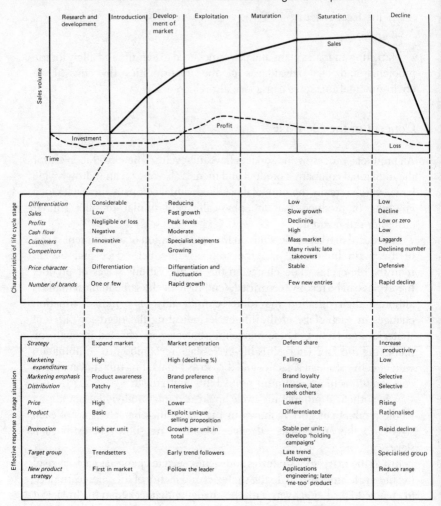

Characteristics of life cycle stage	Introduction	Development of market / Exploitation	Maturation / Saturation	Decline
Differentiation	Considerable	Reducing	Low	Low
Sales	Low	Fast growth	Slow growth	Decline
Profits	Negligible or loss	Peak levels	Declining	Low or zero
Cash flow	Negative	Moderate	High	Low
Customers	Innovative	Specialist segments	Mass market	Laggards
Competitors	Few	Growing	Many rivals; late takeovers	Declining number
Price character	Differentiation	Differentiation and fluctuation	Stable	Defensive
Number of brands	One or few	Rapid growth	Few new entries	Rapid decline

Effective response to stage situation				
Strategy	Expand market	Market penetration	Defend share	Increase productivity
Marketing expenditures	High	High (declining %)	Falling	Low
Marketing emphasis	Product awareness	Brand preference	Brand loyalty	Selective
Distribution	Patchy	Intensive	Intensive, later seek others	Selective
Price	High	Lower	Lowest	Rising
Product	Basic	Exploit unique selling proposition	Differentiated	Rationalised
Promotion	High per unit	Growth per unit in total	Stable per unit; develop 'holding campaigns'	Rapid decline
Target group	Trendsetters	Early trend followers	Late trend followers	Specialised group
New product strategy	First in market	Follow the leader	Applications engineering; later 'me-too' product	Reduce range

Fig. 11.1 A hypothetical life-cycle with stage characteristics and appropriate response (from G. J. Bolt, *Marketing and Sales Forecasting*. Kogan Page Ltd, 1981, pp. 38 and 39)

customer types for whom his/her product/service combinations are most appropriate.

The sales approach in these later life-cycle stages will be affected by the fact there will tend to be more replacement or repeat purchase product/ service customers than new users. It is also a period when, as the demand for the product has 'plateaued' and new competitors' business can only be taken from existing market shares, the sales function will expect considerable support from marketing and advertising functions to help it at least to hold its existing sales volume and market share.

Extensions to product/service life-cycles by improvements/developments of the 'deal' being offered will mean that the sales person has more to offer existing and potential customers, possibly opening a wider market for the overall enhanced product/service.

Another implication of the product/service life-cycle for the sales function is that the type of customer tends to change as the life-cycle progresses, requiring modifications in the sales approach for each type. In the early stages of the life-cycle of a new generic product, the sales strategy must be to sell to the 'personality leadership/trendsetting types' at the personal customer level and to the companies recognised as industry leaders at the corporate level; these are the customers who set the new trends. They do this either to be 'unique/ultra modern' at the personal level or are looking for increased efficiency and/or lower costs at corporate level.

At a later period of time, these initial customer types are followed by the more conservative types who either did not believe the claims made for the new generic product/service or did not see that it immediately applied to them or are waiting for problems normally associated with new products to be resolved. Often, because of initial resistance to the new product/service combination, the most effective sales approach is to provide them with 'plausible rationalisations for climbing down' from their initial stance. Alternatively, testimonial selling (i.e. on the visual or verbal proof testimony of satisfied customers) and showing them what benefits have been achieved elsewhere are also useful sales tactics.

The final stages of life-cycles are populated by customer types who have been described as 'laggards'. They tend not to change unless they are forced to do so by competition or strong customer preference, and the sales approach in this case is not only to 'sell the benefits' of the sales person's proposals but also to highlight what they are losing by not changing/purchasing. By the time of these latter stages of the life-cycle, the 'trendsetters' have normally moved on to the second generation of the product/service or found a new substitute generic product.

These life-cycle implications for the sales function require awareness of them by the sales team and the ability to adopt appropriate strategies and tactics for the various product/service types, especially in a company that has a variety of products all in different stages of their life-cycles.

Concept of market segmentation

This is the basis of the process by which a company partitions its prospective customers (the market) into sub-groups or sub-markets (segments). Companies have found that if they can identify a viable sub-market (segment), they can cater for the special needs of that segment either exclusively or at least specially and gain a degree of dominance that probably would not be possible with the total market.

Recognising that customers are different can enable the sales manager and the individual sales person to achieve a closer matching of customer needs to the firm's product/service offering. Segmentation strategies allow a company or sub-division of a company to relate its strengths and weaknesses to its marketing/sales approach by ensuring a concentration of resources in those areas where the company has the greatest advantage or the least possible disadvantage. The two main strategies are:

(a) to start with an existing product/service/industry field and study customers and potential customers of the generic product/service to determine if there are differences between buyers of different products/services; or

(b) to start with preconceived notions of what the critical segment variables are, i.e. status, industry type etc.

Segmentation bases in consumer products/services may be by consumer characteristics such as:

(a) Socio-economic/demographic factors, i.e. by:
    (1) Social class – identification through income, education, occupation etc.
    (2) Ethnic race – nationality.
    (3) Demographic – age, sex, religion, family size, life-cycle etc.
(b) Life-style dimensions – these being activities, interests, opinion and demography.
(c) Geographic factors, i.e. urban or rural, advanced economies and developing nations.
(d) Psychological factors – these may be based on personality, buyer's motives, attitudes/values etc.

Segmentation bases in industrial products/service combinations may be customer size, geographic location, industrial classification (the Standard Industrial Classification (SIC) is a useful framework for this), usage rate, type of organisation (importer, manufacturer, processor, wholesaler), product type.

Both consumer and industrial segmentation is possible on the basis of customer response to products, quality, brand, performance, price, advertising and sales promotion, distribution etc.

Market segmentation is a valuable help for the sales team as it can indicate where sales are most likely to be found, and for the sales manager it is an aid to management as he/she can indicate to the sales team what type of customers should be canvassed for business.

Market segments can be identified by the marketing/sales function in terms of the immediate customer, the intermediate customer and the final customer. For example, in the case of an aircraft manufacturer, the intermediate customers could be envisaged as airlines and/or tour operators and the ultimate customers the various types of travellers (personal, business, holiday etc.).

Market segmentation can be determined by company decision, e.g. to only deal with wholesalers, to only deal through pharmacies as opposed to supermarkets, to only deal with original equipment manufacturers (OEMs) etc. It can also be determined by the sales manager carrying out analyses of past performance to identify segments in which the sales/profits ratio was optimised and predicting whether the situation is likely to continue.

Concept of market position

This is crucial to the effectiveness of a company in the market-place and should be a fundamental aspect of marketing/sales management planning.

The position in the market of a product/service is difficult to determine and can be both real and/or apparent. Real in the sense that in retrospect it will be possible for the company to see by sales, market share, segment analysis where the product/service position was in a past sales period. Apparent in the sense that although the company may think its product and/or service is in one position in the market, customers may perceive it to be in another. Thus a company which markets and sells what it perceives to be a high-quality/relatively high-priced product/service will have problems if customers perceive it as a medium-quality/high-priced product/service.

Market position factors need not only be price and quality, but also performance, design, discounts, product, service, image (company), image (product/service) and combinations of these; in fact, all the factors that make up the 'total deal' and what the sales team will be selling.

Further, it must be recognised that the market position as perceived by customers in one market segment will be different to that perceived by customers in another; therefore, market position is linked with the concept of market segmentation. The relationship could be viewed through the use of a matrix format as in Fig. 11.2.

In each market segment, the marketing/sales objectives and strategies will be different, particularly in view of existing or potential competition.

The importance of market position to sales management can be seen in Fig. 11.3 where the marketing function believes it has placed a particular product range in position X, i.e. the lowest price in the high-quality market category. But stockists and the ultimate customer perceive it to be the highest-priced product in the medium-quality category, i.e. position Y. It will be difficult for the sales team to persuade stockists to stock and/or the ultimate customer to buy at the high-quality price. There will be similar sales team problems in segment B if a company positions a product range at point W (i.e. relatively low in the high-price, high-quality market) when the need/gap in the market-place is for a very low-priced, low-quality (expendable) product, i.e. position Z.

Market position	Segment A	Segment B	Segment C	
Factor quality/price				
High				
	● X	● W		
Medium	● Y			
Low				
		● Z		

Fig. 11.2 A matrix format indicating market position in the context of quality and price

The concept of market position is important to the sales manager in explaining that price is relative to the quality of products/service offered and appropriate to the market segment. Most sales teams want the highest of all qualities for the lowest of all prices.

Market position is also linked with other aspects of marketing/sales planning, i.e. product/service/packaging description, market/brand share, customer/user target group, basic customer benefits, desired image, media policy, promotional policy, profits policy etc.

Concept of market opportunity

This has been defined as '. . . a marketing/sales opportunity, a challenge to purposeful marketing/sales action that is characterised by a generally favourable set of environmental circumstances and an acceptable probability of success . . .' It should result in providing customer satisfaction at a profit. Thus there may be a gap in the maket for a piece of hi-tech equipment that would meet a market need but, if it requires a 3-year run to introduce and to maximise sales to recoup R & D and/or promotional costs and a further technological breakthrough is predicted in the next 2 years, it may have a low and unacceptable probability of success. Thus the sales team will have difficulty in persuading customers to purchase. Perhaps a better marketing strategy would be to enhance/revitalise existing products and be prepared for the early exploitation of the next anticipated technological breakthrough.

There are other subsidiary market opportunities. For example, there is the opportunity for the company to innovate, to introduce something new, to devise some new product/service combination etc. New innovations need to be considered in the context of the life-cycle concept and the types of customer involved. Sometimes, because of the fact that the innovative product/service is new, it may be hard to sell and the sales team will need considerable promotional support, but it does give them something new to sell to customers and a new product/service combination tends to arouse interest/curiosity in the market-place.

Market opportunities may also arise (or can be initiated) that improve efficiency for customers, create a competitive difference (i.e. that sets a company apart from its competitors) and find a special market segment in which to operate. All these will help a company's sales team exploit a market situation and sell its product/service combination to the best advantage. At the same time, members of the sales team should be encouraged to feed back any opportunities they perceive in dealing with potential and existing customers.

Concept of the marketing mix

This term has been defined as referring '. . . to the apportionment of effort, the combination, the designing and the integration of the elements of marketing/sales into a programme or "mix" which, on the basis of an appraisal of the marketing resources and forces, will best achieve the objectives of an enterprise at a given time'. An example is given in Fig. 11.3.

It will be seen that the component parts of the marketing mix can be categorised into marketing strategy (fact-finding, analysis and planning activities) and marketing tactics (communication and service activities).

The emphasis or mix of the various component parts of marketing (marketing research, forecasting, advertising, public relations, selling etc.) will vary with each stage of the life of a product/service combination.

The concept of the marketing mix is based on the principles of delegation as examined in Chapter 1; as an organisation becomes larger, the various marketing activities are delegated to specialists. It is considered that the activities delegated by the marketing executive will be better performed. In small companies, one person may be responsible for several functions. In large organisations there will be further delegation of activities of the delegated individual marketing functions. In Fig. 11.3, sales (selling) is considered to be part of the overall marketing function.

The importance of the concept of the marketing mix to sales management and the sales team is that if the balance is not right, it will be very much harder to sell the product/service combinations being marketed by the company. For example, if the marketing research function has identified the wrong market segments, or R & D have developed the marginally wrong

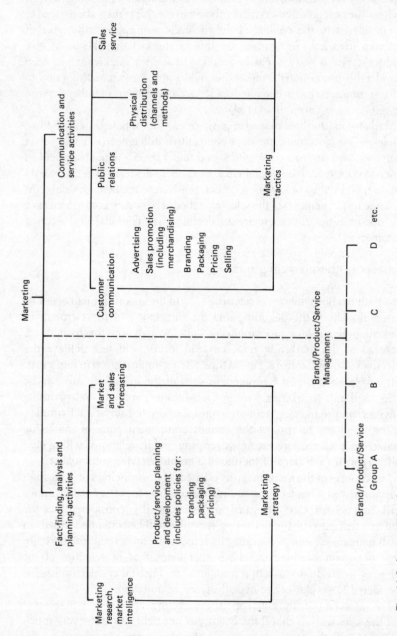

Fig. 11.3 An example of a marketing mix

products/services, or prices are set at the wrong levels, or packaging and branding are inappropriate, or the market and company sales have been wrongly predicted etc., the sales team will not be able to optimise market opportunities. On the other hand, the sales function needs to be organised in such a way to make the maximum contribution to the marketing mix to support the other activities.

Concept of optimum profit product/service mix

A broad group of products intended for essentially similar uses and possessing reasonably similar physical characteristics constitutes a product line. The product mix is the full list of all products offered for sale by a company. The structure of the product mix has dimensions of both breadth and depth. Its breadth is measured by the number of product lines it includes; its depth by the assortment of sizes, colours, models, qualities, prices etc. offered within each product line.

An optimum profit can be achieved by a company when the various product lines offered are sold in relation to a certain ratio that maximises profit opportunity.

Further, the product mix concept has regard for the age of products and their current life-cycle stage; such concern ensures that all the products of a multi-product company do not decline at the same time.

The problem for the sales manager with this concept is that as the sales function of a company does not have control of the costs that go into a product/service combination and has only limited control (none in some cases) of prices and discounts, it is wrong to hold it responsible for the difference between the two, i.e. profits.

Product/service combinations that produce the greatest profit may be the most difficult to sell and so it may be necessary to give each individual sales person sales quotas of each product/service combination in a ratio that makes up the optimum profit product mix in their sales area. This needs to be backed by a geared incentive and/or commission scheme and a high degree of motivation from all levels of sales management.

The various marketing concepts briefly examined can help both the sales manager and the sales team, but in each case their successful application requires some contribution from the sales function.

Marketing research

The component parts of the marketing mix (page 346) individually and collectively affect sales management and the sales function, of which they are also a component part anyway. It is therefore necessary to examine these relationships; the first to be considered is marketing research. This has been defined as '. . . . the systematic and objective search for, and analysis of, information relevant to the identification and solution of any problem in the field of marketing. . . .'*

It has also been defined by reference to a multi-dimensional model relating marketing research information types to research types and the overall marketing research process as shown in Fig. 11.4.†

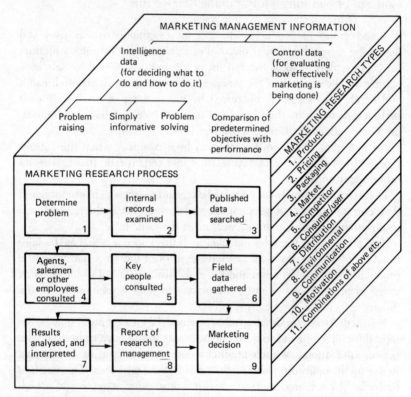

Fig. 11.4 Marketing research as a multi-dimensional model relating information types to research types and the overall process

In the context of these definitions, research into sales and for the sales function is part of marketing research. Therefore the sales manager should be able to expect to receive relevant information but also be expected to contribute sales and other marketing research/intelligence information. The marketing research function needs to be well briefed on the sales manager's information needs, i.e. to identify the nature of a problem, to solve

* P. E. Green and D. S. Tull, *Research for Marketing Decisions*. Prentice Hall, NJ, USA.
† Gordon J. Bolt, *Marketing in the E.E.C.* Kogan Page Ltd, 1973, p. 23.

problems, to provide continuous data that is simply informative about the segments in which the sales team operates. These types of information are shown in Fig. 11.4 under the heading of 'Intelligence data (for deciding what to do and how to do it)'. It is in this area that the sales team contribute market intelligence which the sales manager can obtain from individual sales team members' activity reports, regional/area managers' reports and by making his/her own field visits. Obviously such market intelligence will be used by the sales manager for his/her own use and/or 'filtered' into reports to top management and the marketing research function. In the context of obtaining reliable and relevant information, it does indicate the importance of training and encouraging the sales team to provide market intelligence and of well-designed sales team activity report forms.

The other aspect of marketing management information (see Fig. 11.4), i.e. 'Control data (for evaluating how effectively marketing is being done)', has its equivalent in sales management. The methods and techniques were examined in Chapter 8, i.e. the supervision and control of the sales team.

The actual types of sales analysis that need to be carried out was covered in detail in Chapter 2 in relation to sales management planning and organisation.

The marketing research function (and MR agencies it may use) can be seen to research and collect information on a broad/macro level (i.e. about markets and market segments) whereas the sales function tends to collect information on an individual customer/micro level.

The information from the ten marketing research types shown in Fig. 11.4 (which includes sales research under the title of communication research) are obtained through a variety of methods indicated in the diagram as the 'Marketing research process', and this can be easily emulated or adapted to meet the needs of the sales manager.

In the case of No. 6 (Field data gathered), the methods used are personal interviews, telephone interviews, postal questionnaires, group discussions, panel or audit methods observation, bibliographical and statistical research. The sales manager can and should get his field and internal sales teams, national and branch sales office personnel or himself/herself personally to use these methods to obtain information, but the whole operation must be put into perspective. All sales personnel can, if observant or simply inquisitive, acquire the information they and the sales manager need, but it should not take precedence over their main function, i.e. to sell.

Because of their close proximity to customers, both the sales team and the sales support staff can provide/obtain useful micro sales/marketing intelligence data. Such 'grass roots' information could include customers' or potential customers'

(a) manufacturing, processing, wholesaling, retail methods
(b) rate of production, purchasing or sales

(c) quality requirements (maximum and minimum)

(d) testing procedures and standards used

(e) need for finance and/or general trade credit

(f) names of present suppliers; competitor's equipment in use or product stocked

(g) purchasing procedures and organisation

(h) order/supplier decision-making process and patterns

(i) duration and commencement dates of budget periods

(j) stockholding policy

(k) is the customer company, production or marketing orientated, a 'trendsetter' or a follower?

(l) need for technical and other advice

(m) does the customer rely on demand derived from another industry?

(n) what is the seasonal pattern of demand and are purchases influenced by some medium-term business cycle?

(o) has the customer a new, unusual or different application or appeal for the supplier's products?

(p) what are the customer's future development plans?

(q) in which industrial or consumer goods market segment(s) does the customer operate?

(r) what is the competitive situation of the customer?

(s) what is the current credit rating of the customer?

and many others.

Marketing research serves as professional and/or technical expertise in collecting, classifying and storing relevant information. It should also recommend, execute, interpret and present marketing/sales research studies to marketing/sales management. It is a management tool for reducing managerial risk-taking by providing facts that enable judgements and decisions made by management to be more soundly based. As such, it should be a systematic, continuing study and evaluation of all factors bearing on any business operation which involves management decisions to be made in terms of what is good for the company in the market.

Good sales management decisions must be based on good information; through the interface with the marketing research function, there can be a beneficial two-way process.

Product/service planning

Under this heading are the policies and strategies of product/service development, branding, packaging and pricing. They are dealt with collectively because as they are very much interdependent and in the eyes of the customer they are the product/service.

Medium- and long-term company prosperity needs to be based on a realistic and well-planned new product development policy/strategy programme. As one product/service becomes no longer viable and is phased out, a new or differentiated one must be ready to take its place if the sales/profitability of the organisation is to be assured.

New product/service development

A new product/service is taken to mean a substantial innovation, either in the technological or the marketing/sales sense. The marketing/sales of an existing product/service to a new group of users may call on many of the skills used for evaluating completely new products/services. Development necessarily involves reviewing existing products and/or services, since deletion is just as much a part of the firm's total product/services strategy.

In any firm in a competitive market, new product/service development should be a continuing process. It is, therefore, fundamental that the organisational system should allow sufficient emphasis to this facet of the firm's activities, alongside current operational tasks. The process should germinate in the overall corporate strategy, and comprises the establishment of a product/service strategy, the identification of new ideas and research and development based on these, a marketing analysis and the development of the marketing/sales programme, and a final financial evaluation.

The task responsibility for new product/service development is normally shared between a number of individuals and groups. The chief executive, for example, may be charged with responsibility for corporate strategy; a research and development manager may be briefed to produce 'new' products/services within the overall marketing plan or to fairly 'tight' specifications; the marketing manager may co-ordinate product strategy; and a new product development manager may be responsible for originating, evaluating and launching specific projects. Some firms have a full-time new product manager, or a manager who has responsibility for existing products, to co-ordinate and carry out many of the tasks. Alternatively, this responsibility may be invested in a committee or a venture group, not necessarily permanent, representative of the principal functional areas within the firm; this would necessarily include the sales manager whose contribution as to what will sell in relation to the present tactical market situation, customer types and needs, and the current product/service range, is invaluable.

Every company which manufactures a product or provides a service has the choice of the following:

(a) Buying its new product/service knowledge from outside sources by contract or licence.

(b) Inventing its own entirely new products/services. Because of the individual sales person's close proximity to customer needs and problems, he/she may see a solution in the form of a new product/service.

(c) Developing improved products/services from existing designs/specifications, some of the suggestions for which may come from customers via the sales force.

(d) Engaging some other concern to develop improved products/services for it.

The necessity for taking one of these courses of action arises from the inescapable fact that business is dynamic, that products/services and materials are always improving and, consequently that every product/service has a measurable life-cycle. Occasionally a product/service emerges which is exceptional and which enjoys a highly extended life. Consequently it becomes necessary to consider a carefully designed system dealing with the development of new products/services; for example, its stages could be:

(a) The company decides on a strategy for technological advance over a long-term period or for certain contingencies.

(b) Marketing research and/or the sales function indicates the major directions where successful research effort would bear immediate fruit.

(c) Basic research indicates possible breakthrough areas in the technology.

(d) Applied research expands basic discoveries and applies them to the particular potential customer group.

(e) Design/development produce a new product/service specification either from applied research or direct from market planning.

In the medium/small business, these stages may be 'telescoped' into the activities of one person.

The system is, therefore, highly interactive with new product/service ideas initiating at several points and being developed for eventual production and market launch.

Product/service development covers the revitalisation and development of existing products/services, those new to the company, and new generic ones both for existing and new markets. The information that signals the need for this can originate from a variety of sources, including the sales function. It is important that the sales manager is involved in this type of development. It should also cover the phasing out of products/services when they no longer contribute to the profit or other objectives of a company.

Product/service planning will vary from company to company depending upon customer needs, resources, market situation, objectives etc. It has been suggested that there are four product/service strategy approaches open to most companies in an industry based on changing technology, first to market, follow the leader, applications engineering, 'me-too' (see page 44).

It is important for the sales manager to identify and the sales team to understand the strategy being adopted by the company because the particular choice can affect marketing/sales 'benefits' activity and the performance of the sales team. In different product/service areas, different strategies may apply within the same company/organisation.

There have been many approaches suggested to the concept of product/service portfolio analysis, i.e. where the range (portfolio) of product/service combinations is assessed to produce the most effective/profitable balance.

One such approach that permits the sales manager to decide on the emphasis to be given by the sales team to various product/service groups was suggested by the Boston Group. This enabled the various product/service combinations of a diversified company to be classified on what was called the growth share matrix or product portfolio. The basic matrix* is shown in Fig. 11.5 but in setting up such classifications, consideration must be given to

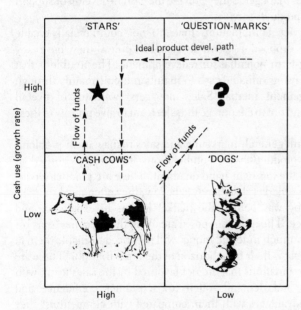

Fig. 11.5 The Boston Consulting Group's growth share matrix or product profile

present and potential market segmentation, the different time horizons for profitability of various product/service combinations, and their relationship with competitors, e.g. a company may be the largest in a particular industry but may not be the market leader in any market segment.

In Fig. 11.5 the product/service combinations that are 'stars' are classified

---

* Adapted from: *The Growth Share Matrix*, © 1970, The Boston Consulting Group, Inc., Boston, USA.

in the upper-left quadrant. They grow rapidly using large amounts of cash to do so, but also generate large amounts of cash because they are leaders in their market segment. Normally, such product/service combinations balance in terms of net cash flow. These are the product/service combinations that the sales team like to sell: high sales volume producers, market leaders, and in great demand; but they tend not to be profit producers. Over a period of time as they move along their individual product/service life-cycle, their growth rate slows down and they either become 'cash cows' or, if they lose market share and/or are overtaken, become 'dogs', i.e. not commercially viable product/service combinations.

Growth tends to be slow for 'cash cows' product/service combinations but market share tends to be high and they can be 'milked' as they generate more cash than is needed to re-invest in their continued development. These lines are popular with the sales team because of high demand and are often attractive to the sales manager as they provide the cash to develop or support new or revitalised products/services.

The product/service combinations that are not commercially viable ('dogs') should be dropped as soon as possible unless they have any immediate or long-term potential for redevelopment. The trouble is that many are retained using valuable cash to maintain them, mainly through reasons of management inertia. Sales managers, watchful of overall profitability, will tend not to encourage the sales team to give priority to these lines.

The really difficult general, marketing and sales management problems are posed by the product/service combinations that are categorised as 'question marks' in the top right-hand quadrant. These are product/service combinations whose market share tends to be low, they often need support, and they are a long way behind the market leaders in experience and customer confidence. The questions posed are: 'Will they become "stars" or "cash cows"?'; 'How much time and money will they need to enable them to catch up?'; and 'What is their time horizon at the top if they do?' These are product/service combinations that are not favoured by the sales team; with low market share and demand, often low customer confidence and awareness, fewer advantages with them compared with competitors, they tend to be hard to sell. Yet if they are to become 'stars' or 'cash cows' eventually, they need all the sales effort the sales team can give; the sales manager may have to consider special incentive commission and management guidance to encourage the sales team to sell these product/service combinations.

Portfolio analysis has wide implications for the sales manager particularly if, as is often the case in new companies, all the product/service combinations are 'stars' (high sales but little if any profit) or alternatively, in more mature and fairly passive companies, they are mainly 'dogs' or 'question marks'.

While it is possible for an organisation to market a service without a product (e.g dry cleaning, design consultancy, travel agency services, maintenance contracts etc.), rarely is it possible to market a product without some aspect of service (e.g. repair and/or spares service, convenience of location, technical advice, performance information, demonstration etc.). The balance between the product/service ratio offered to customers is often crucial in competitive markets and can affect the numbers of products it is possible for the sales function to sell in changing market situations.

The development of new product/service combinations needs to take place within the context of corporate objectives and strategies, following a company situation analysis and possibly a decision to diversify. Analysis of opportunities open to the company will need to be researched, as will the identification of particular market segments. New ideas will need to be screened for viability and profitable commercialisation so that new product/service concepts emerge.

Marketing and profitability feasibility studies of new product/service concepts need to be carried out separately to production feasibility studies, as it may be more appropriate to sub-contract the whole or parts of the production process. On the assessment of this process, a decision to proceed will need to be made.

Product/service development, pack (if appropriate) testing, brand name testing and placement testing either in retailer or user locations and possibly test marketing will need to be carried out before the decision is made to launch the product/service nationally. All these activities should produce an up-to-date, customer-orientated range of product/service combinations that is ahead of competitors and that the sales team will be motivated to sell.

Whenever possible, patents should be applied for and trademarks registered for product/service combinations because they give a type of monopoly and exclusivity, safeguarding unique features and building a company/brand image, which are definite aids to the sales team in presenting a unique 'total deal' to customers.

Branding policy

Branding of products/services is a necessity in highly competitive markets to ensure customer recognition and for the projection of company/product/service images. A brand has been defined as

. . . a combination of all the factors which distinguish one product from another in people's minds and experience. These embrace both physical attributes (such as the quality of basic ingredients, design or formulation, and efficiency) and psychological attributes (the name, company, reputation, packaging and associations aided by, or reflected in, the brand's advertising). Both are relevant in satisfying consumer needs and they are integral to the totality of a brand. . . .*

* Patricia Mann, *Advertising*. A Unilever Educational Booklet, Unilever Ltd, 1981, p. 11.

The importance of branding a company's products to the sales manager and the sales team is that a relationship is established directly between the manufacturer/supplier and the ultimate consumer/user and is therefore not dependent on the actions of middlemen and retailers. Further, through branding, the goodwill originating from the product/service accrues directly to the company. In fact, branding is the basis of 'pull' marketing, i.e. ultimate customers demanding the product/service.

Through branding, a more stable, continuous market and market share is established, making sales relationships easier to maintain, sales forecasting easier to carry out, and production/purchasing easier to schedule.

To be successful, a brand needs three sets of attributes. First, it has to be a coherent totality, not a lot of bits. The physical product, the pack and all the elements of communication (name, style, advertising, pricing, promotions and so on) must be blended into a single brand personality. Secondly, it has to be unique, and constantly developing to stay unique, because it is through this that the brand can offer sustained profit margins. And the uniqueness will depend on both functional and non-functional values: appeals to the senses, the reason and the emotions. The added values beyond the functional may become increasingly important. Thirdly, this blend of appeal must clearly be relevant to people's needs and desires, and be immediate and salient. It must stand out constantly from the 'crowd'; it must spring to mind. This will not, of course, be a static thing: it will constantly have to develop and to take the initiative to avoid 'me-tooism'.

A branding plan should include the statement of objectives, policies and procedures regarding the selection of brand name(s) and trademark(s), individualised or 'family' brand(s) for the product/service range, branding related to quality, geographical areas or market segments, and the degrees of emphasis a company wishes to make on own brand, 'private' label and unbranded products.

Packaging policy

Where appropriate, linked with the product/service research and development plan should be a policy and plan for the development and application of appropriate packaging and labelling linked to a budget and time schedule.

Packaging has been defined by the Institute of Packaging as '. . . a comprehensive term covering the science, art and technology of preparing products for transit to their ultimate point of use, preparing them for anticipated periods and conditions of storage, and of presenting them in such a way that consumers are motivated into purchasing them. . .' In all three roles there are important implications for the sales function; in the first two, it could form the basis of complaints if inadequate, and the opportunity of sales support in the third.

The first steps when considering packaging are to determine the objectives, define the task it is expected to do and state the situation in which the product will be used. Information is required regarding:

(a) The nature of the product to be packed and whether shipment packaging and unit packaging is necessary.

(b) The marketing aims and objectives.

(c) The market–consumer/user types, incomes, needs, fashions, expected product application and usage, attitudes and habits.

(d) The methods and channels of distribution (types and number of stages) to be used, and attitudes of middlemen.

(e) Competitors – their products and their packaging, their market share and image.

From these five information groups, a very good profile of a product's packaging requirements can be obtained. These can be translated into an ideal package policy/strategy by considering its construction, size and shape, labelling copy, design and colour. Incorporated in the packaging plan should be time schedules for review and, if necessary, updating the packaging image, e.g. the existing pack (e.g. colour and design) or changing the type (e.g. from bottle to aerosol) to reflect market needs.

Pricing policy

Pricing policy is another aspect of marketing that has a market impact on the operation of a company's sales team. Prices will obviously affect the number of product/service units purchased by customers, as will changes in the general level of prices of a product/service type relative to other competing types.

In many companies, the 'cost-controlled' price concept is adopted, i.e. a company starts with its own internal costs at a particular moment in time, adds what it calls a 'normal or reasonable' profit margin to arrive at a price. However, in market-orientated companies, prices tend to be set at levels indicated by what the market will bear (this could be higher or lower than a 'cost-controlled price'). It is the maximum price that the consumers/users in the market segment groups at which the company's marketing operations are directed, are prepared to pay.

To survive and prosper, a company has to recover all its costs and earn a profit from its sales, at least in the long term and preferably in the short term as well. Fundamental to most business 'profitability' decisions are:

(a) costs to be incurred (fixed and variable)
(b) prices to be charged and discounts given
(c) volume to be produced/purchased and sold
(d) the breakeven point (the volume point beyond which a profit is made)
(e) the anticipated profit to be earned

While some sales teams are directly involved in pricing through estimating/calculating work/contracts, it is important that the sales manager ensures that everyone in the sales team understands the company's overall pricing policy and on particular product/service combinations. This is to give the individual sales person confidence about prices quoted to customers, i.e. that they are justified, that the 'deal' gives value for money, that some product/service (e.g. 'stars' and 'cash cows') need to be given priority, why some products/services justifiably produce more commission than others, that some products/services will be more highly priced relative to others and how promotional pricing is justified.

It is particularly important that the sales manager and the sales team appreciate how prices will affect the number of units purchased by customers and how changes in the general level of prices in a market, and the individual product/service price in particular, can cause changes in demand patterns. The pricing plan should outline the policy to be adopted during the planning phase, price levels to adopt on launching a new product/service, and price levels considered desirable in later stages of the product/service life-cycle, e.g. skimming, penetration or premium price policy adoption. Trade discount structure, quantity discounts, status pricing etc. would all be included in the pricing plan. The effects of planned and other price changes need to be anticipated in the market and sales forecast.

A very good approach to pricing decision theory has been suggested,* the framework/overview of which is shown as Fig. 11.6. It is based on the need to set objectives or targets for pricing, the selection of a pricing policy from available alternatives, determination of prices and the implementation and administration of the pricing system, including the re-determination of prices, the timing of price changes and discount structures.

Before making pricing decisions, an attempt should be made to understand and appreciate the price decision-making process within the organisation of all main competitors. Often price wars, which can make life very uncomfortable for sales teams, are the direct result of poor, inadequate, distorted information, a situation often exploited by middlemen, retailers and industrial users.

Market and sales forecasting

Market and sales forecasting plays an important role in every major functional area of business and management; every budget, in the last analysis, is dependent on predictions of how many product/service combination units are expected to be sold and/or predictions of anticipated sales revenue. Thus not only does market and sales forecasting have a central

* Professor Dr H. J. Kyhlmeijer, 'Pricing its place in the marketing mix', *Marketing Forum*, July/August 1971.

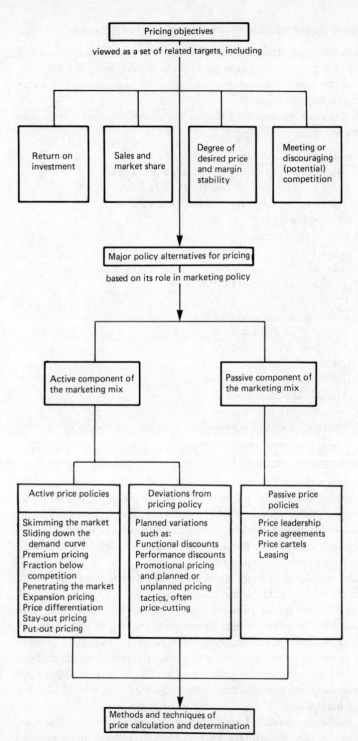

Fig. 11.6 An overview of some of the pricing policy possibilities

role in marketing/sales itself, but also plays a crucial role in other functional areas. For example, for the planning of plant loading in production, for anticipating raw material demand in purchasing, for planning cash flow and capital expenditure in finance.

Forecasting's role in marketing/sales centres around the need to anticipate such items as:

(a) Short-term:
    (1) Sales of each product type (volume and value).
    (2) Sales by geographical area (volume and value).
    (3) Sales by customer type (volume and value).
    (4) Competitors' prices.
    (5) Sales force targets.
    (6) Stock levels.
(b) Medium-term:
    (1) Total sales by product categories.
    (2) Prices.
    (3) General economic conditions.
    (4) Promotional emphasis.
    (5) New product introduction.
(c) Long-term:
    (1) Total sales by product categories.
    (2) Market saturation points.
    (3) New product introduction.
    (4) Existing product withdrawals.
    (5) Marketing research emphasis.
    etc.

Forecasting assumes the ability to identify and understand the forces at work in a market and the ability to predict the future course of these forces. In many companies it is recognised that the sales manager and the sales team, being those in the closest, continuous contact with customers and potential customers, will tend to have the most up-to-date and relevant information regarding their purchasing intentions.

The sales manager, in many companies, will therefore be expected to make, on the basis of information obtained from the sales team and from his/her own research, an important contribution to market and sales forecasting, if not be asked to make the complete forecast. In this situation it would be useful for the sales manager to contact the managers of other functional areas, as often they develop their own methods/forecasts that run in parallel with a company forecast; these 'unofficial' forecasts often yield good forecasting information/comparisons as they are often based on different parameters.

Also, another important forecasting factor is the need for the sales manager to consider not only short-term but also medium- and long-term influences and forecasts. Factors identified in the latter two time horizons can have a gradual but marked effect on the short-term forecast (e.g. a change in technology, availability of particular raw materials etc.).

Market and sales forecast's relationship to budgets can be appreciated by the three definitions:

(a) A market and sales forecast is an estimate of future product/service combination sales in terms of volume (unit forecasts) or value (sales revenue forecast) over a given period of time (short, medium, long term) regarding current and prospective customers.

(b) A budget is a financial statement of forecast revenue and expenditure and/or unit sales over a given period of time.

(c) A market and sales forecast becomes a budget when it is costed and accepted by executives/directors who are responsible for the overall operation of a company.

Forecasts are of two main types: either a 'top-down' approach is taken where a forecast of the total economy and/or the industry is made followed by forecasts for each product/service group or geographic area. Or, alternatively, a 'bottom-up' approach is taken where forecasts are made by individual brand or product managers, or individual sales persons (who submit them to area or regional managers who assemble and 'adjust' them), or from other relevant company personnel; the outcome is a global forecast figure. The sales manager will find that the 'bottom-up' approach is more suited to small/medium companies who cannot afford formal forecasting methods, although these have become fewer as computer power has become more available.

Again the methods of forecasting can be categorised into three groups, quantitative, qualitative and a combination of the two. In Fig. 11.7 the component parts of these two categories have been extracted from a broader analysis of approaches to forecasting. *

Within the broad categories shown in Fig. 11.7, the sales manager has a wide range of methods of varying complexity from which to choose and will be influenced to a certain extent by cost (in terms of time and money), expertise and skill available and by the availability of computer forecasting capacity. Whether this is mainframe or microcomputer capacity, forecasting software packages exist for all business computers. However, their usefulness will depend, if they are 'standard' packages, on whether they are what the forecast needs, e.g. thirteen 4-weekly forecasting periods instead of the 12 calendar months and whether they are interactive. Software packages that include 'spreadsheets' are useful for developing and later adjusting the format to what is needed.

* Reprinted from 'Forecasting: issues and challenges for marketing management' by S. Makridakis and S. Wheelwright, *Journal of Marketing*, October 1977, p. 26, published by the American Marketing Association.

Approaches				Short description
Informal forecasting				*Ad hoc*, judgmental or intuitive methods
FORMAL FORECASTING METHODOLOGIES	*Quantitative methods*	*Causal or regressive*	Single and multiple regression	Variations in dependent variables are explained by variations in the independent one(s)
			Econometric models	Simultaneous systems of multiple regression equations
		Time series	Naive	Simple rules such as: forecast equals most recent actual value or equals last year's same month + 5%
			Trend extrapolation	Linear, exponential, S-curve, or other types of projections
			Exponential smoothing	Forecasts are obtained by smoothing, averaging, past actual values in a linear or exponential manner
			Decomposition	A time series is 'broken' down into trend, seasonability, cyclicality and randomness
			Filters	Forecasts are expressed as a linear combination of past actual values. Parameters or model can 'adapt' to changes in data
			Autoregressive/moving averages (ARMA) (Box-Jenkins Methodology)	Forecasts are expressed as a linear combination of past actual values and/or past errors
	Qualitative methods	*Subjective assessment*	Decision trees	Subjective probabilities are assigned to each event and the approach of Bayesian Statistics is used
			Salesforce estimates	A bottom-up approach aggregating salesmen's forecasts
			Juries of executive opinion	Marketing, production and finance executives jointly prepare forecasts
			Surveys anticipatory research	Learning about intentions of potential customers or plans of businesses
		Technological	Exploration	Uses today's assured basis of knowledge to broadly assess conditions of the future
			Normative	Starts with assessing future goals, needs, desires objectives etc. and works backwards to determine necessary developments to achieve goals etc.

A Immediate (less than one month)   B Short (one to three months)
C Medium (three months to less than 2 years)

Fig. 11.7 Approaches to forecasting

Another factor is how appropriate is the method, whether it is provided/obtained by computers or manually? All forecasting methods have strengths and weaknesses and the sales manager should be aware of these and choose a combination of the most relevant ones with the greatest strengths. Some are objective and tend to be predictions and projections and of a statistical/mathematical nature while others are subjective and tend to be conclusions and based on experience and judgement. The ideal forecast is a combination of both.

The sales manager should have a range of simple and sophisticated forecasting methods available, i.e. to adopt a multi-technique approach, as no one method can include all the parameters or dimensions of a market. Some will need to be carried out in the sales office with additional information either from within the company or from external sources. Others may be taught to sales personnel in training and will be based mainly on historic sales data and/or information regarding customers' future purchasing intentions.

Objective methods of forecasting

The following descriptions of objective forecasting* are relatively easy methods that can be carried out by computer or provided manually by the sales manager or delegated person.

Time series analysis and historical analogy
Examination of relationships between sales data over a period of time is referred to as time series analysis. A good starting point for company sales forecasting is the plotting of sales data on a time series graph. By doing this, the mass of figures assume a visual shape; seasonal patterns can be discerned by superimposing each year's data and general trends by assembling year/monthly data 'end on', and consequent deviations from them investigated. The adage 'History repeats itself' is often very true in consumer/user demand, in the sense that certain demand patterns for products and/or services tend to recur from time to time.

Moving annual totals and moving quarterly totals
An organisation may record sales in monetary or volume terms either daily, weekly, monthly or quarterly. Sales thus recorded can show considerable variations and can mask trends. A longer time interval tends to show a reduction in variation because time has a 'smoothing' effect. The benefit of this smoothing effect of longer time periods can be obtained by identifying a suitable time period (day, week, month, quarter, year) and utilising this on a continuous basis.

---

* Gordon J. Bolt, *Market and Sales Forecasting—a Total Approach*. Kogan Page Ltd, 1981.

A moving total is obtained by adding the value for the most recent day, week, month etc. to the previous total covering a number of the selected periods and subtracting the value of the earliest day, week, month etc. from the total. Alternatively, the difference between the oldest and the most recent values can be added or subtracted to the 'running' total.

Moving annual totals (MATs) are useful forecasting tools as they highlight underlying trends and are easy to use because from any projection of them it is possible to 'read off' a 12 months' sales volume.

Also, MATs are useful to the sales manager in operating a sales force commission scheme where the products have highly seasonal or erratic sales. As the MAT indicates the last 12 months' sales total, payment on this basis could avoid the situation of no commission one month and extremely high commission the next.

Percentage take-off graphs

It is possible in some industries to evolve a reliable percentage take-off graph to enable the forecast to be used for sales targeting, production or purchasing scheduling purposes. This is done by taking the average sales per period (e.g. per month) over the last 3/4 years, and converting them into a cumulative percentage series. The resulting graph enables the sales manager to 'read off' the percentage of sales for a year that should be achieved monthly or weekly throughout that year.

One of the sales manager's forecasting problems is that 'top' management often requires a market and/or sales forecast for the next financial year, well ahead of the commencement of that year, perhaps as much as six months ahead. One technique for projecting current sales to the end of the current year to permit a more informed forecast to be made for next year (as well as being a forecasting tool in its own right) is the percentage take-off graph.

The Z chart

Another method of forecasting to the end of the current year to make possible more informed forecasts for the next year is the Z chart. The Z chart method of short-term forecasting is a combination of the percentage take-off graph and the moving annual total methods.

The name arises from the fact that the pattern on such a graph forms a rough letter Z. For example, in a situation where the sales volume figures for one product or product group for the first 9 months of a particular year are available, it is possible, using the Z chart, to predict the total sales for the year, i.e. to make a forecast for the next 3 months. It is assumed that basic trading conditions do not alter, or alter on an anticipated course and that any underlying trends at present being experienced will continue. In addition to the monthly sales totals for the 9 months of the current year (the bottom line of the Z), the monthly sales figures for the previous year are also required. The data available allows a moving annual total to be calculated and plotted (the top part of the Z) and a cumulative total to be calculated and plotted (the diagonal part of the Z). Both these values will be the same at the end of the year; both lines are extended to complete the Z, thereby forecasting the anticipated value at the end of the year.

Moving average

A simple method of forecasting is the use and projection of moving averages; it considers past sales data in tabular or graphical form and determines a trend which can be projected into the future. The moving average method tends not to give completely straight trend lines, but smooths out any wide fluctuations in a sales data curve. A weakness in using moving average lines is the effect of using non-typical items. If the moving average trend line is superimposed on the basic sales data, a trend can be discerned and projected into the future. As a general rule, a reasonably straight moving average trend line indicates a recurring cyclical pattern, i.e. values above the trend line compensate for similar total values below the line. It can also be used to identify the length of the medium-term business cycle found in many industries.

In most industries, while the annual sales total is a good general indicator, often it is not detailed enough for many forecasting requirements, and in a number of cases full use is not made of the data available. Seasonal fluctuations present quite a problem in sales forecasting and, where possible, a forecaster should make provisions for this by dividing the year into months or into seasons appropriate to his/her industry.

One of the weaknesses in using moving averages is that the trend line value, as it represents an average, is always placed in the middle of the series it represents and is therefore always 'behind' in its projection. For example, the average for a 13×4 weekly annual period will always need to be plotted against item 7 (of the 13 items).

Exponential smoothing

When calculating moving averages, the same weight is given to all periods. Weighted moving averages give more emphasis to more recent periods, but the weighting declines by a constant value, e.g. by the value of 1/10 on each item, 4/10, 3/10, 2/10, 1/10. Exponential smoothing reduces the weighting by a constant percentage or ratio, e.g. by halving the weighting, ½, ¼, ⅛, 1/16, 1/32, 1/64. This produces geometric progression and, when graphed, smooths the raw sales data into an exponential curve. The usefulness to the sales manager is that it highlights the effects of current trends and seasonal patterns and diminishes the effect that past forecasts which have failed (perhaps because of sharp non-typical fluctuations) will have on the current forecast.

The least squares method

Fitting a trend by the least squares method to past sales data ensures that the trend is the estimate of sales values which is subject to the minimum deviation in the circumstances, in other words it is the line of best fit. Its drawback is that if the sales data used is too erratic, the straight trend line will only represent a broad directional trend, and in any case if the data is very smooth there will be no need for a trend line.

Probability control limits can be calculated to discover the extent of error that the estimated trend can experience. It is possible to seasonally adjust the least squares straight line trend and then fit probability control limits two standard deviations either side of the seasonally adjusted trend value to give 95 per cent certainty.

Correlation

If two or more quantities or factors vary in sympathy, so that movements or changes upwards or downwards in one tend to be accompanied by movements of a corresponding nature in the other, they are said to be correlated. But the sales manager must ensure that the correlation is not spurious, as it is possible to get a high numerical correlation where two series have increased continuously, without there being a necessary cause-and-effect relationship at all.

Correlation can be direct or positive with both series of data moving in the same direction, increasing or decreasing, or it can be inverse or negative with the two series moving in opposite directions, i.e. as one increases, the other decreases and vice versa.

There are degrees of correlation (i.e. where data is partially correlated), and this can be shown graphically or, more precisely, by statistical methods.

Correlation techniques are useful in market and sales forecasting with any type of independent variable that appears to be linked with the sales of the product, although the two unit values may not be the same, e.g. the demand for electricity in megawatts and the outdoor temperature in degrees centigrade.

The biggest advantage of correlation is that it is not dependent on the past history of sales and seeks to forecast on the relationship of sales to an external, independent factor, e.g. sales and interest rates, sales and consumer spending power, sales and the weather etc. Its greatest disadvantage is that up-to-date information of external, independent factors is not as readily available as historic sales data.

Subjective methods of forecasting

These tend to be intuitive techniques (conclusions) based on the application of experience, intelligence and judgement to the forecast situation. Some methods are wholly subjective, basically representing an averaging of a variety of opinions, e.g. a survey of consumer/user intentions. Others, although derived subjectively, can be made more useful by the application of an objective method, e.g. the addition of probability values to panel forecasting.

The indicator assessment method

Where particular economic data have been found to reflect the economic climate in a particular industry, the appropriate indicators are listed in two columns. One column will show all those indicators that are favourable towards an extension of trade and the other those that indicate a contraction of trade. The strength and effect of these indicators are assessed and a final conclusion formed and written up.

Survey of consumer/user purchasing intentions

A simple and direct method of forecasting sales is to ask customers and potential customers what they are planning to purchase in the future (e.g. next year). In consumer goods markets where sheer numbers make it impossible to interview everyone, an appropriate representative sample must be approached if the eventual forecast is to be meaningful. It may involve a sample survey at two levels, the consumer intention to buy a particular product or brand and the wholesale/retail intention to stock and promote it.

With industrial products, the number of customers and/or potential customers may be relatively few and sampling may not be necessary. The main problem will be to persuade customers to make such a prediction or to give enough reliable information regarding future production plans, future expenditure, manufacturing capacity, new product development policy, existing stocks etc. so that a forecast can be made.

Panels of executive opinion

Whereas the previous method concerned a prediction of the market from the customers' point of view, this technique obtains a forecast based on the facts and the considered opinion of key executives within a company's own organisation. Executive forecasts are evaluated, combined and averaged, and through discussion a single forecast emerges.

Composite forecasts of the sales force

This must be the most significant method of forecasting for the sales manager in view of the sales team's involvement. The term 'grass roots' has been used to describe the relationship of the sales person, area or regional managers and sales managers to the customer. The close proximity of the sales force to the 'grass roots' of demand is the justification for its use in many cases to carry out research and forecasting functions. This type of forecasting can be used as a prediction technique in its own right, particularly if statistical data from other sources limits the amount of forecasting that can be done by other methods. It can also be used as a practical check on more mechanical methods of forecasting.

Sales persons are asked to give their best estimate of potential sales to each customer; they should also be asked to give their most optimistic and most pessimistic forecasts. From this information, the sales manager can not only obtain a forecast but also can determine the degree of uncertainty involved.

As there always appears to be an air of negotiation about discussions of future sales, especially if targets are to be set and commission paid on the basis of them, individual sales persons tend to enter into them with a low sales forecast so that it will be possible to 'over-achieve'. On the other hand, sales managers tend to commence discussions with high sales forecasts in mind; there is usually a meeting somewhere in the middle of the range.

When considering individual sales persons' forecasts, records should be kept as to what has been achieved in the past compared with the forecast made. Some sales persons are naturally optimistic and will tend to forecast high (unless targets and commission are involved), others are naturally pessimistic and will tend to forecast low. It is possible to calculate a percentage adjustment figure (e.g. one sales person always tends to under-achieve his sales target by 5 per cent, another person always tends to over-achieve by 8 per cent) and apply it to the individual's own forecast. This percentage adjustment figure can be updated annually.

The main weakness of this method of forecasting is that it is highly subjective; although this can be lessened by teaching individual sales persons and managers some of the relatively easy forecasting methods mentioned earlier, e.g. moving annual totals, Z charts. The latter, if used by the individual sales person, can help him/her monitor progress towards achieving an annual sales target; self-realisation can cause a quicker reaction than pressure from the sales manager. The sales person may be given historic data on past sales over an appropriate period of time or may be expected to derive this information from his/her own records.

A further weakness in a large organisation is that if at each level of the composite forecast (i.e. sales persons, area managers, regional managers) everyone carried out excessive contingency forecasting (i.e. under-forecasting in case of problems of commission, so as to over-achieve), the composite forecast may be virtually useless when it is assembled by the national sales manager. This, of course, can be overcome by anticipating the level of contingency forecasts and applying adjustment percentages based on past performance or, alternatively, to motivate the total sales team to forecast realistically.

Other disadvantages claimed are that forecasts by individual sales persons are influenced by recent successes or failures rather than by future sales opportunities.

But an advantage claimed in obtaining forecasts from sales persons is that it is a motivational device. Forecasts by sales persons are made, then discussed with sales executives. Agreement is reached eventually on the forecast, which then becomes the basis of the individual's sales target. The individual sales person feels that he/she has had a part in calculating the target and has been consulted and, therefore, is more likely to reach and pass the agreed sales target than if it had been arbitrarily imposed from 'above'.

Surveys of expert opinion

This approach can range from 'buying-in' forecasts from consultants to running a panel made up of experts from within the company (marketing researchers, sales persons etc.) and specialists from outside (i.e. economists, marketing experts, specialist psychologists, typical customers etc.). Further, the method can be of the kind that each panel member makes a forecast and never meets the other members or, alternatively, they meet as a committee and through discussion arrive at a composite forecast. In the former case, the variations in the different forecasts can be analysed and an eventual forecast obtained (sometimes by the simple device of averaging) but in the latter case, the role of forecasting has been delegated to the committee.

Probability forecasting with large contracts or 'lumpy' items*

Many forecasting techniques require continuous data (weekly, monthly) to enable trend, seasonal and cyclical patterns to be identified and projected. But some sales situations relate to non-continuous data, e.g. large, multiple-item contracts or a potential order for a single high-value item. In such cases there is no 'historic' data to trend, the company either gets the order or it does not. There are several approaches the sales manager can use when forecasting in such a situation.

One is that of ranking particular purchasing decision factors (price, performance, design, delivery etc.) in order of importance, then rating the company's product/service advantage for each. The process is repeated for each known competing bid; a subjective judgement is then made as to the possible success of the company's bid.

Another method involves competitive bidding analysis. Here, the main objective is to identify a contract bid price which maximises the sales revenue/profit pay off.

At the same time, there is a need to determine the probability of success and to calculate the potential loss (or penalty) which will be incurred if the contract is not awarded to a particular bidding company.

Even though these methods are based on many subjective factors, they do provide the company with a considered forecast of the likelihood of being awarded a particular contract. Crucial to such subjective forecasting will be the knowledge/experience/judgement of the situation, customer and competitors.

---

* Adapted from Gordon J. Bolt, *Market and Sales Forecasting*. Kogan Page Ltd, 1981, p. 296.

The multi-technique approach

Although a number of techniques have been mentioned, it is not suggested that any one should be used in isolation. Within the company constraints of acceptable costs, the limits of time and the company's needs in the market, as many forecasting techniques as possible should be used. Each forecast obtained will be different, but investigation of the variances between them will bring to the surface factors contained in one and not in another that are increasing or declining in forecasting importance. In fact, analysis of such variances, horizontally across the board, will often bring to light new trends or the up-turn or down-turn in market or sales values.

A forecasting plan

It would be helpful to the sales manager to develop and use a forecasting plan. The exact plan will reflect particular needs and will vary from one situation/company to another but the basic requirements are covered in the following format:

Forecasting plan

(a) Setting forecasting objectives. What, why, how, where, who and when.

(b) The collection of data for forecasting:

(1) Desk research into internal records.

(2) Desk research into secondary sources of information in published or existing material.

(3) Gathering information by original field research.

(c) Evaluation, analysis and projection of data. The measurement of change. Objective and subjective methods of forecasting. The multi-technique approach.

(d) The application of the forecast to:

(1) Profit centres.

(2) Sales territories.

(3) Industrial markets.

(4) Consumer goods markets.

(5) Distribution channels.

(e) Controlling the forecast and forecasting. Auditing the forecast. Auditing the 'machinery' of forecasting.

By using such a plan, the sales manager will be able to work systematically from setting forecasting objectives to the control of the forecast.

Setting forecasting objectives, standards and goals not only enables the development of policies and programmes to achieve them, but also permits the measurement of every piece of relevant environmental and sales performance data.

Effective control requires the measurement of performance against pre-determined objectives and standards, and the interpretation of trends and results. It also implies knowing where, when and how to take corrective action.

A further aspect of control is recording performance data for use as a guide in planning future operations and to highlight marketing opportunities.

These aspects of control apply to effective forecasting, and take the form of comparing, evaluating, interpreting and auditing the performance of the economy, of the market, the market segment and the company's sales, with the various forecasts. Remedial action can then be taken (if necessary) to update the forecast or change the methods used. Activity in this stage of the forecasting process can be classified into three main areas:

(a) The running audit which makes daily, weekly, monthly or quarterly comparisons of economic data, company sales and/or market performance against forecast.

(b) The annual audit which makes an estimation and comparison over a longer period and in greater detail.

(c) The audit of the 'machinery' of forecasting within the company in terms of the objectives, policies and methods used: some forecasting techniques are more effective in certain market circumstances than others.

Within these three areas, forecasting can be made more effective by obtaining more, or improved, information for the techniques at present in use, or by developing methods, and by improving existing techniques or replacing ineffective forecasting devices.

Effective forecasting control is not simply for discovering how good or bad it has been in the past, but also for determining what action to take today to improve forecasting results tomorrow.

Summary

The nature of the interface of sales with marketing will vary from company to company. In some large companies they are organisationally very separate; in others their nature and function will cause some overlap of activities and need high degrees of integration. In yet others, sales will tend to dominate and the term sales management is a misnomer as it will be responsible for and cover marketing. Consequently, the various marketing concepts examined in the early part of this chapter will apply in some degree to aspects of sales management, but all have important implications for it, making it easier for the sales function to operate if they are recognised and more difficult if ignored.

From the sales management point of view, one significant marketing activity is that of marketing research. It should help to provide (and sales management should contribute to) information that can be described as 'intelligence data' (for deciding what to do and how to do it) or 'control data' (for evaluating how effectively marketing/selling is being done). Although all of the ten marketing research types mentioned will be of differing levels of importance in particular circumstances, all are helpful to sales management, particularly that of communication research which includes sales effectiveness research. The research process and sources of information were briefly examined in this chapter, but the market/micro information that the sales team can obtain will be vital to the operational decisions of the sales manager, as well as to the sales effectiveness of individual sales team members, and should make a direct contribution to marketing research.

Although the individual sales person should be trained to 'sell' the company image and himself/herself as a 'consultant', the key element of the 'total deal' being purchased by the customer is the product/service combination. Effective planning policies, strategies in this area (and in those that the customer associates with it, i.e. branding, packaging, pricing), are crucial to the success of the sales mission. Appropriate R & D, market-orientated strategies, product/service portfolio analysis, pack testing, price confrontation studies, brand name research and testing, placement trials and test marketing, all play a part in product/service development and will involve reactions of the sales person's potential and existing customers.

The final part of this chapter dealt with market and sales forecasting; it emphasised that every budget in a company is dependent on forecasts of how many product/service combination units are expected to be sold and/or predictions of anticipated sales revenue. Market and sales forecasting can be approached in a number of ways: 'top-down' or 'bottom-up', volume (units) or value (revenue); short, medium or long term; and quantitative (objective) or qualitative (subjective).

A variety of forecasting techniques is available to the sales manager ranging from the simple to the sophisticated depending on his/her market/company situation. As no one method covers all the parameters necessary in complex market and sales forecasting situations, a multi-technique approach is necessary.

It will also be helpful to the sales manager to have a forecasting plan so that he/she can work systematically; setting the forecasting objectives, collecting appropriate data, projecting/calculating a forecast, operationally applying the forecast and controlling both the forecasts and the techniques used to obtain them.

Questions

1. There are many basic marketing concepts that affect sales management. Describe three and indicate how they can be used most effectively at the sales/marketing interface.

2. In what ways can marketing research help sales and sales management? Describe also how the latter can make a contribution to marketing research.

3. Why is product/service development important to sales and the sales manager even in currently successful companies and what essential pre-stages are necessary to ensure the effective introduction of a new product/service?

4. Identify the advantages of an appropriate branding policy to the sales team and sales management.

5. What are the three main roles of packaging? Indicate how they can affect the performance of the sales team and show the implications for sales management.

6. What are the main pricing policies available to companies which in practice the sales team will be expected to implement?

7. Why does the sales manager need to become involved in market and sales forecasting? What types of forecasting are possible and what are the techniques available to the sales manager to make feasible predictions?

CHAPTER 12

The sales interface with marketing (2)

Objectives

In this chapter, the examination of the sales interface with marketing is continued by considering the second part of the marketing mix (see page 346), i.e. the communication and service activities associated with a company's tactical presence in its various marketing segments. Specifically examined will be the interface between sales and the other component parts of customer communication (advertising, sales promotion, branding, packaging and pricing), public relations, physical distribution and sales service. Brand or product/service group management is also considered as a sales/marketing interface that can have an effect on the sales function and with which the sales manager needs to develop a close working relationship.

The customer communications mix

There is a wide variety of media which companies can use to communicate with existing and potential customers: advertising, sales promotion (including merchandising), branding, packaging, pricing and, of course, selling. Within these broad categories are large numbers of methods, each with its own advantages and disadvantages, and each must be tailored to particular market/company needs. One medium may transmit the same message as another but its difference in presentation, location, timing etc, may cause it to have greater sales impact and/or reach parts of the market the other medium could not reach. For example, in consumer goods situations where wholesalers and/or retailers are used, often 'push' marketing is necessary to get products into the distribution system and 'pull' marketing is necessary to cause demand by the ultimate consumer. Thus trade advertising, sales promotion and selling activities by the sales team are necessary for the former, but only consumer advertising and sales promotion could be used for the latter by manufacturers/suppliers to enable them to communicate with every consumer. Thus the manufacturer/supplier can control trade and consumer advertising/sales promotion, but can control sales activity only to the immediate customer and will have to rely on the sales personnel of wholesalers and retailers for selling communications in later stages of the distribution chain. Control of the activities of the selling function is one of the justifications of selling direct to the ultimate consumer.

A similar situation can prevail in the marketing of industrial products where components made by one company are included in the products of another. For example, a component for a fractional horsepower electric motor may be sold to the electric motor manufacturer who sells motors to a variety of other manufacturers of equipment. Advertising, sales promotion and selling activity can be used for the immediate customer but in most cases it will be economic only to use advertising and sales promotion to communicate with others further down the manufacturing chain.

It will be seen in both the consumer and industrial goods situations that the sales function is heavily dependent on the other two media to influence the immediate, the intermediate and ultimate consumer/user.

Obviously the 'mix' of media used will have a greater impact/credibility if, rather than conflict or detract, they all tell the same or similar stories. In fact, in many situations it is a question of emphasis; for example, in consumer markets, goods tend to be heavily pre-sold by advertising, supported by sales promotion followed by selling. In industrial markets, the spearhead of customer communications tends to be the technically trained sales force, supported by sales promotion and then advertising. The customer communication mix should therefore be seen as support for the sales team and a source of sales themes/ideas, and the sales manager should not be slow to encourage the sales team to exploit these relationships to the full.

Conversely, selling being a part of the customer communications mix, there will be expectations of contributions from the sales team and the sales manager (e.g. intensive sales visits geographically during an advertising campaign, operating sales promotional devices in retail outlets etc.).

Advertising

Advertising was once described as 'salesmanship in print', indicating the overlap/closeness of the two activities. There are many more detailed definitions; one concise yet all embracing description is: Advertising is the process of developing visual and oral messages and their communication through paid media for the purpose of making specific individuals and groups of people aware of, and favourably inclined towards, a product, brand, service, institution, idea or point of view, with the ultimate intention of influencing action.

Advertising objectives

Because of its flexibility and its many facets, advertising has an important but always changing role to play as part of the marketing 'mix' in all stages of the life of a product/service. It is possible to influence all aspects of demand and supply, together with sales, profits and costs, in the short, medium and long term, by evolving various combinations of advertising objectives which in turn depend upon the task required of advertising. For example, there is an obvious need to get right the balance between trade advertising and consumer advertising with regard to marketing 'fast-moving consumer goods'. Further, the advertising objectives for the introduction of a new product will be different to those for the continued promotion of an existing mature product.

Advertising may be required to establish, protect and expand a company's sales position or market share, and to retain the loyalty of present customers; a direct parallel with the sales function 'mission'.

Certain advertising objectives may be generally necessary to differing degrees of intensity anywhere during the life of a product. For example, the general need to stimulate sales enquiries and orders, or to help establish salesmen when the company adds new products and expands into new geographical markets. Some general advertising objectives aim to improve the overall environment in which a company operates, thus making the more specific objectives more easy to attain. Specific objectives (e.g. to educate customers, to develop awareness and encourage demand, to inform, sell and persuade, to encourage a particular customer reaction etc.) need to be set with the sales team's task in mind.

Advertising expenditure

Before a detailed advertising plan can be evolved, the question of finance must be considered.

In some market/company situations, decisions have to be made as to whether it would be more effective to spend money on an advertising campaign or to employ more sales persons. Obviously the sales manager needs to be able to justify the number and opportunity cost of his sales team and should be involved in any discussions on changes of emphasis in the customer communications mix.

There are a number of methods in use to determine the scale of advertising expenditure: fixed percentage of past sales, moving inverse percentage of past sales, fixed percentage of sales forecasted, fixed sum per past sales unit etc. But there is really only one effective method: ideally, advertising expenditure should be the minimum amount of money necessary to attain the aims and objectives set by a company in its advertising plan.

The advertising plan

An appropriate plan needs to be developed; a basic format is shown in Fig. 12.1* which is also appropriate for public relations and sales promotion.

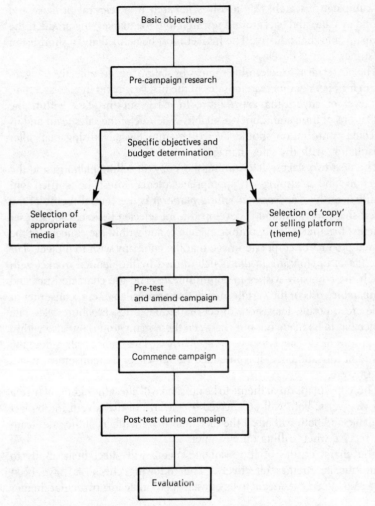

Fig. 12.1 A basic format for an advertising plan

The advertising plan should cover objectives, policies and procedures relating to resources analysis, budgeting, competitive analysis, allocations of funds to brands, product groups, geographical areas and customer types. It should also outline future advertising strategy and tactics relating to audience definition themes, copy, choice of media (weight, frequency,

* Gordon J. Bolt, *Communicating with E.E.C. Markets.* Kogan Page Ltd, 1973, p. 12.

timing), and advertising testing in the light of the desired product and corporate image. It should also state the planned mix of advertising to the trade, through the trade and to consumers/users.

Having determined the basic objectives, the next stage in advertising is pre-campaign research; this involves research into relevant primary and secondary data, and background research into the market, the product, the company and the industry. The market must be defined and a short list of consumers' needs developed.

The next stage is to determine strategy by stating specific objectives (e.g. to obtain a 25 per cent increase in sales in the first year), and then to ascertain the level of advertising expenditure to carry out this task within the limitations of time and money available. The role of the sales team and its expected contribution should be written into the advertising plan after consultation with the sales manager.

The next two stages, determining the 'copy' or selling platform and the selection and planning of appropriate media, must be carried out simultaneously. *The 'copy' or selling platform* is the central theme of the advertising campaign and is developed from selected basic consumer/user benefits, together with supporting evidence, and within the concepts of the desired product or corporate image that the company wish to project. *The selection of appropriate media* is determined by the defined market with which the company wishes to communicate, and the characteristics and comparable costs of the various media that are available, e.g. consumer or trade press, poster, television, direct mail, directories, brochures etc. The choice has to be made not only between these main groups but also within the groups (e.g. *The Times* v. *Daily Mirror*). The choice will reflect the nature of the 'audience' it is intended to influence, i.e. consumer, trade, industry etc.

The 'copy' platform or theme to be pursued will affect the choice of media and vice versa; both will be affected by the size of the advertising budget available and both will affect the reception that members of the sales team will receive when calling on customers.

The characteristics of the available media will affect their ability to communicate themes effectively. The following checklists have been suggested* to enable media to be chosen appropriate to a particular theme:

Six general aspects of advertising media:
  (i) Basic characteristics;
 (ii) Atmosphere;
(iii) Impact;
 (iv) Coverage;
  (v) Cost;
 (vi) Position.

*A. P. F. Swindells, *Advertising Media and Campaign Planning*. Butterworths & Co. Ltd, 1966, p. 36.

Each of these are considered in detail, for example (i) is considered under the following sub-headings:

Basic characteristics (twelve):
(a) Size.
(b) Colour.
(c) Movement.
(d) Sound.
(e) Length of copy.
(f) Length of life.
(g) Repetition.
(h) Impression of medium on groups other than customer.
(i) Amount of assistance to selling.
(j) Flexibility of medium.
(k) Ability to attack through several senses.
(l) Quality and uniformity of presentation.

The 'copy' platform and the pattern of appropriate media will need to be changed during each stage of a product's life; companies are forced to change them as the advertising objectives change. This is because of the changing market situation found in the different stages of life of a product; each stage requiring a different type of message to be communicated to different or changing market segments. The sales team should be informed of pending changes to the copy platform and the choice of media to avoid conflict of sales messages at the point of purchase.

Before a series of advertisements is exposed to a particular market segment, each should be *pre-tested*, i.e. it is shown to a sample of potential customers to assess reactions and to ensure it communicates exactly what the advertiser wants and that it has the desired effect.

After the campaign has commenced in the specific market(s), *post-testing* should commence and continue, if only at intervals, during the whole life of the advertising campaign to ensure not only its immediate impact, but to assess over a period of time its cumulative effect. The ultimate evaluation of a campaign's effectiveness will be in relation to increased sales and overall profitability of the advertised product/service, its effectiveness in maintaining sales and/or the minimisation of losses. Existing and potential customer reaction to advertising campaigns should be reported by individual sales team member's activity reports and collated by the sales manager.

Advertising can produce more sales leads for the sales team either by rousing interest backed by action or by the advertisement including a 'mail in' section to be completed and sent in by an interested customer; interested prospects identify themselves.

The role of the advertising agency
Today, because of the growing acceptance of the marketing concept and the recognition of advertising as a part of overall marketing strategy, no

market-orientated company should consider planning a marketing programme without its advertising expert's advice.

The advertising agency's knowledge, skill and experience in other product fields will often make an invaluable contribution to the planning of a company's marketing strategy and tactics.

The sales manager should ensure that he has adequate contact with the advertising agency's account executive, not only to ensure he/she is aware of what is being developed by the agency but also to ensure that he/she can bring pressure to bear, when appropriate, in relation to the sales team's situation and its feasible contribution.

Sales promotion

Advertising attracts consumers/users towards the product/service and the company, whereas sales promotion is related to activities that 'push' the product/service and company image towards the user/consumer. It acts as a bridge between advertising and direct selling, making both more effective by inducing sales personnel to sell more, middlemen to stock and promote more and the ultimate consumer/user to buy.

Sales promotion and advertising prepare the ground for the acceptance of the sales person by the buyer by creating a better initial atmosphere to the selling interview. Further, sales promotion gives the sales force additional selling points and benefits about which the sales person can talk. Effective sales promotion cuts sales force costs and general selling overheads because it increases the sales interview efficiency rate of the individual sales person to open new accounts, to sell more to existing customers, and to get more display space for his/her products.

Thus the first group concerned with the effects of sales promotion is the sales force; the second group are distributors, wholesalers and retailers; and the third group, consumers.

There is a variety of sales promotional methods/techniques that can be directed towards the latter two groups and which in turn will have an impact on the sales force, and these have been summarised* as shown in Fig. 12.2. Not all these methods are applicable to industrial sales promotion situations (e.g. premium offers, key money etc.) and some will need to be modified (e.g. educational films, packaging etc.) but many shown are used in the industrial situation. For example, demonstrations, factory visits, education and training, literature (brochures, data sheets etc.), 'give-away' samples (where appropriate), free trials, exhibitions and trade fairs etc. are widely used and often involve the sales team.

The impact of the above sales promotional methods and the reaction of distribution channels to them will be reflected in their attitude/behaviour

---

* Gordon J. Bolt, *Communicating with E.E.C. Markets*. Kogan Page Ltd, 1973, p. 27.

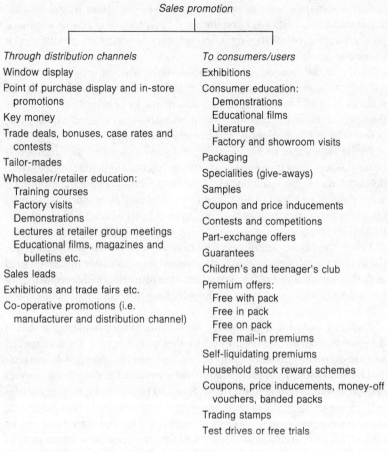

Fig. 12.2 Sales promotional methods/techniques

towards the sales team and to making purchasing decisions. The reaction of consumers/users will be reflected in changes in the volume of sales of the product/service.

Sales promotion campaigns must be planned with the same stages as shown previously for an advertising campaign. The first stage is to determine the sales promotion objectives: what is the aim, why it's necessary, how it is to be achieved, and on what time scale?

Sales managers, sales trainers and individual members of the sales team need to appreciate that sales promotion objectives like these (and others) themes, media and methods change as a product/service life-cycle progresses; consequently they need to be allowed for in sales presentations to customers.

In the early stages of a product/service life-cycle, sales promotion is concerned mainly with devices that 'educate' and inform (exhibitions, demonstrations, trials etc.) and are used to introduce a new or improved product/service or to step-up sales in order to maintain production at economic levels.

In the middle stages, sales promotion takes the form of a mixture of 'education' and inducements (free trials, free technical advice, design services etc.) and may complement advertising in helping to create a new interest, or even to 'cushion' the introduction of a price increase or, conversely, act as a selective form of price reduction.

In the later stages of the life-cycle of a product/service, the emphasis is upon inducements to purchase (premium offers, competitions, free trials, demonstrations, free coupons etc.), perhaps when introducing a product/service into a new area or for the purpose of obtaining broader distribution for a product/service or for equipping sales persons with an additional sales tool.

When the market segment is declining for a particular product/service, the amount of sales promotion is often reduced considerably unless it is used as part of a customer-holding operation in conjunction with advertising, or for reducing excessive stocks or for offsetting the effects of competitors' activities.

A special area of sales promotion in consumer goods marketing is that of merchandising, already examined in depth in Chapter 10 as a special support activity to the sales teams in fast-moving consumer-goods markets.

The sales promotion plan will normally outline the objectives, policies and procedures relating to future strategy and tactics in the marketing/sales activity area. It should include the assessment of promotional resources, gearing them to products/services, customers, sales and seasons. It will be concerned with special selling plans and devices, major and minor promotions, directed at or through trade channels and/or consumers and/or users. It should lay down the degrees of emphasis to be placed on the various sales promotion activities and indicate these through a budget and time schedule. Finally, it should indicate how the sales promotion activity will be evaluated.

Branding

This was defined earlier (page 355) when branding policy was considered. In the marketing/sales strategy context, branding helps advertising, merchandising and display, and the sales function by giving a guarantee of continuity of quality of products/services and assists in making the launching of new or revitalised products/services more effective. It also makes market segmentation easier, facilitates brand loyalty, promotes memory recall, can reduce the amount of selling effort needed and promote acceptance of the product/service.

Further, wholesalers and retailers are forced to stock branded products demanded by consumers and this has the effect of speeding distribution and increasing sales turnover. It is also an aid to the individual sales person who quite logically can demand display and stock space from retailers in relation to the brand's share of the market. A brand also distinguishes a product/service and enables a company to establish a recommended price for the product which cannot be easily compared with those for competing products/services or the importance of price differentials may be diminished. Memory recall is facilitated as well as self-selection, and the amount of personal persuasive selling effort may be reduced.

Branding is not so important to the sales team in the early stages of a new generic product/service life-cycle because the sales team needs to sell hard the acceptance of the new concept. However, in the middle life-cycle stages as more consumers accept the new generic basic product/service concept, the market becomes larger and more 'like' brands emerge, the situation becomes one of brand versus brand. In the later life-cycle stages, branding will be particularly important to the sales team and effective selling if a company introduces a replacement or improved product/service or is simply involved in obtaining repeat orders.

The general rule for tactical branding is that the brand name should be memorable, distinctive, easy to pronounce, not offend, be relatively short (this helps in pack design also) and apt. Further, as there are registers of names in most countries, it should be legally available, i.e. no one else has already registered it. Companies selling/marketing in international markets will obviously need to avoid brand names that have unfortunate meanings in a foreign language.

Packaging

As mentioned earlier when considering packaging policy (page 356), the term covers shipment packaging and/or unit packaging (i.e. for carrying a pre-measured quantity of an individual item). It was also recognised that there are three main aspects of packaging: to protect the product in transit and storage, its persuasive marketing/selling role both to consumers and the 'trade' (which means that it must have a strong identity) and to be helpful to consumers in terms of carrying, product accessibility, safety, repeat usage, information etc. All provide sales 'benefits' and play an important part in the sales operation. If protection in transit and storage is inadequate then complaints will be made, not only costing money (e.g. returns) and valuable sales force time, but also threatening customer confidence in the product/service/company and making it harder for the sales team to sell further units.

The effectiveness of packaging's tactical role will depend on its construction, design, size and shape, labelling 'copy', colour and performance. These factors can be developed, tested and modified by:

(a) developing a pack design brief after consultation with appropriate persons, especially the sales manager

(b) reviewing and modifying packaging roughs

(c) obtaining highly finished roughs

(d) carrying-out a quantitative pack test;

(e) evaluating performance;

(f) modifying pack to finished state.

Packaging companies often give free design advice and provide 'rough' pack examples.

Other aspects that could be used as sales 'benefits' are that the packaging is chemically compatible with the contents, convenient for middlemen to 'break bulk' for small retailers, it conforms to Government regulations (i.e. child-proof packaging for pharmaceuticals), shows the product name clearly, be agreeable for consumers to 'live with', reduced transports costs (lightweight) etc. In fact, an appropriate list of packaging 'benefits' needs to be developed by and for all sales teams.

Pricing

Prices can communicate a variety of messages to potential customers, e.g. value for money, a bargain, quality, cheapness, worth, saving, profit, loss etc. Tactically, companies need to establish a price image for each product/service combination so that movements in price can be related to it. For example, a reduction will not motivate if its original price image has not been 'registered' with the potential customers; at the point of purchase, the original and the new price should be shown together with the actual saving. Also, the price image should be established at the time of the launch of a new or 're-vitalised' product/service so that an introductory offer of 'two for the price of one' (i.e. £2) is used rather than pricing them at £1 each and trying to raise the price to £2 later.

The psychological 'pulling' power of tactical pricing can be seen in the use of prices slightly below the next round figure, e.g. £9.99 is psychologically much cheaper than 1p below £10. It can also be seen in the recognition of price barriers at £1, £10, £100 etc. The tactical approach of charging what the market will bear is often justified by reference to high R & D and launch costs.

Pricing policy was examined earlier (page 357) as part of a product/service strategy, but its role in the communications mix and marketing tactics requires that the basic methods and techniques of tactical pricing are understood by the sales manager and the sales team.

Methods of price calculation will include marginal and total absorption techniques. For example, in a hypothetical case where 1000 units are sold at £2 each, where variable costs (those that increase with the number of products produced, e.g. raw materials, direct labour etc.) per product are £1 and fixed costs (those that do not increase, i.e. are overheads or on-costs such as rent, rates, indirect labour) are £500, the marginal pricing/profit situation would be:

	Price per unit (£)	Total (£)
1000 units sold		
Sales	2	2000
Variable cost	1	1000
Margin or contribution	1	1000
Fixed cost	0.50	500
Profit		500

The key issue is the margin or contribution; in theory at least, as long as the variable costs are covered, prices could be adjusted so that the margin or contribution was (as in the above case) more than necessary to cover fixed costs or, perhaps in the face of fierce competition, lower than the fixed cost. In the latter situation, however, in a multi-product company, other products would need to carry a relatively higher disproportionate amount of overhead/fixed costs.

The sales team also need to be 'sold' on the importance and effect of volume on price and profits, i.e. spreading fixed cost over a larger sales volume will reduce the fixed cost per item thereby making possible either lower prices, or increased profits, or both. For example, in a product/service combination situation where fixed cost is £50,000 and variable cost is £10 per item produced and the company wishes to make a 20 per cent profit mark-up on cost, price will be reduced considerably as the volume increases and fixed cost becomes less 'per each' product.

Number produced (units)	Fixed cost (£)	Variable cost (£)	Plus 20% mark-up (£)	Price (each) (£)
1,000	50,000	10,000	12,000	72
5,000	50,000	50,000	20,000	24
10,000	50,000	100,000	30,000	18
20,000	50,000	200,000	50,000	15

This fall in prices can only continue as long as there is the capacity to increase output, e.g. when a machine is working at full capacity, additional output is not possible. Therefore another machine will need to be purchased which in turn increases fixed cost.

The last example did not, however, show the need to relate costs, revenue and profits. Using the same basic data as in the last example but where the price is £15 per unit, it is possible to indicate the break-even volume, i.e. the point in volume after which profits are made.

Number produced (units)	Fixed cost (£)	Variable cost (£)	Total cost (£)	Sales revenue (£)	Profit or loss (£)
1,000	50,000	10,000	60,000	15,000	(45,000)
5,000	50,000	50,000	100,000	75,000	(25,000)
10,000	50,000	100,000	150,000	150,000	Break-even
20,000	50,000	200,000	250,000	300,000	50,000

The break-even point (i.e. where total cost equals total sales revenue) is therefore 10,000 units; before which a loss is made, after which a profit is made. The sales manager and sales team need to aim for an acceptable profit level above the break-even point.

Market segmentation, the process by which a company partitions its prospective customers (the market) into sub-markets or segments, was mentioned earlier in Chapter 11 (page 341) and in certain circumstances it is possible to charge different prices for the same (or marginally different) product/service in the various market segments. This can be done by varying the amount of overhead (fixed costs) each market segment will bear and/or changing the profit mark-up. An example is given in Fig. 12.3.*

XYZ Co. Ltd. Total Production: 15,000 units. Total fixed costs: £50,000.
Variable cost: £10 per unit

	Market A	Market B	Market C
Fixed cost	£ 50,000	—	—
Variable cost @ £10 per unit	£ 50,000	£50,000	£50,000
Profit	£ 20,000 (20% mark-up) £120,000	£20,000 (40% mark-up) £70,000	£10,000 (20% mark-up) £60,000
	÷	÷	÷
	5000 units	5000 units	5000 units
	‖	‖	‖
Price per each	£24	£14	£12

Fig. 12.3 Price discrimination between markets

It will be seen in Fig. 12.3 that by keeping the fixed cost of the total production of 15,000 units in market segment A, the price per unit will be £24; in the other two market segments, the price difference is the result of product mark-up decisions. While the three are relatively extreme examples, the principle of price discrimination is well illustrated. In practice, all products/services would be normally expected to make some contribution to fixed cost and profits.

* Gordon J. Bolt, *Marketing in the E.E.C.* Kogan Page Ltd, 1973, p. 107.

Market segmentation by price has other implications for tactical pricing in view of the sales team's normal inclination to reduce prices; a product/service priced as the lowest in a particular price band and therefore offering good competitive value may become the highest priced product/service in the next lower price band if price is reduced.

Another approach to pricing is the total or absorption cost approach. This method indicates the price at each level of volume below which the company would make a loss.

Units	Fixed cost (£)	Variable cost (£10) each unit) (£)	Total cost (£)	Minimum unit price (£)
1,000	50,000	10,000	60,000	60
5,000	50,000	50,000	100,000	20
10,000	50,000	100,000	150,000	15
20,000	50,000	200,000	250,000	12.50

The understanding of this method of pricing is important in situations where the sales team are given authority to negotiate on price and a basic minimum price is needed.

In many commodity/raw material markets where there are many sellers and many buyers, prices will be arrived at by the market forces of supply and demand. In such circumstances, the sales manager needs to have information and communication systems that quickly obtain, apply and communicate up-to-the-minute data.

Of great importance to the sales manager and the sales team will be the effect of changes in price on the amount that will be sold; this is referred to in the science of economics as elasticity of demand. Thus a price situation is considered relatively inelastic if a relatively small change in price (up or down) causes a less than proportional change in demand (sales). A price situation is considered to be relatively elastic if a small change in price (up or down) causes a more than proportionate change in demand (sales). For example, a relatively inelastic demand curve is shown in Fig. 12.4(a) and a relatively elastic demand curve is shown in Fig. 12.4(b).*

In Fig. 12.4(a) the situation is that the sales of a product/service (often perceived as a 'necessity') will not be too adversely affected by a slight price increase. But it is the wrong situation for the sales manager to reduce prices in the hope of increasing sales as the reduction will need to be disproportionately large to effect a large increase in sales. Some other form of customer appeal will need to be made.

In Figure 12.4(b) the situation is that the sales manager should avoid a

* Gordon J. Bolt, *Market and Sales Forecasting—a Total Approach*. Kogan Page Ltd, 1981. p. 122.

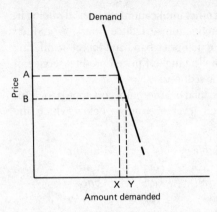

Fig. 12.4(a) A relatively inelastic demand curve – a price increase from B to A causes only a small decline in sales (from Y to Z)

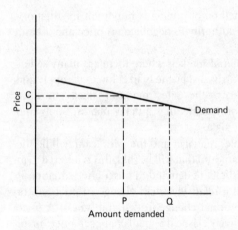

Fig. 12.4(b) A relatively elastic demand curve – a price increase from D to C causes a considerable decline in sales (from Q to P)

price increase if possible as sales will be reduced dramatically, unless everyone else increases price (perhaps because of an increase in raw material costs). On the other hand, in a relatively elastic market a small decrease in price will tend to bring about a large increase in sales.

The shape of any demand curve (i.e. its elasticity) will change over a whole range of prices and in practice it is difficult to set up a demand schedule over a wide range of prices. However, if the results of the last price change are analysed, it is possible to calculate the degree of elasticity of demand (sales) and therefore can guide a sales manager with regard to price changes. The following examples* give the formula and calculate the elasticity of two situations.

1. Proportional change method where

$$\text{Elasticity of demand} = \frac{\text{Proportionate change in amount demanded}}{\text{Proportionate change in price}}$$

For example, if on a demand schedule (or from marketing research) the following two items occurred:

@ £9 per unit   4000 units were sold
@ £8 per unit   5000 units were sold

then using the above formula, elasticity could be expressed as:

$$\frac{\dfrac{1000}{4000}}{\dfrac{1}{9}} = \frac{\dfrac{1}{4}}{\dfrac{1}{9}} = \frac{1}{4} \times \frac{9}{1} = 2\tfrac{1}{4}$$

Where the result is more than 1, demand is relatively elastic; a fall of 1/9th in price caused an increase in sales of 1/4. Alternatively, if the two items from a demand schedule were:

@ £9 per unit   300 units were sold
@ £6 per unit   330 units were sold

then using this formula, elasticity could be expressed as:

$$\frac{\dfrac{30}{300}}{\dfrac{3}{9}} = \frac{\dfrac{1}{10}}{\dfrac{1}{3}} = \frac{1}{10} \times \frac{3}{1} = \frac{3}{10}$$

Demand is relatively inelastic as the result is less than 1. A price reduction of 1/3rd causes only a 1/10th increase in sales.

The sales manager will need to devise a contingency plan of what he/she will do if competitors increase/decrease prices. For example, if the main competitor's prices are reduced or discounts increased to give a net reduction in price of 1–3 per cent, the planned reaction might be to hold prices at present level or to run a temporary price deal to dilute the advantageous effect of the competitor's reduction. If prices are reduced 3.1–5 per cent, the contingency plan might be to run a competition with trade customers and/or a self-liquidating promotion to consumers that attracts a lot of attention. A contingency plan response to a competitor price reduction of 5 per cent or more could be a new advertising campaign, a revitalised product or even reference to the company's marketing committee for a decision as to whether

---

* Gordon J. Bolt, *Market and Sales Forecasting—a Total Approach*. Kogan Page Ltd, 1981, pp. 123 and 124.

the particular product/service affected is worth (in the short and long term) being given financial support.

When it is difficult to predict the volume of sales and if demand for a product is price sensitive, it is important to know how 'break-even' will vary at different levels of output (sales). Lower prices may produce higher sales which may, in turn, produce a lower unit cost. The sales team will usually prefer product/service combinations of the highest quality at the lowest price, relative to its positioning in the market. Alternatively, an increase in stock turn may follow a price reduction and provide increased profits in certain circumstances (see page 323).

Business activities generally operate in an environment which calls for flexibility; success depends on being able to adapt to changes in demand, supply, costs, prices and other variables.

Much of the decision-making information for the five areas of advertising, sales promotion, branding, packaging and pricing will come from the marketing research function. However, the sales function will be able to provide 'grass roots' information reflecting up-to-date customer attitudes and reaction to change in the five areas. It can also be helpful to marketing management if the sales manager is consulted about such changes before final decisions are made as they affect broader sales strategies and tactics.

Public relations

If the simple definition that 'advertising sells the product/service and public relations sells the company or corporate image' is linked with the earlier statement that the sales person has three things to sell, the product/service, himself/herself and the company, it will be seen how close these areas are.

Public relations is not included in the previously examined customer communications mix because, although customer public relations are important, they form only part of a much wider communications role.

A definition by the Institute of Public Relations states that 'Public relations is the deliberate, planned and sustained effort to establish and maintain mutual understanding between an organisation and its publics.'

To the public relations person, the component parts of the population are called 'publics'. This can mean not only the company's customers and/or potential customers, distributors, wholesalers, retailers, the sales force, but also its shareholders, its employees, the trade unions; the press, its suppliers, the local community residents, the financial world etc.

In companies where formal public relations sections exist covering all the above activities, most marketing/sales public relations activities may be left to it. But where no such arrangement exists, then the marketing/sales functions must assume responsibility for customer public relations. A part of the 'bundle of satisfactions' or the total deal that customers buy is the company image and this needs to be 'sold' by the sales team.

Marketing/sales public relations as a part of the marketing 'mix' is concerned with consumers' and potential consumers' attitude towards the company, with trade middlemen such as wholesalers, retailers etc., with building goodwill and a prestige reputation, and presenting the correct company image. In fact, ensuring that a favourable environment exists in which the company and its marketing 'mix' can operate most effectively. The environmental objectives that public relations seeks to achieve can cover a wide range of situations. For example, they may relate to channels of distribution, i.e. to encourage the enthusiastic support of dealers or to gain the confidence of the most desirable distributors. They could relate generally to the sales force, i.e. to help build a strong sales organisation and reinforce the confidence and enthusiasm of the sales person, or to prepare the way for the sales force by creating the right customer attitude and atmosphere. They could be concerned with the need to attract the most desirable suppliers. Alternatively, they may cover a general broad field, e.g. to say things about a company that needs to be widely known, or establish a corporate name and unify under it all present and future products/services. Environmental objectives, if achieved, may make it possible to increase public, press, government support of sound policies favourable to the company, or to make a favourable impression on the various influential segments of the market and/or public, important to the company's success. All other aspects of the marketing operation may be correct but if the company has a poor corporate image, potential customers will tend not to have confidence in the product and optimum results will not be attained.

The public relations task will be performed by presenting facts, news, information etc. through unpaid and paid media, and through organisations and key people so that good relationships are maintained, weak relationships improved and bad ones corrected; activities in which the sales team is involved anyway. Just as the objectives, theme and media of advertising change as the product life-cycle progresses, so will they change as it seeks to achieve the right 'public' climate and attitude and to present the corporate image in the most favourable light.

The marketing/sales public relations plan should cover the objectives, policies and procedures relating to developing the desired corporate image. It should outline the strategy and tactics, specific areas of activity, competitor analysis and the allocation of funds to particular projects and public relations activities in general. For example, sponsorship of sport etc. is a long-term public relations technique for building not only the corporate image but also for building awareness.

Sales managers/trainers should take every opportunity to ensure that the individual sales person 'sells the company' at every possible opportunity as it encourages confidence in the company by customers and an *esprit de corps*, the pride of belonging in the sales person, that develops a good sales team spirit.

Physical distribution

In many companies the total physical distribution function is fragmented and performed in different functional areas. In a number of situations the purchasing department is responsible for the movement of raw material inwards; the production department is responsible for packaging, stock control and factory warehousing of finished products; and the sales function is responsible for strategic field stocks of finished products at branch offices/warehouses. Often a central transport unit is responsible for bulk movement of goods to geographically spread sales/warehouse locations which are responsible for local distribution. This fragmentation of the function can lead to both cost inefficiency and departmental conflicts in the interpretation of the distribution mission of the company. However, even where the physical distribution function is not the responsibility of sales management, there is still an implied sales function responsibility every time an advertisement appears or a salesman accepts an order. Every time a performance/quality claim is made or a delivery date promised, the responsibility is there. It is that of having the right goods in the right place at the right time and in the right condition.

In the circumstances described above, the sales function can only influence indirectly total physical distribution planning.

A particular aspect of physical distribution that has an impact on sales management (structure, organisation, type) is that of the choice of channels. A systematic approach is needed to determine the most effective methods of sales representation and channels of distribution in any market segment.

It is important that company managements view effective representation and channels of distribution as competitive marketing weapons. All other efforts in marketing, production and finance can be negatived by poor and ineffectual representation and inefficient channels of distribution.

The methods of sales representation and the choice of channels of distribution cannot be divorced from each other. In some cases, the ultimate sales representatives and the channels will be the same persons or organisations, but even where they are different the activities involved should be integrated to be fully effective.

The most effective way of determining the best possible sales representation and channels of distribution is to consider the effect that changes in basic factors relating to them will have on each other and on company marketing. Thus by considering the alternatives, certain plus or minus 'trade-offs' will occur. For example, the decision to use an agent with a warehouse, as opposed to a company's own individual sales person and direct delivery from the UK, will give the plus trade-offs of improved customer service and bulk transport loads, but the minus trade-offs of less control of the selling function, no direct contact with customers, and increased stock levels with greater control difficulties.

The trade-off approach to sales representation and methods and channels of distribution in an international sales situation is shown in Fig. 12.5.*

The initial trade-offs would need to be considered at the same time as those surrounding sales representation and distribution channels. A variety of permutations are possible with the criteria being centred around effectiveness in the market-place and cost in terms of money and time.

An objective appraisal is necessary and, stated simply, the steps would be:

(a) Analyse the distribution impact on each cost in a company (i.e. the trade-offs).

(b) Select and carry out a detailed study on those activity costs that are significantly affected by distribution policies and practices.

(c) Consider the availability of alternative distribution decisions.

(d) Develop the data necessary to measure the profit impact that the alternative distribution decisions would have on each of the activities.

(e) Determine which distribution alternatives and combinations of them will maximise profits.

Consideration of the distribution alternatives mentioned in the above sequence would involve not only investigation of individual activities (transport, warehousing, distribution channels etc.) but also the effect that a change in one activity would have on the others.

The choice of the channels of distribution is the prerogative of the individual company, but those available or acceptable will develop as part of the economic structure of a country. The freedom of choice by the individual company may not be as real as it appears for, in the last analysis, the economics of operation, the service offered by competitors and the level of service customers are willing to accept will all be key factors when deciding the choice of channels.

Channels of distribution cannot be considered in isolation; they are inter-related with, and sometimes substituted for, other aspects of physical distribution. For example, if economical, local company warehouses may be substituted for wholesalers, or the appointment of a retail agent (exclusive dealership) may eliminate the need for wholesalers. Alternatively, a powerful voluntary chain or group of wholesalers, through whom a large number of small retailers can be reached effectively, may be substituted for a company local warehouse. The implications are considerable for the size and type of sales force.

Channels of distribution systems can occur either through a conscious change of policy within the existing channel structure or through the emergence of new channels. In actual fact, these two alternatives represent

* Gordon J. Bolt, *Communicating with E.E.C. Markets*. Kogan Page Ltd, 1973, p. 77.

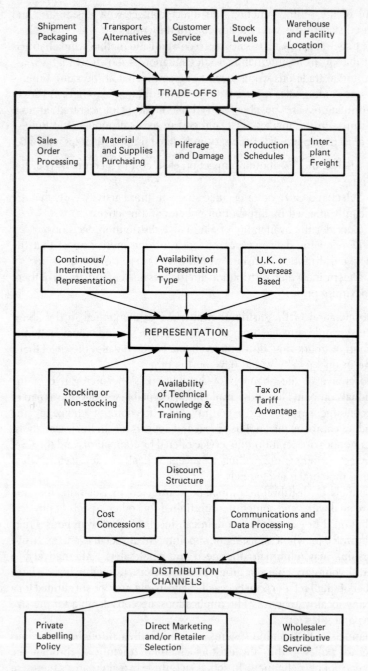

Fig. 12.5 Trade-off approach to representation and distribution

the effect of the same factor, i.e. the dynamic nature of channel systems: they are constantly, though gradually, changing. This change can relate either to the nature of the particular channel level (e.g. the changing role of the wholesaler) or a change in the relationship of levels (e.g. the new relationship between retailer and wholesaler through the emergence of voluntary chains and groups).

In consumer-goods markets, the choice of combinations of the various levels and types of channels of distribution available can be seen in Fig. 12.6.* In sales management, the trends in the volume of business done through the various combinations of channels cannot be ignored. The decline of the share of business done by independent retailers reflects the trend towards 'giantism' in retailing in recent years and the reduction in the number of small retailers.

The channels of distribution for industrial products/services may be less complex (as indicated in Fig. 12.7) but whatever the combination chosen it will have an effect upon the sales function of a company.

The choice of methods and channels of distribution will depend upon a number of factors, including:

(a) The amount of 'control' considered necessary in the retail outlet (merchandising, display allocation etc.).

(b) Whether market coverage is to be intensive, selective or exclusive franchise.

(c) Market needs (before- and after-sales service), market segment size and structure, guarantees needed, availability of stock, choice etc.

(d) Product type and size, frequency, value and quantity of purchase, product range, legal restrictions, usual outlets for similar products, demand etc.

(e) Middlemen/distributor/retailer availability and the profit margins demanded, credit facilities, rapid delivery and stock turn, trouble-free goods, identifiable and well-shaped packs, level of service provided.

(f) The needs of the manufacturing/supplying company and its current economic state, its style of business activity and strategy, location of manufacturing/ distribution points, promotional support and co-operation, price and discount structure, credit policy and terms of sale etc.

(g) Level of competition, methods and channels used by competitors, strategies and tactics of competitors in direct competition (e.g. one oil-fired boiler against another) and those supplying substitute products/services (e.g. an oil-fired boiler against electric heating).

Whatever the methods and channel(s) of distribution chosen, they are bound to affect sales management, i.e. the size, structure, type, organisation, cost, training and management necessary for the total sales function.

---

* Gordon J. Bolt, *Market and Sales Forecasting*. Kogan Page Ltd, 1983, p. 133.

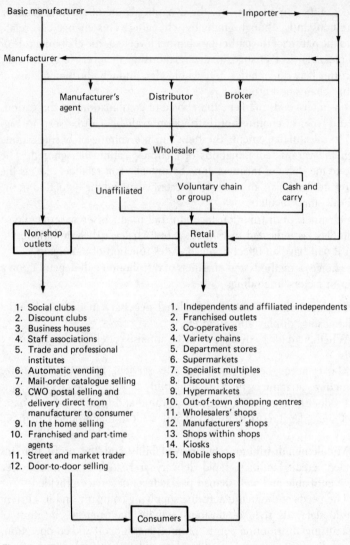

Fig. 12.6 The various levels and types of channels of distribution possible in consumer-goods markets

Sales service

The final aspect of the second part of the marketing mix is that of sales service. This activity is very much associated with a company's tactical presence in the market-place and has been dealt with in great depth in Chapter 10

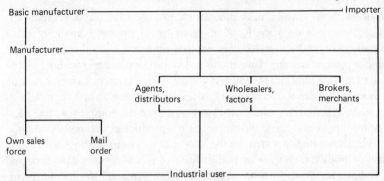

Fig. 12.7 Channels of distribution—industrial goods

(page 309) as a specialised area of sales support activity. It dealt with 'service' as the main 'product' and also before- and after-sales service for product sales. It examined services that were 'performance enhancing, life prolonging, risk reducing', and others.

Service is part of the 'total deal' the customer purchases. By implication, service must be good or it can sour sales/company relationships with customers, and an adverse 'halo' effect can overshadow all the good and positive aspects of the 'total deal' including relationships with the sales team, making it more difficult to sell. Customers expect and tend not to comment on good service but the sales team, including the sales manager, will take the brunt of complaints of poor/bad service.

Brand or product/service group management

Just as the marketing executive delegates the various parts of the marketing mix to specialists, it is necessary, when the number of products increases, to delegate the day-to-day operation of a product or group of products to a brand or product manager. This is seen in Fig. 11.3 on page 346.

Branding or product group management is used to create differentiation of products/services, to sell the brand or product group at a profit, to develop a segment of loyal buyers and to develop unique product/service attributes.

The brand or product manager will, under the general direction of the marketing executive, be responsible for providing guidance, co-ordination and direction in the marketing of the products in his/her product group, to achieve stated profit and marketing objectives within the framework of the organisation's marketing plan and budgets.

The advantage of good brand and product group management to the sales manager and his sales team is that specialised information should be available from brand and/or product managers on the physical characteristics, performance, price, location, promotional support, availability etc. of a particular product/service combination from one central source. Brand and/or product managers are also useful to the sales manager for briefing the sales team on new and revitalised product/service launches and for making visits usually with a sales person to particular customers. This is especially so in industrial markets where problems exist as to the complexity, technical nature, applications/use of the company's product/service combination.

The difficulties that arise for the sales manager from relations with brand and/or product managers are mainly those of allocating sales team time and emphasis to the various brand/product groups in a multi-product/service company. Each brand and/or product manager believes his/her brands/ products warrant special treatment and a favourably disproportionate amount of sales force time. The solution to this problem is for the sales manager to establish 'detail' schedules; these are time schedules of the priorities to be given to particular product groups on each sales team journey cycle visit. Thus depending on promotional timing, needs of particular products/services, profits, seasonality of demand etc., a priority schedule for a company with four product groupings (a, b, c, d) could be devised as in Fig. 12.8. Although priority is given in the order shown, all products/groups may be sold if the opportunity arises.

Detail or priority level	Journey cycle No.	1	2	3	4	5	6	7	8
i		b	b	a	a	c	c	b	b
ii		d	d	b	b	a	a	d	d
iii		c	c	d	d	b	b	a	a
iv		a	a	c	c	d	d	c	c

Fig. 12.8 A product/service detail priority schedule

In some cases, all the company's products/services have to be sold (e.g. to builders' merchants), in others the sales manager may have to direct the sales team to certain customer types, to give priority to certain products and/or services (i.e. computer equipment appropriate to banks or group pension schemes in large companies).

The brand or product/service group method of organisation ensures that no products are neglected. It permits delegation of product/service responsibility and accountability, and makes possible continuous analysis and evaluation of individual brand or product/service performance.

Summary

The concept of the customer communications mix has wide implications for sales management as it emphasises the integration of all the means of communicating with immediate and ultimate customers. This means that the sales function should not be seen as a separate entity in terms of strategy, tactics, content and continuity of sales/marketing theme and message although, because of the nature of its activity, it will normally have a separate organisation.

Advertising, once described as 'salesmanship in print', can in some cases be substituted for sales personnel and vice versa. It should be based on setting basic objectives that link with the rest of the communications mix, doing pre-campaign research, setting specific objectives, determining budgets, selecting the appropriate media together with developing the appropriate theme/message/copy platform and then pre-testing and amending the campaign. After commencing the campaign, it needs to be monitored, post-tested and evaluated for effectiveness. The type of campaign and intended audience will be reflected, not only in the 'message' sent, but also in the category of media chosen, i.e. consumer, trade or industry advertising. The effectiveness of advertising will have a direct impact on demand for the products/services and consequently on the work of the sales team. The importance of the role of the advertising agency and of the need for the sales manager to establish close links with it cannot be over-emphasised.

Advertising attracts consumers/users towards the product/service and the company, whereas sales promotion 'pushes' the product/service and the company image towards the customer. In the sense that the sales person 'pushes' the product/service towards the customer, selling must be an aspect of sales promotion. There are a number of methods for doing this that are appropriate for the industrial buyer, the consumer and channels of distribution being used. A sales promotion plan should be developed (using the same basic stages that were applied to advertising) with due regard to the needs of the company in the market-place, the information and motivational needs of customers, the activities of competitors, the nature of the product etc.

Branding (the policy for which was examined in the previous chapter) is an important part of marketing tactics, making market segmentation easier, promoting customer memory recall, making selling easier, promoting acceptance of the product/service and assuring the continuity of quality. Brand names should be memorable, distinctive, easy to pronounce, not offend, be relatively short and apt.

Packaging should protect a product in storage and transit, persuade the customer to purchase, and be helpful to customer/user. It does this through its construction, design, size, shape, labelling 'copy', colour and performance. All providing the sales team with 'benefits' to sell to customers.

Tactical pricing can communicate a variety of messages to potential customers which add desirable values to a product/service based on price images and psychological pricing. Methods of tactical pricing include marginal and total absorption techniques which involve the consideration of fixed and variable costs, the margin or contribution, profit mark-up, volume, the break-even point, price discrimination (between products/ services in different market segments) and the minimum unit price at different volumes. Elasticity of demand (sales) is also an important issue for the sales manager as it reflects the price sensitivity of products/services and indicates in what circumstance price reductions or increases are viable. The final aspect of tactical pricing is for the sales manager to develop a price contingency plan identifying his/her response to price decreases/increases of competitors.

Public relations is a wider set of activities than customer communications as it involves a broader set of 'publics' than ultimate customers and/or channels of distribution. Many companies have a department/section covering all 'publics' but, if one does not exist or is neglecting marketing/ sales public relations, the sales manager and the sales team needs to take over the responsibility for this activity.

The public relations task will be performed by presenting facts, news, information etc. through paid and unpaid media and through organisations and key people so that good relationships are maintained, weak relationships improved and bad ones corrected. These are activities that are fundamental to the sales team to ensure the most favourable atmosphere in which to sell.

Effective physical distribution means having the right goods in the right place at the right time and in the right condition. The magnitude of the total trade-offs obtained through the choice of the right methods of distribution and the most appropriate channels will influence decisions within companies relating to physical distribution. A number of options is open to the sales manager but, in the last analysis, it will be the economics of operations, the service offered by competitors and the level of service customers are willing to accept that will be key factors when deciding the choice of channels. Whatever the methods and channel(s) of distribution chosen, they are bound to affect sales management, i.e. the size, structure, type of organisation, cost, training and management necessary for the total sales function.

Service, considered as the main 'product' (and also before- and after-sales service), was briefly mentioned as it was examined in depth in Chapter 10.

Brand or product/service group management arises because of the delegation of the day-to-day operation of a brand, product or group of products/services to a brand or product manager who is responsible for achieving the stated profit and marketing objectives for the product(s)/ services.

Brand or product managers can help the sales function in various ways (briefing, customer visits etc.), but problems can arise regarding the time allocation of the sales team to various brands; the answer is a priority schedule. It can ensure that no brand, product or product group is neglected and it makes possible continuous analysis and evaluation of individual brand or product/service combinations.

Questions

1. Why is the concept of the customer communications mix so important to sales management?

2. What is the role of advertising in relation to that of the selling function and sales management?

3. How does sales promotion differ from advertising and what are the means by which it gives support to the sales function?

4. Show how branding and packaging are linked with each other and how they both help and support the sales operation.

5. What are the main factors that affect the sales team in tactical pricing?

6. What is the significance of public relations being a wider concept than just customer communications and what are the implications for the sales team?

7. What are the potential areas of 'conflict' between an individual brand or product/service group manager and the sales manager? How can they be reconciled in:

(a) consumer-goods markets and industrial goods markets?
(b) goods versus service industries?

CHAPTER 13

The sales interface with key external factors

Objectives

The aim of this chapter is to examine the affect that certain external factors have on the sales function in general and sales management in particular. They are seen as environments in which sales management operates which give rise to, and can indicate, opportunities, threats, constraints, relationships which are largely not controllable by the company. They include the economic environment; competition; technology; the legal environment; the international environment; consumerism and social accountability; the political environment; population, culture, social class and consumer behaviour; and organisation/industrial buyer behaviour. They are examined and the implications for sales management indicated.

Implications of key environments

At the beginning of Section Five it was stated that sales management operates within two types of environments/constraints/relationships, internal and external. This chapter examines the latter in the context of the external and largely non-controllable factors identified in the figure on page 334.

All these external environments and factors are changing at different speeds and different orders of magnitude and will have different implications for sales management at different times. Thus a sales manager must have a 'working relationship' with all of them, must be aware of trends and changes taking place and make the appropriate amendments in sales planning, strategies, organisation, operations and control to accommodate them.

It is relatively easy for the sales manager to identify and be aware of major changes. The problem often lies with small, slow-moving changes in external factors which can emerge almost unnoticed by the busy sales manager whose priorities often lie with more pressing/immediate situations. A checklist approach is therefore recommended, i.e. the listing of key relevant factors that is referred to at least every 3–6 months to assess and relate the external factor to the sales function.

Often the interdependent nature of a number of the external factors is apparent, thus market needs, buyer behaviour and competition very much impinge on each other as well as on sales management. Another dimension is that these external factors have a chain reaction/sequential effect on each other, thus a new product obtained by a change in technology can have an effect on consumerism and social accountability, and these may cause government controls or even a change in the law.

Key environments examined

The economic environment

All companies operate in, and are therefore affected by, the international, national and regional economic environments. Even the company that does not market abroad will be affected by imports from foreign producers.

No economy is ever static on all fronts; it is either moving forward or dropping back. Therefore the movements/swings in economic trends reflected in a variety of published economic 'indicators' need to be monitored, analysed and interpreted by the sales manager to ensure that appropriate decisions are made and that the basic economic data on which the sales function objectives were set and the sales plan was made still apply.

Governments, reacting to economic trends, can cause them to be halted/modified or new trends started by various fiscal policies, e.g. manipulation of interest rates, application of tariff and non-tariff barriers, import quotas and licences, exchange controls, credit regulations and taxes. All can affect company decision-making ranging from the decision to borrow, defer or not to borrow money for capital equipment/investment programmes and for extending working capital, to those decisions that have to be made by the sales manager as to how the sales function of a company can accommodate new situations caused by economic trends and/or government fiscal policies.

It will be helpful to sales managers to identify relevant economic indicators that generally affect the business world in which a company operates and those that specifically affect his/her company or markets. Examples of key economic indicators in specific areas are:

(a) Output – published data includes gross domestic product, industrial production, total purchasing by industries, stocks, work in progress etc.

(b) Labour – data on unemployment, vacancies, by industries and region.

(c) Fixed investment – gross fixed capital formation (i.e. money spent on purchase of capital equipment etc.) by industry, such as hi-tech, general manufacturing, processing, distributive and service industries (e.g. banking, shipping, insurance etc.).

(d) Consumption – personal income and expenditure, real personal disposable income and consumer expenditure.

(e) Retail trade – including retail sales by volume, value, region and market, e.g. new car registrations.

(f) Companies – company income (industrial and commercial), gross company income, gross trading profits total or net of stock appreciation.

(g) Balance of payments – on current account and capital account, invisible and visible balances.

(h) Overseas trade – visible trade volume, exported and imported goods, terms of trade.

(i) Exchange rates – sterling exchange rates in relation to US dollar and other major currencies, exchange rate index.

(j) Prices – tax and price index, retail price index, wholesale prices, prices of imported raw materials.

(k) Earnings – average earnings by industry and region, monthly index, increase on year earlier.

(l) Money – money supply levels, sterling M3, interest rates, 3-month interbank rate, minimum lending rate.

Most of the above general economic indicators can be found in one publication, the UK government's *Economic Progress Report*, but a wider range of sources and more specific indicators have been identified. *

Economic indicators can be presented either in unit volume figures or values (e.g. the value of exports shown in pounds sterling), or presented as an index number where increases or decreases are shown as a percentage of the base year figure of 100. Whether actual values or index values are used, data can be further presented either on a period basis (e.g. the level of industrial production over the last 3 months), or on a basis of a particular moment in time (e.g. the total hire-purchase debt as at 31 December 19X3).

Since most economic indicators are, by their nature, general, they often have to be interpreted and evaluated to determine how changes in them will affect a particular company, industry or market. Further, some will be more appropriate for certain markets than others, and in most cases a combination of such indicators will be necessary to provide data to set up an effective composite indicator forecast for a particular company.

Various facets of the economy and the economic climate can be examined through economic indicators and often trends in them can be anticipated, permitting more realistic industry or market forecasts to be made by the sales manager.

---

* Gordon J. Bolt, *Market and Sales Forecasting*. Kogan Page Ltd, 1981, pp. 95–110.

Competition

This can be defined on an intensity scale, narrowly or broadly, ranging from other companies selling exactly the same product (e.g. timber) in exactly the same market segment (e.g. small/medium builders) at almost exactly the same base price, to companies selling very different products (oil versus electricity versus coal) but which can be substituted for each other (e.g. in the field of industrial energy or home central heating). There is a wide range of competitive situations between these two extremes.

The sales manager must therefore identify at the macro level the industries in which the company is operating and in which competition will take place. Information is needed regarding the size of industry, growth rates (historical and future), the key factors in growth, barriers to entry and production facility status to put competition into a contextual framework and to make comparison.

No sales manager will escape the pressures of competition, although its intensity may change from time to time. Sales managers in large companies will be concerned about the activity of small specialist competitors who can operate with lower overheads and who can select and concentrate on lucrative market segments. Those in small companies will be concerned about the activities of large dominant competitors who have large-scale resources and economies of scale to help them meet and beat competition. Even within the same size-band competition will be the constant concern of the sales manager who should know its extent, intensity and effectiveness to enable strategic and tactical decisions to be made.

The objective profiling of competitors helps sales managers to understand/anticipate competitor decision-making, not only because it assembles relevant information but also because over a short period of time it establishes the thinking behind competitor marketing/sales strategies, i.e. the competitor's 'modus operandi'.

At the micro level, developing competitor profiles requires that information is assembled to give as complete a 'picture' as possible of particular competitors and should include details of:

(a) Products/services, existing and planned.

(b) Market segments covered and customer types serviced (e.g. manufacturers, wholesalers, retailers etc.).

(c) Present and future marketing/sales/advertising strategies and tactics.

(d) Type of competition (e.g. price, quality, performance, service, delivery, choice etc.).

(e) Pricing strategies (e.g. skimming policies, 'sliding down the demand curve', penetration price policy, premium pricing etc.).

(f) Price change behaviour.

(g) Costs, sales turnover and profits performance.

(h) Production methods, location and capacity.

(i) Purchasing policies.

(j) Type, structure and operation of sales force and selling methods used.

(k) Distribution policy.

(l) Credit policy.

(m) Company organisation, philosophy and image.

This and other relevant information regarding competitors can be obtained from one's own customers, ex-employees of the competitors, financial pages of newspapers, their chairmen's annual report, their consumer and/or trade advertising, their employment advertisements (and information sent to individuals in response to replies to them), directories, year books, trade fairs, exhibitions, Companies House, assessments of advertising/sales promotion/sales force expenditure, price lists, brochures, service manuals, technical data sheets, house journals etc. There are many other sources including from the actual competitors with whom good relations and an on-going dialogue should be maintained; such relationships can prevent the costly price wars often started or 'fuelled' by other interested parties, i.e. customers, middlemen, large-scale own label companies etc.

Further, it is important to identify established criteria for assessing a company's competitive position through SWOT analysis (i.e. strengths, weaknesses, opportunities and threats). Such criteria should include:

(a) Product/service combination, broad general or narrow specialist range.

(b) Customer spread in terms of turnover, coverage or industry/market types (Standard Industrial Classification for industrial customers, accommodation, socio-economic groups, age, sex, location, for consumer goods/services).

(c) Special relationships with customers (private labelling or large contracts, reciprocal trading etc.), or suppliers ('monopoly' of certain materials or agencies/distributorships) or others (e.g. licensing arrangements either for products or processing).

(d) Market position with regard to product, price, quality, performance, image etc.

(e) Company position with regard to industry/market price leadership.

(f) Credibility of brand and/or corporate image.

(g) Company position with regard to being a low-cost producer.

(h) A measure of profitability – a criterion for operating at the furthest position beyond the break-even point, to the point of optimum capacity.

(i) Where the company stands with technology, i.e. to have the greatest possible advantage or the least possible disadvantage.

(j) Financial strength.

(k) The degree of competitive advantage obtained by backward integration (i.e. with suppliers) or forward integration (i.e. with the next stage of production or with channels of distribution).

(l) The capability of the company to take calculated risks in a particular product/service/market area.

(m) How does the company's management/organisation rate against the competition?

(n) Current effectiveness of the sales force.

(o) Product/service range completeness.

(p) Quality/service performance in relation to target market segments.

(q) Market share trends.

Competition cannot be ignored, it won't simply 'go away'; by developing competitor profiles and establishing criteria for assessing a company's competitive position, the sales manager will have the best information available on which to make strategic and tactical decisions to deal with and gain an advantage over competitors 'in the market-place'.

Technology

Just as there is a need for the sales manager to examine conditions in the market, there is also a need to monitor, examine and allow for existing and potential technology in the immediate industry, in those industries that could compete with substitute products/services and in customer industries.

Technology can be perceived in two ways: it can be the alternative ways in which a particular job/function can be performed or, alternatively, some basic technologies (with variations) will have a range of applications in a variety of products in many different industries.

Technological innovation can create new products/services and require new industries/companies to provide them. It can also transform existing industries (either by forced or natural progression) or even destroy them either abruptly or over a period of time.

Internal new product development/strategy was dealt with in Chapter 11 (page 350) and is the situation in which a company introduces its own technological innovation. But the sales manager must be able to appreciate the implication of technological change/innovation externally as well as internally and carry out medium- and long-term contingency planning

An added complication for the sales manager in accommodating particular technological change/innovation is the varying 'gestation' periods for it to achieve commercial viability and/or recognition. Examples of this are given by Hague* (Fig. 13.1).

There is a need for the sales manager to examine existing technology used in an industry and to forecast the future development of sales of a product, but in the long term a fundamental factor will be the range and type of products that technology generally has evolved.

* Paul N. Hague, *The Industrial Market Research Handbook*. Kogan Page Ltd, 1985, p. 53.

Product	Discovery	Production	Lag (years)
Acrylic plastics	1901	1933	32
Helicopters	1907	1945	38
Penicillin	1928	1943	15
Xerox	1935	1950	15
Acrylic fibres	1938	1948	10
Cumene-phenol process	1945	1955	10
Microchip	1948	1959	11
Isothalic (paint additive)	1951	1958	7
High-strength carbon fibres	1965	1973	8
Sintered high-speed steel	1972	1979	7

Fig. 13.1 Length of time taken between invention and commercial launch of selected industrial products

Many companies attempt to forecast future developments in technology because of their obvious effect on the development of new products/services, and also because of their impact on market/sales forecasting in general and on individual company product forecasting in particular.

It is not only the innovating type of company that needs to forecast technological developments, but also the company that follows the lead set by the innovators. Further, it is also necessary for the company that modifies a basic product concept to the needs of a specific market segment, and the company with the same product as others but which offers a different overall combination of customer satisfactions. All operate a changing technological environment and will be affected by it.

Technological forecasting can be highly sophisticated or very elementary in its methods: but the fact that it is considered at all will cause executives to examine, consider and plan their own product range more effectively.

Generally, technological forecasting is concerned mainly with trends, not precise predictions. Even so, it can be helpful to the sales manager in indicating potentially different technological 'futures' that will affect his/her markets.

The techniques of technological forecasting fall into two categories, exploratory and normative. These have been defined thus:

exploratory forecasting consists in using our present knowledge of science potentialities and technical trends for projection purposes under a ceteris paribus assumption which generally neglects all other possible structure changes. On the contrary, normative forecasting works backwards from the future to the present; it implies a coherent examination of future needs in a future society, which helps define first, socio-economic objectives and then purely technical research objectives and the best way to achieve them.

Some technological forecasting methods have been suggested,* including morphological research, systems analysis, normative relevance tree techniques, brainstorming, the delphi oracle approach, scenario writing, and technological trend extrapolation which includes a variety of approaches (i.e. direct, vector, line of best fit, envelope curve extrapolation, 'S'-curve trend comparison, long/short-term performance graph etc.).

If technological change/innovation in an industry is forecast or has already commenced, the sales manager needs to consider the extent of the threat it may pose, if any, to his/her company and sales and identify alternative courses of action.

The sales manager must be prepared to accommodate the impact of technological change and innovation, and be prepared to use the outcomes arising from them either as 'buying benefits' for customers or to better equip the sales team, or to use them to ensure more effective sales management. In these circumstances, the potential area for technological changes are:

(a) *The product/service* – technological advances in the actual production process (e.g. from mechanical to numerical control to robotics) may not only provide the sales team with better products/services, improved quality, wider choice, lower prices etc., but may also be used to project the image of an up-to-date, modern company. However, the more technologically advanced and complex the product/service becomes, the longer and more technical the necessary product knowledge and applications knowledge training will need to be (e.g. the application of computer systems to banking etc.) and may even need the recruitment of a different type of sales person.

(b) *The pack* – technological advances in packaging and packaging machinery will not only produce better designed, more protective, more economical packaging but may affect product presentation (e.g. from bottles to the use of aerosols) or be used as a sales tool at the point of purchase (e.g. shrink-wrap, 'visible product' packaging).

(c) *The methods of selling* – technological advances in communications has meant that the sales person's visual aids can include video presentations and the use of portable computers to calculate instantly the variety of financial outcomes differing buying decisions can have (e.g. insurance or large contract variations etc.) and for instant design decision. These advances in communication technology will continue and will also affect methods of placing orders (telephone, electronic mail) and of handling/ processing orders.

(d) *Selling by agents/retailers* and technological innovation and application – e.g. the use of microfilm readers to provide up-to-date information on parts for complex machinery, the use of viewdata and/or visual display units to access suppliers' data banks (e.g. regarding stock availability and other data) and to make instant reservations (e.g. travel agents and tour operators,

---

* Gordon J. Bolt, *Market and Sales Forecasting*. Kogan Page Ltd, 1981, pp. 148–53.

hotels, theatres etc.). The use of bar coding of packaged products and their electronic reading by check-out microprocessors affects retailers' cash control, stock control and re-ordering procedures. In large national multiples, it is also reflected in 'after-hours' communication by master and satellite computers to provide top and operating management with profit, sales and stock data. Another example is the installation of interactive videodisc equipment at the point of purchase to provide customers and staff with a wide range of information.

(e) *The operation of sales management* – the effects of technological innovation can affect methods of sales management slightly in some cases and radically in others. The use of viewdata, electronic mail, cellular radio, teleconferencing and paging devices are examples of technological innovation that aids sales management communication to and from the field sales team. The setting up and/or use of databases on the relevant industry segments, customer and potential customers, and the use of micro-computers in an interactive mode will give the sales manager more/better information and suggest alternative courses of action, so that better decisions can be made. Also, there has been technological innovation in the use of computers for stock control, order processing and profit monitoring.

There are potential advantages/benefits for the sales manager in technological innovation in all the five areas above, but it must be remembered that their potential application will be relative to the market that the sales team is covering. For example, the degree of application of technological innovation will be more advanced and sophisticated in the USA and some parts of the European Common Market than in the UK. In others, they will be less advanced and in some developing countries the technological infrastructure, know-how/service is just not available.

The legal environment

The law not only affects the marketing and selling of goods and services but also impinges on other aspects of the role of sales management, e.g. business property (branch offices), employment, business disputes and other business relationships (e.g. agency agreements).

Companies operate in a range of legal environments ranging from those controlled by local by-laws to those operated under the 'law of the land' (civil and criminal), legally enforceable government regulations, EEC laws and regulations, and international law. The company, being a legal entity, will in the main be responsible for acts done in its name by directors and employees although this may not be so where activities are carried out by individuals without authority (*ultra vires*). The individual will certainly be responsible and accountable in addition to the company for criminal activities.

This part of the chapter endeavours to highlight some of the more important legal factors that affect sales management situations, at the expense of considerable over-simplification. Any executive should have reference to the company's legal advisers but at the same time should be aware of the rights and legal constraints and powers.

There is a need for the sales manager to be aware of the law relating to the nature and scope of business contracts in general. It is important to identify and analyse the essential ingredients of business contracts and to critically evaluate the factors which may affect their validity. The sales manager should be able to compare the advantages and disadvantages of standard form contracts for business organisations and be able to identify the available controls over exemptions and limitation clauses in such contracts. The key areas of the basic law of contract of which the sales manager should be aware are agreement, the intention to create legal relations, consideration, formality, capacity, terms and exclusion clauses, vitiating factors, mistake, misrepresentation, undue influence, contracts in restraint of trade, discharge, remedies for breach of contract.

Next there is the need for the sales manager to be aware of the legal framework of business contracts and relationships for the supply of goods and services. This includes the need to differentiate between such types of business contracts as sale, rental and leases, hire purchase and other credit transactions as well as to differentiate between the contracts for the supply of goods and those for the provision of services. The sales manager should be able to identify and compare the essential obligations of the parties in the different forms of contract, i.e. the transfer of title or property rights, acceptance of goods, delivery and especially the applications of the Sales of Goods (Implied Terms) legislation. He/she should also assess the liability (contractual and non-contractual) applicable to the provision of goods and services, and especially the liability of manufacturers when their goods are sold by others (e.g. retailers).

The sales manager should be able to appreciate the different ways in which an agency situation may arise. When such situations do arise, it is important for him/her to be able to analyse the classification of agent's authority and to appreciate the rules governing the inter-relationships of the parties involved.

The key areas of the law relating to specific contracts relevant to sales management are the sale of goods and hire-purchase/credit sales, conditions and warranties, transfer of property and risk, title of goods, delivery and acceptance, remedies, and forms of credit agreements. Also under this particular heading is the creation of agency situations, authority of agents, rights and duties of principal and agent, and termination of agency.

The sales manager should appreciate the legislation surrounding what is known as 'industrial property right protection', to be aware of and/or prevent infringement by others of company industrial property and to prevent sales personnel making the company liable through the infringements of other's rights. The Patents Act 1977 provides that an invention (specifically definable) is patentable provided it is original and has not been used, marketed or sold by others in the UK or any other country prior to making application for a patent which prevents others from copying it for a period of 20 years.

Trademarks are another part of 'industrial property right protection'. They are essentially to distinguish by the use of words or symbols one company's products from those of another. Registration of a trademark will enable a company to stop other people using it for products identical or similar to its own.

In some cases, the company's industrial property to be protected is in written form (e.g. technical data manuals, manuals relating to computer software, or books in the case of publishers) and this is covered by legislation relating to copyright. There is no registration system for copyright; it is granted automatically to authors of original works who could be writing on behalf of companies or who 'invest' their rights in companies, to prevent others copying them. The protection lasts for 50 years and covers not only printed material but others such as photographs and films.

A company's industrial property also includes the design of products and/or packaging and industrial designs such as engineering drawings providing the 'design' is sufficiently original, but a company must apply to register it before it is used. The advantage of registering a design is that a company can prevent (or if the rights are infringed seek compensation for) not only the intentional imitation of it but also its innocent and unintentional imitation.

A company may seek to license the production or use of a product, copyright work, process, business format, trademark, technology etc., and the sales manager of such a company needs to be aware not only of the law relating to licensing agreements but also the legal requirements of their operation.

There are also laws, statutory regulations and orders relating to packaging (e.g. use of certain materials, type, safety requirements and contact in certain circumstances) and to labelling (e.g. description of ingredients, size of lettering, warnings for certain products types etc.). The sales manager should be aware of these for the UK but also for other countries if the company's products are exported, as each country tends to have its own packaging and labelling legislation.

There is wide-ranging legislation under the broad heading of consumer protection of which the sales manager should be aware and operate within. Some examples are the Unfair Contract Terms Act, Sales of Goods (Implied Terms) Act, Trade Descriptions Act, Merchandising Marks Act, Consumer Credit Act, Weights and Measures Act, Fair Trading Act and other Acts and rulings. Also, the comments of the Office of Fair Trading are of direct relevance to sales managers in appropriate areas of sales activity (e.g. claims made in advertisements, the distribution of unsolicited goods etc.).

It follows logically that the sales manager should appreciate the legal implications of methods of settlement in relation to business transactions which in turn suggests the ability to compare and contrast the rights and duties of contracting parties in cash settlements, credit arrangements and payments by cheque. The sales manager should also be able to evaluate the provision of the Consumer Credit Act 1974 as it affects business transactions and also understand the principle of negotiability and distinguish between cheques and other forms of negotiable and transferable instruments and their business uses. He/she should be able to appreciate the legal elements in the relationship between banks and customers, banking facilities available to business customers, and the rights of banker, customer and holder in relation to cheques.

An important area of knowledge for the sales manager is the legal framework of controls over trading activities, e.g. the concept of, and the law relating to, restrictive trade practice and rules governing such. In the same area are the legal and policy rules encouraging competition in business and the EEC aspects of such. There is also the need to differentiate between mergers and monopolies and to recognise the regime of statutory control over them.

It is advisable for the sales manager to be aware of the methods available for resolving business disputes (e.g. the legal and equitable remedies available for breach of business contracts) and the system of commercial arbitration as an alternative method of resolution. There is also a need to appreciate the sanctions of the criminal law applicable to business activities.

In relation to customers, distributors, agents, joint ventures etc., there is a need for the sales manager to appreciate the methods and consequences of terminating business organisations and the grounds for, and formalities relating to, the dissolution of them. Linked with this is the need for an understanding of the rules relating to the payment of creditors of a business, the situation of suppliers providing goods on the consignment stock principle and/or 'sale or return' arrangements, and the priorities relating to the distribution of assets when a business is dissolved.

The sales manager, as an employer of sales personnel, should understand the basic factors regarding contracts of employment, their nature and formation, express and implied terms, termination of employment and its implications.

In situations where the sales manager is involved with the setting up of agencies, distributorships, franchises and related independent business organisations, he/she should understand the means of creating different types of business organisations, the formalities required for setting them up and the penalties for non-compliance. Further, it is important that the sales manager should appreciate the relative merits of each type of organisation and be able to indicate the different methods of raising and increasing capital and the controls over them. There is also the need to be able to distinguish the legal status of the different types of organisation and any EEC aspects of such.

Where the sales manager is involved in business property (e.g. branch sales offices, agents, distributors, franchises etc.) and the law applicable thereto, there is a need to analyse the nature and classifications of property, distinguishing between freehold and leasehold interests in landed property, understand the legal controls over business tenancies and appreciate the liability of the company in respect of defective premises. This latter point is particularly relevant to the presence of customers, potential customers and customers' customers in sales showrooms and/or service premises.

This part of the chapter has been able to deal broadly with certain key aspects of the legal environment in which companies and sales management operate. Obviously the sales manager will need to seek legal advice where any of these (and other) legal factors impinge on the operation of the sales function.

International environment

For many years, economists have been evolving theories of international trade, encouraging on one hand a gradual freeing of it to make more effective use of world resources through such agencies as GATT (General Agreement on Tariffs and Trade) and, on the other, there has been a counter movement towards 'protectionism' restricting it through actions by:

(a) political blocs, e.g. Eastern Bloc countries
(b) customs' unions, i.e. a common pattern of tariffs, import duties, quotas, regulations etc. (e.g. the EEC)
(c) free-trade areas, i.e. the free movement of goods, labour, capital internally but country-specific external regulations
(d) individual countries using import controls, tariff and non-tariff barriers (e.g. strategic lists, delays at restricted points of entry), quotas, regulations, preferential trade deals often government financed etc.
(e) individual companies using patents, trademarks, restrictive licensing of products etc.

In spite of these activities, the basic economic concept of comparative costs tends to operate; it is that countries/regions tend to specialise in the production of goods and services in which they have the greater possible advantage or the least possible disadvantage.

It is obvious that all these factors will have an impact on the sales operation of a company whether or not it is involved in international trade (perhaps because of imports or even the lack of them in particular products) and consequently on the operations of sales management.

The managerial philosophies/policies/structure of the international operations will affect the style and type of sales management depending on type of operations and whether it is static or moving towards another form of operation. Many categories/types have been suggested but the four identified by Stanton* are appropriate and comprehensive because they show recognisable stages and a potential progression.

Ethnocentric stage (home-country orientation): Foreign operations are treated as secondary to domestic operations. Planning for foreign markets is done in the home office, and marketing personnel are primarily home-country nationals. The marketing mix follows domestic patterns. No major changes are made in the products sold abroad. Promotion and distribution strategies are essentially the same as at home. The ethnocentric position is likely to be adopted by a small company just entering the international market, or by a larger firm whose foreign sales are insignificant.

Polycentric stage (host-country orientation): Each foreign country is treated as a separate entity with its own autonomous subsidiary organisation. Each of these foreign subsidiaries does its own marketing, planning and research. Products are changed to meet local needs. Each subsidiary does its own pricing and promotion. Distribution is through channels and a sales force native to the country in question.

Today most international executives probably view the polycentric position as the most desirable one. In marketing, it is very important to adapt to country-by-country differences, and to use local nationals of the country in doing a marketing job. Polycentrism, however, is likely to lead to problems of co-ordinating and controlling the marketing activities among the several countries.

Regiocentric stage (regional orientation): A given region is treated as a single market, regardless of national boundaries. Marketing plans and programmes are set for the entire region. Personnel can come from anywhere. Standardised products are used throughout the entire region. Distribution channels and promotion are developed on a regional basis to project a uniform image of the company and its products.

Geocentric stage (world orientation): The entire world is treated as a single market, so that this stage is essentially an expansion of the regiocentric stage.

A regiocentric approach is probably more economical and manageable than a worldwide programme. From a practical point of view, however, national environmental constraints (laws, currencies, culture, life-style) may severely limit either one of these broad marketing approaches.

In the context of one of the above company philosophies/policies, the international environment for any company can be divided into three main categories:

(a) the countries to whom it would like to market/sell
(b) the countries from whom competition can be expected
(c) the countries that fit into categories (a) and (b)

Rarely will any company have all the countries in the world as its

---

* William J. Stanton, *Fundamentals of Marketing*. McGraw-Hill Inc., 1978, pp. 502 and 503. Reproduced with permission.

international environment. Therefore it will be useful for the sales manager to systematically identify and profile countries as they fit into the above three categories under the following criteria:*

A. *Country*
Size and topography
Climate and other geographical factors
The economy and its trends
Gross national product
Balance-of-payment situation
Foreign exchange restrictions
Industry to agriculture relationship (ratio)
Industrial structure
Type of government and stability
Recent attitude to the UK
Official attitude to private industry and trading
Political parties, number and direction of dominant party
Government controls
Taxation systems
Socio-economic class structures
Religions and their implications
Languages
Population and population changes
Location of population; rural and urban emphasis
Income per capita
Age patterns
Occupational patterns
Criteria and ideals
Domestic structures
Living patterns
Culinary habits
Labour legislation
The general level of prices.

B. *Markets*
Accessibility to market (distance etc.)
Size of market for at least the previous 3–4 years, in units and value; quantities bought, or, in the case of equipment, the number already installed.
Total production or sales
Total exports, F.O.B.
Total imports, C.I.F.
Total apparent consumption (Production + Imports − Exports)
Destination of exports
Source of imports
UK share of imports
Company's sales to territory
Company's share of UK sales and of total sales
Forecast of future sales and company's projected share
Factors affecting demand
Factors affecting types and models bought
Buying practice in terms of timing of purchase, quantities in which the purchase is made, and terms of purchase.

* Gordon J. Bolt, *Marketing in the EEC*. Kogan Page Ltd, 1973, pp. 25–7.

C. *Conditions of Entry into Particular Markets*

Import tariffs and preferential rates

Tax systems, local taxes, variations in tax structure and in fiscal systems

Import quotas and licences

Statutory requirements (e.g. for food and electrical products)

Standards and regulations applicable to the product type or its packaging (e.g. health and safety standards)

Marking of merchandise

Documentation requirements (e.g. certificates of origin, consular invoices etc.)

Transport facilities and charges, including insurance:

(a) From UK port of dispatch;

(b) Transit through ports;

(c) From port of entry to destination.

Patent law and requirements

Trade marks and Branding requirements

Other non-tariff barriers.

D. *Characteristics of the Market*

1. Competitors

    Competitor countries (particularly special affiliations)

    Competitor firms, numbers and names and addresses

    What are their respective market shares?

    Corporate information on competitors, including range of products, capacity and output, affiliations, employment, capital, profits, future intentions.

    What specific advantages do the main competitors have?

    (a) Size

    (b) Geographical

    (c) Industrial

    (d) Associations, affiliations, liaisons

    (e) Related products

    (f) Licensing arrangements

    (g) Reciprocal trading arrangements.

    What marketing and sales methods do competitors use?

    Is price used as an instrument of sales policy?

    Advertising, sales promotion and selling policies

    Usual credit and discount practices

2. Comprehensive and/or substitute products

    (a) Characteristics of product type, performance, output, style, quality, colour, flavour, design, other specifications, and number of alternatives in product range

    (b) Brand image

    (c) Prices, discounts, and subsidies

    (d) Market share by brand, product group or make

    (e) Packaging (as protective and marketing device)

    (f) Advertising, sales promotion and selling support

    (g) Before-sales and after-sales services, spares and replacements, technical advice, etc.

    (h) Guarantees and warranties.

3. Methods of distribution

    (a) Through wholesaler and/or retailer

    (b) Direct to consumer or industrial user

    (c) Product category outlet type, clothing, food, electrical, hardware, etc.

    (d) Organisation types used, government import department, importers, agents, group buying arrangements, department stores, multiple chains, etc.

4. Profitability
   Potential sales volume related to profit potential
   Short-, medium- and long-term profit prospects
   Market price levels related to current and anticipated costs
   Assembling and assessing country/market data.

From the above profiling, a list of 'preferred' countries (in terms of sales potential and opportunity to sell) will emerge.

The dynamic approach to international marketing/selling can be defined as getting through, and profitably selling to, individual markets in any part of the world by any means. It is far wider than simply selling complete products overseas and can include the following approaches/strategies which could be used in overseas markets. *

1. The marketing of complete products (machine tools, cars, processed food products, components and sub-assemblies).
2. The marketing of parts, components, and sub-assemblies where these form part of a complete product that a company sells in other markets.
3. Marketing parts for complete products that will be assembled in overseas markets.
4. Marketing of parts to be matched with locally made parts in overseas markets, to make complete products.
5. Marketing of licences.
6. Marketing of process or production technology, product design or other know-how.
7. Marketing of brand names and trade marks.
8. Marketing in overseas markets through leasing arrangements.
9. Marketing through mergers, joint ventures or co-operation with similar companies in the overseas country or market.
10. Market co-operation and reciprocal trading arrangements with companies in similar markets in overseas countries.
11. Marketing by setting up or taking over a local company for manufacturing, assembling, or marketing products or services.
12. Marketing through pure investment—the establishment of a profit link with a company overseas; in some cases this is done to meet competition in that or another market, or to exchange technical know-how, or for the purpose of reciprocal trading, etc.
13. Marketing through importing certain products, components, materials made in other countries may have a cost, quality or technological advantage and by judiciously incorporating them into its products, it may give a UK company a competitive advantage.

All these various types of approach to international marketing/selling can be used by British companies operating in overseas countries. It is merely a matter of determining which approach, or combinations of approaches, suits the needs of the individual company.

While company marketing strategy, availability of information about countries and markets, and product/service strategy will affect the sales manager's decision-making, a more direct concern may be with the

* Abbreviated from Gordon J. Bolt, *Marketing in the EEC*. Kogan Page Ltd, 1973, pp. 16, 18 and 19.

channels of distribution and company representation, and the degree of control the sales manager can exert over the various options.

(a) Complete control can be effected by total ownership of manufacturing facilities, wholesale distribution networks and retail chains.

(b) Strong control is possible through a company export department either in UK or in overseas countries, sales branches and/or warehouses, joint ventures, own sales force (UK or overseas based), order-getting tours by company executives, exclusive agency or distributorship arrangements.

(c) Moderate control can be expected from shared agency or distributorship facilities, local licensing arrangements, minority shareholding arrangements, franchising etc.

(d) Weak control only is possible when selling through joint or group selling, reciprocal trading, co-marketing, consortia, government agencies etc.

(e) No control is possible of activities in overseas markets when goods are sold to foreign importers/merchants, merchant shippers, international trading companies, buying/indent agents operating in the UK on behalf of overseas manufacturing/trading companies, purchasing tours/missions by overseas companies.

The sales manager needs to balance the desirability of control in overseas markets with the access to particular markets that weaker control options may offer. He/she needs to carry out a cost/benefits analysis of the alternatives.

The identification of appropriate market segments and individual customer types should be pursued by the sales manager in the same way as in the home market, i.e. through marketing research.

Consumerism and social accountability

There has always been some form of consumerism, but in its present form it emerged in the late 1950s and early 1960s and has gathered momentum ever since; it has a number of implications for sales management. Because of market conditions, it is more powerful in developed (USA, Western Europe, Japan) than in developing countries.

Consumerism can be defined as the opinions and actions of the population generally, and individuals, groups, governments, organisations in particular, in response to dissatisfactions/frustrations that arise directly or indirectly from marketing/sales relationships.

Consumerism manifests itself in active and passive protest against what the groups mentioned above see to be malpractice, legal and illegal deception, injustice, and activities that ignore the consequences to a third party. Naturally the protest is followed by efforts to ameliorate, remedy, eliminate these perceived deficiencies.

On one hand there appears to be the attitude that the individual consumer is poorly matched against the business entity (large or small), that companies should have a wider social responsibility and that the profit motive should not be the only criterion. On the other hand, there is the attitude that the supplier is providing a social need by supplying a product/service, that the consumer has the choice of buying or not buying, that caveat emptor ('let buyer beware') should apply and that unless the profit motive is paramount suppliers will not be able to remain in business, which in turn will cause less consumer choice. Consumerism is an attempt to redress the perceived imbalance in this equation.

Stanton* identifies '. . . a series of highly inflammable issues which generate much consumer discontent and frustration. . . .' These are economic discontent (e.g. inflation, unemployment etc.), social discontent (sub-poverty level conditions, racial conflict etc.), ecological discontent (hazardous pollution, traffic congestion, overcrowded cities etc). and political discontent (political, legislative, governmental institutions being either unresponsive to consumer needs or ill-equipped to handle them). He goes on:

> In the business area, discontent with the marketing system was particularly strong and wide spread. The marketing conditions which have fostered modern day consumerism possibly can be summed up in this single observation: Consumers are frustrated, dissatisfied, and indignant because of unfulfilled promises, unrealised expectations, and unstated dangers in the products and services they have purchased. And nobody seemed willing to listen to the complaints or to do anything about them.

Responses to consumerism can be either voluntary, where the 'offending' party agrees in response to pressure to take appropriate action to put right the perceived 'offence'; or compulsory, through legislation by central government or regulation by local or other vested authorities (e.g. water authorities). Inaction, token response, indifference at the voluntary level often leads to legislation.

The individual company can have only indirect or marginal effect on most of the types of discontent mentioned above (economic, social, ecological and political) but can do much to avoid business/marketing/sales discontent. This needs to start at the top by ensuring that decisions, objectives and policies are thought through with a social dimension in mind. Location factors, plant and process implications, research and development into new products/services, safety considerations, cost/benefit balance and others also need to be considered not only from a commercial viewpoint but also from a social perspective.

Thus the root cause of consumerism pressure directed at individual companies needs to be dealt with at the highest level and publicly by either

* William J. Stanton, *Fundamentals of Marketing*. McGraw-Hill Inc., New York, USA, p. 558. Reproduced with permission.

senior directors/executives and/or by the public relations/customer relations functions of a company. However, the indirect effects may have to be accommodated in the market-place by the sales function (and, consequently, sales management).

This may be done by giving more effective information about the company, its objectives, its operation and its products/services not only to potential customers but also to the world at large. It may be achieved by product/service improvements, amendments to commercial and selling practices, improved and less ambiguous advertising and sales promotion, and by adopting a more consumer-orientated approach.

Consumerism tends to lead to better business practices so that all parts of a population may benefit, i.e. not only those directly involved with an organisation but also those who have only an indirect relationship (e.g. non-customers who live near a production plant). The sales manager/marketer needs to monitor the response of consumers (and those indirectly affected) to his/her products/activities in the market-place.

Consumerism and its resultant need for feedback can make the individual sales person and the sales manager the key responsive link in the company's sales/marketing programme. The sales manager who develops sensitively an overall sales plan according to the dictates of the needs and wants of his/her customers and also in the context of other indirectly affected persons will obviously help to avoid problems related to consumerism.

A corollary of consumerism is that of social responsibility and accountability. Most companies acknowledge that they have responsibilities and accountability to shareholders. Some claim they have responsibilities to the workforce and customers, but not necessarily accountability. Some do not acknowledge that they have any direct responsibilities to non-customers and/or the world at large; for example, increased lead/radiation levels in persons living near industrial plant is seen as a health authority problem, recycling of waste is seen as needing a government-led campaign, and unemployment and levels of imports are seen as political/governmental responsibilities.

The concept of social responsibility and accountability is based on the fact that the business entity (large or small) can operate only in the environments set and made available by the social community at large; and derive power, legal protection, economic freedom, the right to own property, independence and flexibility from the social structure. It therefore follows that it has responsibilities to all groups and aspects of the overall social system. A number of these were covered earlier when examining the causes of consumerism.

Stanton* considers that business has not generally assumed its proper social responsibilities and therefore has lost public confidence; his

---

* William J. Stanton, *Fundamentals of Marketing*. McGraw-Hill Inc., New York, USA, p. 569. Reproduced with permission.

comments, supported by quotations from others, pose a question and give answers:

Now the question is how do we reverse this decline in the public's confidence? Business leaders simply must demonstrate in convincing fashion that they are aware of, and will really fulfill, their social responsibility. A cosmetic, lip service treatment will only worsen an already bad situation. Management needs to learn from the mistakes of other firms. These executives must first read, and then heed, the early warning signals of the public's dissatisfaction. Companies must set high ethical standards and then enforce them. Management must perceive the social, political and economic trends and then be willing to adapt to them. In a nutshell, business must turn in a really credible, socially responsible performance.

The failure to act in this fashion will lead inevitably to the alternative of further government intervention. . . . Moreover, once some form of governmental control is established, it is rarely removed.

If the individual sales manager does not agree with company thinking and policies on social responsibility and accountability, he/she has the choice of leaving the company or trying to bring pressure for change from within the organisation. But in practice, sales management cannot 'go it alone', it must reflect company thinking in its policies but be ready to accommodate new situations.

The political environment

The political nature of the environment/country in which sales managers operate, at home and abroad, is bound to have an effect on the overall activities of the sales operation and sales management. 'Left-wing', 'moderate centre party', 'right-wing' are terms that describe only three of the many versions of government types that could be categorised on a broad political spectrum.

The nature of the policies of such political groups will be reflected in the degree of government political and economic controls, the degree of business freedom, the position and power of government purchasing agencies, and the position of a government on a scale between a socialist-controlled economy and a capitalistic free-market system.

The political dimension may be that government is prepared to allow or favour their business/trade efforts with countries/companies whose political sympathies are in line with their own and only partially and perhaps of necessity with others. The political estrangement of a country or the enforcement of partial or total sanctions for political purposes will prescribe the environment in which sales management can operate. There have been many examples of countries which at some period were considered politically undesirable with whom to trade. The sales manager (and perhaps the board of directors) needs to consider at what point the opportunity costs of doing business with companies in a so-called 'politically undesirable' country become too high to continue or when relationships with a country, with which it is politically difficult to do business, move marginally and open up the potential of viable markets.

Changes in government's home or overseas political policy could affect a company's sales/marketing activity and business trends. For example, a political decision to cancel or change a large defence contract could have a devastating effect on some companies/industries, while import controls, tariffs, non-tariff barriers etc. may have (at least in the short term) beneficial effects for companies in the home market but have the converse effect for foreign companies trying to sell in that market.

Governments, through their various ministries, nationalised industries, shareholding, influence in local authorities (and in Eastern Bloc countries through state purchasing monopolies), are often one of the largest purchasers of goods and services in a country. Their purchasing, fiscal, legislative, regulatory policies, membership of multi-national groups (e.g. EEC) and relationships with other governments can affect the national and international economy and/or consumer or industrial markets to varying degrees which may have to be accommodated by the sales manager.

Before general elections (and in some cases before the elections of a head of state), the sales manager needs to consider the alternative sales policies open to his/her company if the various contenders are elected.

Population, culture, social class and consumer behaviour

The sales manager's approach to examining these factors that form yet another external environment within which sales management operates should be under five main headings:

(a) population
(b) cultures and sub-cultures
(c) social and socio-economic classes
(d) reference groups, including face-to-face and family groups
(e) the individual

The sales manager whose sales team sells through wholesalers and/or retailers or direct to consumers needs basic background and decision-making data on all five areas. He/she should be able to identify and anticipate trends that are taking place in them that can have effects on life-styles/needs/wants and consequently on sales.

Population
This refers to the degree to which a country or region is populated, usually expressed as the total number of inhabitants. It is a physical state and can be indicated by a variety of parameters, e.g. volume, location, urban, suburban or rural, regional distribution, age, groups, sex, education, occupation, income, family life-cycle stage (single, married, married plus children,

'empty nest' etc.), births, marriages, deaths, family size, household accommodation/dwelling types etc.

Markets are people; and demography, the study of population, as measured in the various ways shown above, permits comparison of data from period to period or region to region and identifies patterns that are fundamental, when interpreted, to effective sales management decision-making regarding target market segments.

The most detailed statistics on population and households in the UK are collected in the periodic census conducted by the government's Office of Population Censuses and Surveys (OPCS). It is also responsible for publishing *Population Estimates*, *Population Trends* (statistics plus articles on population and medical data topics), *Population Projections* (forecasts of population trends), *OPCS Monitors* (most recent estimates and projections and migration figures), *Family Expenditure Survey* (income and expenditure by type of household, nationally and some regional analyses) and *General Household Survey* (a continuous sample survey of households relating to a wide range of social and socio-economic policy areas). Some population data are also found in the *Monthly Digest of Statistics* and the *Annual Abstract of Statistics*

Cultures and sub-cultures

The effect these environmental factors have on markets and people can be seen in Stanton's* definitions:

Culture may be defined as the complex of symbols and artifacts created by man and handed down from generation to generation as determinants and regulators of human behavior in a given society. The symbols may be intangible (attitudes, ideas, beliefs, values, language, religion) or tangible (tools, housing, products, works of art). Culture is a totally learned and 'handed down' way of life. It does not include instinctive arts, although standards of performing instinctive biological acts (eating, bodily eliminations, sexual relationships) may be culturally established. Thus everybody gets hungry, but what we eat and how we act to satisfy the hunger drive will vary among cultures . . .

As the author has previously stated,† sub-cultures emerge from cultures, diminishing some market segments but causing others with their attendant market/sales opportunities to appear.

A cultural pattern emerges over a period of time and often through successive generations. It is a way of life developed through common ideals and the solving of common problems. It is often based on religion, race, region, patriotism, politics, or combinations of these.

As the population of a culture increases, the broad common ideals no longer satisfy certain minority groups and sub-cultures emerge. They have different problems and ideals, and place a different emphasis on various cultural factors

* William J. Stanton, *Fundamentals of Marketing*. McGraw-Hill Inc., New York, USA, p. 103. Reproduced with permission.

† Gordon J. Bolt, *Marketing and Sales Forecasting*. Kogan Page Ltd, 1981, p. 135.

compared with the majority ; for example, a Moslem culture in a basically Christian country, the negro culture in the US, a Communist culture in a capitalist society. Sub-cultures affect consumer behaviour by influencing the formation of attitudes and are important indicators of the standards and values of the individuals making up the groups.

A relaxation or change in the 'rules' or basic concept of sub-cultures could be of importance to researchers forecasting human behaviour. These changes, and indeed the cultures and sub-cultures, may be difficult to quantify, but even a qualitative assessment is better than no assessment at all.

An appreciation of the effects of cultures and sub-cultures is important to the sales manager where they are part of the total consumer market segments in which a company operates. The culture or sub-culture may need to be reflected in the type/content of the product/service marketed, the way it is marketed/sold, and even the type of sales person involved may be crucial to sales success. This is particularly true in foreign markets where sales management decisions may need to be made that are different to those in the home market culture.

Social and socio-economic class

Social classes emerge because consumers are brought together through certain common characteristics or states either inherent or acquired. Such social grouping factors include status, occupation, job performance, wealth and ownership, skill, power and identification. Often combinations of these factors fashion particular social groups, e.g. the linking of status with occupation or wealth.

Indicators of social class change are more equal educational opportunity, greater social mobility, the impact of modern communication and mass media etc., and they cause some blurring of rigid social divisions and attitudes.

Class structures and their proportionate weighting within the UK have been identified in a variety of forms, e.g. Fig. 13.2 shows social and occupational data linked to percentages of households in the UK. Figure 13.3 shows the cross-referencing of housewives by social grade, age and geographic location.

The consumers in the higher social class groups will not be motivated by the same basic needs as consumers at subsistence level, but will often be searching for such satisfaction as esteem, convenience, prestige, unique-ness, approval of others etc. Often the attainment of these satisfactions can be expressed in the purchases of certain types of products such as status cars, large houses, extreme fashions, leisure pursuit products and even in the reading of particular newspapers and magazines.

In some cases, socio-economic groupings are clearly defined, the social status carrying with it expected attitudes and purchasing patterns and the economic status indicating income which provides the appropriate purchasing power.

	Head of household		
Social grade	Social status	Occupation	Percentage
A	Upper middle class	Higher managerial, administrative or professional	3
B	Middle class	Intermediate managerial, administrative or professional	11
C1	Lower middle class	Supervisory or clerical, and junior managerial, administrative or professional	23
C2	Skilled working class	Skilled manual workers	31
D	Working class	Semi and unskilled manual workers	23
E	Those at lowest levels of subsistence	State pensioners or widows (no other earner), casual or lowest-grade workers	9

Source: IPA

Fig. 13.2   Social and occupational data linked to percentages of the households in the UK

By research, it is possible to determine the buying motives and the purchasing and consumption habits of a particular class. The movement upwards in social classes often means that consumers spend more money on what the lower groups consider to be non-essentials.

A number of approaches to classifying people have developed from the social class concept. One of these is *sagacity* grouping, the basic thesis of which is that people have different aspirations and behaviour patterns as they go through their life-cycle.

It takes standard demographics relating to life-style (including age and situational variables), income (taking some account of spouse's income) and occupation (dividing social class A, B, C.1 (white collar) v. C.2, D, E (blue collar)). It interlaces them, yielding twelve groups relating to family status sub-divided by prosperity and occupation.

Treating demographic data in this way generates sharper discrimination in some areas and identifies groups that mean something in social terms.

Another approach is that of ACORN (A Classification Of Residential Neighbourhoods) which divides Britain's 120,000 census enumeration districts (average 150 households) into thirty-six socio-economic types. Each of these types offers cross-referencing to forty census characteristics. It is basically a method of mapping geographically the concentrations of particular types of people where these are likely to be related to the housing characteristics of their district.

ACORN adds a new multi-sided dimension to techniques of marketing

Percentaged nationally Standard region	Total	Social grade						Age					
		A	B	C1	C2	D	E	15–24	25–34	35–44	45–54	55–64	65+
North	6.62	0.11	0.62	1.04	1.97	1.88	0.99	0.54	1.23	1.10	1.10	1.22	1.42
North West	12.42	0.23	1.06	2.71	3.45	3.28	1.69	1.14	2.10	2.04	2.23	2.20	2.71
Yorks & Humber	9.14	0.24	0.70	1.77	2.70	2.56	1.17	0.77	1.62	1.71	1.67	1.53	1.84
West Midlands	8.97	0.14	0.79	1.94	2.65	2.34	1.11	0.73	1.66	1.62	1.69	1.55	1.72
East Midlands	6.40	0.14	0.60	1.15	2.18	1.62	0.71	0.63	1.15	1.16	1.13	1.16	1.17
East Anglia	3.36	0.05	0.36	0.63	1.12	0.82	0.38	0.29	0.67	0.59	0.51	0.54	0.75
South West	7.24	0.19	0.78	1.63	2.07	1.59	0.98	0.64	1.09	1.13	1.29	1.37	1.73
South East	17.73	0.76	2.77	4.62	4.60	3.40	1.64	1.45	2.98	2.97	3.40	3.32	3.67
Greater London	14.10	0.40	1.69	3.92	3.62	2.86	1.59	1.32	2.09	2.39	2.52	2.77	3.01
Wales	5.00	0.07	0.49	0.99	1.40	1.26	0.79	0.30	0.77	0.85	1.03	0.95	1.10
Scotland	8.93	0.19	0.89	1.84	2.46	2.37	1.24	1.65	1.59	1.57	1.69	1.66	1.82
Total GB	100.00	2.50	10.77	22.25	28.21	23.97	12.30	8.47	16.95	17.14	18.24	18.27	20.94

Source: Population Statistics for Marketing and Survey Research, Research Services Ltd/IPA.

Fig. 13.3 Housewives, by social grade and age within region

research, advertising, marketing and selling. It provides an excellent tool for sampling and survey design, extends social class as a measure of status, shows clear life-style differences between neighbourhoods leading to many differences in consumer behaviour with implications for purchasing, and identifies clearly areas for optimum sales team activity.

The existence of social classes and the way they express themselves in purchasing and consumption indicates differences in attitudes, values and priorities and therefore has important sales management implications in companies in, or supplying to, consumer goods/services markets.

Reference groups

This includes face-to-face and family groups. Consumer buying motives, brand choice, purchasing and consumption patterns are often influenced by what other consumers say or buy, especially those people with whom they compare themselves or whom they use as reference groups. Such groups can be classified as:

(a) *Membership groups.* These are groupings of people to which a person belongs and is recognised as belonging by others. It usually implies identification with the group's ideals, values, tastes and behaviour. Groups such as the family, a club, company, church, college, political party etc. can all fit into this category.

(b) The opposite to (a) is the *dissociative group* with whom an individual does not want to be identified or associated. Reference in this case is to the ideals, values and behaviour he finds acceptable. The group types are the same as for (a).

(c) *Aspirational groups.* These refer to groupings of people to which the individual would like or aspires to belong. The individual's buying behaviour is influenced by how he/she thinks the group behaves or purchases. Reference groups of this type are often made up of TV, film or radio stars, sportsmen or women, astronauts, millionaires, or even particular social sets.

(d) *Face-to-face groups.* These are groups of people small enough for the individual to communicate with face-to-face. This type includes the family, close friends, neighbours, fellow workers or students, and has the most direct influence on an individual's ideals, tastes, values and behaviour.

In many cases the greatest influence on the individual in forming and maintaining ideals, attitudes, tastes, values etc. is the family group. Sometimes the result of the reference is positive, i.e. the individual does the complete opposite to express himself/herself. The sales manager must be alert to the various behavioural and attitudinal patterns that dominate families in particular market segments and to the current trends and how they are expected to change in the future.

The purchases of certain products are more subject to reference group influence than others. For example, branded beer, cigarettes, clothing, cars, toilet soap etc. are products that are associated strongly with reference group influence. Customer communication (advertising, etc.) in this area will be most successful if it stresses the types of people who buy the product, particularly if it is designed to encourage the learning/educational process of product application or usage and is exhibited in media where those who refer to the group form the main audience.

Where reference group influences are weak, the marketing strategy is to stress product innovation and characteristics, functional advantages and performance, price etc.

An appreciation of the influence of reference groups on consumer buying behaviour is an essential for sales managers in consumer-goods markets, or for those carrying out end-use analysis for products being sold into industrial product markets.

The individual

A basic approach to the study of consumer buying behaviour is at the level of the individual. It has been said that:

> Social influences determine much but not all of the behavioral variations in people. Two individuals subject to the same influences are not likely to have identical attitudes, although their attitudes will probably converge at more points than those of two strangers selected at random. Attitudes are really the product of social forces interacting with the individual's unique temperament and abilities.
>
> Furthermore, attitudes – in buying as in anything else – do not automatically guarantee certain types of behavior. Attitudes are pre-dispositions felt by buyers before they enter the buying process. The buying process itself is a learning experience and can lead to a change in attitudes.*

It is necessary to understand why the individual consumer behaves as he/she does so that changes in ideals, tastes, values etc. of groups of consumers can be anticipated and predicted.

Individuals do not buy products, but groups of satisfactions or benefits to satisfy logical and psychological needs. But the individual will only purchase a product if he/she can perceive (hence the concept of perception) that it will satisfy his/her needs. Perception can be aided by physical stimuli including the actual product. But the effect of physical stimuli will be modified and interpreted by the individual's tastes, ideals, temperament, experiences and memory. Often the individual perceives only what he/she wants to, and therefore the physical stimuli must be appropriate and appealing to satisfy his/her logical and psychological needs.

Individual behaviour in purchasing and consumption is to a certain extent a learned response and as such can be influenced and changed. For example, the consumption of branded, ready-to-eat breakfast cereals in

---

* P. Kotler, *Marketing Management, Analysis, Planning and Control.* Copyright © Prentice-Hall, NJ., USA, p. 93.

Britain and North America has been 'learned' over a period of time, in many cases replacing porridge, which needs preparation. Also the type of diet, way of life etc. acceptable in one society may be repugnant in another, and is a learned response.

There are numerous learning theories that seek to explain consumer buying behaviour. They include stimulus response theories that are based on the concept of reward for each correct response; many sales promotional devices are based on this approach.

Other learning theories are based on the concept of cognition. While acknowledging the stimulus response approach, cognitive theories imply that buying behaviour is influenced by habit based on memory, achievement seeking, and insight based on reasoning. Basically, acceptance of the concept of a cognitive decision-making process implies an endeavour by the consumer to reduce risks. By repeat purchasing of a particular brand or the repeated assessment of available information, the consumer is trying to avoid taking undue risks. Cognitive concepts are founded on habit and consistency, and are fundamental to brand loyalty and repeat purchasing.

Inconsistency in cognitive systems has been described as cognitive dissonance. Thus the person who purchases and consumes fattening foods when on a health diet experiences dissonance (i.e. psychological discomfort) and often tries to reduce this and achieve consonance by rationalising his/her actions.

Some other learning theories are founded on the personality of the individual and on the probability of the repetition of past purchasing behaviour. Such theories are based on the premise that if a man's personality can be understood (i.e. his underlying organisation of characteristics and behaviour patterns), then it should be possible to understand also why he behaves as he does, and what the reasons are for some of the superficial inconsistencies that occur in his behaviour. Based on these assumptions, it should then be possible to predict with greater random success how a given individual is predisposed to respond to given circumstances and suggestions.

A wide range of other factors affect the individual consumer's buying behaviour: attitudes, knowledge, faith, opinion, beliefs, economic motivation, rationality etc. Every sale is a reflection of a decision to buy. This decision will be based on the consumer's perception (influenced by the other factors mentioned above) of the proposal related to value, utility and ability to satisfy needs. If the initial impression is unfavourable, it will need to undergo a change before a positive buying decision is made. The consumer's perception depends on his attitude to the subject being considered.

All these theories relating to the individual seek to measure and predict the future response and pattern of consumer buying behaviour. As such, at least a broad appreciation of them is necessary for effective sales management action in decision-making related to product/service development, pricing, branding, forecasting, customer communication (including sales training), distribution and sales service.

This part of the chapter on population, cultures and sub-cultures, social and socio-economic classes, and reference groups can be summarised thus:

The statement 'No man is an island' has empirical support. No man exists who does not reflect interaction with other people. Values, learning patterns, and symbolism are some of the results of the society in which a consumer develops. Sometimes social influences are negative rather than positive influences, but always they are influences. Man evaluates himself against the behavior of others and the values he has learned from others on previous occasions. He depends on others as a source of new information about product decisions and as a reference for evaluating the information.

Organisations seeking to influence consumer behavior should realize that they must communicate not only with an individual but also with a social system. *

Organisation/industrial buyer behaviour

Organisation/industrial buyers are engaged in the purchase of goods and services not for the sake of personal consumption but for use in further production or distribution. Their common denominator is that they are paid to make purchases for organisations with definable needs (often specified by others within a decision-making unit) and operate within a corporate environment that has budgetary constraints.

There are differing views as to the underlying objectives of organisation/ industrial buyers and these were succinctly identified by Kotler. †

. . . Many marketing writers have emphasised the predominance of rational motives in organisational buying. Organisational buyers are represented as being most impressed by cost, quality, dependability and service factors. They are portrayed as dedicated servants of the organisation, seeking to secure the best terms. This view has led to an emphasis on performance and as characteristics in much industrial advertising.

Other writers have emphasised personal motives in organisational buyer behaviour. The purchasing agent's interest to do the best for his company is tempered by his interest to do the best for himself. He may be tempted to choose among salesmen according to the extent they entertain or offer gifts. He may choose a particular vendor because this will ingratiate him with certain company officers. He may short cut his study of alternative suppliers to make his work day easier.

In truth, the buyer is guided by both personal and group goals . . . The corporate man tries to steer a careful course between satisfying his own needs and those of the organisation. . . . He will respond to the persuasive salesmen and he will respond to rational product arguments. However, the best 'mix' of the two is not a fixed quantity; it varies with the nature of the product, the type of organisation and the relative strength of the two drives in the particular buyer. . . .

* Engel, Kollat and Blackwell, *Consumer Behavior*. Holt, Rinehart & Winston, New York, USA, 1978, p. 615.

† Philip Kotler, 'Behavioural models for analysing buyers', *Journal of Marketing*, October 1965, p. 45.

Another dimension to organisation/industrial buyer behaviour was added by Brand* in what was described as the 'task' approach. He identified that there were basically three organisation/industrial buying situations and therefore three approaches in which the sales person should be trained to deal with company sales activities targeted towards them. They were:

(a) *First-time purchasers (the new task)*. He indicated that research into purchasing decision processes has confirmed the importance of 'getting in' early. If a high proportion of calls made are responses to requests for information, the sales force are missing out on the very early stages of the decision to buy that precede such requests.

(b) *Change of supplier (modified rebuy)*. When a change is contemplated in the supplier of products of known and acceptable technical performance, the buyer is the most active and most influential member of the decision-making unit in a purchasing company. The situation is that of a new supplier getting new business from a company dissatisfied with the performance of its existing suppliers.

(c) *Repeat purchase (straight rebuy)*. The volume of purchases and the heavy involvement of leading members of the decision-making unit in new and modified purchasing decisions results in the delegation of repeat purchasing to lower-level personnel acting on instructions as to the required specification and approved supplier previously agreed when the purchase was new to the company or previous changes made.

Because of the organisation/industrial buyer's location in an industry/business structure, it is often assumed that he/she will purchase for shrewd, rational, functional reasons; but, in fact, will make buying decisions on a mixture of logical, psychological and sometimes illogical motives. On another dimension, buying decisions may be made in relation to corporate needs, department needs (the non-standard requirements of a particular department or manager) and the buyer's own personal needs of job satisfaction.

Most industrial purchases are made through a collective buying decision or are influenced or controlled in some way. Even routine non-technical purchases may be controlled by instructions to purchasing department personnel to buy only from companies on an 'approved list' of suppliers.

The purchase of more complex/technical, high-cost plant, equipment, components, materials will inevitably lead to the involvement of functional specialists in formal or informal structures of decision-making. The members of these decision-making units will be influenced in their deliberations/decisions by their own status and specialism. For example, members of boards of directors will tend to view purchases from the point of view of the return on capital invested, the setting of overall design

* Gordon T. Brand, *The Industrial Buying Decision*. Associated Business Press, London, 1972.

parameters (i.e. high quality/high cost or low quality/low cost), compliance with, and the overall effects on, company policy. Operations management will be influenced by performance of machines, output or the ease with which materials and components will fit into present future production processes. Production engineering/maintenance management will be concerned with less machine down-time and lower maintenance costs. With capital equipment, financial management will measure the viability of purchase against pay-back periods and indicators of discounted cash flow and the terms of payment. Components/materials, design and development engineers will assess a purchase against compatibility with, and enhancement of, existing and future products and designs, and determine standards. The purchasing department will be more interested in measuring a potential purchase against price/performance considerations, discounts and delivery dates, and sales management will be interested in how the new purchase, whether equipment, components, materials or services, will enhance the sale of the range of product/service combination the sales team has to sell and may be instrumental in setting 'saleable' design parameters, selling price constraints and therefore manufacturing costs.

All these views of the various specialist functional 'influencers' or decision-makers then have to be put in the context of the background situation or reason why a need to purchase exists. For example, with equipment purchasing for expansion of production capacity or replacement of worn-out or obsolete machinery; for components and/or materials, the change of product design or to be part of a new product. The combinations of the various 'influences' or decision-maker's underlying motives and potential buying situations are considerable but need exploring.

Organisation/industrial buyer behaviour is yet another of the environments in which the sales function has to operate. Careful study will enable the individual sales person to identify all those involved in a company in the often intricate process of buying organisation/industry goods and services. Further, sales managers need to ensure that the sales team is trained to identify the key-dominant members of a purchasing company's decision-making unit and explore their motives.

Summary

There are a variety of external environments in which the company and sales management operate and which are changing at different speeds, different orders of magnitude and which have different implications for sales management at different times. The identification and listing of relevant key external factors and the examination of their current performance at regular intervals is crucial for the sales manager to effectively accommodate them in planning operation and control. However, operating a checklist often implies that they are separate/discrete factors whereas in practice they are often interdependent and impinge on one another.

An appreciation of the economic climate and trend in the various international, national and regional environments in which a company operates is crucial to sales management decision-making. But, additionally, an element of anticipating government's reaction to economic trends is necessary. From the wide range of economic indicators available, the sales manager needs to identify those most appropriate to the company's customer, market, industry and own needs.

A company's competitive environment is constantly changing and should be assessed at both a macro and micro level. At the macro level, industries/market segments should be identified in which the company has the greatest possible advantage and/or the least possible disadvantage. At the micro level, competitors should be 'profiled' against particular competitive criteria to enable comparison. In both cases, checklists should be established and continuously updated. The company's own competitive position should be established by using a competitive SWOT analysis.

Technology is a constantly changing environment in which the sales manager operates, and technological change can come from initiatives started internally and from forces/situations external to the company. There is therefore a need to monitor, forecast, appreciate, accommodate or allow for, and make use of, technological change as it affects not only the company but particularly sales management. Strategic and contingency plans need to be considered to accommodate technological innovation in the five main areas relating to the product/service, the pack, methods of selling, selling by agents/retailers and the operation of sales management

The legal environment in which sales management takes place is controlled by local by-laws, civil and criminal law in the form of common, case and statute law, legally enforceable government regulations, EEC laws and regulations, and international law. At the expense of considerable over-simplification, the chapter considered the key areas of the nature and scope of business contracts, supply of goods and services, industrial property right protection, packaging legislation and regulations, consumer protection, settlement of business transactions, trading activities, business disputes, setting up and termination of business organisations, employment legislation and property. An appreciation of these legal areas is important to the sales manager to avoid/deal with situations and to operate within the law but does not obviate the need to obtain advice from the company's legal advisers in doubtful and/or unusual situations.

In spite of frequent statements that countries intend to 'free' trade, various restrictions/constraints exist. Even so, there is a tendency for countries/companies to specialise in/produce products for which they have the greatest possible advantage and/or the least possible disadvantage. The broad type of international trading tends to be reflected in management policies that are reflected in four recognisable stages: ethnocentric, polycentric, regiocentric and geocentric.

Information regarding, and the profiling of, countries will produce a list of those with whom it is most profitable and/or easiest to sell. This will need to be in the context of the dynamic marketing/sales approach, i.e. getting through, and profitably selling to, individual markets in any part of the world by any means. Such markets will also need to be considered in terms of the availability of appropriate channels of distribution, effective methods of company representation and the potential degree of control over the chosen markets. Marketing research, however elementary, will be needed to identify market segments and individual customer types.

Consumerism reflects the opinions and actions of the population generally, and individuals, groups, governments, organisations in particular, in response to dissatisfactions/frustrations that arise directly or indirectly from marketing/sales relationships. It manifests itself in active and passive protest against what the groups mentioned see to be malpractice, legal and illegal deception, injustice and activities that ignore the consequences to a third party.

Social responsibility and accountability is based on the fact that the business entity can operate only in the environments set and made available by the social community at large and derive power, legal protection, economic freedom, the right to own property, independence and flexibility from the social structure. It therefore follows that it has responsibilities to all groups and aspects of the overall social system.

The nature of the political environment in which a company and consequently the sales manager makes decisions and operates will be reflected in home and overseas markets in the degree of government political and economic control.

Markets are people and the sales manager will need basic background and decision-making information on people viewed from five perspectives, population, cultures and sub-cultures, social and socio-economic classes, reference groups, and the individual. By selecting appropriate/relevant data, the sales manager will be able to identify and anticipate trends that are taking place within the five perspectives because these have effects on life-styles/needs/wants and consequently on sales.

An understanding of organisation/industrial buyer behaviour is crucial to a sales manager whose sales team is selling industrial product/service combinations. They are not purchasing for their own sake but for use in further production and/or distribution; they are paid to make purchases for organisations with definable needs and operate within a corporate environment that has budgetary constraints. Industrial buyer behaviour can be positioned on a scale ranging from complete company motives and considerations to complete personal motives and considerations. The buying task can be seen as new (i.e. first-time purchases), modified rebuy (change of supplier) and repeat purchase (straight rebuy). Because a number of specialists will form the decision-making unit, they will tend to be influenced by motives relevant to their individual status and specialism which will vary with the underlying need/reason to purchase.

There are other external/non-controllable environments within which sales managers and their sales teams have to operate that will be highly specific to particular industries/markets/customers. An awareness of their possible existence is important so that the sales manager and sales team can accommodate/allow for them in their approach to the market-place.

Questions

1. Why is it important for the sales manager to identify and accommodate certain changing external environments/factors/relationships?

2. What are the main indicators of the economic climate and how do they help in sales management decision-making?

3. Identify the types of competition that can face a company and show how assessing it at macro and micro levels can help the sales manager in developing effective competitive strategies and tactics?

4. Why should technology affect and be of interest to the sales manager?

5. What are the main areas of the legal environment that are relevant/appropriate to sales management operation?

6. The international environment will not include all countries for a particular company. How are appropriate countries selected and what can the sales manager do to ensure a company's effective sales presence in foreign markets?

7. Identify the ways in which the concepts of consumerism and social responsibility can affect the sales manager.

8. What are the five perspectives from which 'people as markets' can be viewed and show their relevance to sales management decision-making?

9. Indicate why the organisation/industrial buyer behaviour environment is different to the consumer goods area. Identify the specific differences and show how the sales manager can accommodate them.

CHAPTER 14

The future of sales management

Objectives

The purpose of this chapter is to acknowledge that while many of the basic principles and practices of sales management will continue relatively unchanged in the future, temporary changes in some cases and more fundamental changes in others will be necessary in sales management thinking, objectives, strategies and organisation structures to accommodate changing market, company or environmental situations. Change rarely occurs suddenly in marketing/selling situations, but tends to emerge. This chapter signals changes that are reflected in certain situations/trends that have emerged, are emerging or are accelerating in key environmental areas in which sales management operates. It also looks at the impact on selling of changes in other aspects of the company 'communication mix' and considers future likely changes in sales force organisations and training. A widened marketing research role for the sales function is predicted in some areas, and the expected scope and impact of the use by buyers and sellers of information technology (including computers) on the role of the sales force is examined.

Underlying changes

Markets are dynamic and ever-changing, so sales management, to be effective, will need to change to accommodate/allow for emerging situations. Some apparent changes will be short-lived and need a contingency/holding response until a 'new' former situation is restored. Others will be the beginning of a more fundamental change which will need a complete rethink of sales objectives, strategies and organisation structures. Potential developments in markets and the key environments (examined in the last chapter) in which organisations operate will need to be analysed to ensure that sales managers recognise and identify the various causes and/or change agents, thereby enabling them to anticipate the future role of sales management and the selling function.

The shift in international comparative costs of producing and/or processing basic raw materials (e.g. steel) in countries of low labour cost and/or in conditions that would be unacceptable to 'western' trade unions has meant, in some cases, a shift in 'western economies' to 'high-tech' and service industries from basic processing, raw material processing industries. This has caused (and the trend continues) changes in products/services offered, fewer customers and lower sales volume in the latter, but increases in the former with obvious implications for the sales manager. Further, it has led to home industries producing more complex and sophisticated product/service combinations which in turn demand new types of selling from new types of sales organisation staffed by a new breed of sales person, with the same or different objectives and strategies.

The speed of development of new technology is another accelerating factor also causing more complex and sophisticated product/service combinations. Product life-cycles tend to be getting shorter so that past levels of profit realisation over a longer period of time are not being achieved before new substitute/replacement product/service combinations emerge. The sales management response is increasingly to sell intensively to try to obtain high market share early in the life-cycle, requiring higher levels of customer education in sales presentations.

In consumer-goods markets, as consumers become more 'international-ised' through foreign travel and foreign country TV exposure, there is less 'brand' loyalty to 'home produced' product/service combinations. Consumers (with changing priorities) are demanding, and getting, a wider choice of products or alternative ways of spending their scarce resources of money and time. For example, the choice between increased quality or quantity of basic necessities and a wide range of leisure pursuits. All of which requires adjusted sales activity.

There is an accelerating shift towards active consumerism, ecological and conservational awareness and demand for social accountability and more information from companies. Much of this causing government intervention and increasingly being required/enforced by law, e.g. the wide range of consumer legislation, new Companies Acts requiring increased disclosure of information, and data protection legislation that requires more information on company-held data. All these not only bring pressure to bear with regards to products/services and company activities generally, but also on sales management and the selling function in particular.

The previous paragraph merely reflects one aspect of the increased use of information technology. In fact, the impact of the increased use of information technology on the selling function is examined later in this chapter. But in some industries the information-giving role of the sales force is being eroded by developments in information and transportation technologies which have allowed and encouraged manufacturers' searches for new raw and processed materials, components, plant and equipment to move from the traditional local, regional or 'home-country' markets to an international, worldwide one. This has in turn encouraged the operations of multi-national companies and spurred on worldwide competition. This should provide worldwide opportunities for sales teams but also increases competition in the home market.

There are obvious implications for sales management of worldwide and national economic problems, of over-production/over-capacity in some industries. Recession, stagnation, low growth, inflation, high unemployment are indicators of economic conditions that are likely to continue in many markets for some time with a depressing influence on demand. Likewise, the emergence and development of political (e.g. 'Eastern') and economic (e.g. EEC) blocs and the potential emergence of trade protectionist policies as countries try to cope with long-term economic recession need to be accommodated in sales management plans and strategies.

The increase in 'giantism' in retailing and distribution (i.e. the continuing trend of dominance by large groups) is merely symptomatic of a larger problem that faces sales management in the future. Increasing trade concentration in almost all categories of business creates fewer customers and prospects (and admittedly fewer buying points) for most industrial and/or organisation to organisation 'sellers'. The sheer volume, if not monopoly power, of large purchasers to dictate on all matters (e.g. product design/content, prices, profit margins, curtailment of suppliers to others and other concessions) will require very different sales management strategies and organisation structures and the development of totally new customer relationships than if the particular market-place was more diverse or more highly populated. This is increasing on a national, regional and worldwide basis and is often reflected in the growth and success of some multi-national groups.

Future consequences for sales management

As long as business is about exchange relationships between buyers and sellers, companies will need to:

(a) communicate facts, ideas and opinions
(b) give information
(c) get information
(d) express corporate policies, attitudes, feelings
(e) arouse customers' interest
(f) persuade

all with the aim to change attitudes and/or behaviour of the 'receiver'.

This must take place with:

(a) potential customers
(b) existing customers
(c) customer's customers
(d) those who can influence customers' buying decisions
(e) trade channels
(f) employees
(g) regulatory bodies (compulsory or voluntary)
(h) trade associations
(i) pressure groups

either through

(a) selling
(b) advertising
(c) sales promotion
(d) merchandising
(e) packaging
(f) branding
(g) pricing
(h) public relations
(i) combinations of the above

The degree of emphasis in the 'communications mix' on selling and the sales function, at the present and in the future, will depend on a number of factors, including:

(a) The need for a physical presence during the selling process, e.g. for demonstrations or to give specific advice on alternatives, perhaps presented on a portable computer.

(b) The need for sensitive, interactive negotiation supported by visual material.

(c) Expectation of clients/customers of a social relationship with the sales person or sales manager or company.

(d) The cost of operating a sales team either in the field or as a telephone sales operation.

(e) The relative costs of alternatives, e.g. agents, direct mail.

(f) Technological developments, e.g. the video telephone, interactive viewdata systems (availability of instant information/technical data).

Wherever there is a sales function, there will need to be sales management to plan, operate and control it.

In the future, the same number of options of methods of sales force organisation will exist as are available today but (because of economic climates/circumstances, the speed and scope of technological change, market/customer needs, the need to negotiate major contracts at high level, changes in the relative costs of communicating with customers and potential customers, the demand for specialist advice, and others) the sales manager will have to reconsider the present mode of organisation and choose one or a combination of the following structures:

(a) Allocation of field sales personnel by geographic area, sales potential rather than county boundaries.

(b) Allocation of field sales personnel by TV area to get the best sales/advertising impact/support.

(c) Creation of product or technology specialisation sales groups/teams, particularly relevant in industrial situations where complex/advanced technology and/or systems are involved.

(d) Allocation of field sales activities by functions, for example:

(1) sales representatives supported by sales engineers;

(2) pioneer or 'missionary' sales persons to open accounts and hand them over to 'maintenance' sales persons or wholesalers'/agents' sales forces;

(3) Sales representatives supported by merchandisers.

(e) Creation of key/major account sales teams.

(f) Creation of 'new accounts' sales teams.

(g) Creation of industry/market-centred sales teams which allocate sales duties around particular industries/markets/market segments which they serve.

(h) The allocation (especially in consumer goods) of duties to sales teams on the basis of the types of retail outlets to be serviced, e.g. small grocers, grocery chains at local, regional or national level etc.

Sales managers at frequent intervals in the future need to ask whether their present sales team structures are relevant/appropriate to newly emerged markets and rapidly changing situations.

Some sales managements may consider dispensing with a field sales team (in any of the forms shown above) either partially or in total for some aspects or the whole of company customer communication. This is done by examining the use of agents or brokers, telephone selling operations or direct mail substituted for the activities of the field sales team. The main disadvantages of these alternative forms of customer communication is that with:

(a) Agents/brokers, there tends to be lack of direct control.

(b) Telephone selling operations (outgoing or incoming), there is no physical presence and there are difficulties of visual presentation/communication.

(c) Direct mail, it is not interactive and cannot deal with immediate reaction/response. Although 'mail shots' can be personalised, the tendency is to appeal to groups of customers rather than the individual client that the field sales person can accommodate. Also, with the 'direct mail only' approach, there is the problem of maintaining an up-to-date mailing list particularly related to personnel and of keeping in touch with customers/the market-place normally done through market intelligence/sales reports of sales representatives.

As sales force costs continue to escalate, there is an increasing use of all three of these options, and their successful operation in many industries will encourage sales managers to consider them as valid substitutes or at least support for field sales force activity.

Methods of sales training have changed in recent years and will continue to change and, if the training needs of the sales team change, those of the sales managers are unlikely to stay the same.

The clarification and constant reappraisal of future sales team objectives and market situations will help not only to identify the sales training needs and the most cost-effective way of training, but will also pose such basic questions as does the training needs/objectives require development of skill or simply the acquisition of knowledge?

The greater the need for skills training and personal development, the greater will be the need for job-related, problem-centred/solving activities in the formal 'training centre' location. It also implies the urgent need for personal tuition, involvement and 'on-the-job' field training.

The more the training objective is aimed at giving information/ knowledge, the greater the need for the sales manager to examine the possible uses of programmed learning and packaged training. In the present and future, there will be pressures on sales department budgets to be reduced in many areas of sales training. There are many formal course cost savings that can be achieved through the use of programmed learning and package training.

As Malcolm Higgs* suggests:

. . . Such training packages will draw heavily on the theory, development and application of programmed learning. However, they also draw on other methodology, especially the use of audio/visual presentational techniques. The principles underlying training packages are suitable to the application of a range of approaches to the presentation of structured material, including:
(i)   Tape/slide presentations.
(ii) Audio cassette presentations (with or without visual material).
(iii) Video presentations.
(iv) Printed text presentations.
(v)   Interactive video.
(vi) Computer-based learning.
(vii) Combinations of the above methods.
It is important that a clear distinction is made between designing the training, and determining the methods of presentation and delivery. . . .

One of the problems with training packages is that there is a tendency to

* Malcolm Higgs, 'Developing training packages', in *Banking and Financial Training*, p. 15, published by Philip Thorn Associates Limited.

treat them in the same way as many regional, area, district managers treat centrally organised formal courses, i.e. the training appears to be the responsibility of someone else. Also, as the particular manager is not involved, there is neither commitment, credibility or accountability, particularly if training packages contradict some practical aspects covered in field sales training.

Higgs continues:

. . . Training packages may be designed to be delivered by (sales) line management. In addition, (Sales) Management can often be involved in developing the package and thus become more committed to its successful implementation.

The essence of package training lies in the way that the subject matter expert works together with the training design expert to produce effective training material which may be used without the need for either to be present. This process becomes more effective when line managers are involved from the outset, including at the needs analysis stage. . .

In some industries there is an increasing trend, which is expected to continue, to adjust the role of the sales force to become an increasingly powerful market information source not just for the individual sales person and the sales manager, but also for marketing and other functions of the company. Moss* indicates the trend of companies to:

. . . utilise their salesmen to acquire intelligence concerning the following:

(a) The structure, organisation, and future development of the customer company forward investment plans; inventory plans; inventory policies; capacity utilisation levels; inspection and quality control policies; manufacturing assembly operation; 'make or buy' capabilities etc.

(b) The role of competition in the market place, e.g. the number of companies competing at each supply point; the organisation of competitor sales forces; the types of contract proposals being issued by competitors.

(c) The reasons for the loss of 'major' orders.

(d) The problems, faults, complaints concerning products which emanate from the customer, and an assessment of the business at risk unless difficulties are resolved.

(e) The structure of the customer decision making unit – the special contribution of the industrial salesman in identifying the specific individuals and their goals in the buying decision process . . .

(f) The future volume levels likely to be attained at customer and prospect locations. . . .

The same marketing intelligence approach is apparently increasingly being applied in many consumer goods industries. The approach appears to be the reverse of the earlier trend which was to cut back the marketing intelligence/reporting activity of the sales team in the interests of reduced cost incurred in reporting back (and reading) and the release of administrative time for selling purposes, i.e. to only report when some action by others was needed.

* C. Moss, 'Industrial sales forces – trends and developments', *Quarterly Review of Marketing*, Vol. 7, No. 2, Winter/January 1982, p. 21.

Future impact of information technology

At the same time, the trend in the more intensive use of the sales team for market research purposes is gathering momentum in some companies. More far-reaching changes in the role and type of sales force activity are beginning to emerge.

Buying and selling is based to a large extent on the giving and receiving of information. The speed of technological change in information gathering, processing, disseminating and communication is today threatening the traditional buyer/seller relationship. In doing so, it threatens to change the nature, scope, importance and role of the sales force activity in some areas, especially in industrial/organisation-to-organisation type selling. The cause/reason for these threats is the wide range of information technology that has become, or is becoming, available.

In Chapter 10, information technology was suggested as essential support for the sales manager and covered the use of computer databases, word-processor systems, telex, intelligent photocopiers, facsimile communication equipment, interactive video disc technology, telephone systems that have memories and carry electronic data traffic as well as voice, cellular radio systems, videotex (including teletex and viewdata), electronic mail, teleconferencing etc. But if these are available to the sales manager and the sales team, they are also available to buyers and companies making purchases.

It is envisaged in some seller/buyer relationships that the purchaser, with the aid of information technology, knows as much, or perhaps more, about a product/service performance applicability and relevance to his needs than does the seller. The traditional concept of the sales person bringing to the buyer information on new ideas, new products/services, new concepts, new uses, new applications and information on prices, discounts, deliveries, availability etc. may not apply today, or increasingly in the future, when, because of information technology, buyer and seller are on equal information terms.

With more information technology, literate purchasers aided by desk-top computers/IT workstations, differing purchasing decisions make some sales approaches inappropriate or irrelevant. As R & D, designers, engineers and even purchasing personnel use, increasingly, computers, databases and videodata systems to (a) aid new product or revitalised product design, and (b) to use them to help their materials and component search for alternatives/substitutes/sources, a new dimension has been added to selling. A basic evaluation/decision-making stage has been added to the total purchasing process, one which, because of its nature, will be difficult for an individual sales person to be a party to or even know how, when or what criteria were used in making a decision.

It follows, therefore, that where sales organisations have not changed to meet these new situations they will become obsolete. In the circumstances, a sales organisation/team which is unable to work with, or relate to, the new type situation of IT-informed buyers needs to be trained in new approaches to selling; this has wide implications for sales managers. The sales organisation cannot be simply scrapped; it has a role to play and must therefore be re-modelled and re-trained.

But it is not only whether the sales team can cope with the newly emerging IT situations but also whether fundamental marketing decisions (and particularly those that affect the sales function) are based on adequate up-to-date information and are more speedily arrived at through the use of IT systems in the selling company. This will affect the 'deal' the sales team can offer in the market-place.

Additionally, the adequacy, in IT terms, of the administrative sales support systems such as immediate handling of enquiries and/or sales leads, immediate order processing, inventory control, speedy despatch and delivery systems, invoice and credit control etc. must be assessed not only in terms of customer needs and expectations, but also compared in terms of services being offered/provided by competitors that have been enhanced by more advanced IT systems.

The key to the whole issue is IT literacy. Whether or not the sales team and sales manager have the appropriate level of IT literacy (e.g. the overall ability to utilise computers) will depend on the levels needed to deal with customers and competitors as well as the basic content. Where the levels of IT literacy are compatible in the selling/buying relationship, linked bidding, pricing, total deal negotiations will be possible without the aid of the personal presence of an individual sales person. Where they are not, or competition alone has the IT compatibility, a company will be at a distinct market disadvantage.

The availability of IT power and literacy is increasingly affecting the behaviour of distribution channels, i.e. agents, distributors, wholesalers and retailers. Through IT they can have available comparative supplier data regarding location and availability of stocks, and price and discount levels that enable them to bring pressure to bear on suppliers to increase discounts, charge lower prices, enter special joint sales promotion deals, engage in co-operative advertising or tailor advertising campaigns to meet their specific needs. The more dominant individual channels become through the use of IT, the greater will be the reduction of a supplying company's capacity to negotiate through its sales team.

In some areas the threat to the sales function will emerge as purchasing companies move closer to electronic database comparison of alternative 'deals' and with it an increasing acceptance of non-personal sales contact. The reactive response will need to be through more sophisticated personal sales methods, e.g. computerised presentations on portable computers, pre-recorded interactive sales presentations, electronic mail and on-line communication. The change is that some customers will find it no longer acceptable for suppliers to provide product, application, sales information at the speed and convenience of their sales departments.

Conclusion

The variety of future trends that are emerging are not contradictory but merely indicate and emphasise the diversity of sales management and its activities. The nature of the responsibilities of sales management is such that it must be 'market driven' and reflect not only present but emerging future needs relevant to specific market segments and the company. The conceptual and operational criterion must be what is good for the company in the market-place.

It is expected that the sales manager will continue as an important participant in the marketing management group. Sales managers will continue to be responsible for the management of the selling function in whatever form the future dictates and for maintaining relationships with customers either directly or through distributive organisations. In discharging future responsibilities, the sales manager will continue to plan and control sales operations and will be a key implementor not only of sales programmes but also of important aspects of marketing strategy.

The successful sales manager, in continually planning for the future, needs good market intelligence systems and inspired forward thinking to ensure that his objectives, strategies, organisation structures are appropriate for the 'sales mission' in particular market segments.

Ideally, he/she should not only be reacting to the leads taken by competing companies and/or other sales managers but should be intelligently pro-active, i.e. setting the pace so as to have some measure of control or at least major influence on the sales initiatives needed.

This can be done by the early identification of market and other environmental changes, emerging needs and situations and not only accommodating them but developing unique but appropriate sales objectives, policies, strategies and tactics that make the particular sales manager the recognised leader in his/her field in providing the quality service, to the customer and the company, known as sales management.

Sales management was once described as an art form in search of a science. While there is still an element of an art and flair about it, sales management has had to become more scientific not only in its approach to management of resources (personnel, financial, physical) but in its approach to management science generally and to information technology in particular, and its use for planning, organisation and control. If sales management has not become a science (and by its nature it is difficult to see it becoming so totally), it has to be scientific in its approach to survive in today's and tomorrow's market-place.

Summary

The ever-changing nature of markets means that sales managers need to identify and gauge the speed of those conditions that are changing and to re-think objectives and strategies, and to develop organisation structures to accommodate them.

Changes in international comparative costs are causing shifts in national economies and industries, leading to companies within countries in some cases changing from traditional products. Changed products also result from changed technology, and 'internationalised' consumers lack the former levels of home-country 'brand loyalty' and in any case have different priorities in spending on leisure and necessities from one time period to another.

Active consumerism and other pressure groups have led to increased legislation and information being made available. Developments in information technology can, and increasingly do, provide suppliers, distributors, customers and competitors with increased market, product and marketing decision-making information. The problems of the international and national economies tend to lean towards potential trade protectionist policy solutions, and the increase in trade concentration in many markets leads towards fewer available customers and prospects, and permits market dominance by a few groups. All these background factors will have a greater or lesser impact on the future of sales management depending on the particular market segment.

The future role of selling must be seen as a component part of the future role of, and developments in, the total 'communications mix'. Within the sales operation itself, cost and/or market factors may require one or a combination of several sales team organisation structures. Changes in the sales person type and the cost of the training of sales managers and members of their sales team, particularly with highly dispersed team members, will need changes in methods of training. There is a likelihood of distance learning and training packages becoming increasingly more important in the training of sales personnel.

An increasing marketing research role is envisaged in some areas of selling, developing the sales force as a powerful market information source. The impact of the wide-scale use of IT could fundamentally alter the role of the sales function in some areas. Where customers and potential customers can obtain all or most of the product and/or market information they require from computerised or other IT systems to make purchasing decisions, the role of the sales team is likely to diminish. However, coping with IT will depend upon the levels of customer, competitor and sales team information technology literacy and how the sales manager can turn IT to his/her own advantage.

The diversity of sales management, indicated by the many trends which are emerging, means that all sales managers need to treat their own situations as special cases, monitoring the economy and the market for indications of change, the anticipated magnitude and momentum of which require new thinking, new objectives, new strategies and new organisation structures.

Questions

1. Why does the sales manager need to be pro-active in considering new objectives, strategies and organisation structures for future market situations and not merely react to competition?

2. What do you consider to be the most important underlying changes in key market environments in which companies operate and to which sales managers must respond?

3. Selling as part of the company total 'communications mix' will be affected by present and future developments in other component parts of the 'mix'. Which of these do you see to be the most crucial to the future of sales management?

4. Sales organisation structures are expected to change to meet market needs. Identify the benefits of the many methods of sales force allocation shown in this chapter.

5. What are the advantages of distance learning or training packages to the sales manager and to sales personnel?

6. What are the advantages and disadvantages to the sales manager of more progressively using the sales team as a source of marketing research information?

7. What are the advantages to the sales manager of using information technology to manage?

8. How will the use of information technology by the supplier, customers and competitors affect the sales team in general and the sales manager in particular?

9. How do you suggest that the sales manager should cope with predicting the future of sales management?

Index